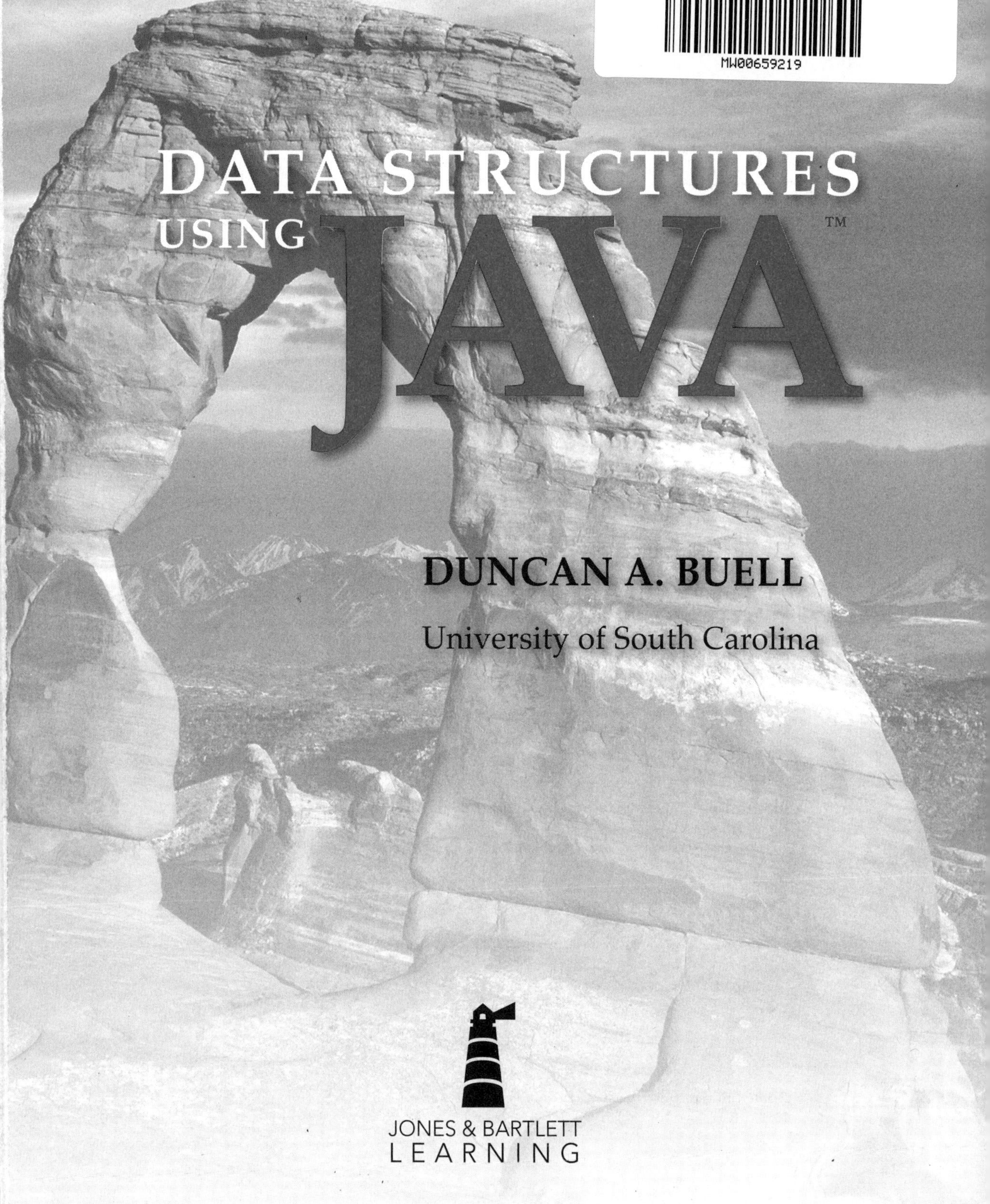

DATA STRUCTURES USING JAVA™

DUNCAN A. BUELL

University of South Carolina

JONES & BARTLETT LEARNING

World Headquarters
Jones & Bartlett Learning
5 Wall Street
Burlington, MA 01803
978-443-5000
info@jblearning.com
www.jblearning.com

Jones & Bartlett Learning books and products are available through most bookstores and online booksellers. To contact Jones & Bartlett Learning directly, call 800-832-0034, fax 978-443-8000, or visit our website, www.jblearning.com.

Substantial discounts on bulk quantities of Jones & Bartlett Learning publications are available to corporations, professional associations, and other qualified organizations. For details and specific discount information, contact the special sales department at Jones & Bartlett Learning via the above contact information or send an email to specialsales@jblearning.com.

Production Credits
Publisher: Cathleen Sether
Senior Acquisitions Editor: Timothy Anderson
Managing Editor: Amy Bloom
Director of Production: Amy Rose
Marketing Manager: Lindsay White
V.P., Manufacturing and Inventory Control: Therese Connell
Composition: Laserwords
Cover Design: Scott Moden
Cover Image: © Mike Norton/ShutterStock, Inc.
Printing and Binding: Malloy, Inc.
Cover Printing: Malloy, Inc.

Library of Congress Cataloging-in-Publication Data
Buell, Duncan A.
Data structures using Java / Duncan A. Buell. – 1st ed.
p. cm.
Includes index.
ISBN-13: 978-1-4496-2807-9 (pbk.)
ISBN-10: 1-4496-2807-9 (pbk.)
1. Data structures (Computer science) 2. Java (Computer program language) I. Title.
QA76.9.D35B84 2013
005.2'762–dc23

2011033497

6048

Printed in the United States of America
15 14 13 12 11 10 9 8 7 6 5 4 3 2 1

For Mary Ann

Contents

Preface

This text is intended for a second-semester course in computer science, the course that is often referred to as "CS2" in the ABET/ACM/IEEE standard curriculum. At my own university, this course has the title "Introduction to Algorithmic Design II," and I suspect the titles are similar at many other institutions. What this course is *not intended* to be is "Introduction to Programming II," although there will be a lot of programming discussed in the book. The conceptual material here is on the design and use of algorithms and data structures. The programming vehicle happens to be Java, but it could in fact be almost any language, and this course has no doubt been taught at some college or university in the past in FORTRAN (and probably Fortran), PL/I, Pascal, Basic, C, and C++.

What is important is that *some* programming language be used so that a rigorous use of the concepts is made and that students become facile with the basic ways in which information is manipulated to create an efficient data structure. What is hard to convey to the general public, and sometimes to students, is that the goal is to develop rigorous thinking, using a computer and a programming language so as to enforce the rigor through practice. Although familiarity with the specifics of how to be rigorous in a particular language will come from that practice, this is a secondary goal.

There are two basic methodological premises behind the treatment of the material in this book. The first is that there is no substitute for the school of hard knocks when it comes to understanding why we have some of the more sophisticated features in a modern programming language. A student who writes a program with a global variable that is updated by three different functions, and then changes the updating in two but not all three functions, with a program crash as the inevitable outcome, will learn through that experience why we want to encapsulate data into objects and limit access on what amounts to a "need-to-know" basis. A student who has never had that experience is much less likely to appreciate fully the concept of objects. The pedagogical problem is that it is difficult, in a fifteen-week semester, in a first-year class, to create assignments that are sufficiently difficult as to create the controlled failure mode that will lead to learning. Much of what we have to say is tantamount to telling students that they ought to eat their vegetables because years later they will appreciate having done so.

In response to this first problem, I have tried to limit the discussion of metaphysical, moral, and theological aspects of Java (or any language) to those concepts that can be firmly grounded in practice in the second semester of a computer science curriculum. Yes, the compiler writers have done some very cool things. No, I don't see that this is necessary in a second-semester course.

The second premise of the book is that necessity is the mother of invention and that sophisticated algorithms and data structures have their natural place in the world. If one is never going to do anything more complicated than a program to balance one's personal checking account, it's not clear that anything more sophisticated than bubblesort or linear search will ever be needed. It is when the naive methods fail us that we implement more clever approaches, and I have tried to emphasize this point. I have always been of the opinion that a program that executes without crashing, even if it doesn't do exactly what is desired, is much more valuable than a program that has all the sophisticated logic programmed in ... except for a few bugs that crash the program every time. This opinion is what is usually used in the "bottleneckology" of high-performance computing—focus on the most time-consuming part of the code and make that part disappear. Since something else will now become the most time consuming, this is an iterative process until the law of diminishing returns sets in. Similarly, a program that does what is needed, albeit perhaps only on data sets of test size, can be improved piecemeal, method by method, class by class, until it can handle the real job.

For the convenience of the instructor, I have tried to map the contents of this book against the learning objectives of the curricular guidelines from ACM and IEEE in *Computer Science Curriculum 2008*. We have assumed that this is a second-semester text, and thus that the PF/FundamentalConstructs and PF/DataStructures (objectives 1, 3, 4, 5, and 7) areas have already been covered. We also assume some familiarity with DS/FunctionsRelationsAndSets. For the material in Chapter 6 and the discussion of algorithm analysis in general we assume a familiarity with differential calculus. Although we do need differentiation of logarithms and exponentials on a few occasions, we do not need any trigonometry. The crucial part of calculus that is used repeatedly at least in Chapter 6 is L'Hôpital's rule. The numbers in parentheses after the topic area in the following table are our estimates of the coverage of this book compared to the number of hours estimated in *Computer Science Curriculum 2008* to be necessary for minimal coverage of the topic.

Topic Area	Objectives	Our Chapters
DS/GraphsAndTrees (4)	1–4	9, 10, 12, 13
PF/AlgorithmicProblemSolving (6)	7–11	throughout
PF/DataStructures (7)	3–9	throughout
PF/Recursion (4)	1–6	Chapter 8
PF/ObjectOriented (7)	1–4	throughout
AL/AlgorithmsAndComplexity (2)	1–3	Chapter 6
AL/AlgorithmicStrategies (4)	1–4	3, 4, 6, 10, 11, 12
AL/FundamentalAlgorithms (6)	1, 4–7	3, 4, 6, 8, 10, 11, 12
PL/ObjectOrientedProgramming (5)	1–3, 4, 6–7	throughout

On the flip side, most of the Programming Fundamentals (PF) topics are covered throughout this book. For the topics that are covered more in selected chapters but are not pervasive throughout, we also index the other way around.

Chapters	Topic Area
Chapter 3	AL/AlgorithmicStrategies AL/FundamentalAlgorithms
Chapter 4	AL/AlgorithmicStrategies AL/FundamentalAlgorithms
Chapter 5	
Chapter 6	AL/AlgorithmsAndComplexity AL/AlgorithmicStrategies AL/FundamentalAlgorithms
Chapter 8	PF/Recursion AL/FundamentalAlgorithms
Chapter 9	DS/GraphsAndTrees
Chapter 10	DS/GraphsAndTrees AL/AlgorithmicStrategies AL/FundamentalAlgorithms
Chapter 11	AL/AlgorithmicStrategies AL/FundamentalAlgorithms
Chapter 12	DS/GraphsAndTrees AL/AlgorithmicStrategies AL/FundamentalAlgorithms
Chapter 13	DS/GraphsAndTrees

I have generally found that I can teach straight through in chapter order, although the vagaries of semester scheduling sometimes make it necessary to move the position of Chapter 6 around. Chapters 7 and 8, except for Section 7.5 on priority queues, do not depend on the chapter on asymptotics, and I sometimes move that material ahead of Chapter 6 in order to do the first midterm exam only on completed chapters. A decision like this is usually based on the calendar, and I have found our fall and spring semesters to be slightly different.

Additional resources for students and instructors are provided at go.jblearning.com/Buell. Students and instructors may download source code related to the text. In addition, PowerPoint Lecture Outlines, Solutions to end-of-chapter Exercises, and a Test Bank are available for free instructor download.

For the mistakes and failings of this book I will take full responsibility, but for whatever is good about this book I must thank in part all the people who have helped me become a better programmer and a better teacher. The students of the last three years who have looked at versions of this text and made comments have all contributed. My colleagues at the Institute for Defense Analyses have played a part in this text, as have the reviewers and the students who have commented, caught my errors, and helped this be better than it might have been. Thank you to Dr. Alice Armstrong, DSc, Shippensburg University; John Boyland, PhD, University of Wisconsin–Milwaukee; and Hélène Martin, Garfield High School for reviewing the manuscript. I owe a special debt to the copyeditors and proofreaders at Jones & Bartlett Learning. Their work has greatly improved the consistency of the text. We all might like to think we write well; the editors are those who make it appear that we actually do. I would also like to thank the editors at Jones & Bartlett Learning; Tim Anderson, Senior Acquisitions Editor; Amy Rose, Director of Production; and Amy Bloom, Managing Editor. Finally, I thank my wife Mary Ann for being patient with me for my many hours spent in the office staring at the screen.

Duncan Buell
Columbia, South Carolina

1 Introduction

1.1 The Course of This Course

In a nutshell, this course has two foci: The first is the efficient management and manipulation of data. The second is the ability to implement methods for efficient management and manipulation of data in a modern high-level programming language, which in this case happens to be Java™. This is not intended to be "a course in Java"; rather, it is a course in the use of data structures and algorithms that uses Java as the vehicle for turning concepts into the details of implementations. In the final analysis, most people do not get paid to talk about how one might compute something; they get paid to facilitate the actual computation of something. Really knowing the details of implementation is thus very important. Students in computer science should actually be happy that computers, compilers, and programming languages are as rigid as they are. This allows the rigorous testing of ideas, because "the computer" is the final arbiter of correctness, and one can do one's own testing for correctness, unlike, say, mathematics, chemistry, or the law.[1]

Many of the basic problems of data structures immediately present themselves when dealing even with so simple a thing as an address book. Much of the purpose of this text and the course it is intended to support is to present algorithms and methods that are better in one way or another than the naive approaches that one might take without thinking very hard.

We assume that a student who has entered an intermediate course already has experience at an introductory level in the manipulation of data and in writing programs to manipulate data. The most fundamental, and most naive, view of data is usually that of a *flat file*. A flat file is simply a two-dimensional data array like a spreadsheet. Each line can be viewed as a *record*. Each column can be viewed as a *field*. In a simple example, one can think of an address book. Each record is an individual "person," and each record possesses fields for last name, first name, street address, city, state, zip code, telephone number, and so forth. Actions that

[1] Actually, there is nothing in the law that says one cannot determine what is legal or illegal by the experimental method, but the penalties can be more substantial than having the compiler simply inform you that your program has a bug.

would reasonably be taken on such a structure would be to sort it into alphabetical order, to add new records and delete old ones, and to retrieve entries based on one or more *search keys* like last name or city of residence. In Chapter 3, we will present the basics of a naive flat file implementation, and then in later chapters we will introduce the structures and algorithms that allow for more sophisticated and more efficient management of the data.

1.1.1 Layers of Software

A central theme in the development of software in a modern setting is that software exists in layers. This is critical to understanding concepts of how and why software is developed the way it is and why there are right ways and wrong ways to develop code.

If you, for example, are the programmer developing an address book implementation, your job is to develop code that handles "address-book-ness." This will include adding, deleting, and editing records; sorting, displaying, and printing copies; perhaps adding and deleting fields in the record; and (in many current applications) linking to web pages or sending text or making phone calls. What you as the address book programmer ought not to be concerned about is how the data is stored in detail. That takes place one level down in the software hierarchy. Although you need to be aware of the *existence* of the data storage methods that have been chosen for use, your code need not be concerned with the *implementation* of those storage methods. Implementation of the storage methods should take place one level down, and that code should be written so as to be independent of the application that is using it.

This layering of code allows programmers to concentrate on the tasks at hand without being distracted by other issues, and it allows code to be used by different programs. You have by now used library code for things like input and output. Your program need not be concerned with *how* the `println` statement gets your data to the console; it need only be confident that the code will accomplish that task correctly and consistently. In this course, we will extend that concept to higher structures that you write as well as to further structures built into Java in the large.

1.1.2 Algorithms and Efficiency

Computers demonstrate their real value not when doing small amounts of work on small amounts of data, but when doing large amounts of work on large amounts of data or when doing the same small task over and over again. Modern computers are very fast, much faster than their predecessors of even 10 or 20 years ago. But as fast as computers are, it is still usually the case that we *do* need to make programs run at least reasonably efficiently. For this reason, we will cover some of the background of how we measure the efficiency of an algorithm or program and why some algorithms are inherently more efficient than others. Almost invariably, no matter how powerful the computer, a person intending serious use of the computer to support some activity will run up against the performance limitations of the machine and will need to use better algorithms.

There are two ways in which computational performance can be improved: One can change from an inefficient algorithm to an efficient algorithm, or one can change from a poor implementation to a good implementation. It is usually argued that the real improvements in performance (factors of 10 and 100) come from improved algorithms, and that improved implementations usually provide factors of perhaps 2 to 4. One should therefore look for a good algorithm and implement that, and one should do a good implementation. That being said, it's also possible to overdo both of these. The really good algorithms will also be more complicated to implement (and thus more prone to error), and the benefit of the algorithms is usually only on large input sets. If the input data is small, then a good algorithm is better than a naive algorithm and a great algorithm is probably overkill. Similarly, if a small improvement in performance can be achieved by an implementation that makes the code impossible to read, understand, and maintain, then maybe that's not good either.

1.1.3 Sorting

It will normally be the case that we want to keep an address book in sorted order, usually by last name, because that is how we identify records for retrieval. It has been estimated that perhaps a third of the CPU cycles expended in all of computing are spent in sorting records to keep them accessible in a desired order. For this reason, sorting records is an extremely important subject in data structures and in computing in general, and thus we will spend an entire chapter on sorting.

There are sorting methods that are very simple to implement. Generally, since there is no free lunch in this world, these are also the methods that are not very good. The good sorting methods are somewhat more complicated, but it turns out that a reasonably simple method—quicksort—is actually quite effective. Although we can prove (and will prove) that *quicksort* is not the best method for all sorting problems, it is quite good on average. We will spend a little more time on the bigger picture of sorting because the comparison of the major sorting methods—quicksort, *heapsort*, and *mergesort*—provides a good introduction into the trade-offs that good software people need to make

- between good algorithms that might be hard to implement and poorer algorithms that are easy to implement;
- between the *best-case behavior*, the *worst-case behavior*, and the *average-case behavior* of algorithms;

- and between the different implementation characteristics of algorithms when we move beyond a "theoretical" description of the algorithm and actually write a program that runs on a real computer.

1.1.4 Maintaining Sorted Order

Change is a constant fact of life. No matter how careful one is to anticipate all possibilities, something unanticipated will also happen. In the case of data, we know that change will happen. As soon as we create an address book with all our contacts in it, we will encounter a new individual who needs to be added to the file. Since we will want to maintain our contacts in sorted order, we will probably need to insert the new contact into the data file in the correct location.

If our flat file is in fact a spreadsheet, we could do this by adding the new record at the bottom and then using the "sort" function to move all the data into the proper locations. In a simple spreadsheet, the sort will quite literally move all the records, and for an individual's address book of a few hundred records, this can be acceptable behavior. However, if the data records are the entire database of the U.S. Internal Revenue Service, then physically moving all the data on disk so as to insert one record is not acceptable. Part of the study of data structures, therefore, is the study of how to maintain sorted order in the presence of change.

1.1.5 Indexing, Search, and Retrieval

Although in many instances there is a natural *primary key* on which to retrieve records (such as last name for our address book), it is often important to be able to retrieve records from a (conceptual) flat file in an order other than the order in which they are stored conceptually. If one is maintaining a mailing list, then in addition to having records sorted by last name, one may well need to be able to retrieve records sorted by zip code so as to get the benefit of bulk mail postage rates. To do this, one would *invert* the file on the zip code field and create an index that can be used for retrieval on the secondary key instead of the last-name primary key.

More importantly, one of the primary features of any complex computer program is that it will search for and retrieve a data item, based on a *key*, from a "collection" of data. The key might be a Social Security number, a name, or even a request for "the next" item in some sorted order. We will therefore deal with the organization of data so that search and retrieval of data can be done efficiently.

In working with data, what matters a great deal is whether or not that data is structured. A retail receipt for purchases at the grocery store represents structured data. Each such record has date, time, and store information, as well as some number of lines of transaction information for the item purchased, the individual price, and the number of items that were purchased. One can easily imagine a template for a receipt record. The boilerplate store information would be easy to add; the date and time would change but would be easy to obtain from an internal clock; and the only complexity comes from the fact that one has a variable number of items to record.

This kind of structured data is very different from a web page or a collection of web pages forming an entire website, for example, which would have free text, links, internal horizontal references, etc. In a retail store, one would assume that the list of items for sale could be found somewhere in a file on a master computer. For a randomly chosen website, though, no master list of the words used on the site would be expected to exist. That list of words would have to be built dynamically by reading through the pages. With a retail transaction, we expect header and footer information and a list of items and prices in the middle. With the pages of a website, we have no reason to know what to expect in terms of the internal and external URL references. We have no reason to know the length of the pages or where the content will occur. If we are to build a data structure to hold that information, we must use a structure that can adapt automatically as we read the data.

1.1.6 Dynamic Versus Static Behavior

As soon as one introduces the notion of change to a data file (or more generally to a data object) and sets about to decide upon a data structure for that file, one is forced to consider the operational characteristics of the dynamic activity on that data. The questions that need to be addressed include the following:

- What is the size of the data object?
- What is the size of the object relative to the ongoing change to the object?
- What happens to data items when they are "deleted" from the collection of data?

With the data file of IRS records on U.S. taxpayers, for example, it is probably a reasonable assumption that the base file is enormous relative to the daily changes to the file. There are hundreds of millions of taxpayer IDs, and no doubt billions of individual records of tax payments, but the rate of change of the data object is probably relatively small. If the data object consists of the active processes in a computer, however, the number of processes will be small (in the low hundreds at most), but a large number of the processes will be very short lived and the turnover will be very high. Similarly, the servers of an ISP will have at any time a collection of individual packets of Internet transmissions, but the set of packets at any given time will be constantly changing. Different rates of change will require different data structures.

What are the access and retrieval patterns? Is the data[2] stored once and retrieved a large number of times, as in an address book? Or is the data stored on an ongoing basis and then retrieved only occasionally? Is there a need to make retrieval of some (more popular) records more efficient than the retrieval of other records? Is it the case that there are usually only a few updates to be made, as with a university transcript database, but then there are times (such as the end of the semester) when bulk updates occur?

Google™, for example, will want to index everything, but part of the success of Google has been its ability to quickly point to what the user community has determined to be "relevant" data. The use of last name as the primary key in a personal address book is due to the fact that this is (for most people, at least) the normal way in which the data would be identified and searched for. Retrieval by zip code for bulk mailing purposes can be useful, but it is not going to be the common method for retrieval of names and addresses.

Similarly, in an operating system, the available processes to execute can probably be sorted by priority, but with only one or perhaps two CPUs, there will be a high priority placed on being able to identify very quickly "the next" process in the data structure to execute since any time spent on deciding which process to execute will not be viewed as productive work for the user. A similar situation will exist if the data object that is being built is a game tree of potential moves. We will want to build as large a tree as possible of our potential moves, the opponent's potential responses, our responses to the responses, and so forth, together with a measure of our game status after each move and countermove.

1.1.7 Memory and Bandwidth

Increasingly, software is focusing on mobile devices. Because these devices are mobile, and usually mass-marketed, they have limited resources in processor power and in memory or longer-term storage. As mobile devices, they gain their utility largely by being connected wirelessly, which means that the bandwidth from the device to the rest of the universe is limited. Anyone who has downloaded large files or accessed the Internet from a slow telephone line knows that some things just don't work well due to a mismatch of the program and the bandwidth of the machine. This is most apparent with images and video. It is virtually impossible to access mere text in sufficient quantity to make bandwidth an issue, but it is relatively easy to do this

[2]The author generally tries to be strict in his grammar, and he is aware that "data" is officially the plural of "datum," is therefore plural, and should take the plural verb "are" and not the singular verb "is." However, even though the author generally tries to be strict about correct grammar, this is one instance in which the common singular usage, treating data as a mass noun, especially with regard to computer data, seems appropriate.

with images. Anyone who has seen a video buffered up or played back in a bursty fashion will recognize the problem.

To counteract the problems with bandwidth, most programs for mobile devices must make careful use of memory and data structures, freeing up and then reusing memory space when possible, and delaying execution of certain functions for as long as possible.

Consider something as simple as a slideshow of photos for a museum tour. If the program is written to run on mobile devices owned by the museum, the photos can be downloaded to the devices long in advance and kept in a memory card. If, however, a museum visitor can use her own smart mobile device, then the program designer has to consider whether it will be acceptable to users to have to wait 2 or 3 minutes to download the entire collection of images and then display them. Or should the download be delayed as long as possible, in hopes that the visitor will linger over photo n long enough to permit photo $n+1$ to be downloaded just before it is needed?

1.1.8 Heuristics

Finally, we recognize that there are times when the best becomes the enemy of the good. In any given application, how good is good enough? We have already mentioned that quicksort, to be covered later, is usually the "standard" sorting method used for practical applications, not because it is theoretically the best method available (it is not) but because it is a relatively simple method with good average-case behavior.

Similarly, it is probably unusual for someone to print a new paper copy of an address list just because one person has been added to the electronic list. More likely the electronic list is updated and the paper copy is simply annotated with a handwritten reference. When so many changes to the paper copy have been made that the paper copy is too messy to be convenient, a new paper copy will be printed. In truly serious data-intensive applications, the same principle might well apply. If there is enormous effort involved, for example, in a one-time sort of the entire data object, then one might plan to maintain the changes as an addendum to the main object and then incorporate the changes in a block only at intervals, perhaps daily, weekly, or monthly. For such applications, the heuristics of how to do *incremental* updates can be very important.

A *heuristic* in computer science is a general guideline, based on experience and an understanding of the problem, that leads to the implementation of specific algorithms or design features in the software meant to solve the problem or provide the service. Especially when performance is an issue, we usually write programs whose execution is based on normal, average use. We will include the code to deal with *pathological cases* (because we have to cover all possible inputs), but we will not usually write code that assumes that the one-in-a-billion worst case is going to happen. For example, the first time we create a sorted telephone book, we might want to assume that the records are in a reasonably random order, but if we are adding new records to a telephone-book-sized address list, we can safely assume that we are starting with a large list that is already sorted and then adding a small number of records to that list. These assumptions might well lead to the use of a different sorting algorithm for the incremental updates than was used for creating the list in the first place.

A different version of the heuristics issue is that programming for performance requires identifying the most serious bottlenecks and then applying some better brainpower to those bottlenecks first. There is probably no point in using a complicated algorithm for a task that is done infrequently and is not time-critical. In software, as in life, there is always a list of the most important things to be accomplished, and we should be attacking those before we go about making cosmetic changes or changes that will have no real effect.

1.1.9 Templates, Generics, and Abstract Classes

We have described a flat file that comprises records (lines in a spreadsheet), each record of which has fields (the columns). In any real programming situation, field items will exist as strings, integers, floating-point numbers, and other less primitive types. To avoid writing almost the same code over and over again, Java can provide *generic* constructs and `abstract` classes that will simplify the coding process (that is, the process will be simpler once one learns how to use generics and abstract classes). In sorting, for example, the structure of a sort is independent of whether one is sorting integers as integers or sorting strings (like last names) lexicographically; the base step in sorting an array into "increasing" order is to compare two data items and exchange the order of the two items if necessary so that the "smaller" item comes first. Good programming practice will therefore put off until the very last moment any code that specifically deals with one data type or another, and only at the very last moment use an appropriate compare-and-exchange method for two data items.

One issue of data structures that does not necessarily present itself in a flat file but is so important that it warrants mention here is the nature of tree structures and then eventually of recursion. One canonical use of a tree structure is the directory structure on a modern computer. In Unix, the "root" data structure is the "/" directory, and all the directories and files live underneath that. Users will have a "home" directory and create under that various files and subdirectories, with the subdirectories then having files and subdirectories, and so forth. In Windows, most user data starts at the My Documents folder (Windows uses the term "folder" instead of "directory") and descends from there.

1.2 Examples

1.2.1 Card Catalogs

Although it is not necessarily one of the more exciting applications of data structures, the card catalog of a library is one example of a large data file that needs to be properly organized to be useful to the user community. These used to be physical cards, as shown in Figure 1.1, but are now almost always kept entirely online in large libraries.

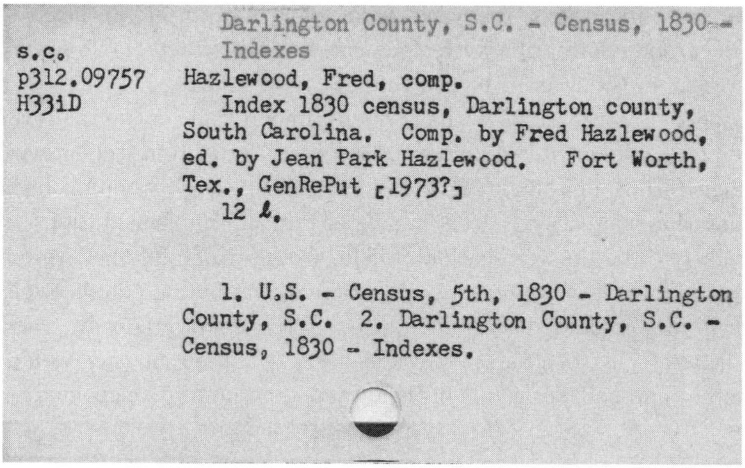
Darlington County, S.C. - Census, 1830 - Indexes
S.C.
p312.09757
H33iD
Hazlewood, Fred, comp.
Index 1830 census, Darlington county, South Carolina. Comp. by Fred Hazlewood, ed. by Jean Park Hazlewood. Fort Worth, Tex., GenRePut [1973?]
12 l.

1. U.S. - Census, 5th, 1830 - Darlington County, S.C. 2. Darlington County, S.C. - Census, 1830 - Indexes.

FIGURE 1.1 ■ A card from a library card catalog.

The first thing to note is that the card catalog data is stored essentially only once (unless there are corrections to be made, and these should be rare). Except for a data field indicating whether the document is or is not checked out of the library (and the possible checkout history that we will ignore), the data file, although perhaps large (libraries in major universities have collections numbering in the millions of volumes), is very static. The issue with this kind of data is not constant updating but rather that the data can be accessed by multiple search keys. In this case, access by author name, document title, Library of Congress classification number, keywords, perhaps accession date, and perhaps also due date for documents checked out, would be necessary. We will want to use a data structure that permits records to be added over time, and there will be records that occasionally get deleted, but the major issue is not the change in the data file but in the efficient retrieval of record information.

Data such as card catalog data is usually very highly structured. Indeed, substantial effort has been expended by the U.S. Library of Congress to standardize card catalog data so that records are uniform in all libraries in the country.

1.2.2 Student Records

A classic kind of record to be stored and manipulated are the student records at educational institutions. Each record contains several different kinds of data. Name, student ID number, and such are going to be almost static. Address information, major, and such will need to be updatable, but this together with the identity information will be data "local to the student." This will differ from the transcript information. Both for privacy and efficiency reasons some information is likely to be stored in different files from the address information. We would also not expect the individual course grades to be stored with the student information; rather, we would expect all the grade information for a given course to be stored in one place, with the student record indexing into the course data.

In the case of student records, then, we have the likelihood that, unlike the card catalog information for a document in a library, "the record" for a given student will not consist of a single record, in a single array, in a single Java class (assuming Java to be the implementation language). Indeed, in most significant implementations, a single "record" is likely to be the aggregation of fields from several different stored collections. One reason for this is to prevent duplication of data because duplication leads to the problem of consistency across instances. If one list of grades by class were kept and a separate list of grades by student existed, then changes would have to occur in more than one location. This is always something to be avoided in designing software.

1.2.3 Retail Transactions

A number of standard data processing environments constitute *transaction processing*. For example, both a large retailer, such as Walmart, and a credit card processor, such as Visa, deal with millions of individual transaction records every day that come in on a pretty much nonstop basis. Characteristics of the data records will be that they are small, with several fixed fields (date, payment method, purchase location, and such), and a variable number of individual item purchases made. The data records need to cataloged and stored, with multiple indexing and retrieval patterns made possible, but it is unlikely that the individual items will be accessed randomly or very often.

1.2.4 Packet Traffic

Internet packets resemble transaction records in many ways. One characteristic of Internet packets is that they are more or less fixed size (a primary reason for packetizing an Internet transmission is to keep the packet size small) and have a number of fixed fields (source, destination, etc.). One characteristic somewhat unique to packet traffic is that what the user views as a single transmission is broken into packets at the source to be sent, possibly through different routes, to the destination. The packets arrive at the destination in no particular order and then must be reassembled in the proper order before the complete message is delivered to the destination user.

This kind of data is different from all those mentioned previously in that the data records (packets) are not standalone items but must be aggregated into complete transmissions in real time at high speed. Student records are expected to be persistent and long term, but Internet messages are packetized, sent, collected, and then discarded. This kind of processing requires a much different data structure from that used previously in order to accommodate these different needs.

1.2.5 Process Queues

Similar in some ways to Internet packet traffic are the process queues managed by the operating system in any modern computer. In even a standard desktop there will be dozens of processes in a *state of execution* at any point in time. Some of these are processes that are always running; some are processes created when the user fires up a word processor, an edit window, an Internet browser, and so forth. The task of the scheduler for the operating system is to determine which process to execute next. As with packet traffic, these process queues must be managed in real time with as little effort as possible expended by the scheduler. Processes need to have their priorities updated at intervals, and the effects of the updated priorities need to be available immediately. The data structure used to implement the process queues needs to be highly dynamic and easily changed, and the processes with the highest priorities need to be quickly accessible.

1.2.6 Google

All the preceding examples of data are of *fixed-format records*. These are records that can be thought of in spreadsheet form; each record has a list of fields, and each field has a specific data type. Although some fields might be of variable length, the sequence of the fields and the data type for each field are the same across all records. Further, there is some reason to believe that the data as stored will actually make sense because the records have been created by an authoritative source or by means of software that has presumably been written so as to produce reasonably correct records.

All that goes out the window when one considers the Google problem of analyzing all the web pages in the world. Web pages are not fixed-format; they are highly changeable over time; they are not created by an authoritative source; they may be rife with misspellings or typographical errors; and they are not guaranteed to be organized. All these complications require greater thought when deciding how to craft a data structure that contains the information that must be processed and presented to a user.

1.2.7 Game Trees

A large number of computing applications can be described simply as involving the optimizing (either minimizing or maximizing) of an *objective function* over a *tree search*. A game tree for chess or a similar game falls into this category. At any point in the chess game, White has a number of possible moves. Black has a number of possible responses, to which White has responses, and so forth. White's objective function for the game would be a function that would assign to any given board position a "goodness" value for White for that position; this goodness function is the objective function, and White's game-playing strategy is to determine which moves maximize that function. Given any possible move, one can recompute the goodness of the new board position, then compute the goodness of the board position after Black's response to the particular move, and so on. Structurally, the options resemble the branching of a tree from the *root* (the current position) down through the options of move and countermove.

Such a tree search is *combinatorially explosive* in the total number of possibilities, because even if we restrict ourselves to a fixed number k of possible moves at every level, the number of possible moves for n levels is k^n and thus grows exponentially with n. Most game programs are thus implemented with some sort of *heuristic search* in which the heuristics of the search strategy limit the number of choices at each decision point and thus limit the total number of possible paths that might be explored.

1.2.8 Phylogenetics

Phylogenetics is the subdiscipline of biology in which one computes backward through time from a list of current species (called taxa) to determine the best possible evolutionary tree back to the common ancestors of today's taxa. This is a variant of a classic example of tree search; the current taxa are the leaves of the tree and, moving backward through time to a common ancestor, the length of each edge is proportional to time. The problem is that, as with most tree searches, the number of possible paths is astronomically huge and thus efficient data structures as well as heuristic algorithms must be applied in order to perform any sort of serious computation.

1.3 Summary

As we shall see in Chapter 3, a standard way to begin to program an application is to use the simple and naive algorithms and data structures. These would be simple to program, would work correctly, and would almost certainly work so inefficiently as to be unacceptable in practice.

An implementation under development will usually move from simple-but-inefficient to efficient-but-harder-to-program in stages, with each stage providing better efficiency at a cost in complexity. This complexity usually involves management of subscripts, control over memory usage, and great care with endpoint conditions and null values. To control this complexity, most modern programming languages come bundled with solid implementations of the standard data structures.

In Java, these are the classes in the Java Collections Framework. Virtually all the data structures in this text exist in the JCF. If mere use of the structures and algorithms were all that was needed, there would be no need for you as the programmer to reinvent the code for a linked list, for example. That code already exists in the JCF, and it is highly unlikely that your code will be as general purpose, as robust, and as thoroughly tested as that in the JCF.

You, the programmer, do not really need to rewrite the code; in a professional setting, you would probably choose to use the existing code, leaving you free to concentrate on implementing code for the actual application instead of simply for the underlying data structures and algorithms. However, really understanding the structures and algorithms requires a deeper knowledge than that of mere usage, and you are unlikely to really learn how these data structures work without implementing them in code yourself. We have thus written the text and set the exercises as if the reader were going to implement all the data structures and algorithms. Many of them are quite similar, and perhaps it is not necessary to do all of them; having implemented the code for a stack, perhaps implementing the code for a queue is not as good a use of your time as would using the JCF queue in a more interesting application. Nonetheless, we encourage practice in writing code. We believe strongly that gaining a real understanding both of the programming process and of the algorithms and data structures necessary for applications of significant size requires the trial and error of programming and the knowledge acquired through the fingertips in the school of hard knocks.

2 A Review of Java

Objectives

- A Java code refresher
- Basic structuring of a program into classes
- An introduction to documentation requirements
- A brief look at UML, the Unified Modeling Language

Key Terms

constructor	parse	static variable
data payload	primitive type	token
encapsulation of data	religious issues	UML diagram
instance variable	spaghetti code	

Introduction

Rather than try to break down Java into its constituent parts, we show in Figures 2.1–2.6 the code[1] for a complete program, and we will refresh your memory of Java from that example. This program has two classes and reads a data file of name-and-course-number pairs and prints that data back to the console.

2.1 The Basic Data Payload Class

In keeping with Java's object-oriented nature, we have one class, named `Record`, that handles the *data payload* of one instance of a name-and-course-number pair (see Figures 2.1–2.4). The payload would be the data (our data) carried by the structure.

[1] The code is also available on the website at go.jblearning.com/Buell

```
import java.util.Scanner;
/*********************************************************
 * Class for handling the data in a <code>Record</code>.
 * This is the class to handle a single phonebook-like record.
 * @author Duncan A. Buell
 * @version 1.00 2010-07-05
 * Copyright (C) 2010 by Duncan A. Buell.  All rights reserved.
**/
public class Record
{
/*********************************************************
 * Instance variables for the class.
**/
  private final String TAG = "Record: "; //for testing
  static private final String DUMMYSTRING = "dummystring";
  static private final int DUMMYINT = Integer.MIN_VALUE;
  private String name;  // instructor's name
  private int teaching; // course number being taught

/*********************************************************
 * Constructor.
 * We create the record and assign dummy values so as not to
 * have null values.
**/
  public Record()
  {
    this.setName(Record.DUMMYSTRING);
    this.setTeaching(Record.DUMMYINT);
  }
```

FIGURE 2.1 ■ Part 1 of the `Record` class for the phone book example.

In the simplest instances of an array or an `ArrayList`, it is necessary to declare the data type, perhaps as `ArrayList<Integer> myList`. In this case, the data payload would be a set of `Integer` values. If the list were declared as `ArrayList<Record> myList`, then the data payload would be a set of `Record` values. In general in this course, we will be emphasizing the fact that, if we were using an `ArrayList`, or perhaps extending an `ArrayList`, or implementing a different structure entirely, everything that happens to the data should happen inside the payload's class, and everything that involves the methods of `ArrayList`, or its extensions or analogs, should take place independent of what the payload is.

In Chapter 5, we will cover the Java generic construct. This allows one to write code that refers symbolically (generically) to a data payload type without specifying the type, so that code that handles data payload classes can truly be written independent of the data inside the payload.

```
/***********************************************************
 * Accessor method to get the <code>name</code>.
 * @return the value of <code>name</code>.
**/
  public String getName()
  {
    return this.name;
  }
/***********************************************************
 * Accessor method to get the <code>teaching</code>.
 * @return the value of <code>teaching</code>.
**/
  public int getTeaching()
  {
    return this.teaching;
  }

/***********************************************************
 * Mutator method to set the <code>name</code>.
 * @param what the value of <code>name</code> to be set.
**/
  private void setName(String what)
  {
    this.name = what;
  }
/***********************************************************
 * Mutator method to set the <code>teaching</code>.
 * @param what the value of <code>teaching</code> to be set.
**/
  private void setTeaching(int what)
  {
    this.teaching = what;
  }
```

FIGURE 2.2 ■ Part 2 of the `Record` class for the phone book example.

Everything in Java is enclosed within braces, and the

```
public class Record
```

line is matched at the end with the closing brace. After some initial documentation about this particular class and file of code, we declare the *instance variables* for the class. Some of these are declared to be *static variables*, meaning that regardless of how many instances of the class we have at any point in time, we only have the one copy of that variable. Since we use this for read-only `final` information, this

```
/**************************************************************
 * General methods.
**/
/**************************************************************
 * Method to compare the <code>name</code> values of records.
 * This does a lexicographic comparison on the data stored, so
 * if the data stored is not in last-name order we will get
 * something different from what might be expected.
 * @param that the "that" record to compare to
 * @return -1, 0, or +1 depending on how the comparison goes.
**/
  public int compareTo(Record that)
  {
    if(this.getName().compareTo(that.getName()) < 0)
      return -1;
    else if(this.getName().compareTo(that.getName()) > 0)
      return +1;
    else
      return 0;
  }
```

FIGURE 2.3 ■ Part 3 of the `Record` class for the phone book example.

seems entirely appropriate. We believe it is not good form to create variables and then not assign them some dummy value, so we create dummy values for the initial assignment.

That initial assignment is made in the *constructor*, the method that is invoked every time the `new` command is issued in the main program.

In a more sophisticated phone book, we would have more than just the name and course being taught (we might even have phone numbers). For the purpose of this illustration, we have limited ourselves to just the two instance variables, one of `String` and one of `int` type. The other common types are `boolean` and `double`. The lowercased `boolean`, `int`, and `double` types are *primitive types*; if one needs classes of these types together with methods for converting from one type to the other, or converting to and from a string representation, then the capitalized `Boolean`, `Integer`, and `Double` classes can and must be used.

We will use the `Scanner` throughout this book for input and the `PrintWriter` or the system console for output.

Some thought must be given to the simplest way to get data into and out of an instance of a class. In general, the reading of data into an instance of a class should be done by a method in that class because there is no reason for the details of reading data, verifying correctness, or converting it into more usable forms to be

```
/**********************************************************
 * Method to read the flat file from an input
 *   </code>Scanner</code> file.
 * Note that this is more or less hard coded. Also that we
 * don't bulletproof the input; among other things we assume
 * that partial records don't appear in the input data.
 * @param inFile the <code>Scanner</code> from which to read
 * @return the <code>Record</code> that was read
**/
  public void readRecord(Scanner inFile)
  {
    int n;    // local <code>int</code> variable
    String s; // local <code>String</code> variable
    if(inFile.hasNext())
    {
      s = inFile.next();
      this.setName(s);
      n = inFile.nextInt();
      this.setTeaching(n);
    }
  }
/**********************************************************
 * Usual <code>toString</code> method to convert a record to a
 *   <code>String</code>.
 * @return the <code>toString</code> value of the record.
**/
  public String toString()
  {
    String s;
    s = String.format("%-10s %4d",
                 this.getName(), this.getTeaching());
    return s;
  }
} // public class Record
```

FIGURE 2.4 ■ Part 4 of the `Record` class for the phone book example.

shown outside the class. Further, the reading of a data item usually requires us to know the type of that item. Modern programming practice is to limit as much as possible the exposure outside the class of information about variables. This practice of *encapsulation* requires us to put everything possible inside the class in which the variables are defined and used, and export as `public` only that which is really necessary to be public.

Although reading and writing the data for the variables in the class should be confined to the class itself, the instance of the class probably ought *not* have to worry about opening the data file and checking that the open procedure worked correctly. That is a more global issue, not an issue local to one instance of the `Record` class. We therefore do the file handling in the main program. In the next chapter, we will move these utility functions to a separate class. The code for that can then be written and tested once for all time, which will minimize the chance of an error in copying or in retyping the code, and the clutter of the code for the standard methods that open and close files won't distract from the flow of the application program being written.

The `readRecord` method is passed a `Scanner` (and in this method the `Scanner` is tacitly assumed to be open or else an error will be thrown) and then reads from that file into the "current" (that is, `this`) instance of the class. (Note how the calling is done from the main program.) For proper programming, error checking should be done here. Similarly, every data payload class should have a `toString` method that converts the data in the payload into a printable (and usually formatted) string. The beauty of the `toString` construct in Java is that the `Record` class can and should know how to format the data in the class, but it need not know anything about what will be done with that formatted string. There is no need even for an output file to be passed in, analogous to what is done for `readRecord`. We can simply leave it to the calling program to use the returned string as it sees fit.

Finally, there is perhaps no method that exemplifies the "need-to-know" encapsulation of data into an abstract data type (the `Record` class) more than does the `compareTo` method. For many purposes, we will want to arrange lists of data items into a sorted order, sorted perhaps by last name, by keyword, by Social Security number, or some other mechanism. Although we do not use it in this simple example, we have included a `compareTo` that will compare "this" instance of a `Record` class against "that" instance of a `Record` class. Notice, however, that a program that invokes the `compareTo` method knows, and needs to know, nothing about the details of how the comparison is made, and without reading the documentation for the method the invoking program knows nothing about what makes one record sort earlier than another. It is sufficient that two records can be compared and that one will be determined to be "less than" another in a sorted order.

2.2 The Main Program

Throughout this book the primary purposes of the "main" program will be to

- set up the program for input and output by prompting the user for input, and/or opening (and later closing) any files necessary, and/or checking that files, filenames, and such are valid; and
- invoke a method that can loosely be given the name `doTheWork`.

```
import java.io.File;
import java.io.FileNotFoundException;
import java.util.ArrayList;
import java.util.Scanner;
/*********************************************************
 * Main class for reading and printing phonebook records.
 * Copyright(c) 2010 Duncan A. Buell.  All rights reserved.
 * @author Duncan Buell
 * @version 1.00 2010-07-05
**/
public class Main
{
  public static void main (String[] args)
  {
    final String TAG = "Main: "; // for debugging
    String fileName = "mydata";
    Scanner inFile = null;
    ArrayList<Record> phonebook = null;

    // INNER CODE GOES HERE

//*********************************************************
// Although terminating the program will close open files,
// we will follow good form and explicitly close files.
///
    inFile.close();
  }
} // public class Main
```

FIGURE 2.5 ■ Part 1 of the `Main` class for the phone book example.

One reason for keeping the main program so simple is that the details of what is being done with the data can be encapsulated in the subordinate classes. For example, the main program does not need to know which individual instance variables exist in the `Record`; it needs only to know that all the instance variables can be read for a given instance of the class by invoking the `readRecord` method.

In this particular instance, as shown in Figures 2.5 and 2.6, the main program has a slightly expanded purpose. We have declared an `ArrayList` of `Record` items in the main program, and the main program thus handles the file access, runs a `while` loop to read the data, and then runs a `for` loop to print the data.

In most cases in this text, we will have not one but probably three basic classes. At the top of the hierarchy will be the main program, which functions mostly as a driver and handles issues of the source of input and the destination for output.

```
//************************************************************
// Open the data file, catching the exception.
///
    try
    {
      inFile = new Scanner(new File(fileName));
    }
    catch (FileNotFoundException ex)
    {
      System.out.println(TAG + "ERROR opening inFile "
                             + fileName);
      System.out.println(ex.getMessage());
      System.out.println("in"+System.getProperty("user.dir"));
      System.out.flush();
      System.exit(1);
    }

//************************************************************
// Read in the data and store it in the <code>ArrayList</code>.
///
    phonebook = new ArrayList<Record>();
    while(inFile.hasNext())
    {
      Record rec = new Record();
      rec.readRecord(inFile);
      phonebook.add(rec);
    }

//************************************************************
// Print out the <code>ArrayList</code> data.
///
    for(int i = 0; i < phonebook.size(); ++i)
    {
      System.out.println(phonebook.get(i));
    }
    System.out.println("Record count: " + phonebook.size());
```

FIGURE 2.6 ■ Part 2 of the `Main` class for the phone book example.

At the bottom of the hierarchy will be the data payload class. The data payload class is much the same regardless of whether the payload is a phone book record, a retail transaction, an item to be sorted, a web page HTML tag, or data. The payload class comprises instance variables, accessor and mutator methods, a method to read an entire record, and a `toString` to format the data in a record for printing. Sometimes there may be comparison methods—a phone book record would perhaps be sorted by last name, phone number, or street address, so there will need to be methods to compare two records and indicate which is "smaller."

Finally, of course, there may well be helper methods in the data payload class for converting raw data into parsed[2] data (one line of data for a name might have to be parsed to identify the last name, deal with "Jr." or "Sr." suffixes, and such), for verifying correctness, or for producing derived data from the instance variables (a retail transaction record need not store the total as a separate value if it is more convenient simply to sum the individual costs into a total as needed).

At the top of the code hierarchy is the main program. At the bottom of the hierarchy is the data payload. In the middle will usually be one or two classes that actually implement classes for a data structure. In this simple program, there has been no need for these intermediate classes because the "data structure" is really just the `ArrayList` of the records.

Note that we have used an `ArrayList` and not an array in this program. For one-dimensional lists of items, especially for those whose size is not fixed at compile time, the `ArrayList` is much to be preferred over the more restrictive array.

This example main program has about a dozen lines of code to open the `Scanner`, given the name of a file, and check that the file exists and the `Scanner` can in fact be opened. In the next chapter, we will move this code to a `FileUtils` class that has methods for opening and closing files given filenames passed as arguments. This makes it unnecessary to do all the error checking in-line and thus cleans up the appearance of the code. This also makes it more likely that error checking will in fact be done correctly, since a utility method can implement correct code once for all time and make it unnecessary for the programmer either to retype the details every time or to feel guilty about having been too lazy to do it right every time. It's a reasonably safe bet that once this dozen lines of code with all the appropriate error checking is written, it will be used over and over again but not modified. That makes it an ideal candidate for becoming part of a utilities class or even an archived library routine.

2.3 Comments about Style and Documentation

There are a number of stylistic characteristics common to the program code presented in this book. Many of these are *religious issues* and are thus neither technically right or wrong. In the course of many years of writing programs, we have come to the conclusion that a large fraction of the errors that are made are the result of carelessness or forgetfulness. For that reason, habits that reduce the likelihood of such errors should be cultivated.

First, each of your code files needs to have your attribution in it in the code. Under U.S. copyright law, once you write the code, you hold the copyright. Although

[2]In computing, a *parser* is an application, or part of an application, that takes raw data as input and breaks it down into its component parts. The first step in compiling a Java program, for example, is to parse the text of the program, separate the parsed *tokens* into Java reserved words, variable names, operator symbols, and such, and then verify that the input program is syntactically correct.

you are not *required* to put in the copyright statement in order to claim copyright, it is a good practice because it will notify others that you are aware of the law. You should also maintain an audit log of when the code was last updated. It is increasingly the case for such things as security logs, health care code, and financial code (to name only a few) that a complete provenance of the code is necessary in order for the owners to obtain certification that the code is acceptable for use.

The most important character traits for someone developing code would then seem to be a serious discipline and an attention to avoiding the human errors that one knows one is prone to making. If you know you make the same mistake over and over again, you should try to find ways to write code so that it's harder to make that same mistake.

We tend to group methods first by type and then alphabetically. There are two schools of thought on accessors and mutators. One school of thought is that the accessor and the mutator for a given instance variable should appear together. Another school would group all the accessors and then all the mutators. In this example, we have grouped all the accessors, then all the mutators, and then all the "general-purpose" methods, and we have sorted the methods in each group alphabetically by method name so we know more or less where the methods will be located in the code. Again, this is one school of thought and not the only one. However, you should choose an overall organization plan for your code and get in the habit of following that plan. It isn't necessary, but it might well help cut down on the number of silly errors that you, like all of us, would otherwise make.[3]

We tend to be very precise in using the `this` qualifier to refer to variable and method names inside the current class. The reason for this is to force us to notice whether or not a symbol is an instance variable or a method of the class. The compiler will prevent us from using `this` on a symbol that is not defined to the entire class. If we always use `this`, then we would expect to be able to distinguish class symbols, labeled with the `this`, from local symbols without that label. That will help us avoid mistakes due to improper scoping of symbols.

We also tend to put a comment on a closing brace that has worked its way some distance from its opening brace. The closing brace on the `Main` and `Record` classes, for example, has a comment telling us what that brace is supposed to close. It is always possible to make mistakes and have improper nesting, but at least if we label what we think is the proper nesting, it might help us if we make a mistake later.

We also tend to put a constant class label (in this case, a `String` variable named `TAG` and with values "`Main: `" and one with value "`Record: `") in a class

[3]Long ago, in the days when programs had `GOTO label` statements that allowed one to write convoluted *spaghetti code* that was very hard to read and follow, one of my colleagues used the `GOTO` liberally. But to make life a little easier (for him), he always branched south on the New Jersey Turnpike. The code was read top to bottom, and the branch labels went north to south, exit by exit. To others, this was not necessarily a big help, but to my colleague, who had been raised in New Jersey, it was a great help to his understanding of the code.

definition. In the process of testing,[4] if it becomes necessary to print something out, then we have ready-made a label on the output that will tell us from where that output is coming.

We tend to put a comment header before methods and before blocks of code. This isn't necessarily a standard technique, but we do it because the line of asterisks provides a demarcation that guides us as we skim the code.

Note also the two different kinds of comment headers in the `Main` class. At the top, the header reads

```
/***********************************
 *
**/
```

In the body of the code, however, the comment header is written with the alternative double-slash

```
//**********************************
//
///
```

As standalone comments, both are identical. The difference between the two comes when one tries to nest comments. It is not permissible to nest the slash-star–star-slash comments. That is,

```
/***********************************
 *
  /***********************************
   *
  **/
**/
```

triggers a compiler error but

```
/***********************************
 *
  //**********************************
  //
  ///
**/
```

does not. If it should happen that in testing you want to comment out a large chunk of code because things really went wrong, you can do that with `/* ... */`, and if your comments in the body of the code have been done with the double-slash, then

[4] In keeping with what seems to be Google's approach, we will talk about "testing" but not about "debugging" in this text. The former word has the positive outlook of producing code that has been verified to do what it's supposed to do, while the latter word refers in some sense only to the process of determining that the code does not do what it's not supposed to do.

the nesting is permissible and the only change you need is to put the slash-star at the beginning and the star-slash at the end of the block of code you want to avoid for the moment. It's a hack, but it can be a useful hack.

2.3.1 Javadoc

One reason for being careful about documenting Java programs is that the Javadoc documentation generator will produce "standard" documentation pages

Package Class Use Tree Deprecated Index Help

PREV CLASS NEXT CLASS FRAMES NO FRAMES
SUMMARY: NESTED | FIELD | CONSTR | METHOD DETAIL: FIELD | CONSTR | METHOD

Class Record

```
java.lang.object
  └Record
```

```
public class Record
extends java.lang.object
```

Class for handling the data in a Record. This is the class to handle a single phonebook-like record.

Version:
1.00 2010-07-06 Copyright(C) 2010 by Duncan A. Buell. All rights reserved.

Author:
Duncan A. Buell

Constructor Summary
`Record()` Constructor.

Method Summary	
`int`	`compareTo(Record that)` Method to compare the `name` values of records.
`java.lang.String`	`getName()` Accessor method to get the `name`.
`java.lang.String`	`getOffice()` Accessor method to get the `Office`.
`java.lang.String`	`getPhone()` Accessor method to get the `phone`.
`int`	`getTeaching()` Accessor method to get the `teaching`.
`Record`	`readRecord(java.util.Scanner inFile)` Method to read the flat data file from an input `Scanner` file.
`java.lang.String`	`toString()` Usual `toString` method.

Methods inherited from class java.lang.Object
`equals, getClass, hashCode, notify, notifyAll, wait, wait, wait`

FIGURE 2.7 ■ Part 1 of the Javadoc for the `Record` class.

Constructor Detail

Record

`public Record()`

Constructor. We create the record and assign dummy values so as not to have null values.

Method Detail

getName

`public java.lang.String getName()`

Accessor method to get the `name`.

Returns:
the value of `name`

---

getOffice

`public java.lang.String getOffice()`

Accessor method to get the `office`.

Returns:
the value of `office`

---

getPhone

`public java.lang.String getPhone()`

Accessor method to get the `phone`.

Returns:
the value of `phone`

---

getTeaching

`public int getTeaching()`

Accessor method to get the `teaching`.

Returns:
the value of `teaching`

FIGURE 2.8 ■ Part 2 of the Javadoc for the `Record` class.

automatically—*provided* that the programs have been documented in the way that Javadoc expects. The Javadoc output for the code in Figures 2.1–2.4 is presented in Figures 2.7–2.9. Careful use of the `<code> ... </code>`, `@param`, and `@return` tags results in font changes for method and variable names and appropriate documentation of parameters passed in and values returned sent back by the methods. The initial sentence of documentation (with "sentence" defined to end at the first period) for any method also triggers a special response in the generated documentation.

compareTo

`public int compareTo(Record that)`

Method to compare the `name` values of records. This does a lexicographic comparison on the data stored, so if the data stored is not in last-name order we will get something different from what might be expected.

Parameters:
`that` - the "that" record to compare to

Returns:
−1, 0, or +1 according as how the comparison goes.

---

readRecord

`public Record readRecord(java.util.Scanner inFile)`

Method to read the flat data file from an input `Scanner` file. Note that this is more or less hard coded and that we don't bulletproof the input; among other things we assume that partial records don't appear in the input data.

Parameters:
`inFile` - the `Scanner` from which to read

Returns:
the `Record` that was read

---

toString

`public java.lang.String toString()`

Usual `toString` method.

Overrides:

`toString` in class `java.lang.Object`

Returns:

the `String` value of the record.

Package Class Use Tree Deprecated Index Help

PREV CLASS NEXT CLASS FRAMES NO FRAMES
SUMMARY: NESTED | FIELD | CONSTR | METHOD DETAIL: FIELD | CONSTR | METHOD

FIGURE 2.9 ■ Part 3 of the Javadoc for the `Record` class.

■ 2.4 UML

It is becoming standard for code to be presented as a *UML diagram.* Such a diagram indicates in a standard shorthand notation the instance variables, method names, values returned, and parameters, and whether these are public or private. The UML diagram for the code in this chapter is shown in Figure 2.10.

The uppermost section of the class diagram is the class name. Next comes the list of instance variables, together with their types and a + or − depending on whether the variable is `public` or `private`, respectively. Finally, in the lowest of the three sections of the diagram the methods are listed with their signatures of parameter types and the type of the return value (if any).

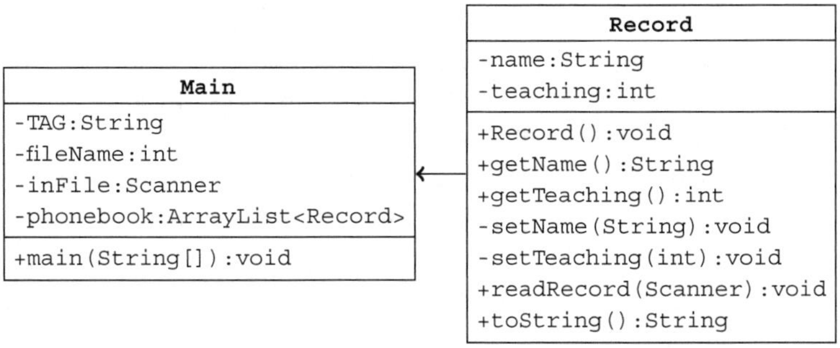

FIGURE 2.10 ■ The UML diagram for the phone book.

From the class diagrams one can generate at least the boilerplate for variables, accessors, mutators, and general methods. Indeed, there are a number of software tools that will do exactly this for you.

■ 2.5 Summary

We have attempted a brief refresher on Java by means of an example of a complete program. This includes an introduction into the structuring of programs into classes and the appropriate functionality to include in each of those classes.

We have also undertaken a first look at the requirements for documenting programs both for program maintainance needs and because software that makes decisions for the real world is increasingly coming under legal scrutiny as to what decisions are made and whether the code can be verified to do only and exactly what it is intended to do.

Finally, we introduced UML, the Unified Modeling Language that is now the standard for describing software modules and how they interrelate with each other in larger software systems.

■ 2.6 Exercises

(Sample data for many of these exercises can be found on the website at go.jblearning.com/Buell.)

1. If you have not used the `Scanner` class already, write a program to read date data. Create a file with a dozen or so lines of data. Each line should have a month, day, and year, followed by a day of the week, such as

```
10 23 1982 Monday
```

The month, day, and year should be integers, separated by spaces, and the weekday should be a `String`. Verify that you can open the file, read the data into variables in a separate class from the main program that opened the file, and then output the data in a format identical to the input.

2. Augment your code in the previous exercise so it parses data from an input `String` variable into `int` data items for month, day, and year. Use the `substring` method to read lines such as

```
10/23/1982 Monday
```

into two `String` variables and then parse the first to extract month, day, and year as integers.

3. Do the same as the first two exercises, but this time use data that would resemble retail transaction data, such as

```
3 $2.49 notebooks
```

that has the number of items (an integer), the price of each item (a string that needs to be parsed), and a text description for the item (that can be taken as written). Use the `substring` method to parse the price, and then print a total of the cost.

4. Read the date data file and find the earliest date, the latest date, and the number of earliest and latest dates. This should refresh your memory on loops and `if` statements.

5. The phonebook code as presented has only name and course teaching number in the data payload. Augment the data payload to include phone number and office number, together with accessors and mutators and updated versions of the `readRecord` and `toString` methods.

6. The phonebook code as presented has the `ArrayList` as part of the `main` program in the `Main` class. Improve this application by creating an actual `PhoneBook` class "between" the `Main` and `Record` classes. Your new class should implement the `ArrayList` as well as a method for each of the three blocks of code in the current `main` method.

7. Begin to create a "utilities" class, perhaps named `FileUtils`, that will have a static method for opening a file when passed the filename as a parameter. Your method should handle the error checking that is currently in the `Main` class and should return the `Scanner` that is the opened file. After you have created a method to open a file, create another method to close a file. Now update the code in this chapter to use the utilities and thus clean up the appearance and readability of the `Main` class.

3 Flat Files

Objectives

- An outline of a program to manage flat files of records
- A simple sorting algorithm
- A look ahead to improved methods for sorting and searching
- A look ahead to more sophisticated approaches for abstracting computations to make programs more general and more reliable
- A binary search algorithm, the first "mature" algorithm covered in this text

Key Terms

abstract class	dynamic data structures	probe
asymptotic analysis	flat file	pseudocode
binary search	generics	recursive divide and conquer
bubblesort	index	semantics
discipline of programming	optimal	syntax
driver program	portable code	

Introduction

One of our guiding principles is that students at this stage in a computer science curriculum have probably learned how to do basic computations and now need to learn more sophisticated methods for writing programs and producing computational results. We start in this chapter, then, with a summary of what might be considered to be a reasonably full and complete implementation of an application but an implementation that uses only the techniques usually covered in a first course in computing. After presenting this "naive" version of a program, we will then discuss the ways in which it would be improved upon through the methods and analysis developed later in this text.

3.1 A Basic Indexed File

Let us now look at an example of the naive implementation of a *flat file* with an index, complete with a method for looking up an entry in the file. But before we do that, we make a disclaimer of sorts by directing the reader to Appendix A, where a number of the author's idiosyncrasies of coding are presented. We emphasize that none of these idiosyncrasies should be taken as absolute dogma. Style is a religious issue, and there are many competing religions. Anyone taking this course and writing programs should, however, adopt one of the standard styles and apply it consistently. The more predictable and routine the presentation of code is to a reader, the less likely that tricky points will be overlooked and silly errors made.

Before embarking on the writing of a program, we should first have an idea of what it is that we want our program to do. In the case of this example, the program is an address book. We could implement this with a spreadsheet, and indeed a spreadsheet and a flat file are very similar. We will want to add records to and delete records from our file. We will want to be able to do lookups into the file, which means we will need a "find" capability. Usually we will keep something like a phone book in sorted order by last name, so we will need a way to sort the records in the file.

Although a simple flat file phone book may appear to be an example too simple to be of real value, most of the issues involved in the use of mature algorithms come up once we think of our flat file growing in size from a few hundred records to tens of millions of records. Adding and deleting records in a large file, searching for records, and keeping the file in sorted order all become tasks that can no longer be done in a naive way or else the processing time will become a problem for the user of the software.

3.1.1 A Basic Program

We take the view in this course that a program generally consists of four basic parts.

1. **The Data Payload**
   As in the example from Chapter 2, the lowest level in the hierarchy will be a set of "payload" records that contain the actual data. The class for the payload will usually be named `Record`, or `Payload`, or occasionally something more meaningful. All the instance variables and methods for managing the actual data will reside in this class. The goal in this text is to learn to manage data. For the most part, the means for managing the data are independent of the data being managed, so most of the higher-level constructs will work with virtually any payload class. Indeed, that's the point of good programming style and part of the justification for object-oriented languages like Java. The code that does

the sorting of records, for example, really doesn't need to know what is in those records.

2. **The Data Structure Class**
   At the next level up, the "data structure" class will contain the instance variables and methods to manage the data structure that is the particular object of study. In the case of our example program, the data structure begins not as a separate class but simply as an `ArrayList`, and the data structure in this example is embedded in the code of the next higher "application" level. This is not an unusual style for many simple applications, and indeed not a bad program development technique either. If the `ArrayList` in the previous chapter's code turns out to be too inefficient and an improvement to the code is necessary, then having a working application is a great benefit. It allows the programmer to concentrate on just the parts of the code being improved, confident that the rest of the code that drives and tests the application has already been found correct.

3. **The User Application**
   Next higher in the hierarchy is the "application" class that will contain the code implementing the features of the desired application. In the case of our example flat file with an index, the application is that of a phone book. Typical user actions with a phone book are to add records, to delete records, to update records, and to search for records (usually by name). The need-to-know principle of information encapsulation and hiding applies here just as it does everywhere else. The phone book application needs to know that there is a method to add records, but it doesn't really need to know the details of what happens when a record is added. The application layer thus usually creates an instance of the data structure and then invokes its methods.

4. **The Main Program/Driver Program**
   Finally, we will always use a *driver program*, which will contain the `Main` class. The driver will normally do three things:
   - The driver will open files for input of data and will open files for output or otherwise establish that an output mechanism exists.
   - In the `Main` class of the driver program, we will create an instance of an "application" class to perform some useful task. The application class will in turn create and use the data structure under discussion. After creating the application instance and arranging for input and output, the driver program will then exercise the data structure to verify that the other two parts of the program (at least two classes but sometimes more) are working correctly.
   - The driver will then clean up after the test and terminate the program naturally.

In the case of our first main example, the application is that of an address book or phone book of directory information. In this case, the payload for the data structure is an individual `Record` item containing the last name, office number, phone number, and current teaching assignment of a list of faculty members. These four fields of a `Record` are the instance variables of the `Record`, and their declaration together with their accessors and mutators should normally be done inside the `Record` class. We can thus view a single directory item about a single individual as an abstract data type and encapsulate all the management of the information for that class inside the `Record` class. This is the simplest form of data encapsulation: Beyond the code inside the `Record` class itself, there is usually no need for any program to deal with the payload record in any way other than as a single entity. Exceptions would exist if one were to sort on multiple fields; if there is only one "correct sorted order" on the data, then programs outside the class do not necessarily need to know what that order is, but if one wants access by last name and by office number, then programs outside the `Record` class would, of course, have to know that these were data fields and that one could access the data in those orders. Generally, though, since there is no "need to know" beyond the confines of the `Record` class, we encapsulate inside the `Record` class all the code that handles its variables. Figure 3.1 shows the UML diagram for the `Record` class; this differs from the `Record` of the previous chapter only in that more instance variables exist and that some comparison methods have been added to allow us to sort the list.

The middle two levels of our application are a data structure of `Record` data. In our initial version, that structure is simply an array of `Record` type and we combine the data structure (the array) with the user interface and methods (add a record, etc.). By analogy with a simple spreadsheet, the spreadsheet itself is the data structure, each row of that data structure is a unique instance of a `Record`, and each column of the spreadsheet is a field within the `Record`.

In general, you should always consider the code hierarchy with an eye to writing *portable code*. The phone book application, for example, is really just a program for handling records that look like a spreadsheet. Very little should need to be done if those records changed from being phone book records and became retail transactions instead, perhaps sorted now by date and not by last name. It should be possible, then, to swap out the payload `Record` class for a retail transaction record class, with different variables, and to have all the intermediate code need no changes. The only change that would be necessary is that the search in the `main` method would have to search on some different variable. This is part of the reason for our restricted notion of a `Main` class. The `Main` class should be used for driving and testing the code below it. If the data payload is changed out, then the driver code may need to change in order to conduct a slightly different sort of test, but the application code should need little or no change.

3.1.2 The `Record` Code

Figure 3.1 shows the UML diagram for the **Record** class.

Record
-DUMMYSTRING:String
-DUMMYINT:int
-name:String
-office:String - added
-phone:String - added
-teaching:int
+Record():void
+getName():String
+getOffice():String - added
+getPhone():String - added
+getTeaching():int
-setName(String):void
-setOffice(String):void - added
-setPhone(String):void - added
-setTeaching(int):void
+compareName(String):boolean
+compareTo(Record):int
+readRecord(Scanner):Record
+toString():String

FIGURE 3.1 ■ The UML diagram for the `Record` class.

The **Record** class handles everything connected with a single record and the individual fields inside that record, and the code for this class differs little from the code in Chapter 2. We have additional instance variables and therefore additional accessors and mutators, and the **readRecord** and **toString** methods must be different to include the new variables. The real difference, though, is in the comparison methods; the **compareTo** and **compareName** methods are new. Code for these methods is shown in Figure 3.2.

Comparison of numbers and comparisons of variables of primitive types (**boolean**, **int**, **double**)[1] are usually done with the standard arithmetic symbols $<$, $\leq$, $>$, $\geq$, and $=$ (and the computer version ==). Java comparison of the values

[1]There are other primitive types, but we will use them only sparingly in this book. The **float** data type, for example, is largely unnecessary these days. The only good reason for using a **float** variable in the past was to save memory space (4 bytes instead of 8). Memory has become cheap, however, so there is little practical reason for not doing more accurate computations, and the standard for real scientific computing has been **double** variables for some years now. There are, however, some classes of Java (the **Color** class is one) that use **float** and not **double** values, so a **float** value must be used when required.

```
/************************************************************
 * Method to compare the <code>name</code> values of records.
 * This does a comparison on the last name stored against the
 * string passed in, returning true or false.
 * @param thatName the string to compare last name against
 * @return true or false for the comparison
**/
  public boolean compareName(String thatName)
  {
    return this.getName().equals(thatName);
  }
/************************************************************
 * Method to compare the <code>name</code> values of records.
 * This does a lexicographic comparison on the data stored, so
 * if the data stored is not in last-name order we will get
 * something different from what might be expected.
 * @param that the "that" record to compare to
 * @return -1, 0, or +1 depending on how the comparison goes.
**/
  public int compareTo(Record that)
  {
    return this.getName().compareTo(that.getName());
  }
```

FIGURE 3.2 ■ The comparison methods in the `Record` class.

stored in `String` variables, however, is done with a `compareTo` method that returns −1, 0, or +1 depending on whether the "first" string is less than, equal to, or greater than the "second" string lexicographically. We will maintain this construct for comparisons, as well as the asymmetric syntax:

```
thisObject.compareTo(thatObject);
```

By implementing one or more `compareTo` methods in a class, we can sort the class on different fields. For an address book, last name would be one obvious choice, but one might also want to sort on the course number in this file. The fact that the course number `teaching` is an instance of `int` data means that a different comparison would need to be made. As we will see later, the various generic, `abstract`, and overriding or overloading features of Java are designed specifically to make this kind of thing easier to do. What we really want to do is to make it easy to perform comparisons—regardless of data type—on any of the fields in the record, without exposing to a calling program any information or details that the caller doesn't need to know. In a later example, we will create a `compareTo` method that could be written and rewritten to make any desired comparisons of the `Record` data.

In addition to the `compareTo` method that we use in the bubblesort routine (to be discussed shortly), we also have a `compareName` method; when passed a `String` value as a parameter, this method will compare the parameter against the last name and return either the first record that matches that last name or a null value.

3.1.3 A Driver for the Application

At the top level of our application is the driver code, presented in Figures 3.3–3.5 as the code for the `Main` class. Nothing very special happens here. We open input and output files, create the `FlatFile` object, and print out its contents to show

```
import java.io.PrintWriter;
import java.util.Scanner;
/***************************************************************
 * Main class to drive the <code>FlatFile</code> application.
 * This program opens an input <code>Scanner</code> file and an
 * output <code>PrintWriter</code>, creates an instance of a
 * <code>FlatFile</code> structure, and then writes out the
 * <code>FlatFile</code> to show that it is indeed empty.
 * The program then reads the input into the structure,
 * writes out the structure as read, sorts the structure,
 * and writes out the sorted structure.
 * Two searches are then done, and the program terminates.
 * @author Duncan A. Buell
 * @version 1.00 2010-07-06
 * Copyright (C) 2010 by Duncan A. Buell.  All rights reserved.
**/
public class Main
{
  public static void main (String[] args)
  {
    final String TAG = "Main: ";
    String inFileName = null;
    String outFileName = null;
    String searchString = "";
    Scanner inFile = null;
    PrintWriter outFile = null;
    FlatFile theFlatFile = null;
    Record foundRecord = null;
    inFileName = "myinputfile";
    outFileName = "myoutputfile";
    inFile = FileUtils.ScannerOpen(inFileName);
    outFile = FileUtils.PrintWriterOpen(outFileName);
```

FIGURE 3.3 ■ Part 1 of the driver `Main` class for the phone book example.

```
//*********************************************************
// Create the flat file and read and write it.
outFile.printf("%s create and write out the empty file%n",
               TAG);
theFlatFile = new FlatFile();
outFile.printf("%s%n", theFlatFile.toString());
outFile.printf("%s empty file was created%n", TAG);
outFile.printf("%s read the data%n", TAG);
theFlatFile.readFile(inFile);
outFile.printf("%s the data has been read%n", TAG);
FileUtils.CloseFile(inFile);
outFile.printf("%s write out the file%n%s%n",
               TAG, theFlatFile.toString());
outFile.printf("%s done with the write%n", TAG);
//*********************************************************
// Finally, sort the file and write out the sorted file.
outFile.printf("%s sort the file%n", TAG);
theFlatFile.sortFile();
outFile.printf("%s after sorting, write the file%n%s%n",
               TAG, theFlatFile.toString());
outFile.printf("%s done with the write%n", TAG);
```

FIGURE 3.4 ■ Part 2 of the driver `Main` class for the phone book example.

that the object is in fact empty (and that our code handles the case of an empty object). After reading in the data, we echo the data to make sure that our read has been successful.

Because data is generally more useful when it is sorted, we call a sort routine to sort the `ArrayList` of data.

We then perform two searches, one on the name "Smith" that we know is the name of someone in the data file, and one on the name "Buell" that we know is not in the data file. (We are ignoring the issue of multiple records with the same last name as key; that is, we assume that we have no *duplicate keys.*)

■ 3.1.4 The Original `Flatfile` Code

The code at the bottom of the hierarchy for this application is the `Record` class that handles the data payload of our flat file. At the top of the hierarchy is the driver program. As will be typical in this book, the data structure, that is, the flat file itself, is managed by the code in the intermediate `FlatFile` class, whose UML diagram is given in Figure 3.6 and whose code is shown in Figures 3.7–3.12.

```
    //*****************************************************
    // Find a particular item and print the record if found.
    searchString = new String("Buell");
    outFile.printf("%s find the data item '%s'%n",
                    TAG, searchString);
    foundRecord = theFlatFile.findRecord(searchString);
    if(foundRecord != null)
    {
      outFile.printf("%s found record '%s'%n",TAG,
                              foundRecord.toString());
    }
    else
    {
      outFile.printf("%s record %s not found%n",TAG,
                              searchString);
    }
    outFile.printf("%s done with first search%n",TAG);
    searchString = new String("Smith");
    outFile.printf("%s find the data item '%s'%n",
                    TAG, searchString);
    foundRecord = theFlatFile.findRecord(searchString);
    if(foundRecord != null)
    {
      outFile.printf("%s found record '%s'%n",TAG,
                              foundRecord.toString());
    }
    else
    {
      outFile.printf("%s record %s not found%n",TAG,
                              searchString);
    }
    outFile.printf("%s done with second search%n",TAG);
    //*****************************************************
    // We're done.  Close up and go home.
    outFile.printf("%s done with main%n", TAG);
    FileUtils.CloseFile(outFile);
  }
}
 // public class Main
```

FIGURE 3.5 ■ Part 3 of the driver `Main` class for the phone book example.

FlatFile
-index:ArrayList<Integer>
-recs:ArrayList<Record>
+FlatFile():void
+getRecord(int):Record
+getSize():int
+findRecord(String):Record
+readFile(Scanner):void
+sortFile():void
+toString():String

FIGURE 3.6 ■ The UML diagram for the `FlatFile` class.

```java
import java.util.ArrayList;
import java.util.Scanner;
/*********************************************************************
 * Class for handling activity at the level of the flat file.
 * This class has an <code>ArrayList</code> of
 * <code>Record</code> data and an index list for sorting,
 * methods to access, the two <code>ArrayList</code>s,
 * methods to read and to <code>toString</code>, and a
 * simple bubblesort method for sorting the list.
 * @author Duncan Buell
 * @version 1.00 2010-07-05
 * Copyright(c) 2010 Duncan A. Buell.  All rights reserved.
**/
public class FlatFile
{
/*********************************************************************
 * Instance variables.
**/
  static final String TAG = "FlatFile: ";
  private ArrayList<Integer> index;
  private ArrayList<Record> recs; // the records to be stored

/*********************************************************************
 * Constructor.
 * Initialize the <code>ArrayList</code> variables.
**/
  public FlatFile()
  {
    this.recs = new ArrayList<Record>();
    this.index = new ArrayList<Integer>();
  }
```

FIGURE 3.7 ■ Part 1 of the `FlatFile` class for the phone book example.

```
/*******************************************************************
 * Method to get an individual <code>Record</code>.
 * @param which the subscript of the <code>Record</code> to return
 * @return the <code>Record</code>
**/
  public Record getRecord(int which)
  {
    return this.recs.get(this.index.get(which));
  }
/*******************************************************************
 * Method to get the size of the <code>ArrayList</code> of
 * data.  We are going to call this an accessor, although it
 * is actually generating derived data.  One of its other
 * purposes is to make sure that the size of the data list
 * and the size of the index list are the same.
 * @return the size of the arrays
**/
  public int getSize()
  {
    if(this.recs.size() != this.index.size())
    {
      System.out.println("ERROR: unequal list sizes " +
                         this.recs.size() + ", " +
                         this.index.size());
      System.exit(0);
    }
    return this.recs.size();
  } // public int getSize()
```

FIGURE 3.8 ■ Part 2 of the `FlatFile` class for the phone book example.

We store the `Record` data and its index using `ArrayLists`. It would be reasonable in a more complicated program to have a separate class for the different index arrays, but in this simple example we have included the index as an array inside the `FlatFile` class. Note that as we read the data in we set the initial value of the index to the physical record number in the file, so that all our references to the array can be made not as `recs.get(i)` but as `recs.get(index.get(i))`.

The accessor and mutator for the `Record` array are not bulletproofed to prevent errors if an invalid subscript is provided to the methods (we will take care of this in a moment). Similar to what we did in Chapter 2, we include methods

```
/*********************************************************************
 * Method to find a record in the flat file.
 *
 * This is a linear search.
 * @param name the last name to look up the record of
 * @return the found record, or null if not found.
**/
  public Record findRecord(String name)
  {
    Record returnValue = null;

    for(int i = 0; i < this.getSize(); ++i)
    {
      if(this.recs.get(index.get(i)).compareName(name))
      {
        returnValue = this.recs.get(index.get(i));
      }
    }

    return returnValue;
  } // public Record findRecord(String item)
```

FIGURE 3.9 ■ Part 3 of the `FlatFile` class for the phone book example.

```
/*********************************************************************
 * Method to read the file from an input <code>Scanner</code>
 * file.  This reads the entire file.  As we read and store
 * the records, we also store the subscripts in the index.
 * @param inFile the <code>Scanner</code> from which to read
**/
  public void readFile(Scanner inFile)
  {
    int sub;
    Record rec = null;

    sub = 0;
    while(inFile.hasNext())
    {
      rec = new Record();
      recs.add(rec.readRecord(inFile));
      index.add(sub);
      ++sub;
    }
  }
```

FIGURE 3.10 ■ Part 4 of the `FlatFile` class for the phone book example.

```
/*****************************************************************
 * Method to sort a file.
 * This is, embarrassingly enough, simply a bubblesort,
 * but it works and is useful for demonstration purposes.
 * Note that we sort keys and adjust the index but do not
 * actually move records around in the list.
**/
  public void sortFile()
  {
    int tempIndex;

    for(int length = this.getSize(); length > 1; --length)
    {
      for(int i = 0; i < length-1; ++i)
      {
        if(this.recs.get(this.index.get(i)).
              compareTo(this.recs.get(this.index.get(i+1))) > 0)
        {
          tempIndex = this.index.get(i);
          this.index.set(i, this.index.get(i+1));
          this.index.set(i+1, tempIndex);
        }
      }
    }
  }
```

FIGURE 3.11 ■ Part 5 of the `FlatFile` class for the phone book example.

```
/*****************************************************************
 * Usual <code>toString</code> method.
 * @return the <code>String</code> value of the file.
**/
  public String toString()
  {
    String s = "";
    for(int i = 0; i < this.getSize(); ++i)
    {
      s += String.format("%s(idx,rec) (%d,%d) %s%n",
                         TAG, i, this.index.get(i),
                         recs.get(this.index.get(i)).toString());
    }
    return s;
  }
} // public class FlatFile
```

FIGURE 3.12 ■ Part 6 of the `FlatFile` class for the phone book example.

to read an entire input file and to convert the entire array into a `String` for printing. The former method extends (and invokes) the `readRecord` method, and the latter method extends and invokes the `toString` method of the underlying `Record` class.

We reiterate what was said in Chapter 2, that the `toString` method allows for the data of the `Record` to be formatted and returned exactly in the format declared to be official by The Powers That Be without any details of the inner workings of the `Record` class being exposed to the user of the method.

Because we intend to call a sort method from the driver program, we include a `sortFile` method that will sort the data. (We will discuss sorting and the details of this code in a moment.) In this case, we don't sort by actually moving the records around (although we could). Instead, we sort by setting up an *index* `ArrayList`; the integer at subscript `i` in the index is the subscript of the `i`th record in the actual `ArrayList` of data.

Finally, we have in our driver program a call to a search method to look up an entry by last name, so we need the `findRecord` method to implement this functionality.

3.2 An Analysis of the Code

Using the input data file `myinputdata` presented in Figure 3.13, we get the output shown in Figure 3.14. We have left in some of what would normally be considered testing information for demonstration purposes. All of this is well and good, but clearly this is only the first step in producing an address book program that someone would want to use.

```
Herbert  2A41 789.0123 390
Lander   2A47 789.7890 146
Winthrop 3A71 789.4667 611
Marion   2A13 789.1536 750
Adams    3A56 789.8702 522
Smith    2A46 789.5275 101
Axolotl  3A22 789.2749 102
Zokni    3A39 789.9111 350
Igen     2A21 789.6050 240
Nem      2A89 789.3383 790
```

FIGURE 3.13 ■ Input data for the indexed flat file example.

```
Main:  create and write out the empty file
Main:  empty file was created
Main:  read the data
Main:  the data has been read
Main:  write out the file
FlatFile: (idx,rec) (0,0) Herbert    2A41  789.0123   390
FlatFile: (idx,rec) (1,1) Lander     2A47  789.7890   146
FlatFile: (idx,rec) (2,2) Winthrop   3A71  789.4667   611
FlatFile: (idx,rec) (3,3) Marion     2A13  789.1536   750
FlatFile: (idx,rec) (4,4) Adams      3A56  789.8702   522
FlatFile: (idx,rec) (5,5) Smith      2A46  789.5275   101
FlatFile: (idx,rec) (6,6) Axolotl    3A22  789.2749   102
FlatFile: (idx,rec) (7,7) Zokni      3A39  789.9111   350
FlatFile: (idx,rec) (8,8) Igen       2A21  789.6050   240
FlatFile: (idx,rec) (9,9) Nem        2A89  789.3383   790
Main:  done with the write
Main:  sort the file
Main:  after sorting, write the file
FlatFile: (idx,rec) (0,4) Adams      3A56  789.8702   522
FlatFile: (idx,rec) (1,6) Axolotl    3A22  789.2749   102
FlatFile: (idx,rec) (2,0) Herbert    2A41  789.0123   390
FlatFile: (idx,rec) (3,8) Igen       2A21  789.6050   240
FlatFile: (idx,rec) (4,1) Lander     2A47  789.7890   146
FlatFile: (idx,rec) (5,3) Marion     2A13  789.1536   750
FlatFile: (idx,rec) (6,9) Nem        2A89  789.3383   790
FlatFile: (idx,rec) (7,5) Smith      2A46  789.5275   101
FlatFile: (idx,rec) (8,2) Winthrop   3A71  789.4667   611
FlatFile: (idx,rec) (9,7) Zokni      3A39  789.9111   350
Main:  done with the write
Main:  find the data item 'Buell'
Main:  record Buell not found
Main:  done with first search
Main:  find the data item 'Smith'
Main:  found record 'Smith     2A46  789.5275   101'
Main:  done with second search
Main:  done with main
```

FIGURE 3.14 ■ Output data for the indexed flat file example.

■ 3.2.1 Sorted Data?

First off, we notice that the records are not presented to the program from the input file in sorted order. This is normal; life doesn't always present things to us in the order in which we would like them to happen.

We have two choices when presented with unsorted data. One is that we can read the data and physically move the records into their proper order.[2] This is what is normally done on library shelves; the books are physically kept in a defined order based, for most university libraries, on the Library of Congress indexing system. This physical sorting of data is acceptable only if the following three conditions are met:

1. We don't have a lot of data that would have to be moved.
2. The records are to be accessed in only one order (last name, in this case).
3. The data will be fairly static, because we don't want to have to keep moving things around all the time.

The problem of sorting data by moving data around and then keeping the data physically in sorted order is increased when one takes into consideration the problem of deleting records. In a flat file image such as we have created in memory so far, a record that is deleted in the middle presents a problem. The naive way to fill the empty space left by the deleted record would be to shift the records up one space as needed. If the deleted record is the last record in the physical order, there is actually nothing to do (except adjust the size counter), but if the deleted record is the first record in the physical order, its deletion requires the entire array to be shifted up. That's a lot of work with no benefit except to take out a blank space.

The three conditions that make it reasonable to sort by moving data are rarely met in practice, so the customary way to deal with this kind of data—and your second option—is to use an *index*. We will read the data and store it into an array in the physical order in which it presents itself, but then we will *invert* on last name as a *key* to get an index. The ith index value will be the subscript of the record that should appear in position i in sorted order. If we were to sort and produce an index, we would get the second column of Figure 3.15; this would be produced by code like the following. The important thing to notice here is the *indirect reference*; we don't access the record at subscript `i` but rather the record at subscript `index[i]`.

```
for(int i = 0; i < size(); ++i)
{
  System.out.printf("%d %d %s%n",
                    i, index[i], record.getName(index[i]);
}
```

---

[2] In the pre-Cambrian era of microcomputers, the author had an outside consulting job that required sorting an address book on an early "personal" computer. The sort implemented by the vendor for use on 1979-era $5\frac{1}{4}$-inch floppy disks was horrendously inefficient. Putting a full disk of records even once into sorted order required so much reading and writing to and from the disk that the disk became scratched to the point that it was no longer readable.

Sorted Order Subscript	Physical Order Subscript	Last Name
0	4	Adams
1	6	Axolotl
2	0	Herbert
3	8	Igen
4	1	Lander
5	3	Marion
6	9	Nem
7	5	Smith
8	2	Winthrop
9	7	Zokni

FIGURE 3.15 ■ Indexed file.

■ 3.2.2 A Simple but Inefficient Sorting Algorithm

Our data is not presented in sorted order, so we have implemented a simple *bubblesort*[3] whose code is shown in the `FlatFile` code.

The index array is implemented as an instance variable

```
private ArrayList<Integer> index
```

whose values run in parallel with the `recs` of `Record` data; the value of `index.get(0)` is the subscript of the `Record` with the alphabetically first `name`, which is subscript 4 in Figure 3.15; the value of `index.get(1)` is the subscript of the `Record` with the alphabetically next `name`, which is subscript 6 in Figure 3.15; and so on. When we read the record with subscript `i`, we initialize `index.get(i)` to have the value `i`. When we walk through the array in the `toString` method, the code becomes:

```
for(int i = 0; i < this.getSize(); ++i)
{
  s += String.format("%n(%3d,%3d) %s",
                     i, this.getIndex(i),
                     recs.get(this.getIndex(i)).toString());
}
```

[3] With small apologies to the English teachers of the world, we will write the names of the various sorting algorithms without a space before the word "sort."

Note also that we have implemented a `getSize` method that returns the size of the `ArrayList recs`. In fact, both the `ArrayLists recs` and `index` have their own `size` method. But since these values are supposed to always be the same (except during execution of the two lines of code between adding a new `Record` to the `ArrayList` and then adding a new entry to the `index`), we have implemented and used our own method to return the size of the lists and included code in that method to check each time that the two sizes are the same. This kind of defensive programming can reduce the number of silly errors in programming and make life easier.

Most importantly, we need to implement a sorting routine, the code for which is shown in the `FlatFile` program. This bubblesort is, as we shall see later, not a terribly good sort, but it is simple to explain and it happens to get the job done for the small data file on which we apply it.

As the following pseudocode shows, a bubblesort consists of a doubly-nested loop.

```
for(length from arraysize to 1 exclusive stepping backwards)
{
  for(i from 0 to length-1 exclusive)
  {
    if(record(i) > record(i+1))
    {
      swap record(i) and record(i+1)
    }
  }
}
```

Let's take a look at what this *pseudocode* does, where we read the "exclusive" in the first `for` loop to mean

```
for(i = arraysize; i > 1; --i)
```

and similarly in the second loop. In the first iteration of the outer loop, with `length` set to the length of the original array, we run the inner loop from `i = 0` through `i = length-2`. (We have to be careful to stop one short since we are accessing both subscript `i` and subscript `i+1`.) If any pair of values is out of order (by this we mean that the key value on which to sort is smaller in `record(i+1)` than it is in `record(i)`), then we exchange `record(i+1)` and `record(i)`. The effect of this is that at the end of this first iteration of the outer loop the largest value in the entire array will have been placed in the last location. When we decrement the outer loop variable and run the inner loop again, the next-largest value will be placed in the location for the penultimate subscript. When the two loops finish, the array will be sorted in increasing order.

In keeping with our desire not to move the data records themselves, we are sorting *keys* instead of sorting the data itself. The assumption is that an index is really just an array of integers, that the index array is likely to be stored in memory, and thus that moving keys around is efficient, whereas moving data that might be stored on disk would be inefficient and slow. It is also likely to be the case in a serious application that we would want to sort and then retrieve on *multiple keys*, perhaps Social Security number and phone number in addition to the last name, and for this reason we would need to have an index of keys for each field because the actual data array cannot, after all, be stored in sorted order in more than one way.

3.2.3 Searching Through a List

From the main program we have twice issued a `findRecord` request to find a complete data record whose key is the `String` last name value provided to the method as a parameter. Our code implements a *linear search*. That is, we simply walk through the array looking for a record whose `name` matches the value for `compareName`. This is certainly a simple method to write, but like most simple methods its performance is not very good. We have included the code to count the number of tests performed because we wish to illustrate that the performance is relatively poor. If we are searching in an unordered list for a random value of `name`, and the value happens to be in the list, then on average we would expect to have to look halfway through the list in order to find what we are looking for. If we are searching for a value that is in fact *not* in the list, we will have to search all the way through in order to determine that the value just isn't in the list.

If we take the time to sort the list, our search can end either when we find what we are looking for or when the next name in our list is alphabetically greater than the one we are looking for. With the sorted list, for example, we can quit looking for the name "Buell" as soon as we encounter "Herbert," because "Herbert" is greater than "Buell" and therefore all the names past "Herbert" in the sorted list will also be greater than "Buell." On average, therefore, a search for a record will require looking at half the list whether or not the record is present.

3.3 A Foreshadowing of Things to Come

The indexed flat file example, although it is a simple enough program, provides a good starting point for mentioning where this course is headed.

A large part of this course is about the storage, management, manipulation, and retrieval of information in efficient ways. The general rule is that there is probably a simple data structure or algorithm that could be implemented, and that there is no free lunch: because the structure or algorithm is simple, it will be inefficient. Generally, you do indeed get what you pay for in life. A bubblesort is simple and easy to code. Performing a sequential search through a pile of records is simple, but even if the records are in sorted order, you will on average have to search through half the pile to find what you are looking for. Simple and thus inefficient is OK for small-scale implementations—if one's purpose really is to manage a list of records in a personal address book, then the code presented here is not a bad start. But if the records list gets large (like the Los Angeles phone book) or the records are retrieved constantly (like merchandise looked up on the Amazon.com website), then simple and inefficient is unacceptable.

Similarly, the storage of data can be done efficiently or inefficiently, and simplistic methods are usually inefficient. Just as with a shelf of books in a library, the standard flat file poses problems as records are inserted and deleted. The simplest method for "deleting" a record would be to leave the record in place but add a flag that indicates the record has been deleted. After a large number of deletions, though, a sequential search might waste a lot of time walking past deleted records, and the total space required would be much larger than is actually needed. Closing up the holes takes work, and it takes more work to open a hole to insert a new record into sorted order. In this course, we will study several methods for *dynamic data structures* that permit efficient insertion and deletion and that allow for continued efficient search and retrieval of the valid records in the structure.

The other part of this course is the development of good programming skills and techniques. Just as good data structures are used for organizing the actual data to be managed, good programming style is in part an *intellectual* organization of the software that manages and accesses the data. A main program, for example, should deal only with things at the very top level of the program: Get the information from the user, console, or input file; call the method `doTheWork` to do the work; and then tidy up at the end and finish. The main program has no need to know the implementation details of *how* the work is accomplished; it only needs to know that the work will be done and the results will be returned in a standard way. The `FlatFile` code thus can be reused to handle an entirely different `Record` class with no changes at all.

This *information hiding* is central to good programming style. The code that implements the flat file need not know anything about the "records" that it is handling; it need only know that there are things called records and that there is a linear list of them. Java, as with other object-oriented programming languages, enforces at the syntactic level a compliance with the strictures of the program design "religion" that it supports. You may feel that this is restrictive and prevents you from exercising your artistic freedom in how programs are designed. That's entirely the point; the idea is that if the compiler and the IDE can impose constraints on what is *syntactically* correct, then it is more likely that a syntactically correct program will also be *semantically* correct.

Looked at another way: We all make mistakes, and in writing programs each of us is likely to have our own short list of mistakes that we will make repeatedly if we aren't careful. Part of the *discipline of programming*, to borrow a term that Dijkstra used, is for each of us to recognize what those mistakes are and try consciously to remember not to make them. Part of the discipline imposed by Java and languages like Java is that many mistakes that are easy to make and are commonly made are harder to make in Java because the syntax of the language makes it harder to make those mistakes.[4]

3.3.1 Effective Sorting Techniques

One of the methods in `FlatFile` implements a bubblesort for the purpose of creating an index by sorting keys. It is not hard to show that a properly implemented bubblesort requires a constant (fixed for the given implementation) times N^2 comparisons in order to sort an array of N data items. It can be proved (and we will prove it in this course) that any sort that works by comparing values (as does bubblesort) requires *at least* a constant times $N \log N$ comparisons, and there are several sorting algorithms that achieve this lower bound. Since we know from calculus that $\log N$ is much smaller than N as N gets large, clearly a bubblesort is not the most efficient sort for large data arrays; its only virtue is its simplicity. We show in Figure 3.16 the graph of N^2 against $N \log N$, for N running from 0 through about 10000. Without even looking at the actual numerical values, it is clear from the figure that a good sorting algorithm with a running time of $N \log N$ "steps" (we will define later the concept of "step" for sorting algorithms) is faster than a bubblesort for all but the very smallest of problems, and the superiority of the better algorithm is increasing.

We shall study some different sorting algorithms. Our interest is in algorithms that are efficient in terms of both the number of comparisons and the extra storage space needed. Bubblesort, for example, needs only the one extra storage location to store the temporary value of a key when the ith and jth items are being swapped. Mergesort, for example, works in $N \log N$ time, but it requires as much as $N/2$ extra storage locations.

The problem of sorting records is still an active research area, and we will only scratch the surface of the topic.

---

[4]In George Orwell's *1984*, the government strove to remove from the language all those words with which "thoughtcrime" could be committed. Once all the words with which thoughtcrime could be expressed were removed from the language, then thoughtcrime itself could not exist. Java works much the same way. If the language won't let you write something that The Powers That Be have determined to be Bad Form, then it becomes that much harder to write code that possesses Bad Form.

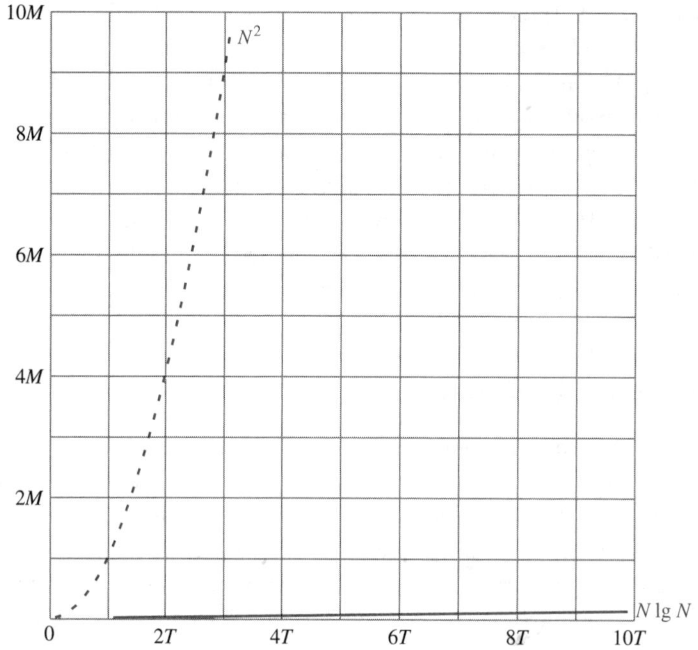

FIGURE 3.16 ■ N^2 graphed against $N \lg N$ ($T = 10^3$, $M = 10^6$).

■ 3.3.2 Effective Search Techniques and Data Structures for Maintaining Priority

One of the methods in `Flatfile` implements a linear search to find an item in a sorted list. The first of the more sophisticated things we will learn, later in this chapter, is *binary search*, a *recursive divide-and-conquer* technique that is almost always a win when computing things.

Divide and conquer is a basic theme in computation: To solve a problem, recursively cut the size of the problem in half at each stage. We begin in binary search with a list of N data items. We cut the problem in half by determining whether the data item is (or rather, could be, since we don't know that it is actually present in the list) in the first half of the data or the second half of the data. We then ask the same question of the data array that is now only half as big as we started with.

In general, it is not hard to show that binary search in a sorted array of $N = 2^n$ items can be done with at most n tests (called *probes*), and that no similar search can be done any faster than that. That is, binary search is *optimal.* We will see later, for example, that cutting the array into thirds and doing a recursive search on the one-third of the data in which a sought-for element might appear will not go any faster, and it would require two tests at every stage, rather than one, to determine which third might hold the item for which we were searching.

3.3.3 Static Versus Dynamic Storage Structures

One of the main questions to be asked when dealing with a computational problem is whether the data is essentially static or dynamic, that is, whether the data as a whole changes slowly or rapidly. A transcript file at a university, for example, is essentially a static collection of data. Although there will be additions and deletions and updates of grades, local addresses, and such, the data collection is largely static. Contrast this with the queue of processes ready to be executed in a computer. In a modern computer, a large number of processes will be active at any point in time, listening for mouse movements, clicks, and keystrokes; managing the display of multiple windows that might even have ongoing updates or audio or video playing; as well as the processes that are more realistically viewed as having been initiated by the user. The goal of the scheduler in the OS is to keep these processes sorted by priority (we don't want any hiccups in the Internet radio that plays in the background) and to cycle through those ready processes quickly and efficiently.

A similar task awaits the computer whose job is to collect Internet packets and assemble them into messages for delivery. Packets are discrete data items, each one being part of an entire Internet transmission. They may take different paths from source to destination, they may arrive out of order, and in a large operation they will be coming in at a tremendous rate. It is the job of *some* computer in the flow of traffic to reassemble these packets into their original messages, with the data payloads in order, and to be able to handle simultaneously the assembly of packets for multiple messages at a time. This is a classic dynamic data processing problem: A payload of unknown size is broken into packets; the packets must be sorted as they come in; and when the message is fully reassembled, we can send on the complete message and delete that data from storage.

Handling these two different kinds of problems usually takes different kinds of data structures as well as an assessment of the overall characteristics of the problem. Having all the data before we begin can be a very good thing; being forced to organize data before we have any idea what the data looks like can lead to pathologically bad performance. We have seen the value of having data in sorted order. If we have data that undergoes updates only once a week, for example, and it takes an hour to sort the data from scratch, then it is perfectly reasonable to consider that hour an investment worth making. If the data is updated once an hour, and it takes an hour to sort, then the time spent sorting is not an investment but an ongoing expense.

3.3.4 Generic and Abstract Classes

Java has a powerful capability in its *generic* construct and *abstract classes* that allow common methods to handle different data types. We have already seen with the `compareTo` method the power of having a standard syntax for a common operation: we implement comparison of objects as

```
thisObject.compareTo(thatObject)
```

with a returned result that is a negative number if `this` is less than `that`, a positive number if `this` is greater than `that`, and a zero if they are equal.

You have probably already used, without necessarily being made aware of them, some of this abstraction capability of Java. The Java generics and abstract classes permit the programmer to define templates and general-purpose methods that act on objects whose data types are not specified at the time the code is written. This provides another vehicle for separating the data structure that supports efficient computation from the underlying data on which the computation is performed.

3.3.5 Arrays Versus `ArrayList`s

The experienced Java programmer will recognize that we have implemented the `FlatFile` program using an `ArrayList` instead of an array. This is because for one-dimensional lists of things, whose size might not be known at compile time, the `ArrayList` is a much simpler construct to use than an array. Storage for an `ArrayList` is done dynamically, with no preallocation needed and no out-of-space errors from allocating too little space for the input data. The `size` method allows one to determine the actual number of items stored and decreases the chance of writing code that steps out of bounds. The deletion of items (which we didn't happen to do here) is done with a `remove` method that does the list compression to remove the hole caused by deletion.

A Java `ArrayList` also has a `contains` method that does the lookup that we implemented with the linear search method, and that should in fact implement a binary search as described in the next section.

We note, however, that there is no inherent sorting function for an `ArrayList` and thus we would still need to sort the records and create an index if we wanted to deal with the `ArrayList` in sorted order. There are other Java collection classes that *do* implement sort order capabilities. Just as with the binary search for the `contains` method, we would have to assume that the implementors of the sort methods had used an efficient algorithm. Indeed, it is fair to say that all the algorithms and techniques presented in this course have already been implemented in Java in some class.

3.4 Binary Search: Our First Mature Algorithm

The first "mature" algorithm we will consider, as a prelude to the rest of the text, is a binary search. We are going to introduce this now, although this may seem to be a bit off-topic at the moment, because we want to contrast the basic nature of binary search against a more naive linear search.

In our earlier search method, we did a linear search, entry by entry, through the `ArrayList` until the desired record was found. For a randomly chosen record for which to search, we would expect to have to search on average halfway through a list of N entries. It is equally likely that we would have to search through to location k as it is that we would have to search to location $N - k$. Since these two searches together require $k + (N - k) = N$ "probes," they each require on average $N/2$ probes into the list.

A *binary search* proceeds by a *recursive divide-and-conquer* approach to searching for an element. If we have paid the initial price of sorting the data, then binary search is the most natural algorithm to use for searching because it is relatively simple (although not totally trivial) and because it can be shown to be the fastest search possible.

In a recursive divide-and-conquer search, we start with a list of N entries in a list `L`, which for the moment we can assume to be simply a list of *sorted* integers, with no repeated values. We want to know if a given integer k is one of the elements in the list, and if it is, what its subscript value is.

Our first probe is to compare k against the entry stored halfway into the list at location `L[N/2]`, whose value we will call m. If $k < m$, and the list `L` is assumed to be sorted, then k, if it exists in the list, will be found in the first half of the list because all the entries in the second half of the list are larger than m and thus larger than k. If $k > m$, and the list `L` is assumed to be sorted, then k, if it exists in the list, will be found in the second half of the list because all the entries in the first half of the list are smaller than m and thus smaller than k.

With one probe, then, we have reduced the problem of searching a list of N entries to the problem of searching a list of $N/2$ entries. We now do a second probe to cut the list from size $N/2$ in half again to size $N/4$. And again. And again.

Consider the example in Figure 3.17. Assume we have a list of 16 names in sorted order (history buffs will note that we skipped one in order to have unique surnames): Let's say we do a lookup on "Tyler." We compare Tyler against the

Loc.	Name	Loc.	Name
0	Adams	8	Madison
1	Buchanan	9	Monroe
2	Fillmore	10	Pierce
3	Harrison	11	Polk
4	Jackson	12	Taylor
5	Jefferson	13	Tyler
6	Johnson	14	Van Buren
7	Lincoln	15	Washington

FIGURE 3.17 ■ A sorted list for a binary search.

name at subscript 8, which is "Madison" (we are indexing zero-up, just like Java, and we arbitrarily choose always to round up to the first subscript in the upper half of any list or sublist if we have to break ties). Tyler is larger than Madison, so we know we have a record in the second half of the list (if it's there at all). Since we have retrieved the record at subscript 8, we test equality as well as greater-equal/less-equal, and find that we don't have equality. The second half of the list has subscripts 8–15, and we know we didn't get a match at subscript 8, so we are looking at subscripts 9–15. The midpoint (and this time it's actually the midpoint) is 12, and the entry at subscript 12 is "Taylor." Tyler is still larger than Taylor, so we continue searching in the short list of subscripts 13–15, since we know it's not at subscript 12. Comparing against subscript 14, "Van Buren," we know we are in the first half of that sublist. The sublist has length 1, though, so when we compare against subscript 13, which is "Tyler," we get a match.

If we look for the name "Clay" (remembering that Henry Clay very much wanted to become a U.S. president but never managed to do so), we compare against subscripts 8 (Madison), then 4 (Jackson), then 2 (Fillmore), then 1 (Buchanan). Since we don't find a match, we know that Clay is not in the list.

As should be obvious, the difficult part about writing a method for this is getting right the concept of "halfway." With an odd number of items in the list, there is a midpoint. With an even number of items in the list, one has to decide whether to take the last entry in the first half or the first entry in the second half.

If the list is of $N = 2^n$ entries, then it will take at most $n = \log_2 N$ probes to reduce the problem to looking at a list of one entry, which is merely a single test. To verify that Clay was not in the list of $2^4 = 16$ items, for example, we checked the four entries at subscripts 8, 4, 2, and 1.

Now we need to clarify a couple of points on which we have been a little sloppy. First, when we execute a probe, we can test both

```
if(this.compareTo(that) < 0)
```

and

```
if(this.compareTo(that) == 0)
```

If we find the entry for which we are looking, then of course we have solved the problem. If not, we continue. Technically this would split the list not into two halves but into one sublist larger than the probed value, one sublist smaller than the probed value, and the probed value itself. If we test in this way, we can shorten our sublist by one by not including the probed value, since we have already tested it.

Similarly, if N is not an exact power of 2, the length in time of the binary search is really no worse than it would be for the next larger power of 2. If we were to increase the size of the array to the next larger power of 2 by padding at the end with values of MAXIMUM_INTEGER (whatever that value is), we will increase the total cost of the search by at most one extra probe.

The code for a binary search method that could be substituted for the linear search in our `FlatFile` example is given in Figure 3.18.

```
/**************************************************************
 * Method to find a record in the flat file.
 * This is binary search. Start with lower and upper subscripts.
 * Compute the middle subscript.  If the value in the middle is
 * larger than the item sought, move the upper subscript down.
 * If the value in the middle is smaller, move the lower subscript
 * up.  Then repeat until found or until we meet in the middle.
 * @param name the <code>String</code> value to search for.
 * @return the subscript of the found record, or -1 if not found.
**/
  public Record findRecordBinary(String name)
  {
    final int NOTFOUND = -1;
    int lowerSub, midSub, returnSub, upperSub;
    Record returnValue = null;
    lowerSub = 0;
    upperSub = this.getSize()-1;
    midSub = (lowerSub + upperSub)/2;
    returnSub = NOTFOUND;
    while(lowerSub < upperSub)
    {
      String thisMidName = this.recs.get(this.index.get(midSub)).getName();
      if(0 > thisMidName.compareTo(name))
        lowerSub = midSub + 1;
      else if(0 < thisMidName.compareTo(name))
        upperSub = midSub - 1;
      else
      {
        returnSub = midSub;
        break;
      }
      midSub = (lowerSub + upperSub)/2;
    }
    if(NOTFOUND != returnSub)
      returnValue = this.recs.get(this.index.get(returnSub));
    return returnValue;
  }
```

FIGURE 3.18 ■ The binary search code.

The use of a divide-and-conquer approach is so pervasive in computing that a new mathematical symbol is used to describe the running time of algorithms of this sort. We know that if $N = 2^n$, then $n = \log_2 N$, which we write as $n = \lg N$. In Chapter 6, we will do more formal *asymptotic analysis* of algorithms, but the power of binary search over linear search is easily seen from the graph in Figure 3.19, showing $N/2$ graphed against $\lg N$. Clearly binary search is superior, and it becomes better and better the larger the size of the list to be searched. The graph of $\lg N$ is barely noticeable. This is not entirely surprising—2^{23} is about eight million, so the binary log of 10^6 at the right edge of the graph is only a little larger than 23, and clearly will barely register on a y-axis measured in millions.

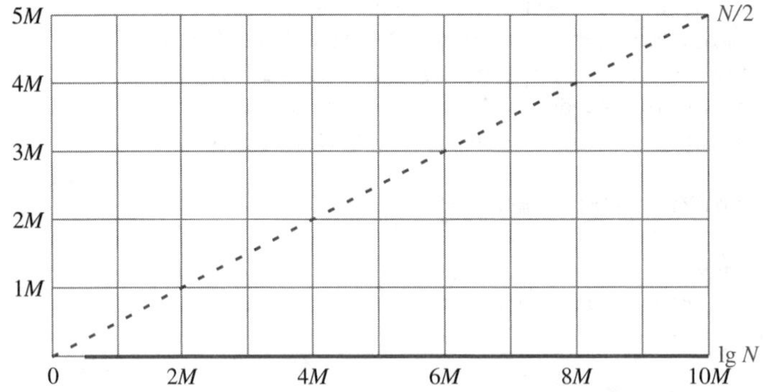

FIGURE 3.19 ■ $N/2$ graphed against $\lg N$ ($M = 10^6$).

■ 3.5 Summary

We have covered in this chapter a program for managing, in a naive way, basic data records in a flat file or spreadsheet-like structure. A large number of computer applications have essentially this purpose: to maintain a file of records, with the ability to add records, edit records, delete records, sort records in any of a number of different ways, and search and retrieve records that match some search field.

For small files of no more than a few thousand records, a simplistic program such as the one presented here would be more than adequate. For large software systems, however, all the functions—adding, editing, deleting, sorting, searching, and retrieving—must be done more efficiently. The purpose of this course and this text is to introduce data structures for more efficient management of data, together with algorithms that process data in more efficient ways or on those more efficient structures. We began the process of increasing the sophistication of skills by introducing binary search.

3.6 Exercises

(Sample data for many of these exercises can be found on the website at go.jblearning.com/Buell.)

1. The current code has the input and output filenames hard-coded. Modify the driver `main` method to ask the user for these filenames. Make sure you catch the exceptions on opening the files, since that is very important for correct execution of programs.
2. The current `FlatFile` code has a `findRecord` method that uses the `compareName` method of the `Record` class. Modify this method to call a more general-purpose `findByKey` method, and implement the `findByKey` method in the `Record` class.
3. If you have done the previous exercise, you will notice that you can overload the `findByKey` method in the `Record` class to allow for either `String` or `int` variables as parameters. Write these overloaded methods.
4. If you have done the previous two exercises, you will notice that you still cannot search both by name and by office, since those two `String` variables are going to be indistinguishable to `findByKey`. This can be fixed. Create a separate class for the name, making sure to include a nondefault constructor that takes a `String` variable as parameter and assigns that to a `String` instance variable inside your `Name` class. Do the same for the `office` variable. Now you can create an overloaded `findByKey(Name whatName)` method that searches on the `name` variable and a different `findByKey(Office whatOffice)` method that searches on the `office` variable. Do this, and modify `FlatFile` to do the appropriate searches. The key point here is the information hiding: nowhere in the `FlatFile` code should the fact that `Name` and `Office` are in fact `String` values be used. All that is used in `FlatFile` is that one can create instances of `Name` and `Office` by passing in a `String` when constructing an instance.
5. Replace the `Record` class with a class that handles names of CDs and artists performing on the CDs, as if you were making a database of your own collection. Except for changing the method calls for the search, the code outside the `Record` should not have to change at all.
6. If you have done the previous exercise, you know that your `Record` class is insufficient. You really want all the tracks in your record, so add an `ArrayList` variable inside `Record` that allows you to read the track names and outputs the track names when `toString` is called.
7. If you have done the previous two exercises, modify the search capability to allow searching by track name. Since it is highly unlikely that the number of

tracks per CD is larger than about 20, and since it is highly unlikely that the tracks are in alphabetically sorted order, you can probably do just fine with a linear search.

8. You probably want to search your CD list both by artist name and by CD label name, but you probably used a `String` variable for both of them. Modify your CD code following the changes for the `findByKey` methods in the earlier exercises to allow you to search either way.

9. Modify your linear search to count the number of tests you have to do. Increase the size of the input data to 100 items, say, so you have enough data for the code to chew upon. Then perform several searches. What is the average number of tests? It should be about 50 if you are searching for items both early in the list and late in the list. Swap out the linear search for the binary search and do the experiment again. This time your average count of tests should be closer to 7, since $100 \approx 128 = 2^7$.

10. Modify the sort method so that you count the number of comparisons performed, and output the number of comparisons for the original input data. You should get $(10^2)/2 = 50$. Now double the number of items in the input data and run the experiment again. This time you should get $(20^2)/2 = 200$. Double the data input again, and check that this time it takes $(40^2)/2 = 800$ comparisons (make sure you have unique items, as this can affect the count).

4 Arrays and Linked Lists

Objectives

- A discussion of the differences between arrays and `ArrayLists` and why the `ArrayList` is the preferred structure to be used in programs
- The concept and implementation of linked list data structures using several underlying methods for implementation
- Exception handling for anomalous conditions
- Insertionsort as a primitive but useful algorithm for sorting, especially when adding individual items to an existing sorted list

Key Terms

array	free list	palindrome
collection classes	insertionsort	random access
deprecated	linked list	singly-linked list
doubly-linked list	misfeature	
dynamic data structure	node	

Introduction

The primitive data types of Java (and of most programming languages) are individual instances of data items of values of `boolean`, `int`, or `double` type. The usual next step in allowing for the representation of data is a linear data structure of entries. The simplest such linear structures in Java are the array and `ArrayList`, and in Java these can be lists of objects of any type, not just of the primitive types. This chapter covers the concept and implementation of another linear structure for storing data—the linked list. The concept of a linked list is quite old in the history of computing and, although it has been somewhat superseded by the `ArrayList` for applications programmed in Java, all computer scientists need to be familiar with the concepts used in linked lists and the methods by which those concepts are implemented.

4.1 Arrays and `ArrayLists`

If we assume that a single data item of a particular type (an `int`, say) is a trivial kind of data "structure," then it could certainly be said that the simplest nontrivial data structure is that of an *array*. If a key feature of computer programs that makes them useful is the ability to execute a task repeatedly, then the simplest structure that provides the sequence of data on which the iterative part of a program executes is a linear array of data.

Arrays, `ArrayLists`, and linked lists provide three different ways to organize and store lists of data items or data records. Each has advantages, and, as always, each also has disadvantages. As with any data structure, the simpler structures are easier to use but provide fewer features; the trick in design is to use a structure that nicely performs the functions needed without requiring the implementation of extraneous features that will never be used.

We have implemented the list of records in our flat file example as an `ArrayList` of records; unlike in primitive languages,[1] we can in Java allocate an array of data records just as easily as we can allocate an array of `int` or `double` data items. One of the main advantages of an array or an `ArrayList` is that one can perform *random access* to retrieve a particular data record in the array using the subscript. That is, given the subscript i, we can access the ith element of the array with a single fetch from memory. This is very powerful, and not all data structures have this property. We will see later in this chapter that a linked list does *not* allow for random access, and instead requires that a user walk through the list from the first item onward, item by item, until a particular item is encountered. Binary search of a sorted list either as an array or an `ArrayList` is possible because we can directly access the ith entry in a list of N entries. We will see that a linked list does not provide this capability, and thus searching a linked list is an inherently sequential process.

There are several major negative aspects to an array, however. The first is that arrays in Java, and indeed in many languages, require a static *a priori* allocation of space before the array can be used. This static preallocation of space has been the bane of programmers since the dawn of time[2] because in a Java program, if we allocate space for 20 records and then try to add the 21st record, the normal result is that the program will crash. If we think we need a hundred million records and thus allocate the vast space necessary for a hundred million records, then we pay the performance price for having used that much space even if we do not actually use it. The penalty for underestimating the amount of space needed is severe, so programmers will always overestimate and thus allocate more space than is needed, which can degrade system and program performance.

---

[1] (for example, Fortran)

[2] (that is, the late 1940s when computer programs began to exist)

A second disadvantage with arrays, that is *not* an implementation issue peculiar to Java, is that arrays provide only a linear look at the data, subscripted item by subscripted item. An array of phone book records, sorted by last name, is a perfectly good data structure if the only access method is by last name, but if the data is also to be accessed by street name, then performance is instantly degraded because the only way without adding more code to find all the records with a given street name is to search the entire array and compare street names. Indeed, if one has the array stored by last name but wants to be able to access by street name, the standard method is to create an index as was done in the previous chapter, but this requires sorting the list, which could be a substantial investment in time if the list is large.

A slight annoyance of Java that is not quite a *misfeature* is that the Java `length` attribute for arrays returns the space that has been *allocated*, not the space that has actually been *used*. On the one hand, this is annoying because we are usually only interested in the space we actually used for storing data. On the other hand, there really is no way for the compiler at compile time or the program process in execution to determine exactly how much space was "intended" to be used. In some algorithms, for example, the initial data will fill only part of an array, and the rest of the array will be filled as the program executes, but the space needs to be thought of as reserved because if more initial data were present, more array space would be necessary to avoid run-time errors. No compiler or run-time environment will be able to know this, so the only sensible thing for a `length` attribute to return is the preallocated length of the array.

Many of these annoyances disappear when an `ArrayList` is used instead of an array. The `ArrayList` structure is part of what are called the *collection classes* in Java. An `ArrayList` allows one to implement an arraylike list structure for which storage management is done for the user behind the scenes. It is a dynamic data structure that adapts easily when data is added to it or removed from it, and this is a major advantage over the more static structure of an array. For example, when a variable is created as a `new ArrayList`, a small fixed storage is allocated (the current Javadoc says that the initial size is 10). Instead of placing a data record specifically in the `i`th storage location, as with an array, one can add a record to the `ArrayList` with the `add` method, using code something like `myArrayList.add(myRecord)`, and the `myRecord` data item is automatically added to the end of the list. If the addition of this new item would require the `ArrayList` to exceed its initial storage capacity, more storage is allocated automatically. Storage and retrieval in the specific `i`th locations can be done with the `set` and `get` methods, and the `size` method will return the number of items actually stored in the list. Perhaps most convenient of all is that the `remove` method will not only delete that item from the list but also will shift the subsequent data items forward in the list to close up the gap. Although this is a bad thing to do in terms of performance, it is a good thing from the point of coding complexity and avoidance of programming errors to have this simple task coded correctly once and for all in the implementation of the `ArrayList` code. This ability of an `ArrayList` to handle simple management of data in *dynamic* situations in which data is regularly entering and leaving the structure is one of the major advantages of the `ArrayList` over the more primitive array.

Another problem with arrays, and in many ways the most serious, is that arrays can provide inherently less security than the `ArrayList` structure and can lead to inherently less reliable programs. Although Java makes it a little harder than does C++, for example, for a programmer to create security flaws through bad programming behavior, it is nonetheless still true that using an `ArrayList` instead of an array makes it harder to make silly mistakes. For example, we recall that arrays are allocated statically with a fixed maximum size and then accessed by subscript. A common error in array processing would be code like the following. (This code has several problems, but we will focus on the loop at the bottom and the fact that the variable values used were assigned in different places, at different times, and possibly by users who didn't know about the array or didn't need to know.)

```
int myArray[100];
//  enough code that we might forget about the length

int mySubscript = 95;
//  enough code that we might forget about the value above

initializationLength = System.console.in();
//  enough code that we might forget about the value above
//  and that we allowed humans to enter a value

// and now we put all the pieces together, and they may
// not simultaneously make sense
for(int i = 0; i < initializationLength; ++i)
{
  myArray[i] = System.console.in();
}
int n = myArray[mySubscript];
```

The problem is that since allocation lengths and subscripts are all simply numbers, it is up to the programmer to ensure that the program is internally self-consistent, and there is greater freedom for error with arrays than with `ArrayLists`. Among other problems in the preceding code, one problem is that it is up to the programmer to ensure that `initializationLength` is at least 96 or else that nothing will go wrong if a zero is fetched for the value of `n` in the line following the loop. That's the sort of thing that leads to errors; because the code and its input data are going to be in separate files, it's easy to imagine situations in which the two can become incompatible.

For reasons such as these the use of arrays is currently *deprecated*, that is, specifically recommended against, and the recommended structure is the `ArrayList`. By now it should be clear that an `ArrayList` has a number of useful properties that are not possessed by simple arrays. The space used by an `ArrayList` is dynamic, in that the size grows and shrinks automagically as records are added and deleted, and the user need not have any preconceived notions of allocated space. The `get(i)` and `set(i)` methods work exactly as does reference to the ith location in an array, and the `size` method is actually easier to use than the `length` variable because its value is the size actually used and not the size preallocated.

On the other hand, there is one use of arrays that has no clean counterpart in `ArrayLists`, and that is the multidimensional array. In truth, a two-dimensional Java array is really an array of arrays, but a reference to

```
array[i][j]
```

is obviously less tedious to write and is easier to read than a reference to

```
array.get(i).get(j)
```

Although Java has not been widely used in scientific computing, there does exist an extensive package at `http://jblas.org` that implements a standard package of two-dimensional array methods that supports the kind of computations widely done in science.

We will also find that even though arrays and `ArrayLists` are rather simple data structures, they can be used—and for many years were used—to implement many more complicated data structures. In part, this is due to the history of computing and programming languages. For many years the only multiple-instance data structure that was built into a programming language was the array, so methods for using arrays were developed and continue to be standard practice in writing software. The `ArrayList`, for example, is really implemented as an array; the `add` merely adds an entry at the end of the array, and the `get` really just does a subscripted lookup. However, the "wrapper" of methods around an `ArrayList` that are necessary to use this structure leads to programs that are less prone to error than if simple arrays were used. When the allocated memory is exhausted, more is allocated automatically, but this is done by code compiled and tested once by the implementers of Java; when the length of the `ArrayList` is needed, the `size` method returns that value, making it unnecessary for the programmer to remember this throughout his or her code, and so forth.

4.2 Linked Lists

If we view an array as a trivial data structure for handling multiple instances of data items, then the first nontrivial data structure to be taken up is that of a *linked list.* The conceptual notion of a linked list is shown in Figure 4.1. To create a linked list, we start with a `head` that points to the first element in the list. After that, every data item contains a `next` pointer that points to the next data item. To make sure we don't walk off the edge of the earth, the last data item has a `next` pointer that is a null pointer. We traverse the linked list by starting with the `head`, following it to the first data item, and then chasing down the `next` pointers until we hit the null pointer.

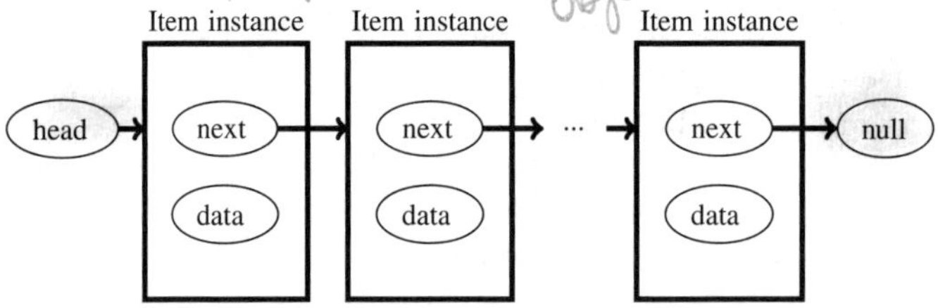

FIGURE 4.1 ■ A linked list of "items."

4.2.1 Linked Lists and Pointers

A key theme throughout this course is the use of *dynamic data structures* whose sizes grow and shrink as needed. If we were to treat a linked list as a completely static structure, created once and then only subject to reads and not writes, there would be little need for this kind of data structure in the first place. We would simply use an `ArrayList` instead. The power of structures like linked lists comes from their use in storing lists of data items of variable and changing size.

We usually refer to the individual "boxes" of data items as in Figure 4.1 as *nodes.* Each box is an instance of a class. In the *singly-linked list* of Figure 4.1, each node has an instance variable that is the data payload of the node and a pointer to the "next" node in the list. We will almost always use the *doubly-linked list* of Figure 4.2, in which there is both a "next" pointer and a "previous" pointer. It turns out in practice that more often than not we want to be able to traverse the list both forward and backward.

A diagram for a doubly-linked list is given in Figure 4.2, and example code for a class for a node in a doubly-linked list is given in Figure 4.3.

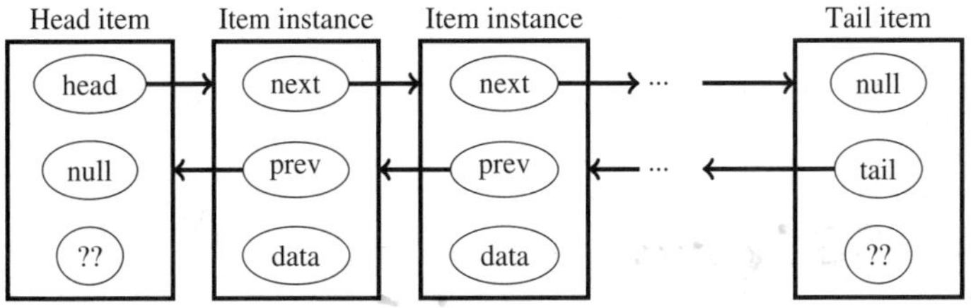

FIGURE 4.2 ■ A doubly-linked list of "items."

Note several characteristics of this code. First, we create a class `DLLNode` for a "node" in a linked list. This particular class will have the instance variables and methods that are specific to the management of the linked list of nodes. This class will *not* have the instance variables and methods that manage the data payload itself; we will leave all that to the `Record` class, and we will provide an example shortly in which the data payload code is made "generic" by using the generic construct built into Java.

Second, we have done nothing more than leave a placeholder for the constructor. If we are to view the linked list as a list of nodes that point to other nodes, we need to decide when and how to create the nodes and how to deal with differences between initial conditions and steady-state conditions of node management. This is the topic of the next section.

Next, what we have here is a *doubly-linked list* and not the *singly-linked list* of Figure 4.1 because we have both links that go forward from a node to the next node and links that go backward to the previous node. The cost of the previous link is extra space in memory and on disk and the cost of writing code for handling "previous" links that is entirely symmetric to the code for handling "next" links. The most obvious use of the link to the previous node comes when one is deleting a node from a list. If the link to the previous node is explicit in the instance of the node, then when deleting a node we avoid the "come from" complication of holding on to the location of the previous node. If we are to manage a doubly-linked list, then in addition to the `head` pointer to the first node in the list, we will need a `tail` pointer to the last node in the list.

Finally, notice that Figure 4.2 reflects the code of Figure 4.3 and is different from Figure 4.1. The head and tail are now actual instances of nodes, because the "pointer" is really a `DLLNode`. We will implement our doubly-linked lists with actual nodes as dummy nodes at the head and tail. This can often make for simpler programming. We will explain shortly why dedicated dummy head and tail nodes can make it easier to link and unlink nodes.

```
public class DLLNode
{
  private DLLNode next;
  private DLLNode prev;
  private Record nodeData;

  constructor code ...

  public Record getNodeData()
  {
    return this.nodeData;
  }
  public void setNodeData(Record newData)
  {
    this.nodeData = newData;
  }
  public DLLNode getNext()
  {
    return this.next;
  }
  public void setNext(DLLNode newNext)
  {
    this.next = newNext;
  }
  public DLLNode getPrev()
  {
    return this.prev;
  }
  public void setPrev(DLLNode newPrev)
  {
    this.prev = newPrev;
  }

}
```

FIGURE 4.3 ■ Code fragment for a node in a doubly-linked list.

■ 4.2.2 A Linked List Class

In keeping with our mantra that the main program should confine itself mostly to file opening and closing, creation of an instance of a class for a data structure, and invocation of "do the work" methods, we assume that the main program creates an instance of the data structure perhaps by means of a doubly-linked-list (DLL) class

```
DLL myDLL = new DLL();
```

The main program need only know that the structure is a doubly-linked list and thus that it can grow and shrink dynamically, but the main program does not need to know *how* that DLL is actually implemented. All those details we will keep private to the class for the DLL.

We thus need a DLL class that could look something like the code fragment in Figure 4.4. There are several observations and comments to be made.

```
public class DLL
{
  private int size;
  private DLLNode head;
  private DLLNode tail;

 constructor code ...

  public void add(Record dllData)
  {
    this.addAtHead(dllData);
  }

  private void addAtHead(Record dllData)
  {
    DLLNode newNode = null;
    newNode = new DLLNode();
    newNode.setNodeData(dllData);
    this.linkAfter(this.getHead(), newNode);
  }

  private void linkAfter(DLLNode baseNode, DLLNode newNode)
  {
    newNode.setNext(baseNode.getNext());
    newNode.setPrev(baseNode);
    baseNode.getNext().setPrev(newNode);
    baseNode.setNext(newNode);
    this.incrementSize();
  }

  private void unlink(DLLNode node)
  {
    node.getNext().setPrev(node.getPrev());
    node.getPrev().setNext(node.getNext());
    node.setNext(null);
    node.setPrev(null);
    this.decrementSize();
  }
}
```

FIGURE 4.4 ■ Code fragment for a doubly-linked list.

We will assume that our linked lists are implemented with an actual node as the `head` as well as an actual node as the `tail`.

The `add` method is public and takes as its input parameter an instance of the data payload. We also will need a `contains` method and a `remove` method, and we will discuss these in a moment. Unlike the `add` method, the three methods `addAtHead`, `linkAfter`, and `unlink` that actually operate on nodes in the linked list are declared as `private` methods because the manipulation of nodes need only be done at the level of the linked list code; calling programs should be concerned with the data payload and not the linked list implementation.

Second, we examine the three `private` methods. The `linkAfter` method will add a node `newNode` to the list immediately following a given node taken as the `baseNode`. The first two statements set the `next` and `previous` pointers to the `next` node pointed to by `baseNode` and to the `next` node pointed to by the successor to `baseNode`. Having done that (and we must do this first or else we will overwrite the values stored in those pointers), we can set the `next` pointer of `baseNode` to point forward to the `newNode` and the `prev` pointer of what had been the successor to `baseNode` to point back to `newNode`.

Let's look carefully at the addition of a node after a given node, as shown in Figures 4.5–4.10. We are adding node C after node A, and when we execute the `linkAfter` code our`baseNode` is node A. We must be careful to add the links to the new node first and to change the pointers at `baseNode` last, or else we might lose any way to reach node B.

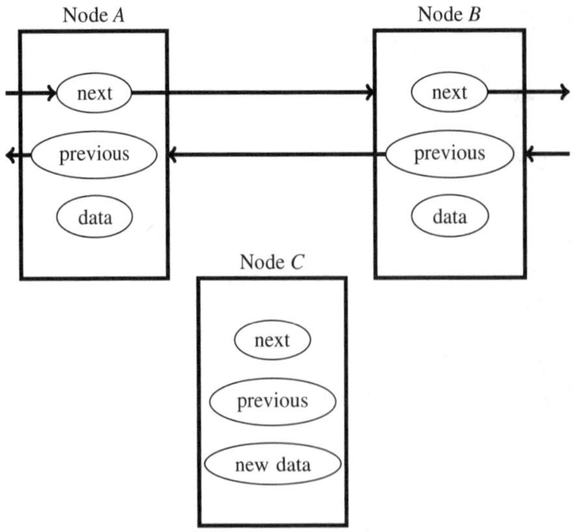

FIGURE 4.5 ■ Inserting node C after node A.

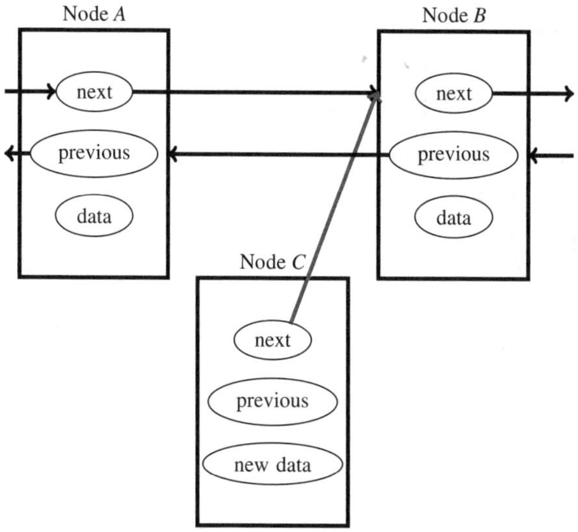

FIGURE 4.6 ■ Inserting a node, step 1.

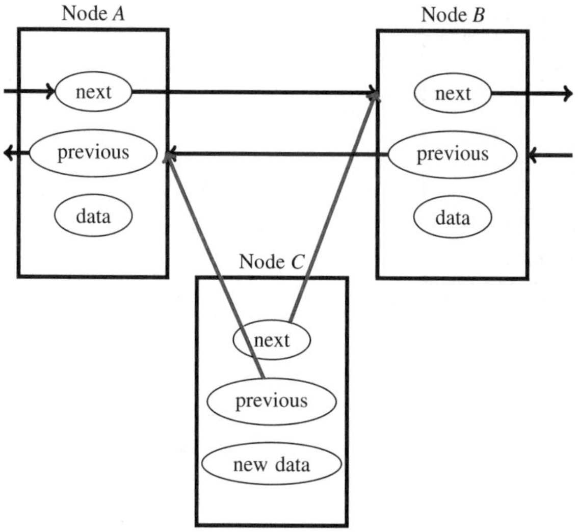

FIGURE 4.7 ■ Inserting a node, step 2.

After first looking at the code for `linkAfter`, the code for `addAtHead` and for the general `add` methods is clear. We choose for the general-purpose addition of a node to the list to add the node at the front, that is, immediately following the `head` node. In looking at this, for example, the convenience of having a real node as dummy for `head` and `tail` is obvious; it means that all the method calls will

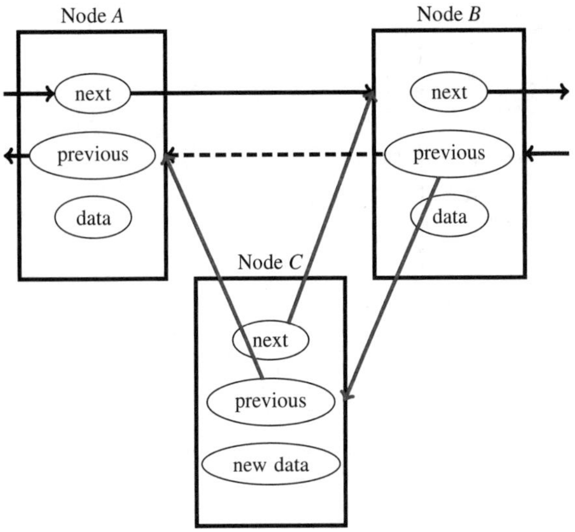

FIGURE 4.8 ■ Inserting a node, step 3.

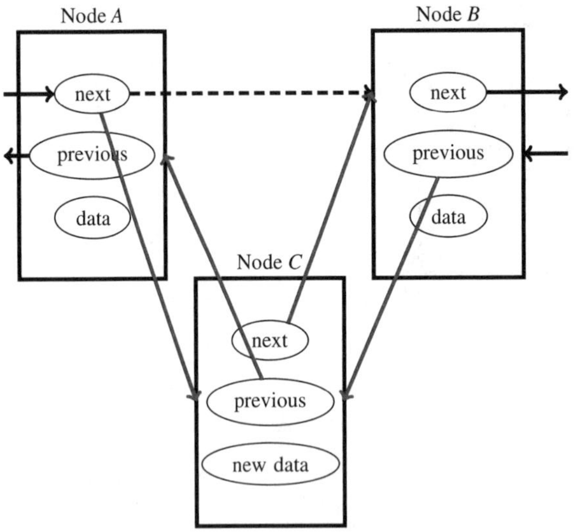

FIGURE 4.9 ■ Inserting a node, step 4.

actually work, and no special code needs to be written to cover the possibility that one is linking or unlinking at the head or tail.

A comment on the `size` variable. If actual nodes are used as the dummies, then the coding and interpretation of the `size` value needs to correspond. Our sample code includes the count for the head and the tail node, so internally our value for

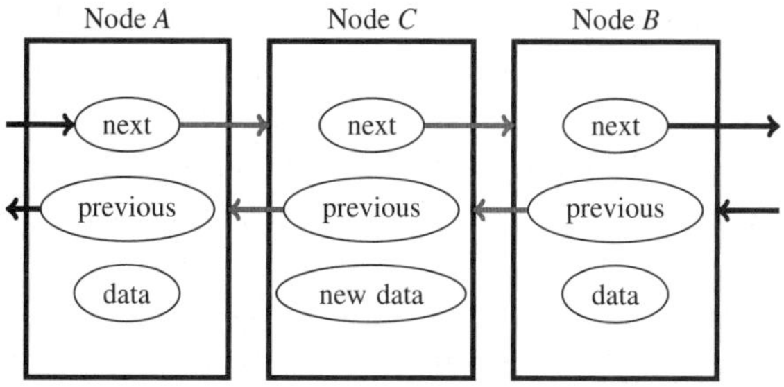

FIGURE 4.10 ■ Inserting a node, final status.

`size` begins at 2 and not 0 for an "empty" list. Since the existence of the dummy nodes ought to be hidden from users of the DLL, the private code inside the DLL must use the `size` that begins with 2 in order to be correct, but the value returned by public methods to programs using the DLL must return the value as if the dummy nodes did not exist.

Figure 4.2 shows question marks instead of data for the data payload of the dummy head and tail nodes. Sometimes it will be appropriate that the dummy nodes carry no data or carry `null` values. On the other hand, sometimes the "data" of the dummy node can be used to advantage. If we are using a list to keep data in sorted order, perhaps based on the value of an `int` variable, for example, then one can store in the dummy `head` node the value `Integer.MIN_VALUE` (usually -2^{31}) and in the dummy `tail` node the value `Integer.MAX_VALUE` (usually $2^{31} - 1$). In this way, an insertion in sorted order can always compare against the values stored in two nodes. If the current minimum value in an actual data node is -123456789, for example, and the value to be inserted is smaller than this, the new node would need to be inserted at the head, and the comparison against the actual value -123456789 in the actual first node and the dummy value `Integer.MIN_VALUE` stored in the dummy head node works properly with no need for special case testing.

Finally, we point out that some care must be taken when dealing with nodes in a linked list. The nodes are independent of one another and can be reached only through `next` and `prev` links. If, for example, in unlinking a node as in Figure 4.4, one sets `next` to `null` before using the current value to link a node's predecessor to its successor, one will have lost the only access to the `next` node and thus the only access to the rest of the linked list. This requires the programmer to develop and exercise a reasonable mental discipline about how such code is to be written to ensure that it can be tested properly.

■ 4.2.3 Exception Handling

Now is as good a time as any to start discussing the handling of exceptions. One of the fundamental problems in getting good software written is ensuring that error conditions will be handled appropriately. In the DLL code, that means we need to look for the methods that could generate exceptions if the parameters passed or the actions to be taken happened to be impossible or to be done in error. Consider the code in Figures 4.3 and 4.4. The `public` methods in Figure 4.3 all either set or return data payload values or node values in the linked list. If we assume that the constructor for the `Record` class always initializes its data values to `null`, then none of the accessor methods for data values will generate exceptions. This assumption should be carefully documented in the `Record` class, however, and the reliance upon the assumption should be documented in the linked list code.

This is what we refer to as a "gotcha." Invariably, it is at the interface between the work of two different people that technical problems occur. The problem that would occur at this point would be if the person who wrote the `Record` class did not initialize data values to `null`, but the person writing the `DLL` code was expecting that initialization to have been done. This is why we insist that code be documented. If the person writing `Record` does not initialize, it isn't fatal unless the person using `Record` assumes that the initialization has been done.

In looking at the code in Figure 4.3, then, we know that no exceptions will be generated as long as initialization to `null` has happened. And even for the `getNext`, `setNext`, `getPrev`, and `setPrev` methods, if we have implemented the DLL so that dummy nodes are used as head and tail, then the methods will return dummy nodes, yes, but they will return nodes rather than throw errors, and then these methods pass off the error checking to the code that uses the `DLL` code.

What about the code in Figure 4.4? All but the last of the methods of this code will execute without error, again assuming that the `DLLNode` initialization has returned a proper node, albeit one with default values, and assuming that we do not run out of memory when we add nodes. Since running out of memory is only likely to happen if we have a runaway loop in some other program, it's not clear, for a naive application, that we ought to be concerned with that.

The bigger concern ought to be with the `unlink` method. What should we do if for some reason we try to unlink the dummy head node or the dummy tail node in our linked list? Should this be allowed? No, because we have other code that assumes that a valid head and tail node exist. If we try, in error, to delete either the head node or the tail node, then we should throw an error.

But how do we determine that we are trying to delete either the head or the tail? One way to make this determination, which also happens to work to detect a "rogue" node, is that a valid node in the linked list will have a non`null` value for `next` and `previous`. If we test for non`null` values there, we will detect not only head and tail but other spurious nodes as well. An improved `unlink` method is shown in Figure 4.11, and the exception class is shown in Figure 4.12.

The choice of what kind of exception to throw can be somewhat subtle. We have written the code of Figures 4.11 and 4.12 as if we really wanted to throw our own

```
private void unlink(DLLNode node)
  {
    if((node.getNext() == null) || (node.getPrev() == null))
    {
      throw new BadNodeException("null value for next or previous");
    }

    node.getNext().setPrev(node.getPrev());
    node.getPrev().setNext(node.getNext());
    node.setNext(null);
    node.setPrev(null);
    this.decrementSize();
  }
```

FIGURE 4.11 ■ A better method for `unlink`.

```
/*********************************************************************
 * Copyright (C) 2010 by Duncan A. Buell.  All rights reserved.
 * An exception to be thrown for bad nodes without a valid next or
 * previous pointer.
 *
 * @author Duncan A. Buell
 * @version 1.00 2010-12-24
**/
public class BadNodeException extends RuntimeException
{

/*********************************************************************
 * Constructor.
**/
  public BadNodeException()
  {
    super();
  } // public BadNodeException()

/*********************************************************************
 * Constructor with a message to be printed.
 *
 * @param message the message to be printed with the exception.
**/
  public BadNodeException(String errorMessage)
  {
    super(" " + errorMessage);
  } // public BadNodeException(String errorMessage)

} // public class BadNodeException extends RuntimeException
```

FIGURE 4.12 ■ A class for exception handling.

exception, in this case the `BadNodeException`. There are many built-in exceptions that could be thrown; the exception that is generally thrown when an enumeration fails is `NoSuchElementException`. As with all exceptions built into Java, this has a constructor both with and without a user-specified detail message, so we could use it directly in the code shown in Figure 4.11. On the other hand, there will be times when we write code to throw several related exceptions. In this case we might choose to bundle up all the exceptions (for example, all the exceptions that would be thrown by a linked list class) into an exception class that then threw the various desired exceptions, possibly including a user-defined exception for problems for which none of the built-in exceptions seemed appropriate.

4.2.4 Linked Lists Using Arrays

Until programming languages caught up with the notion of embedding data structures in the basics of the language, linked lists were usually implemented using arrays. A simplistic version of this, for an array of `int` data, would be as follows. Assume we have an array (remember that we index zero-up in Java):

```
int[] myData = {10, 9, 4, 15, 23, 19, 7, 1, 18, 22};
```

We can put the data into sorted order as a linked list by setting up a parallel array

```
int[] next = {3, 0, 6, 8, *, 9, 1, 2, 5, 4};
```

of the subscripts of the "next" items and including a `head` pointer whose value is set to 7. The `head` points to the array element with the subscript 7, which has value 1. Since the value of `next[7]` is 2, we know that data value 1 is followed in the list by `myData[2]` of value 4. The next item after data value 4 is found at subscript `next[2]`, which is 6, and `myData[6]` has value 7. And so forth.

This is easily seen with a table

subscript	0	1	2	3	4	5	6	7	8	9
`myData`	10	9	4	15	23	19	7	1	18	22
`next`	3	0	6	8	*	9	1	2	5	4

and with the corresponding table sorted not by increasing value of *subscript* but by increasing value of `myData[*]`.

subscript	7	2	6	1	0	3	8	5	9	4
`next`	2	6	1	0	3	8	5	9	4	null
`myData`	1	4	7	9	10	15	18	19	22	23

Note that, rearranged this way, the value of `next[i]` is the $i + 1$st subscript.

Note also that this is *not* the same thing as creating an index for the array. An index for this array would be an array whose values were the same as the list of *subscript* values in the second table, namely $7, 2, 6, 1, 0, 3, 8, 5, 9, 4$.

Finally, we point out that this style of programming, although still present in code, is almost universally agreed upon to be A Very Bad Idea. Setting up parallel arrays in the code requires that these arrays be synchronized at all times, and programming history has shown that this is not something that gets done right much of the time. There were times in the history of computing, and there have been many programming languages, in which an array could only be an array of numbers, not an array of instances of an object. Even if one were to use an array to create a linked list, the right way to make the list shown here would be to create a class for each list item, to have an instance variable for the next subscript, and to use the data as the data payload. In that way, one would have a single array, not two (or more), and the subscript for the next item would be part of the instance of the item's class, not stored in a parallel array that could get out of synchrony.

4.2.5 Arrays, `ArrayList`s, and the Free List

The astute reader will have recognized that in our discussion of linked lists implemented using arrays we have omitted a crucial element. A linked list is a *dynamic* data structure. Unlike an array of known length, a linked list is intended to be created from nothing by adding nodes, and it is intended that nodes be added and deleted over time. If, then, a node is to be created dynamically and added to the list, or deleted dynamically, from where does the node come and to where does it go when it is no longer needed?

The answer, in the case that the underlying data structure is an `ArrayList`, is that an `ArrayList` is a Java construct that is an inherently dynamic construct. When a new `ArrayList` of `DLLNode` entries is created, for example, Java actually creates an array of 10 `DLLNode` entries. The underlying code for the `ArrayList` will keep track of the number of actual nodes in the `ArrayList`, returning that value from a call to the `size` method. If an 11th node is added to the `ArrayList`, the underlying Java code recognizes that more space is needed, and the array of 10 items is doubled in size, with the old entries copied over to the new array.

In this way, we can implement a linked list with an `ArrayList` and also get the benefit of subscripted access to a list without having to manage the length and underlying memory space needed.

If we were to implement a linked list with a Java array,[3] however, we would be forced to manage the space ourselves. This was often done in the past by means

[3] or in ancient times with primitive languages, when there was no alternative

of a *free list* of array-allocated nodes ready to be used. We actually use two linked lists to implement one. One list is that which we populate with data; the other is the free list and comprises the storage locations that have been preallocated but not yet used to hold data.

For example, we might preallocate an array of length 100 and then create the free list by having a `topOfFree` variable point to node 0 and node i point to node $i + 1$ as the `next` node. In essence, we would now have a linked list of free nodes to be used. When a new node is needed, we unlink the node pointed to by `topOfFree` and return it, providing space for the data included in a node and adding that node to our "actual" linked list. When a node is deleted, the data variables are given dummy values and the node space is linked back onto the free list.

The methods needed to implement a linked list with an array and a free list of nodes require little change from the code needed for an `ArrayList`, since the free list is managed as a linked list by itself, with nodes linked and unlinked as they are needed. This kind of implementation of a linked list is rarely needed anymore, but if you have occasion to read code from years past it is entirely likely you will see something like this.

4.3 Insertionsort

The primary difference between an array or `ArrayList` and a linked list is that the array or `ArrayList` permits *random access* into the list structure using a subscript; each data item has a "named" storage location (named by the subscript). In contrast, with a linked list all locations are *relative* to the next or previous locations. With an array or `ArrayList`, we can access the 10th data item, say, with one probe to subscript 9 (indexing zero-up). With a linked list, we cannot access the 10th item without first traversing the first nine items. Searching through a linked list is thus inherently a sequential process.

On the other hand, because all locations are relative, additions and deletions to a linked list can be made without affecting any of the data items already stored in the list. Insertions and deletions require only that the next and previous pointers be changed exactly as needed; no data needs to be moved. When a deletion takes place, no hole is left. The deleted node becomes unused memory, and Java will clean up the unused memory space that was used for storing the now-deleted data.

This dynamic capability permits one to create and maintain a dynamic list in sorted order by using an *insertionsort*. The idea of an insertionsort is quite simple. If we have a linked list of records that are sorted according to some key, we can insert a new record as follows. Beginning with the head node, we traverse the list by following the `next` pointers. At each record, we compare against the key to determine whether to insert the new record into the list at the current location. Specifically, if the data records are sorted in increasing order of keys, we can do this in one of two ways. Either we code the insertion as

```
while(newRecordKey < currentRecordKey)
{
  follow pointers from the current record to the next record
}
insert the new record before the current record
```

or we can code the insertion as

```
while(newRecordKey < nextRecordKey)
{
  follow pointers from the current record to the next record
}
insert the new record after the current record
```

Done in this fashion, one can dynamically add records to a linked list and do the insertionsort at the same time. It is important to note that with a linked list of nodes, linking a new node into the appropriate location requires on average that half the list be traversed in order to find the appropriate location, starting from either the head or the tail of the list.

An insertionsort can also be done dynamically using an `ArrayList` to manage the existence of storage space. The `add` method for `ArrayList` adds a record at the end of the list. We can now "pull" that record toward the front to insert it into its proper location. We compare the new item at the end of the list with the item that immediately precedes it, and we exchange if necessary. Continuing to move toward the front, we exchange as needed until the new item is in the proper location. By beginning at the end of the array, we need only move those items that need to be moved; were we to have inserted the new item at the beginning of the array, we would have had to move down one space every item that followed the new item in the eventual sorted list.

Insertionsort is not an especially efficient sorting method because each insertion requires on average that half the existing list be traversed. However, for short lists that must be constantly maintained, it has the advantage of being simple. Where insertionsort has a genuine place in the stable of algorithms is in situations in which one starts with a relatively long list of N sorted items and then needs to insert a relatively small number n of items, where n is much smaller than N.

A sample code fragment that inserts an element into an `ArrayList` called `recs[]` while performing an insertionsort so the array stays in sorted order is shown in Figure 4.13.

```
public void insertAndSort(newElement, insertionSub)
{
  recs.set(insertionSub, newElement);
  for(int i = insertionSub-1; i >= 0; --i)
  {
    if(recs.get(i) > recs.get(insertionSub))
    {
      swap elements at subscripts i and insertionSub
      insertionSub = i;
    }
  }
}
```

FIGURE 4.13 ■ An insertionsort on an array.

It is worth restating the different strategies that should be considered when looking at insertionsort. If the data structure is an array, new entries should be added to the end of the array and pulled forward until they fall into the proper location, as is shown in Figure 4.14. Inserting them from the beginning of the array requires moving down all the entries in the rest of the array once the proper location is determined, and this can be costly. The same strategy applies for an `ArrayList` because an `ArrayList` is actually an array. However, the `add(int index, E element)`

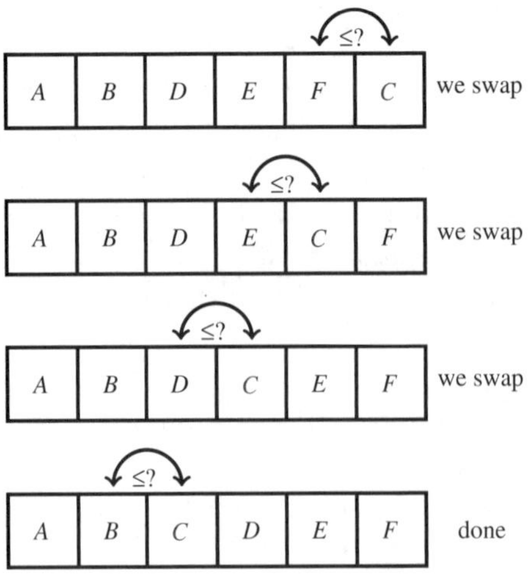

FIGURE 4.14 ■ Inserting a node into an array.

method allows one to insert an element at a given `index` location, just as one would want to do; in this case, the execution time penalty is still present because the data must still be moved, but the programmer doesn't have to write the code to finish moving the data and is thus saved from potential coding errors.

Finally, with a true linked list, there is no underlying array or `ArrayList` structure; the nodes are simply nodes, each of which points to the next one in the list, so linking a node into the list changes only the local pointers of the nodes where the insertion is made.

4.4 Summary

We have discussed in this chapter the array and the `ArrayList` data structures. Both can be used for implementing more advanced data structures, but the `ArrayList` is generally the preferred mechanism because the `ArrayList` has built into the class a number of features that make it harder to make mistakes and easier to implement secure and reliable code.

We have also covered linked lists, both as a concept and as a structure that can be implemented using one of several underlying data structures, including arrays or `ArrayLists`. The linked list is a very common structure to be used for handling data that grows and shrinks in size and has the characteristics of a "to-do" list. As part of implementing linked lists, we discussed how to handle exceptions and throw errors when, for example, one tries to delete from a list that is already empty.

We also discussed the insertionsort. This is not an especially efficient sorting algorithm, but it is commonly used in structures like a linked list in which items are added dynamically and the user expects the items to be kept in a sorted order.

4.5 Exercises

1. Write a method `isEmpty` that will return a `boolean` to answer the question of whether or not a linked list is empty.
2. Rewrite the `FlatFile` code in Chapter 3 to use a linked list instead of an `ArrayList`. You should not need to change either the driver program in `Main` or the data payload program in `Record`. You can still sort the records with a bubblesort if you want, but then you will have to change the code slightly to access the individual nodes in a different way.
3. Take either your code from the previous exercise or the `FlatFile` code directly and change it so that nodes are stored in a linked list and inserted in sorted order using an insertionsort.

4. Let's say you have implemented the code of either of the previous two exercises. Why can't you implement binary search on the linked list?

5. Using your code from either of the first two exercises, adapt the search to look for a node and then, if it is found, delete the node.

6. In implementing a linked list, one can either use an actual node as the head and the tail, storing dummy values in the instance variables, or have a head and tail pointer in the `DLL` class that point to the first and last node containing real data. Implement a constructor that creates a dummy-valued node instead of a node with `null` data.

7. Implement a `clear` method to get rid of all the entries in a linked list. Remember that Java will clean up memory that is no longer being used, so this requires only that you adjust references to the head and tail nodes.

8. Implement a method to remove all duplicate entries in a linked list. Note that if the list is not assumed to be sorted, this will closely resemble the looping structure of a bubblesort and be very inefficient.

9. Create a `Set` class that uses a linked list as the underlying data structure to store sets of words. Remember that a set does not store multiple instances of a given element. You will need to implement at least the methods `addToSet`, `isElement`, and `deleteFromSet`. For further credit, implement a method for set union.

10. Start with the `FlatFile` code that uses a linked list to store the data. You already have a method to add a single instance of a `Record` to the data structure. Write a method `appendData` as a method of the `FlatFile` class that will take a `FlatFile` as a parameter and append the data to the original structure. Think of this as the analog of the concatenation of `String` data.

11. Start with the `FlatFile` code that uses a linked list to store the data. You already have a method to add a single instance of a `Record` to the data structure, and you have a method to sort the list. Write a method `mergeData` as a method of the `FlatFile` class that will take a `FlatFile` as a parameter and merge the two lists of data. The result should be a single merged list, in sorted order, even if the original two lists were not sorted.

12. A *palindrome* is a sequence of characters that reads the same both forward and backward, like the number 12344321, the word "radar," or the famous expression, "Able was I ere I saw Elba" (ignoring capitalization). Write code to read character strings, store them in a linked list, and then determine if the strings are palindromes. To simplify things so you can concentrate on the linked list part of this exercise, go ahead and break out the strings into individual characters separated by spaces (like "1 2 3 4 4 3 2 1") so you can parse them quickly with the standard methods of a `Scanner`.

13. Write a program to read numbers, store them in a linked list, and then split the original list into two linked lists of even and odd numbers.

14. Write a program to read words (as in a dictionary), store them in a linked list, and then split the original list into different linked lists based on the lengths of the words. If you set this up using an `ArrayList` of linked lists, so that subscript `i` in the `ArrayList` was the linked list for words of length i, then you will have to figure out a way to manage possibly empty lists. What you do not want to do is have a separate variable for each length because you will not know in advance how long the longest word is going to be.

5 Generics, Collections, and Testing

Objectives

- An introduction to the use of the Java generic construct
- An introduction to the Java Collections Framework, including the Java `LinkedList` data structure
- An introduction to the use of the Java `iterator` construct
- Implementation of a user-constructed Collection class
- Testing using `JUnit`

Key Terms

collection	foreach	iterator
elements	generics	JCF

Introduction

We claimed at the outset that this was a text on computing using Java as the vehicle, not a text on programming in Java. This chapter will come closest to violating that principle because we will cover three specifics of Java that aid in the writing of correct and understandable programs. By using generics, one can write general-purpose code that operates on more than one underlying data payload type. By building collections, one can create code packages (such as code for a linked list) that can be used as an extension to the base language by other programmers. And by creating test suites with `JUnit`, one can provide standard modules for testing code both now and after future modifications.

5.1 Using Generics for the Data Payload

In our code fragments in Figures 4.3 and 4.4 the use of the `Record` class was pervasive; this class was the data payload carried by a `DLLNode`. However, in this code we did something that is contrary to our general mantra that details of data should be confined to the code that has a clear need to know about details. Namely, we included in our `DLLNode` a specific textual reference to the `Record` class. However, the linked list data structure should concern itself not with the *nature* of the data payload but only with the *existence* of a payload of some definable data type.

Think of the cases in which this is true. The `DLLNode` code refers in a few places to the instance of the `Record` class that is the payload for that particular node. It does not, however, actually do anything with the *contents* of the instance of `Record`. Similarly, the `DLL` code makes no reference to the contents of a `Record`; it, too, handles the instance of `Record` simply as a pass-through entity.

Consider also the inner loop code of the bubblesort in Figure 3.10. There is a `compareTo` method that is called to determine which of two instances of the data is "smaller," but otherwise the code is moving entire instances of the data class around.

Java provides through its generic feature the ability to write code to manipulate entire instances of a class without specifying what that class is. For example, what one really wants to write as a `swap` method for the bubblesort (or any other sort, for that matter) is

```
void swap(ArrayList<T> list, int sub1, int sub2)
{
  T temp;
  temp = list.get(sub2);
  list.set(sub2, this.get(sub1));
  list.set(sub1, temp);
}
```

where `T` is replaced by whatever happens to be the data type/class name of the moment. In fact, this is exactly what we write. The `T` is taken by the compiler to be a generic data type, and only if someone were to invoke this method from a code fragment like

```
ArrayList<String> myList;
...
swap(myList, i, j);
```

would the compiler then finish the job by creating a `swap` method to swap instances of `String` data.

We can rewrite the simplistic code in Figures 4.3 and 4.4 to make use of the generic construct of Java. We have already used generics in this text, probably without knowing that this is what we are doing—the `ArrayList` is defined with a generic data type that is instanced, for example, when we define an `ArrayList` of `Record` type with the line

```
ArrayList<Record> myList;
```

The basic syntax for using generics is exactly the syntax we have been using for an `Arraylist`. The code that would *define* the use of a generic would look something like `Arraylist<T>`, with the `T` being essentially a symbolic reference to a data type. When we use an `Arraylist`, we have to supply an actual data type as in the preceding `Arraylist` declaration.

Our rewrite of Figures 4.3 and 4.4 to define classes `DLL<T>` and `DLLNode<T>` using generics appears in part in Figures 5.1–5.5.

```
public class DLL<T extends Comparable<T>>
{
  private int size;
  private DLLNode<T> head;
  private DLLNode<T> tail;

  public DLL()
  {
    this.head = new DLLNode<T>();
    this.tail = new DLLNode<T>();
    head.setNext(this.tail);
    tail.setPrev(this.head);
    this.setSize(2);
  }
  private DLLNode<T> getHead()
  {
    return this.head;
  }
  private void setHead(DLLNode<T> value)
  {
    this.head = value;
  }
    CODE FOR THE SIZE VARIABLE HERE ...
  private DLLNode<T> getTail()
  {
    return this.tail;
  }
  private void setTail(DLLNode<T> value)
  {
    this.tail = value;
  }
    MORE CODE ...
}
```

FIGURE 5.1 ■ Code fragment for a doubly-linked list using generics, part 1.

```
private void linkAfter(DLLNode<T> baseNode, DLLNode<T> newNode)
{
  newNode.setNext(baseNode.getNext());
  newNode.setPrev(baseNode);
  baseNode.getNext().setPrev(newNode);
  baseNode.setNext(newNode);
  this.incSize();
}
private void unlink (DLLNode<T> node)
{
  node.getNext().setPrev(node.getPrev());
  node.getPrev().setNext(node.getNext());
  node.setNext(null);
  node.setPrev(null);
  this.decSize();
}
```

FIGURE 5.2 ■ Code fragment for a doubly-linked list using generics, part 2.

We note that the only change needed in the code to use these classes is that the `dll` instance variable that is the linked list must be declared and constructed with `DLL<Record>` in a manner entirely analogous to the `ArrayList<Record>` mentioned previously.

The use of the generic for the type of the data payload permits the linked list class and the node class to include a payload of a type that is unspecified (one might almost say "generic") until the point at which the code is compiled and executed. Since neither the linked list class nor the node class actually *do* anything with the payload other than pass it forward and backward and move it around as an entire unit, these two classes need not know anything about what that payload is. This permits these two classes to be written once and for all (just as the `ArrayList` class was) without having to specify much of anything about the nature of the payload. You can almost view the `T` of the generic as a variable name that is passed to the compiler; unless and until the compiler actually needs to do something that depends on the value of the variable (the three things that we will deal with here are comparison, input, and output), the compiler does not need to have that variable given a value. Things like copying are legal for any variable, so code for copying instances of a variable is legal without knowing what the value of the variable happens to be.

A close comparison of the code in Figures 4.4 and 5.1 shows that essentially nothing has changed except a slight bit of syntax. The major changes, however, come from the fact that the code for `DLL<T>` and `DLLNode<T>`, since they no longer explicitly reference the `Record` class, can now no longer make use of the knowledge of the specific methods that are implemented for the `Record` class; the compiler

```
/*****************************************************************
 * Method to find if a list has a given data item.
 * @param dllData the <code>T</code> to match against.
 * @return the <code>boolean</code> answer to the question.
**/
  public boolean contains(T dllData)
  {
    boolean returnValue = false;
    DLLNode<T> foundNode = null;
    foundNode = this.containsNode(dllData);
    if(null != foundNode)
    {
      returnValue = true;
    }
    return returnValue;
  }

/*****************************************************************
 * Method to remove a node with a given record as data.
 * @param dllData the <code>T</code> to match against.
 * @return the <code>boolean</code> as to whether the record was
 *         found and removed or not.
**/
  public boolean remove(T dllData)
  {
    boolean returnValue = false;
    DLLNode<T> foundNode = null;
    foundNode = this.containsNode(dllData);
    if(null != foundNode)
    {
      this.unlink(foundNode);
      returnValue = true;
    }
    return returnValue;
  }
```

FIGURE 5.3 ■ Code fragment for a doubly-linked list using generics, part 3.

will not accept the use of methods that it cannot guarantee will exist for *every* type that might possibly be passed as `T` to `DLL<T>` and `DLLNode<T>`.

Consider that one of our basic operations is to search the `Phonebook` for an entry, that is, to use a `contains` method. Such a method was achieved in our early version of the code by walking through the array and using a `compareName` method to compare the `name` variable of a target entry against the `name` variable of the entries in the list. Almost no data types, however, will possess a `compareName` method, and yet the compiler, were it to see a reference to `nodeData.compareName(*)`, would

```
/*****************************************************************
 * Method to return the node with a given data item in it, else null.
 * This method eliminates duplicate code in <code>contains</code>
 * and <code>remove</code>.
 * @param dllData the <code>T</code> to match against.
 * @return the <code>DLLNode</code> answer, else null.
**/
  public DLLNode<T> containsNode(T dllData)
  {
    DLLNode<T> returnValue = null;
    DLLNode<T> currentNode = null;

    currentNode = this.getHead();
    currentNode = currentNode.getNext();
    while(currentNode != this.getTail())
    {
      if(0 == currentNode.getNodeData().compareTo(dllData))
      {
        returnValue = currentNode;
        break; // we violate the style rule against 'break'
      }
      currentNode = currentNode.getNext();
    }

    return returnValue;
  }
```

FIGURE 5.4 ■ Code fragment for a doubly-linked list using generics, part 4.

accept this as legal only if it could be assured that all the generic data types `T` used in the linked list classes were to be guaranteed to possess a `compareName` method.

We cannot guarantee to the compiler that all data types used for `T` will possess all possible methods. There is a way, however, to guarantee that some obviously useful or otherwise necessary methods will be supplied. The

```
T extends Comparable
```

in the declaration

```
public class DLL<T extends Comparable>
```

in Figure 5.1 is our promise to the compiler that any data type used for `T` will have implemented the `compareTo` method of the `Comparable` interface.[1] Having

[1] In general, `extends` is a guarantee that the data type will implement *all* the methods required by the interface, but in this case the `Comparable` interface requires only the one method `compareTo`.

```
public class DLLNode<T>
{
  private DLLNode<T> next;
  private DLLNode<T> prev;
  private T nodeData;
  public DLLNode()
  {
    super();
    this.setNext(null);
    this.setPrev(null);
    this.setNodeData(null);
  }
  public DLLNode(T data)
  {
    super();
    this.setNext(null);
    this.setPrev(null);
    this.setNodeData(data);
  }
  public T getNodeData()
  {
    return this.nodeData;
  }
  public void setNodeData(T newData)
  {
    this.nodeData = newData;
  }
  public DLLNode<T> getNext()
  {
    return this.next;
  }
  public void setNext(DLLNode<T> newNext)
  {
    this.next = newNext;
  }
  public DLLNode<T> getPrev()
  {
    return this.prev;
  }
  public void setPrev(DLLNode<T> newPrev)
  {
    this.prev = newPrev;
  }
}
```

FIGURE 5.5 ■ Code fragment for a node in a doubly-linked list using generics.

guaranteed that compareTo will exist, the compiler permits us to write without error the line

```
if(0 == currentNode.getNodeData().compareTo(dllData))
```

because the call to currentNode.getNodeData() returns an instance of type T, and we have instructed the compiler that T will extend Comparable and thus will have a legitimate compareTo method implemented for it.

The T extends Comparable is a contract we have made with the compiler. The compiler promises to hold up its end of the contract by accepting the use of a compareTo method. We in turn must fulfill our part of the bargain by ensuring that that method exists. To do this, we change the declaration of the Record class to read

```
public class Record implements Comparable<Record>
```

and we rename the old compareName method compareTo because that's the more general method name that Comparable uses and that the compiler is now expecting to see. The compiler will now be happy, sure in its knowledge that whatever data type is used for T, the comparison we have asked for will be syntactically correct. (Of course, if we write the wrong code for the compareTo method, it could still produce the wrong *results*, but the compiler isn't going to worry about that.) The two classes for DLL<T> and DLLNode<T> can be written without saying anything in detail about what kind of data payload to expect except for the fact that payloads can be compared.

Now that we have guaranteed that we can compare payloads, we can also do a search for a specific payload, and we can therefore implement the contains and remove methods in Figure 5.3. In implementing a contains method, unlike previous methods for this application, we have to consider which values ought to be returned to the calling program. We are shortly going to move from code that is entirely under our control to the implementation of code that must follow the strictures laid down by standard classes in Java, so we will take the opportunity to ensure that what we do now will not have to be changed later. For this reason, we will implement the add, contains, and remove methods to accept a Record (actually an item of type T) as the input parameter and to return a boolean value indicating whether the operation was successful. The use of a boolean both for the answer to the contains question and to indicate that a remove operation actually did find and remove an entry is obvious. Less obvious is the use of a boolean response to an add method. However, in the Java collection classes there are classes for such things as the equivalent of a mathematical set. Adding an entry that is already present does not change the contents of a set, and thus the result of adding a duplicate entry should be false to indicate that no change occurred to the data structure implementing the set. For the sake of consistency with the rest of the Collections framework, we will implement add as a method that returns a boolean. The value `true` is returned if and only if the underlying structure has changed as a result of the `add`. In the case of the current class, this will always be true.

The `contains` and `remove` methods in Figure 5.3 take as parameters an entire instance of an object of generic type `T`. This is often not what we want to do; we will frequently want to pass in only a key (like a last name) and have a version of a `contains` method respond that yes (or no), an item with that `String` as last name happens to be in the data (or not). We can easily write methods to do this by overriding the original `contains` method. As a practical matter, though, we then have to consider whether returning just a `boolean` is the smartest thing to do. The original `contains` and `remove` methods are unambiguous; an entire instance of an object is passed in, and the comparison is presumably done on the entire instance. In the case of the `ArrayList` methods, these two methods return `true` only if the exact object matches (and not just the values of the instance variables in the object). If we are passing in a last name, it may well happen that we have multiple records with the same last name. We probably don't want to remove any arbitrary record just because the last name matches, and we won't get all the information we need if our `contains` terminates a search and returns `true` the first time it hits a match on last name. There will, therefore, be good reasons to write methods that differ from the standard methods for adding, removing, and searching. Perhaps we would want the method to return a subscript if we knew we were dealing with a subscripted list. If we were dealing with something like a linked list, though, without formal subscripts, we might want to have our methods return the entire instance of the object.

5.2 Objects and Equality

We have said it already, but it is worth saying again, because this is the point at which it starts being a big deal: When two instances of an object are compared with the == symbol, the two instances are considered to be equal if they are absolutely identical. This means that the "two" instances must in fact be references to the same location in memory. The code

```
Record one = new Record();
Record two = new Record();
if(one == two)
{
  System.out.println("equal");
}
else
{
  System.out.println("not equal");
}
```

results in the message `not equal` because these are two `Record` instances with the same (default) contents, not the same object, and Java would only return `true` for the `==` if these were the same object. That would happen with the following code fragment because variable `two` would be assigned to be identical to variable `one`.

```
Record one = new Record();
Record two = new Record();
two = one;
if(one == two)
{
  System.out.println("equal");
}
else
{
  System.out.println("not equal");
}
```

The basic `equals` method implemented in the `Object` class works this way—it does the most narrow possible comparison to determine equality, and it requires that the two objects point to the same location in memory before it will return a value of `true`.

Probably in your earlier work in Java this was only an issue when dealing with `String` data. Although the `equals` method for an instance of an `Object` returns `true` only when the two objects are identical, the `equals` method has been overridden for data of `String` type so that the method will return `true` if the two sequences of characters are the same, that is, if the *contents* of the two `String` objects are the same. This allows us to compare two strings of characters, and it is exactly this kind of override that we will have to implement in order to use generics for an arbitrary class. Any class that we declare is a subclass of `Object` and thus inherits by default the `equals` method that is usually too strict for our purposes. We will almost always, especially when using generics, have to override that method with our own appropriate `equals`.

5.3 The Java `LinkedList`

It turns out that Java, straight out of the box, comes replete with classes and interfaces that are part of the *Java Collections Framework*, or JCF. A *collection* is nothing more than a representation for a group of objects known as the *elements* of the collection. There exists, for example, a Java `LinkedList` class that can be used instead of the code that we have presented so far in this text. The `LinkedList` class has methods for `add`, `contains`, and `remove` that function (almost) exactly as do our methods for the same functions. The `LinkedList` also has a great many other methods that are documented on the Java website. By including

```
import java.util.LinkedList;
```

in our `Phonebook.java` code, we can remove all reference to our own `DLL.java` and `DLLNode.java` classes and replace them with references to `DLL` from `LinkedList`. If we do this, the only complication is that we no longer have the hand-coded `toString` method for the entire linked list. This method exists in the `LinkedList` class, but its output is different from what we wrote ourselves. Our `toString` produced formatted output that used the `toString` that we knew existed (because we had written it) of the data payload. The built-in version of `toString` for the `LinkedList` is much cruder because it must be more general purpose; it uses the `Object.toString()` method that works for all objects. The documentation for `Object.toString()` says in part "It is recommended that all subclasses override this method," but the creators of Java obviously did not feel it was necessary to *require* that this be overridden.

To create the same output from `LinkedList` that we had before with our own class, we also need to use the `listIterator` method that comes with the `LinkedList` class; this requires us to include in our code

```
import java.util.ListIterator;
```

to ensure that the `listIterator` method is found by the compiler, and then the `Phonebook.java` version of `toString` can be written as in Figure 5.6.

```
/*********************************************************************
 * Method to <code>toString</code> a complete Phonebook.
 * @return the <code>toString</code> rep'n of the entire DLL.
**/
  public String toString()
  {
    String s = "";
    Record rec;
    ListIterator<Record> iter = this.dll.listIterator();
    while(iter.hasNext())
    {
      rec = iter.next();
      s += String.format("%s%n", rec.toString());
    }
    return s;
  }
```

FIGURE 5.6 ■ Code fragment for a `toString` method.

5.4 Iterators

The code presented in Figure 5.6 uses a Java feature known as an iterator. We have been using an iterator repeatedly in this course for input of data with a `Scanner`, and it is now time to look one level deeper to see what this construct really does for us and how to implement one.

An *iterator* is nothing more than a class that implements two (and sometimes three) methods for accessing the elements of a data structure. We present in Figure 5.7 the code for a `DLLIterator` class that could be implemented separately and that would provide an iterator for the `DLL` code in this chapter.[2] The interface for an `Iterator` class requires that methods `hasNext` and `next` be implemented; these perform the same function as do the methods that we have used for the `Scanner` class for input. The interface does not require that the `remove` method be implemented, so we include code for that but throw the `UnsupportedOperationException` as required.

We have in our `toString` method in Figure 5.6 used not an `Iterator` but a `ListIterator`. The `ListIterator` is intended for use with a collection (like a linked list) that has some notion of "sequential" access as opposed, say, to a collection that implements a mathematical set for which no sequential ordering of the elements is obviously appropriate. A `ListIterator` has more required methods than does an `Iterator`, but the basic concept is the same, and we use both extensively.

An iterator is also present when the Java *foreach* construct is used. Instead of the code in Figure 5.6 that resembles what we use with the `Scanner` class, we could make our linked list "iterable" and write

```
for(Record rec: this.dll)
{
  s = String.format("%s%n", rec.toString());
}
```

In either case, what we have done is to use a construct that allows us to access directly the data payload in the structure without having to provide (or even think about) subscripts.

5.4.1 The Justification for Iterators

It is conceivable at this point that the eyes of many readers are glazing over and readers are wondering whether this concept of an iterator is just something dreamed

[2] In fact, we would probably *not* want to implement this as a separate class, but the reasons for that will appear shortly. For now, it is sufficient that this code will in fact work.

```
import java.util.Iterator;
public class DLLIterator<T extends Comparable<T>> implements Iterator<T>
{
  private DLLNode<T> current;
  private DLL<T> theDLL = null;

  public DLLIterator(DLL<T> dll)
  {
    this.theDLL = dll;
    this.current = this.theDLL.getHead();
  }

  public boolean hasNext()
  {
    boolean returnValue = false;
    if(this.current.getNext() != this.theDLL.getTail())
      returnValue = true;
    return returnValue;
  }

  public T next()
  {
    T returnValue = null;
    this.current = this.current.getNext();
    returnValue = this.current.getNodeData();
    return returnValue;
  }

  public void remove()
  {
    throw new UnsupportedOperationException(
                          "'remove' not supported);
  }
}
```

FIGURE 5.7 ■ Code for an `Iterator` class for a doubly-linked list.

up by compiler writers and language designers because they thought it would be neat to have this kind of feature. Although we may agree with the readers some of the time with regard to compiler and programming language people, this time we have to admit that they got it right. Compare the following two bits of pseudocode, for example.

```
// code fragment one
node = head;
while(node != tail)
{
  Record rec = node.getRecord();
  s = String.format("%s%n", rec.toString());
  node = node.next();
}

// code fragment two
for(Record rec: this.dll)
{
  s = String.format("%s%n", rec.toString());
}
```

The big difference is this: In the first fragment, we knowingly traverse a sequence of *nodes*, fetch the data payload for each node, and then use that payload. (In both fragments all we do is create the `toString` of the payload, but this code could be replaced in both fragments by code that actually used the data.)

In the second fragment, we simply fetch the data. The code at this level in the second fragment is entirely ignorant of the underlying data structure. The data structure has been hidden from this code fragment, and all that is visible is the ability to move from one data element to the "next" data element.

This is[3] the essence of an iterator—instead of fetching the data structure element and then the data in that element, we fetch the data element directly and can ignore the implementation issues below the fetch. The `Iterator` interface requires no more than a `hasNext` and a `next` method (with an optional `remove` method).

Even if no more than the required methods are implemented, this is a powerful technique that eliminates one level of indirect reference (data payloads accessed immediately instead of data payloads accessed within linked list nodes) by focusing directly on the data payload itself. By focusing on the data itself, and removing that one level of indirection, we would hope that programs would become simpler, more likely to be correct, and easier to write.

It would be dishonest, however, to stop here and not point out one more unfortunate fact. What we gain with an iterator, in the ability to reference a data item and then "the next" data item, we must also pay for at the time we need to remove an item or move it around. If we manipulate a sequence of data items with the first code fragment, and what we really want to do is to remove the item from

[3] at least at the level of this course

the linked list, then we have the actual node to be unlinked, which means that we have access to the `next` and `previous` nodes and can do the appropriate unlinking and relinking of nodes. If we have gone beyond the concept of nodes, to deal only with the data items themselves, then in order to unlink and relink, we will need to implement methods that revert to linked list notions. There's never any free lunch.

5.5 Implementing Our Very Own Collection

It is now time to convert our code for a doubly-linked list into the sort of code that would be expected of real Java programmers. We will not push this all the way through to a complete implementation, but we will go far enough to show what could be completed with only a SMOP,[4] and we will leave that SMOP to the student, who will no doubt benefit immensely from the experience.

First, we observe that only two classes need to be changed—the `DLL<T>` class and the `Record` class. The `DLL<T>` class must now begin

```
import java.util.AbstractSequentialList;
import java.util.List;
import java.util.ListIterator;
public class DLL<T extends Comparable<T>>
                    extends AbstractSequentialList<T>
                    implements List<T>
```

and we are now required to implement several methods in order to satisfy the requirements of `AbstractSequentialList` and `List`. We notice that the requirement for the built-in `add` method specifies that elements are to be added at the tail and not the head, so we write an `addBeforeTail` and a `linkBefore` method entirely symmetrical to the two methods we have already written, and we use these instead so as to comply with the rules for the classes and interfaces of the JCF. A brief mention of the hierarchy is in order. The ancestral notion is of a Java `Collection`, which is an interface that prepares the way for dealing with collections of data items (that is, in a way more complicated and providing more underlying support than are present with a simple data array). Three of the subinterfaces that have intuitive meaning are the `List`, `Set`, and `SortedSet`. There is a built-in class `AbstractList` that provides an abstract notion of a "list" data type, and then more specialized than that is the `AbstractSequentialList` class that implements the notion, as the

[4] Small Matter Of Programming; search online for the "Jargon File."

name implies, of a list of data items that are to be thought of in a sequential manner. Indeed, the `LinkedList` class we used in a previous section is itself a subclass of `AbstractSequentialList`.

To complete our nascent abstract sequential list, currently embodied in our linked list code `DLL`, we need only supply in `DLL` a method `listIterator`. This code is simple:

```
public ListIterator<T> listIterator(int index)
{
  ListIterator<T> iter = new DLLListIterator(this);
  return iter;
}
```

although we admit that all we have done is to pass off the work to the implementation of a `DLLListIterator` class. That class is found in Figures 5.8–5.10 as a class *embedded within* the `DLL` class.

In a footnote early in Section 5.4, we said that we would explain soon why we wouldn't really want a separate class; the time is now to explain why we have chosen to embed this class inside the `DLL` class. Our earlier class for an iterator made a copy of the linked list when an instance of the iterator was created. This is not only somewhat clumsy but also highly unsafe; to eliminate this problem, we have embedded the new iterator class inside the `DLL` class so the iterator can have direct access to some of the variables of the `DLL` class. The `unlink` method is used, for example, by the `remove` method. More importantly, we can with the embedded class get direct access to the linked list itself, so the only instance variable inside the iterator class that we need in order to maintain a sense of context with the linked list is the `current` pointer.

Finally, we have chosen in this implementation not to implement the optional methods for `add` and `set` and we have not shown the implementations of `nextIndex` and `previousIndex`. We have, however, implemented the `remove` method together with its subtleties of when it is and is not legal to be issued.

The change to the `Record` class is significant, yet subtle. We note that the `List` possesses methods

```
boolean contains(Object o)
```

and

```
boolean remove(Object o)
```

```
private class DLLListIterator implements ListIterator<T>
{
  private boolean removeInvalid_Add;
  private boolean removeInvalid_NextPrevious;
  private DLLNode<T> cursor;
  private DLLNode<T> lastReturned;
/*********************************************************************
 * Constructor.
**/
  public DLLListIterator(DLL<T> dll)
  {
    this.cursor = dll.getHead().getNext();
    this.lastReturned = null;
    this.removeInvalid_Add = false;  // we don't implement 'add' here
    this.removeInvalid_NextPrevious = true;
  }
/*********************************************************************
 * Method to answer the question of a "next" element.
 * @return the <code>boolean</code> answer to the question.
**/
@Override
  public boolean hasNext()
  {
    boolean returnValue = false;

    if(this.cursor != getTail())
      returnValue = true;

    return returnValue;
  }
/*********************************************************************
 * Method to answer the question of a "previous" element.
 * @return the <code>boolean</code> answer to the question.
**/
@Override
  public boolean hasPrevious()
  {
    boolean returnValue = false;

    if(this.cursor.getPrev() != getHead())
      returnValue = true;

    return returnValue;
  }
```

FIGURE 5.8 ■ The list iterator code, part 1.

```
/*********************************************************************
 * Method to return the "next" element.
 * @return the next data element.
**/
  public T next()
  {
    if(this.hasNext())
    {
      this.removeInvalid_NextPrevious = false;
      this.lastReturned = this.cursor;
      this.cursor = this.cursor.getNext();
    }
    else
    {
      throw new RuntimeException("ERROR: hasNext fails");
    }
    return this.lastReturned.getNodeData();
  }

/*********************************************************************
 * Method to return the "previous" element.
 * @return the previous data element.
**/
  public T previous()
  {
    if(this.hasPrevious())
    {
      this.removeInvalid_NextPrevious = false;
      this.cursor = this.cursor.getPrev();
      this.lastReturned = this.cursor;
    }
    else
    {
      throw new RuntimeException("ERROR: hasPrevious fails");
    }
    return this.lastReturned.getNodeData();
  }
```

FIGURE 5.9 ■ The list iterator code, part 2.

whose functions are exactly as the methods of the same name that we have implemented already. However, it is here that we must take special note once again of the way that Java defines the concept of "equals." Two objects are considered equal, that is,

```
this.equals(that)
```

```
/*****************************************************************
 * Method to remove the element returned by the most recent "next"
 * or "previous" operation.  This is invalid if it has already been
 * called once since the last "next" or "previous" operation or if
 * "add" has been called since the last call to "next" or "previous".
 * @throws IllegalStateException if this method is invalid now.
**/
  public void remove()
  {
    String s  = "";
    if(this.removeInvalid_NextPrevious)
    {
      s  = String.format("%s","illegal call to 'remove'");
      s += String.format("%s","--already called since the ");
      s += String.format("%s","last call to 'next' or 'previous'");
      throw new IllegalStateException(s);
    }
    else if(removeInvalid_Add)
    {
      s  = String.format("%s","illegal call to 'remove'");
      s += String.format("%s","--'add' called since the ");
      s += String.format("%s","last call to 'next' or 'previous'");
      throw new IllegalStateException(s);
    }
    else
    {
      // If we got the "lastReturned" from a "next" then we
      // already bumped the "cursor".  But if we got the
      // "lastReturned" from a "previous" then we need to bump
      // the "cursor" explicitly to the next node.
      if(this.cursor == this.lastReturned)
        this.cursor = this.cursor.getNext();
      unlink(this.lastReturned);
      removeInvalid_NextPrevious = true;
    }
  }
```

FIGURE 5.10 ■ The list iterator code, part 3.

returns a `boolean true`, if and only if `this` and `that` *are the same object, unless we override the default code for* `equals`.

The `contains(Object o)` and `remove(Object o)` methods test for exact equality of objects, and these methods always work because everything in Java is a thing of `Object` type. It is almost never the case, though, that this is what we will want in a program. If we had an `ArrayList` of three strings, say `pepperoni`, `mushroom`, and `sausage` for types of pizza, and if we then read input `mushroom` from a user ordering pizza, the `contains` method will return `false` when it does the lookup on `mushroom`. The problem is that the `mushroom` instance of the object stored in the `ArrayList` is a *different* instance of the object from the `mushroom` instance provided by the user, and `contains` looks at the equality of the objects, not equality of the data contents. (For `String` data, that test is done by the `equals` method in the `String` class.)

If we want to test for equality of the data contents, we must override the default for `equals`, which is what we did in our `Record` class because we wanted to consider two records to be "equal" if the last names in the data were the same. In any search using a search key, we will want to do exactly this because we will be searching for the complete record using only the key—if we had the entire record, we wouldn't need to be searching for it!

The second subtle but important change to our `Record` is to ensure that we will in fact override the built-in method for `equals`. Java is very fussy about type-checking, and our earlier code for the `Record` class read

```
public boolean equals(Record that)
```

which is not what the JCF needs. That method has a different signature than the built-in method because the parameter is of type `Record` and not of type `Object`.

In order to use our own version of `equals` to override the default in the requirements for the `List` interface, we must change our code to read as in Figure 5.11.

```
/*********************************************************************
 * Method to override the <code>equals</code> method.
 * We will declare two records to be equal if their data values are
 * equal, not if they are identical objects.
 * NOTE THE PARAMETER TYPE.  THIS IS ESSENTIAL TO HAVING THE METHOD
 * PROPERLY OVERRIDE THE DEFAULT <code>equals</code>.
 * @param that the <code>Object</code> to be compared against.
 * @return boolean answer to the question.
**/
  public boolean equals(Object that)
  {
    boolean retVal;
    retVal = true;
    retVal &= this.getName().equals(((Record) that).getName());
    retVal &= this.getOffice().equals(((Record) that).getOffice());
    retVal &= this.getPhone().equals(((Record) that).getPhone());
    retVal &= (this.getTeaching() == ((Record) that).getTeaching());
    return retVal;
  }
```

FIGURE 5.11 ■ The `equals` node in the `Record` class.

The parameter is passed as an instance of Object type, but it then must be cast to an instance of Record type in order to invoke the correct equals method. Because the signature of the method is now the same as that of the default equals method, we will in fact be overriding the default instead of creating a new equals method that would be valid only for parameters of type Record.

5.6 Testing with JUnit

The last part of converting our code so that it resembles professional code[5] is to implement unit tests with JUnit. The Java JUnit capability is not inherent in Java, but it is relatively easy to add the jar for JUnit; for example, when using Eclipse™ it is necessary to add the external jar into the compiler's build path for the project.

A JUnit unit testing module for the Record class is presented in Figures 5.13–5.16. The class is a standard Java class, except that the jar for JUnit is part of the build path; we import part of that jar into our class; and the class extends TestCase in the jar.

We have a number of methods, each of which has a name that begins with test and continues with a method name from Record. Each of these methods will be executed after a call to setUp, and the tearDown method will be executed afterward each time, so these two methods should be written to provide each testing method a clean environment with no context held over from a previous method.

The method calls that we will use from JUnit are given in Figure 5.12. The syntax is almost self-explanatory. For the

```
assertEquals(messageString, expectedValue, actualValue)
```

method, for example, the expectedValue might be the returned parameter expected from a method called with a certain set of arguments, and the actualValue argument would in fact be the call to that method with those arguments. If the values are not equal, then either a default or (in this case) a user-specified messageString is printed along with the failure information. As with any other Java class, output to the console is possible if the user is unsure as to the progress of the testing.

In order to test the Record class with JUnit, we did have to make a few small changes. A JUnit test is yet another class in Java and can thus see only the public methods and variables. In our earlier code, for example, we had declared

[5] We use the word "resembles" because we are still not going to be done and would not go so far as to suggest that it might actually *be* professional code.

```
assertEquals(expectedValue, actualValue)
assertEquals(messageString, expectedValue, actualValue)
assertFalse(booleanCondition)
assertFalse(messageString, booleanCondition)
assertNotNull(object)
assertNotNull(messageString, object)
assertNotSame(expectedValue, actualValue)
assertNotSame(messageString, expectedValue, actualValue)
assertNull(object)
assertNull(messageString, object)
assertSame(expectedValue, actualValue)
assertSame(messageString, expectedValue, actualValue)
assertTrue(booleanCondition)
assertTrue(messageString, booleanCondition)
failNotEquals(messageString, expectedValue, actualValue)
failNotSame(messageString, expectedValue, actualValue)
```

FIGURE 5.12 ■ Assertion methods in `JUnit`.

the `DUMMYSTRING` and `DUMMYINT` variables to be both `private` and `static`. In order to use them as class variables in the `testConstructor` method in Figure 5.13, we had to change the declaration to `public`. We note that we have not explicitly tested the `getName`, `getOffice`, `getPhone`, and `getTeaching` methods. We have, however, used each of these in testing other methods, so it can be argued that these methods have been tested implicitly.

Further thought together with a look at the code for testing the `equals`, `readRecord`, and `toString` methods shows that testing is an art, not entirely a science. How much testing is enough? What should be tested in which test method? For example, in testing the `equals` method, we have not tested (once again) the fact that our constructor works correctly, but we have included lines to verify that the `setName` method worked as intended. If the test methods are ever intended to be broken apart and used separately, they should test all aspects of the code, but if the test class is intended only to be used as a single class, then we could assume, for example, that the `setName` method has been tested elsewhere and does not need further testing in the `testEquals` method. (This does, of course, lead to the possibility that the test methods will begin by being treated as a block and then some methods will be yanked out for use in another testing class. Such actions cannot be predicted, and such improper later use of code cannot be prevented. The prudent programmer,[6] though, will include in the documentation of a test method a sufficient number of caveats about what is and what is not tested so as to avoid being blamed later for a poor test method.)

---

[6]Those who are unfamiliar with this sort of expression should look up "prudent mariner" in a nautical context.

```
import junit.framework.*;
import java.util.Scanner;
/**********************************************************************
 *
**/
public class RecordTester extends TestCase
{
  private Record rec1, rec2;
/**********************************************************************
 *
**/
  public RecordTester(String name)
  {
    super(name);
  }
/**********************************************************************
 *
**/
  protected void setUp()
  {
    rec1 = new Record();
    rec2 = new Record();
  }
/**********************************************************************
 *
**/
  protected void tearDown()
  {
    rec1 = null;
    rec2 = null;
  }
/**********************************************************************
 *
**/
  public void testConstructor()
  {
    System.out.println("Test the constructor");
    rec1 = new Record();
    assertEquals(Record.DUMMYSTRING, rec1.getName());
    assertEquals(Record.DUMMYSTRING, rec1.getPhone());
    assertEquals(Record.DUMMYSTRING, rec1.getOffice());
    assertEquals(Record.DUMMYINT, rec1.getTeaching());
  }
```

FIGURE 5.13 ■ A JUnit testing class for Record, part 1.

```
/*******************************************************************
 *
**/
  public void testCompareTo()
  {
    System.out.println("Test compareTo");
    rec1 = new Record();
    rec2 = new Record();
    assertEquals(Record.DUMMYSTRING, rec1.getName());
    assertEquals(Record.DUMMYSTRING, rec2.getName());
    rec1.setName("duncan");
    assertEquals("Failure compareTo set", "duncan", rec1.getName());
    rec2.setName("duncan");
    assertEquals("duncan", rec2.getName());
    assertEquals("Failure compareTo equals", 0, rec1.compareTo(rec2));
    rec2.setName("aaaa");
    assertEquals("aaaa", rec2.getName());
    assertEquals("Failure compareTo greaterthan", 1, rec1.compareTo(rec2));
    rec2.setName("eeee");
    assertEquals("eeee", rec2.getName());
    assertEquals("Failure compareTo lessthan", -1, rec1.compareTo(rec2));
  }
TEST FOR compareName IS SIMILAR
/*******************************************************************
 *
**/
  public void testDefaultInstances()
  {
    assertEquals(Record.DUMMYSTRING, rec1.getName());
  }
TESTS FOR getPhone, getOffice, getTeaching ARE SIMILAR
/*******************************************************************
 *
**/
  public void testSetName()
  {
    assertEquals(Record.DUMMYSTRING, rec1.getName());
    rec1.setName("duncan");
    assertEquals("Name Failure","duncan", rec1.getName());
    assertFalse("messagefail name", rec1.getName().equals("Someone"));
  }
TESTS FOR setPhone, setOffice, setTeaching ARE SIMILAR
```

FIGURE 5.14 ■ A `JUnit` testing class for `Record`, part 2.

```
/*********************************************************************
 *
**/
  public void testEquals()
  {
    System.out.println("Test equals");
    rec1 = new Record();
    rec2 = new Record();
    assertEquals("Failure equals one", true, rec1.equals(rec2));
    rec1 = new Record();
    rec2 = new Record();
    rec1.setName("duncan");
    assertFalse(rec1.equals(rec2));
    assertEquals("duncan", rec1.getName());
    rec2.setName("duncan");
    assertEquals("duncan", rec2.getName());
    assertEquals("Failure equals two", true, rec1.equals(rec2));
    rec1.setOffice("myoffice");
    rec2.setOffice("myoffice");
    rec1.setPhone("myphone");
    rec2.setPhone("myphone");
    rec1.setTeaching(1248);
    rec2.setTeaching(1248);
    assertEquals("Failure equals three", true, rec1.equals(rec2));
  }
/*********************************************************************
 *
**/
  public void testToString()
  {
    String dummy = "";
    Scanner inFile = null;
    System.out.println("Test toString");
    inFile = FileUtils.ScannerOpen("zin");
    rec1 = new Record();
    dummy = inFile.next();
    assertEquals("add", dummy);
    rec1 = Record.readRecord(inFile);
    assertEquals("Herbert", rec1.getName());
    assertEquals("2A41", rec1.getOffice());
    assertEquals("789.0123", rec1.getPhone());
    assertEquals(390, rec1.getTeaching());
    assertEquals("Herbert    2A41  789.0123   390", rec1.toString());
    FileUtils.closeFile(inFile);
  }
```

FIGURE 5.15 ■ A JUnit testing class for Record, part 3.

```
public void testReadRecord()
{
  String dummy = "";
  Scanner inFile = null;

  System.out.println("Test readRecord");

  inFile = FileUtils.ScannerOpen("zin");
  rec1 = new Record();

  dummy = inFile.next();
  assertEquals("add", dummy);
  rec1 = Record.readRecord(inFile);
  assertEquals("Herbert", rec1.getName());
  assertEquals("2A41", rec1.getOffice());
  assertEquals("789.0123", rec1.getPhone());
  assertEquals(390, rec1.getTeaching());

  dummy = inFile.next();
  assertEquals("add", dummy);
  rec1 = Record.readRecord(inFile);
  assertEquals("Lander", rec1.getName());
  assertEquals("2A47", rec1.getOffice());
  assertEquals("789.7890", rec1.getPhone());
  assertEquals(146, rec1.getTeaching());

  dummy = inFile.next();
  assertEquals("add", dummy);
  rec1 = Record.readRecord(inFile);
  assertEquals("Winthrop", rec1.getName());
  assertEquals("3A71", rec1.getOffice());
  assertEquals("789.4667", rec1.getPhone());
  assertEquals(611, rec1.getTeaching());

  FileUtils.closeFile(inFile);
}
```

FIGURE 5.16 ■ A `JUnit` testing class for `Record`, part 4.

5.7 Reflection

Contrary to popular belief and misunderstanding, this text and this course are not about "how to program." Computer science is largely about the management and organization of information. The implementation of decisions about management and organization will be made on a computer using specific programming languages, and thus the implementation will require that one know how to program. Now is a good time to step back and think about the various kinds of information floating around.

This course and its predecessor are not courses on how to program. They are about the design of algorithms, and they use the particular syntax of a programming language (in this case, Java) to force you to be crisp and precise in your thinking and your design. You should by now be familiar with the information about the computational task to be performed and about its implementation in Java. Iterating through a `for` or a `while` loop is a standard process in computer science, with a particular syntax required by Java. Storing data in an array or `ArrayList` and then iterating to swap entries that are in the wrong order, as in the inner loop of the bubblesort, is a standard process in computation, using code such as

```
for(int i = 0; i < list.size()-1; ++i)
{
  for(int j = i+1; j < list.size(); ++j)
  {
    if(list.get(i) > list.get(j))
      swap the i-th and j-th entries
  }
}
```

These are algorithmic processes that require you to manage the actual information of the computation.

What we have covered in this chapter goes one level deeper. The use of the Java generic construct requires you to think about the information used in the *compilation* process. Iterating through the two loops and swapping two entries requires only that we know about the existence of the entries in the list, not that we know anything about the essence of those two entries. It is the test, to see if we need to swap, that requires that we know about the data types to be tested so that we can know how to implement the test.

The double loop with the test as a method call and the swap can be written once for all time using the generic construct to indicate symbolically the data type with which we are dealing. Because the Java compiler will try to compile code that will always work, regardless of what the data type happens to be, you the programmer must manage the information provided to the compiler so that it can function correctly.

It is this metainformation about your computation, the information not about the computation itself but about the compiling process, that you must manage in using the generic construct and the various interfaces provided as part of Java. In order for compilation to take place, the information that is available to the compiler about the program must be internally self-consistent. To use something like the `Record` class in the linked list implemented with generics and to be able to do the lookup of a `contains` method, we must guarantee that we extend `Comparable` and provide some version of a `compareTo` method. Containment requires a test for equality. The `ArrayList` construct, built using generics, has inherited the test for equality of instances of `Object` type all the way at the top of the hierarchy, but that's a test that looks at the actual object, not the data contents. (Remember also that one cannot create an `ArrayList` of `int` variables; it must be an `ArrayList` of `Integer` variables, so that in fact each entry will be an object.)

Designing programs involves a constant tension between the need to keep everything as simple as possible but not too simple and the desire to make everything as general and abstract as possible so as not to have to write nearly identical bits of code. At some point the ability to write general-purpose code (like the loop, test, and swap of the bubblesort) bumps up against the need to handle data in specific ways (like the exact nature of the test), and much of the Java framework has been established to allow you to separate parts of the program based on what information is necessary for proper functioning of each part.

5.8 Summary

Software systems of any reasonable size are not usually coded from scratch any more. One of the justifications for Java as a programming language is the claim that modules can be implemented once, tested carefully, and then repurposed for use in other software projects without modification. The Java generic construct is part of what allows classes to be built, including the Java Collections Framework, that operate on objects whose types are specified at a later time. Facilitating this is the use of iterators that allow one to move from one data payload to another inside a structure without actually knowing what the underlying structure is. Finally, testing of programs using `JUnit` permits a standard test suite to be built and used to ensure that all parts of a method's code have been exercised.

5.9 Exercises

1. Create a `Pair` class using generics that will store an ordered pair of elements of any data type. Pass in the initial values as parameters to a constructor. Create a method `swap` inside `Pair` that will swap the first element and the second element. You will need a driver program to test this adequately.
2. Verify the correctness of the `Pair` code in the previous exercise by writing `JUnit` test functions instead of using just a driver program.

3. Instead of a Pair class that has just two values, write a RotatableList class using

```
public class RotatableList<E> extends ArrayList<E>
```

to extend ArrayList and allow you to write a method rotate that rotates the stored values, putting the first value in the last position and moving all the others up one position.
4. Look up the Class class in the Java documentation online, and notice that there is a getClass method and a getName method so that your program can in fact dynamically test the data type of a variable. Use this to implement a select method in the Pair class that will return the first element if the data type is Integer, the second element if the data type is String, and null for all other data types. Notice that this works because we are still doing nothing that requires us to look at the *values* of the elements.
5. Notice in the previous exercise that you can't really deal with the data stored in Pair because the compiler will insist that anything you do will work with all data types. For example, you can't compare the two elements and return the smaller. Similar to what was done with the Record class in the text, modify Pair to have it read Pair<T extends Comparable<T>>. You should now be able to compare elements of Integer and String type because these both have implemented a compareTo method. Now change the driver and try to create a Pair of elements of some other type that does not extend Comparable, and the code will not compile.
6. Follow up on Exercise 4 to resolve the problem. Similar to what was done with the Record class in the text, modify Pair to have it read Pair<T extends Comparable<T>> and create a wrapper class MyString (making sure that this class extends Comparable). Your MyString class need do nothing but be a wrapper for one instance variable of String type, perhaps named localString. Comparing pairs of String values is possible because the String class has a built-in compareTo that sorts data alphabetically. Override this with your own compareTo method for the MyString class so that the string data is compared according to the *length* of the string.
7. This exercise will allow you to build a prototype of classes using generics so you can steal code from yourself later. Start with an interface named ITinyTest that reads

```
public interface ITinyTest<T>
{
  public boolean isTiny();
}
```

Implement both a `MyInteger` and a `MyString` class that are wrappers for the `Integer` and the `String` classes, respectively. Each of these should implement `ITinyTest`, which means that you must include a method `isTiny`. For `String` data, a string is tiny if it is equal to the word "tiny." For `Integer` data, an integer is tiny if it is equal to or less than −999999999. In between your driver main program and the two data classes, write a `MyData` class that uses generics and will allow you to test a generic `MyData` element for tininess. What you get from this is a class that handles instances of data defined as generic, together with an interface that you have defined and that requires looking at the values of the instance variables and underlying data payload classes that implement that interface.

8. Verify that you understand all the linked list code in this chapter by packaging all the linked list pieces together using generics. At the end, you will have a prototype of how to write linked list code as well as how to work with generics.
9. Verify that you understand all the iterator code in this chapter by packaging all the pieces together and testing them with `JUnit`.
10. Instead of using the `ListIterator` to implement your own iterator, use the `Iterator` interface.

6 Estimating Asymptotic Efficiency

Objectives

- An introduction to the mathematics for determining the theoretical efficiency of an algorithm or computation
- The different orders of magnitude that commonly occur when analyzing the efficiency of different algorithms
- Basic principles that can be intuitively applied without further rigorous proof to determine the efficiency of an algorithm
- An introduction to the differences between the leading contributors to the asymptotic running time of an algorithm and how to distinguish the leading contributors that must be analyzed from the lesser-order terms that can be ignored without affecting the analysis of the running time
- The matching of order-of-magnitude efficiency analysis to the loops in real program code to aid the programmer in developing efficient code
- A demonstration that the binary divide-and-conquer strategy is an optimal strategy for computation and exhibits $O(\lg N)$ complexity

Key Terms

analysis of algorithms	divide and conquer	natural logarithm
asymptotic notation	exponential time	one-time work
average case	linear search	quadratic time
binary logarithm	linear time	Stirling's Formula
common logarithm	logarithmic time	worst case
constant time	main term	

Introduction

In spite of the fact that modern computers, even desktop computers, are powerful and resource rich, it is still important in most applications and software that the programs be written so as to run efficiently. In an operating system, for example, the scheduler and dispatcher that select which processes to run next are running all the time and, because the system is switching from one process to another many times a second, a moderate improvement in the efficiency of selecting which process to run can have a genuine improvement in the overall response time of the machine. At the other end of the scale are the very large applications in computational science that might take weeks or months of compute time. To a discipline scientist, getting results back in one month instead of two can have a major change on the pace of scientific discovery.

Much of this course is about efficient algorithms and about implementation issues for efficiency that are improvements on the naive flat files, bubblesort, and linear searching of Chapter 3. In order to discuss efficiency, we need to ensure that we have mathematically precise statements of what we mean when we say that one algorithm is more efficient than another.

6.1 Analysis of Algorithms

The *analysis of algorithms* has been for some time a major part of the discipline of computer science. The goal in analysis of algorithms is to quantify the efficiency of an algorithm and to be able to compare algorithms that accomplish the same purpose. For example, in our indexed flat file, we did a *linear search* through the records when we were looking for a record with a particular key value. On average, this requires us to search half the records to find a particular record of interest. With a random uniform distribution of search queries, we would expect to search for the record located at position k in a list of N records just as often as we were to search for the record located at position $N - k$. The search for the kth record would take k probes, and the search for the $N - k$th record would take $N - k$ probes. If, for every two searches, we need $k + (N - k) = N$ probes, then on average we would need $N/2$ probes for a randomly chosen search.

We contrast this with the binary search implemented in the code at the end of Chapter 3. Let's assume for the sake of simplifying the argument that the record we are looking for happens to be the first record in the list. If we have $N = 2^n$ records, we will probe to look first at the midpoint record with subscript $N/2 = 2^{n-1}$. We will decide that we want to look further in the first half of the list, so our next probe will be at location $N/4 = 2^{n-2}$. We will then look at locations $N/8$, $N/16$, and so forth until we find the value we want after n probes. Since $n = \lg 2^n = \lg N$, the difference in the number of probes required is reflected in the graph in Figure 3.19; in essence, $\lg N$ is negligibly small compared to N for very large values of N.

In doing the analysis of an algorithm, there are two results we generally will want to obtain. The first is the *worst-case* behavior of an algorithm. That is, in the pathologically worst case (which may have an infinitesimally small probability of happening in a real situation), what is the worst possible running time of an algorithm? The other result that is often of greater interest but also usually harder to get is the *average-case* behavior. That is, of all possible inputs to a program, what is the statistically likely running time? Clearly, the worst case is the worst possible scenario, and the average case is what we would see in a randomly chosen "ordinary" situation.

In the case of linear search of an array of N items, the worst case is that we will search the entire array, doing N probes. This is what will happen if we search for an item that isn't there because we won't know it isn't there until we check the entire array without finding it. The average case, as mentioned previously, in searching for an item that is present in the array is $N/2$ probes, which we will see shortly is not really better than N probes. We can contrast this with binary search of a sorted array, which requires n probes for searching an array of $N = 2^n$ items in the worst case. We shall see in a moment that this difference is crucial to good performance of an algorithm.

The analysis of the running time of an algorithm is done as a function of the "size of the problem." In many cases, this is the size of the data list to be handled in the computation. For sorting data lists or searching in them, it is obviously the case that we would expect more work to be needed to sort or search $2N$ items than was needed to sort or search N items. Thus, for these tasks we measure the running time as a function of the size of the data input to the program. In other problems, there may be other measures that are appropriate.

6.1.1 The Definition of a "Logarithm"

It is a general truism among those who teach calculus that one can determine a student's major based on what they think the term "log" means. Science and math students will generally take this to mean the *natural logarithm* $\ln x = \log_e x$. Engineering students will generally take this to mean the *common logarithm* $\log_{10} x = \ln x / \ln 10$. For the purposes of analysis of algorithms, the role of binary divide-and-conquer algorithms has become so important that computer scientists become accustomed to thinking in terms of the *binary logarithm* $\lg x = \log_2 x = \ln x / \ln 2$.

6.1.2 A Few Comments about the Real World

This chapter is largely about the mathematical analysis of algorithms, but it's worth taking a few sentences here to comment on real-world issues of performance.

It has been said that the litmus test for whether one is really involved in high-performance computing is whether or not that person knows how many seconds there are in a year. The answer is about 30 million, or for those who work in binary, $3 \cdot 10^7 \approx 2^{25} = 33,554,432$. On a smaller scale, there are $86,400$ seconds in a day, which we can sometimes approximate with 10^5. Remembering that 2^{10} is about a thousand, 2^{20} is about a million, and 2^{30} is about a billion, we can build out some ballpark estimates on running times. We can be a little more precise if we remember that $\log_{10} 2 \approx 0.301$, so $2^k \approx 10^{0.301k}$ (as in the preceding estimate that $2^{25} \approx 10^{7.53}$). There is a lot of serious smoke and mirror action about clock speed, CPU pipeline depth, threads, cores, and such, but we can nonetheless note that modern computers have a clock speed of about 1 GHz, so a baseline would be 1 nanosecond per instruction, or 10^9 instructions per second.

Putting all this together, we would get about 10^{14} instructions per day at 1 nanosecond each, or about $3 \cdot 10^{16}$ per year. It is rarely true that "one unit" of computation takes only one machine instruction, so we might get less than $3 \cdot 10^{16}$ "units" of computation per year. On the other hand, modern machines run at perhaps 3 GHz and not 1 GHz, and use threads, pipelines, and multiple cores, so maybe we get more than that. This kind of analysis should not be used for anything much beyond a sanity check. If a computation is going to take 10^{14} operations, it might well be doable overnight (like payroll processing), but it is not likely to be useful for packet processing on an Internet server or for mobile phone connections to a tower. Similarly, the old (vintage 1977) Data Encryption Standard (DES) from the National Institute of Standards and Technology (NIST) had a 56-bit cryptographic key. Assuming that on average one has to test half the keys exhaustively in order to crack the cipher, that means testing about $2^{55} \approx 3.6 \cdot 10^{16}$ keys. At one instruction per test, that's 1 machine for a year, or 100 machines for about three days. It turns out that the DES crackers took some tens of hours for about 100 machines, well within the bounds of this kind of sanity check.

6.2 Some Rigor

With the notation used in the previous section, we note that if $N = 2^n$, then $\lg N = n$. We can thus say that a binary search of N sorted records takes in the worst case not $N/2$ probes of linear search but $\lg N$ probes. What is important in the analysis of the algorithms is the quotient

$$f(N) = \frac{\lg N}{N/2}.$$

Using L'Hôpital's rule we have

$$\lim_{N\to\infty} f(N) = \lim_{N\to\infty} \frac{2\lg N}{N} = \lim_{N\to\infty} \frac{2/N}{1} = \lim_{N\to\infty} \frac{2}{N} = 0.$$

Thus, as N gets larger and larger, the relative benefit of binary search over linear search gets better and better because the quotient of "work needed for binary search" and "work needed for linear search" goes to zero. We also note, with this analysis, that the relative costs for the basic operations of linear search versus binary search don't matter. To go from one linear search step to the next requires only that we add one to a subscript. To go from one binary search step to the next we need to shift some boundary pointers and then compute the subscript in the middle of our boundary range. One can imagine that this might take five to eight machine instructions instead of the single machine instruction needed to increment a subscript for linear search. Thus, a more fair analysis of the two might be that binary search costs perhaps $8 \lg N$ instructions executed for each probe because each probe might cost as many as 8, compared to the 1-instruction cost of linear search for each probe. In the limit, this just doesn't matter:

$$\lim_{N \to \infty} \frac{8 \lg N}{N/2} = \lim_{N \to \infty} \frac{16 \lg N}{N} = 0.$$

In a more practical mode: If binary search and linear search each cost one instruction per probe, then binary search is twice as fast as linear search for $N \geq 16$. If binary search costs twice as many instructions as linear search, then binary search will be twice as fast as linear search for $N \geq 64$. For any fixed relative cost of probes for binary search versus probes for linear search (and the relative costs are fixed and are independent of N), there will be a data set size larger than which binary search is as least twice as fast as linear search.

This motivates the following notation that was first used by Edmund Landau in the 1890s in studying the distribution of prime numbers.

Definition 6.1 We write

$$f(x) = O(g(x))$$

if $\exists$ constants c and C such that $x > c \implies |f(x)| \leq C \cdot g(x)$.

We say that "$f(x)$ is *big Oh* of $g(x)$." Our goal with this use of *asymptotic notation* is to capture the essence of the growth in the work done by computational processes as the size of the data sets on which they operate grows. In the context of search discussed earlier, we can certainly say that $\lg N = O(N)$.

The formal mathematical definition of big Oh (and of little oh, which is defined later) involves absolute values of functions, in the case of the expression $|f(x)|$ in Definition 6.1. Mathematicians, when doing order-of-magnitude estimates, must always keep the absolute value symbol in place because their functions $f(x)$ might be either positive or negative. Computer scientists, in contrast, are usually using the big Oh notation to measure the cost of an algorithm in terms of the work necessary to run a program that implements an algorithm. Such a cost function $f(N)$ for a data set of size N will be inherently positive, so we can be slightly careless at times and omit the absolute value symbols.

We also have to point out that the big Oh notation functions in a manner similar to a "less than or equal to" in mathematics. That is, we may have $f(N) = O(g(N))$ for the constant function $f(N) = 0$ and for $g(N) = e^N$, even though $f(N)$ is always zero and $g(N)$ goes off very rapidly to infinity. In this case, it is certainly true that $0 \leq e^N$ for *any* value of N, but we know that this doesn't really say very much. For the next few paragraphs, we will be dealing with the big Oh as a "less than or equal to," although we will make some effort to say something more meaningful than a trivial statement like $0 \leq e^N$.

For the most part, for this course and indeed for most applications in computer science, the mathematical analysis needed here is limited to some basic calculus of limits, and especially the use of L'Hôpital's rule. Theoretical computer scientists in their research may well use more advanced analysis in order to prove running times of new algorithms. We shall see shortly, though, that the running time of most algorithms we will encounter involves basic polynomials (for nested loops), logarithms (for divide-and-conquer methods like binary search), and some exponentials (for things that go horribly wrong).

6.2.1 An Apology for Some Audacity

We titled this section "Some Rigor" and then proceeded immediately to pull back somewhat from that rigor. Namely, we defined linear and binary search in terms of discrete numbers of probes, counting in integers to get N probes, and yet we then applied L'Hôpital's rule as if we had a continuous variable x and not a discrete variable N.

In fact, for all the discussion that will take place in this book, we can substitute x for N everywhere and it will make no difference. In general, to make our arguments totally rigorous, we could be very careful and bound a continuous value x on which we can apply the rules of calculus by discrete values $N-1$ and N, but this would add complexity to the arguments without actually affecting what we hope is a burgeoning intuitive feel for how the arguments ought to be made.

6.2.2 Basic Orders of Magnitude, and Some Intuition

At the level of this basic introduction, and indeed for most practical work in computer science, we are normally concerned with the asymptotics of six basic functions. We will show in this chapter that each of these is big Oh of the next one and more strongly that each of these is asymptotically genuinely smaller than the next.

6.2.2.1 $\lg N$

This is the cost that we would hope would be associated with a divide-and-conquer approach like the binary search that we added to the indexed flat file code.

6.2.2.2 N

This is the cost of a single `for` loop that runs from 1 to N and does a constant amount of work inside the loop. For example, a loop like the following, that computes the sum of the entries in an `ArrayList`, will require N addition steps.

```
sum = 0;
for(int i = 0; i < N; ++i)
{
  sum += myList.get(i);
}
```

6.2.2.3 N^2

This is the cost of a nested double `for` loop that runs from 1 to N in both loops. This is also the cost of a doubly-nested loop that doesn't quite run all the way to N, such as in the following sort routine.

```
for(int i = 0; i < N-1; ++i)
{
  for(int j = i+1; j < N; ++j)
  {
    test and maybe swap the i-th and the j-th entries
  }
}
```

As we saw in Chapter 3, this requires $N^2/2$ executions of the test-and-swap statements inside the loops.

6.2.2.4 N^3

This is the cost of a triply-nested `for` loop that runs from 1 to N in all three loops. Such loops occur frequently in physics and chemistry codes that might loop over x, y, and z coordinates in three-dimensional space.

6.2.2.5 2^N

This is said to be *exponential time* and we will say a little more about this next. For now, we mention only that 2^N is the number of subsets of a set S of N elements, so the naive enumeration of all such subsets would take 2^N "steps."

6.2.2.6 N^N

This is exponential time, but in fact it is even worse than the exponential time of a 2^N algorithm.

6.2.2.7 Intuition

The study of asymptotics is part of the research done on algorithms and complexity. We will need for this course, however, only a very limited set of basic facts about asymptotic growth. To help illustrate this, we present a table of some commonly used functions in asymptotic analysis. We would also provide graphs, but as Figures 3.16 and 3.19 show so well, each of these functions grows so much faster than the next smaller that, for example, on a graph that would actually display N^2 as a meaningful curve, the graph for N would be almost indistinguishable from a flat line.

N	$\lg N$	N	N^2	N^3	2^N
16	4	16	256	4,096	65,536
32	5	32	1,024	32,768	4,294,967,296
64	6	64	4,096	262,144	1.8×10^{19}
128	7	128	16,384	2,097,152	3.4×10^{38}
256	8	256	65,536	16,777,216	1.2×10^{77}

6.2.3 Constants Don't Matter

Now we will present some basic theorems together with their intuitive interpretations. At the level of asymptotic analysis needed for this course, we don't have to use any deep mathematics. For the most part, we can prove some basic truths about logs, polynomials, and exponentials, convert those truths into simple intuitive principles, and then just cite those principles over and over again without having to go back to doing the math from the beginning.

The first basic intuitive rule is this:

Principle: The constants out front don't matter.

Theorem 6.2

For any fixed constant K, any function $K \cdot F(N)$ is big Oh of $F(N)$.

Proof Let $f(x) = K \cdot F(N)$, and choose $c = 1$ and $C = K$. This provides us with a function $g(x) = C \cdot F(N)$ for which for any N whatsoever

$$f(x) = K \cdot F(N) \leq C \cdot F(N) = g(x).$$

By definition, this means $f(x) = O(g(x))$. □

It is this principle that allows us to ignore the "divided by 2" part of the bubblesort's $N^2/2$ comparisons and say simply that bubblesort runs in $O(N^2)$ time. The definition of big Oh allows us to swallow up the out-front constant K into the constant C of the definition of big Oh. Another way to think of this is to look at the graph in Figure 6.1. The graphs of $N^2/2$, N^2, and $2N^2$, have the same basic "shape," and the constant out front will not matter when we compare those functions against functions with decidedly different asymptotic behavior. Notice that $N^3/1000$ starts out smaller than all three of these, but eventually crosses all of them and has a steeper slope and growth rate. What doesn't matter in the long run is the factor of 2, 1, or 1/2 in the N^2 graphs or the factor of 1/1000 in the N^3 graph. What does matter as we will see now is the difference in the exponents.

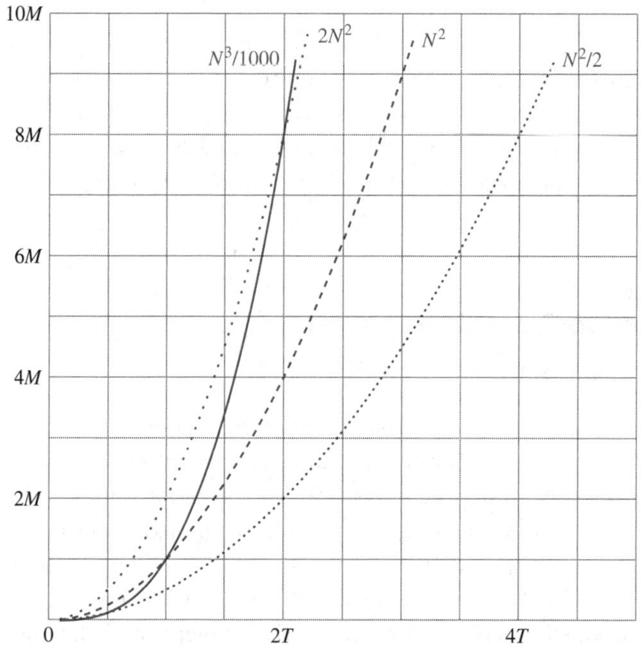

FIGURE 6.1 ■ $N^2/2$, N^2, and $2N^2$ ($T = 10^3$, $M = 10^6$).

As a practical matter of analyzing the running time of code, it does not matter asymptotically whether our binary search algorithm takes 5 machine instructions per probe, or 10, or a hundred million. The asymptotic growth in execution time for binary search and for linear search depends on the lengths of the arrays being searched. If we compare a badly implemented search and a well-implemented search, it may be that the badly implemented search takes twice as many machine instructions for every probe of the array. However, as can be seen by visualizing a graph of the growth or by doing the algebra, doubling the constant pushes out the point at which binary search is faster, but it does not change the essential fact that binary search will be faster for large arrays.

Instead of bubblesort, consider an implementation of linear search that takes 6 machine instructions for every probe. We can argue that the worst-case cost of this search is

$$Linear\_Search = 6N$$

for a search on N items because in the worst case we will have to search the entire array. Binary search is a more complicated algorithm, so let us assume that a well-implemented binary search takes 12 instructions per probe, so the cost of binary search is

$$Binary\_Search = 12 \lg N.$$

These two functions are equal for $N = 2$, and then $Binary\_Search < Linear\_Search$ for all larger values of N. In this case, the binary search would always be better. But even if we implement binary search badly, it is still better in the long run: If $Binary\_Search = a \lg N$ for some constant a, and $Linear\_Search = bN$ for some constant b, then elementary calculus shows that $Binary\_Search < Linear\_Search$ for all large N.

The constants out front don't matter.

6.2.4 Constant Startup Costs Don't Matter

The second basic intuitive rule is this:

Principle: A constant amount of startup or shutdown cost doesn't matter.

In general, there are three parts to a serious computation: an initialization phase, a processing phase that invariably involves loops, and a termination phase. The initialization and termination (such as booting up a computer and turning it off, respectively) are *one-time work* compared to the time spent in running the loop and doing the iterative process that is the reason for doing it on a computer, so their costs are constant additions to the overall work. As the principle and theorem show, startup and shutdown costs do not affect overall efficiency.

Mathematically, if the iterative loop-based part of the computation has running time $f(x)$, then a constant amount K of startup or shutdown work is an additive constant, so the overall computational cost becomes $f(x) + K$.

Theorem 6.3

If $f(x) = O(g(x))$, and if $\lim_{x\to\infty} f(x) = \infty$, then $f(x) + K = O(g(x))$ for any constant K.

Proof By definition, $f(x) = O(g(x))$ means that there are constants c_1 and C_1 such that for all $x > c_1$, we have $|f(x)| \leq C_1 g(x)$. If $\lim_{x\to\infty} f(x) = \infty$, then there is clearly a point x_1 at which $K < f(x_1) < C_1 g(x_1)$, and we can use $2C_1$ as our constant instead of C_1. □

We note that the second condition that $f(x)$ go off to infinity is mathematically necessary because the conclusion is not valid, for example, if $f(x) = 1/x^2$ and $g(x) = 1/x$.

This is a mathematical nicety, however, similar to the use of the absolute value symbols in the definition of big Oh. If our function $f(x)$ is measuring the work to be done inside a loop in the middle of the computation, then the work to be done by a single instruction costs at least 1 regardless of the length of the loop. For the purposes of algorithm analysis, then, it will always be the case that our costs go off to infinity with the size of the data.

6.2.5 Big Oh Is Transitive

Another important rule is that big Oh does in fact act like a "less than or equal to" function. If algorithm A is big Oh of algorithm B, and algorithm B is big Oh of algorithm C, then algorithm A is also big Oh of algorithm C.

Principle: Big Oh is transitive.

Theorem 6.4

If $f(x) = O(g(x))$ and $g(x) = O(h(x))$, then $f(x) = O(h(x))$.

Proof By definition, $f(x) = O(g(x))$ means that there are constants c_1 and C_1 such that for all $x > c_1$, we have $|f(x)| \leq C_1 g(x)$. Similarly, from the second assumption we have constants c_2 and C_2 such that for all $x > c_2$ we have $|g(x)| \leq C_2 h(x)$. For all $x > \max(c_1, c_2)$, then we have both assumptions true and thus

$$|f(x)| \leq C_1 g(x) \leq C_1 C_2 h(x).$$

To conclude that $f(x) = O(h(x))$, then, we can choose $c = \max(c_1, c_2)$ and $C = C_1 C_2$. □

This property is used to simplify our arguments about algorithms. If algorithm A runs in less time than algorithm B, and if algorithm B runs in less time than algorithm C, then we can immediately conclude that algorithm A runs in less time than algorithm C without having to go back to prove this directly.

6.2.6 All Logarithms Are the Same

One of the more useful principles is that mathematicians, engineers, and computer scientists are not in fact speaking different languages when they talk about logarithms.

Principle: Asymptotically, all logarithms are the same.

Theorem 6.5

For any fixed base a, the function $\log_a N$ is $O(\lg N)$.

Proof Let $f(x) = \log_a N = \lg N / \lg a$ by the usual rules of logarithms. Then choose $c = 1$ and $C = 1/\lg a$, and we have a function $g(x) = C \lg N$ for which $f(x) = \log_a N < C \lg N = g(x)$. This is true for all $x > 0$, so we may choose $c = 1$ and conclude that $f(x) = O(g(x))$. □

Again, this is a principle that simplifies things greatly. To prove asymptotics, we use calculus, and in calculus we want to use natural logs and powers of e because the derivatives and integrals do not introduce any constants. In computer science, we tend to count things using the binary log because divide-and-conquer algorithms like binary search are so common. If we are to be mathematically and pedantically precise, we have to account for this difference. What happens, though, is that the difference is a constant multiplied out front times an expression, and for algorithm analysis we simply swallow up that constant in the C of the big Oh definition.

6.2.7 All Polynomials of the Same Degree Are the Same

This is one of the most important principles of all, and it means that we need only pay attention to the *main term* in an expression.[1] If the main term costs us N^3 work, for example, we get no benefit from an implementation detail that might save us N^2 work and cost us $O(N^3 - N^2)$ time.

Principle: All polynomials of the same degree are the same.

---

[1] At least for polynomials, but we will see shortly that this is generally true for analysis at this level of complexity in computer science.

Theorem 6.6

Let $f(x) = a_k x^k + a_{k-1}x^{k-1} + \cdots + a_1 x + a_0$ be a polynomial of degree k. Then $f(x)$ is $O(x^k)$.

Proof Here, at least to prove this principle, we do need to worry about absolute values. Let $A = \max\{|a_i|\}$ be the maximum in absolute value of the coefficients of $f(x)$. Let $g(x) = k \cdot A \cdot x^k$. By our choice of A we have for all $x \geq 1$ that

$$\begin{aligned} f(x) &= a_k x^k + a_{k-1}x^{k-1} + \cdots + a_1 x + a_0 \\ &\leq |a_k x^k + a_{k-1}x^{k-1} + \cdots + a_1 x + a_0| \end{aligned}$$

since any value z is less than or equal to its absolute value $|z|$. We can apply the triangle inequality[2] to distribute the absolute values:

$$\begin{aligned} f(x) &= a_k x^k + a_{k-1}x^{k-1} + \cdots + a_1 x + a_0 \\ &\leq |a_k x^k + a_{k-1}x^{k-1} + \cdots + a_1 x + a_0| \\ &\leq |a_k|x^k + |a_{k-1}|x^{k-1} + \cdots + |a_1|x + |a_0| \end{aligned}$$

and now we get to be rather sloppy. We are interested only in positive values of x (which is n, after all), and for any positive x we have $x^{m-1} \leq x^m$. So we can raise all the exponents to the highest power exponent to get

$$\begin{aligned} f(x) &= a_k x^k + a_{k-1}x^{k-1} + \cdots + a_1 x + a_0 \\ &\leq |a_k x^k + a_{k-1}x^{k-1} + \cdots + a_1 x + a_0| \\ &\leq |a_k|x^k + |a_{k-1}|x^{k-1} + \cdots + |a_1|x + |a_0| \\ &\leq |a_k|x^k + |a_{k-1}|x^k + \cdots + |a_1|x^k + |a_0|x^k. \end{aligned}$$

Now we can be sloppy yet again. Each of the coefficients is smaller in absolute value than A, so we replace all the coefficients with A:

$$\begin{aligned} f(x) &= a_k x^k + a_{k-1}x^{k-1} + \cdots + a_1 x + a_0 \\ &\leq |a_k x^k + a_{k-1}x^{k-1} + \cdots + a_1 x + a_0| \\ &\leq |a_k|x^k + |a_{k-1}|x^{k-1} + \cdots + |a_1|x + |a_0| \\ &\leq |a_k|x^k + |a_{k-1}|x^k + \cdots + |a_1|x^k + |a_0|x^k \end{aligned}$$

[2] $|A + B| \leq |A| + |B|$

$$
\begin{aligned}
&\leq Ax^k + Ax^k + \cdots + Ax^k + Ax^k \\
&= kAx^k \\
&= g(x).
\end{aligned}
$$

By definition, $f(x) = O(g(x))$. □

Let's also prove this a different way, showing that we can be sloppy in a slightly different way. We can clearly write

$$
\begin{aligned}
f(x) &= a_k x^k + a_{k-1}x^{k-1} + \cdots + a_1 x + a_0 \\
&\leq |a_k x^k + a_{k-1}x^{k-1} + \cdots + a_1 x + a_0| \\
&\leq |a_k|x^k + |a_{k-1}|x^{k-1} + \cdots + |a_1|x + |a_0| \\
&\leq Ax^k + Ax^{k-1} + \cdots + Ax + A.
\end{aligned}
$$

But instead of being heavy handed as before, let's roll up the terms from the right one by one, repeatedly using the fact that for positive x we have $x^{m-1} \leq x^m$:

$$
\begin{aligned}
f(x) &= a_k x^k + a_{k-1}x^{k-1} + \cdots + a_1 x + a_0 \\
&\leq |a_k x^k + a_{k-1}x^{k-1} + \cdots + a_1 x + a_0| \\
&\leq |a_k|x^k + |a_{k-1}|x^{k-1} + \cdots + |a_1|x + |a_0| \\
&\leq Ax^k + Ax^{k-1} + \cdots + Ax + A \\
&\leq Ax^k + Ax^{k-1} + \cdots + Ax^2 + 2Ax \\
&\leq Ax^k + Ax^{k-1} + \cdots + Ax^3 + +3Ax^2 \\
&\ldots \\
&\leq Ax^k + (k-1)Ax^{k-1} \\
&\leq kAx^k.
\end{aligned}
$$

The result is the same.

In practice, producing efficient programs is a process of applied bottleneck-ology. We start by looking at the most expensive part of the computation and trying to make that more efficient. If we have a triply-nested loop and a doubly-nested loop, then (all else being equal) the triple loop will have an $O(N^3)$ running time and the double loop an $O(N^2)$ running time, and we will look first at the triple loop, since $O(N^3 + N^2) = O(N^3)$ according to this principle.

6.2.8 All Reasonable Cost-of-Work Functions Go Off to Infinity

Finally, we have the following general principle:

Principle: All reasonable functions measuring cost of work go off to infinity.

We required in Theorem 6.3 that our functions $f(x)$ and $g(x)$ went off to infinity. In general, we can assume this to be true for the following intuitive reason: It always costs us at least "one" just to look at a data item, and if we don't look at a data item, then clearly we can't say anything about the value of that item.

This is easily seen when considering linear search of an unordered list. If we have N items, then in order to determine that a value does *not* appear in the list, we need to at least look at all N data items. We obviously can't say that a value does not appear in the list if we haven't looked at all the values. And if we add one data item, then our worst-case cost for the search *must* increase by at least one, because how else would we be able to know that the new data item is not the item for which we are searching?

6.3 Some More Rigor

6.3.1 Little oh

We have already mentioned that the big-Oh notation is one-directional. That is, if we know that $f(x) = O(g(x))$, for example, we know that asymptotically speaking $f(x)$ is no larger than $g(x)$. The $O(\cdot)$ notation is a "less than or equal to," saying that $f(x)$ is no larger than $g(x)$. However, one can observe that it is perfectly true that $N^2 = O(N^3)$ and yet somehow we *know* that these are not the same orders of magnitude. And although it's perfectly true that we can be sloppy and say that bubblesort is $O(N^{100})$, because $O(N^2) = O(N^{100})$, this is being too sloppy. We usually do want to be reasonably careful about our analysis.

The following definition allows us to show that a function $f(x)$ is *asymptotically smaller than* another function $g(x)$.

Definition 6.7 We write

$$f(x) = o(g(x))$$

if $\lim_{x\to\infty} \frac{|f(x)|}{|g(x)|} = 0$.

We say that $f(x)$ is "little oh" of $g(x)$. Intuitively, what this means is that the relative size of $f(x)$ becomes vanishingly small compared to $g(x)$ as x gets large.

Our first theorem is that little oh implies big Oh.

Theorem 6.8

If we have $f(x) = o(g(x))$ and $g(x)$ is a positive function everywhere, then we have $f(x) = O(g(x))$.

Proof If $\lim_{x\to\infty} \frac{|f(x)|}{|g(x)|} = 0$, then by the definition of limit we have that for any positive constant C, there exists a constant c such that for $x > c$ we have $|f(x)| \leq C \cdot g(x)$. This is much stronger than what we need to show big Oh, which is only that we have such a bound for *some* C. □

Our next theorem is that what we would all have felt to be completely obvious is in fact true.

Theorem 6.9

For any positive integer k and for any $\epsilon > 0$, we have

$$x^k = o(x^{k+\epsilon}).$$

Proof Clearly,

$$\lim_{x\to\infty} \frac{x^k}{x^{k+\epsilon}} = \lim_{x\to\infty} \frac{1}{x^\epsilon} = 0.$$ □

We can also prove that $\lg N = o(N)$ by using L'Hôpital's rule. We have

$$\lim_{N\to\infty} \frac{\lg N}{N} = \lim_{N\to\infty} \frac{1/N}{\ln 2} = \lim_{N\to\infty} \frac{1}{N \ln 2} = 0,$$

and thus we can assert that $\lg N$ is asymptotically genuinely smaller than N. Indeed, the same argument shows that for any $\epsilon > 0$, no matter how small ϵ might be, we have $\lg N = o(N^\epsilon)$. The logarithm grows asymptotically more slowly than any positive power of N.

Theorem 6.10

For any $k > 0$ and for any $\epsilon > 0$, we have

$$\log^k x = o(x^\epsilon).$$

Proof What we need to show is that for any fixed k and ϵ, we have

$$\lim_{x\to\infty} \left| \frac{\log^k x}{x^\epsilon} \right| = 0.$$

We do this with L'Hôpital's rule, by differentiating the numerator and denominator.

$$\begin{aligned}
\lim_{x\to\infty} \left| \frac{\log^k x}{x^\epsilon} \right| &= \lim_{x\to\infty} \left| \frac{(k/x)\log^{k-1} x}{\epsilon x^{\epsilon-1}} \right| \\
&= \lim_{x\to\infty} \left| \frac{k \log^{k-1} x}{\epsilon x^\epsilon} \right| \\
&= \lim_{x\to\infty} \left| \frac{k(k-1)\log^{k-2} x}{\epsilon^2 x^\epsilon} \right| \\
&= \lim_{x\to\infty} \left| \frac{k!}{\epsilon^k x^\epsilon} \right| \\
&= 0.
\end{aligned}$$

□

In practice, we are going to use either the following truths or other truths very similar to these. All the little oh truths imply the same as a big Oh truth, and transitivity implies that each of these subsumes the previous one.

- $\lg N = o(N^{1/2})$. Actually,
  - $\lg N = o(N^{1/2})$
  - $\lg N = o(N^{1/4})$
  - $\lg N = o(N^{1/8})$
  - $\lg N = o(N^{1/16})$
  - and so forth.
- $N^{1/2} = o(N)$
- $N = o(N^{3/2})$

- $N^{3/2} = o(N^2)$
- $N^2 = o(N^{5/2})$
- $N^{5/2} = o(N^3)$

We also have the following.

- $N \lg N = o(N^{3/2})$. Actually,
  - $\lg N = o(N^{3/2})$
  - $\lg N = o(N^{1+1/4})$
  - $\lg N = o(N^{1+1/8})$
  - $\lg N = o(N^{1+1/16})$
  - and so forth.
- $N^{1/2} \lg N = o(N)$
- $N \lg N = o(N^{3/2})$
- $N^{3/2} \lg N = o(N^2)$
- $N^2 \lg N = o(N^{5/2})$
- $N^{5/2} \lg N = o(N^3)$

6.3.2 Big Theta, and Some More Simplifying Theorems

In what has gone before we have defined an asymptotic "less than or equal to" with the big Oh notation, and an asymptotic "less than" with the little oh notation. It remains for us to define the asymptotic notion of "equal to." As we said before, it is true but not very useful that bubblesort is $O(N^{100})$ because $O(N^2) = O(N^{100})$, but what we would really like to know is that the algorithm is $O(N^2)$ and not, say, $O(N^{3/2})$. To be able to make this kind of statement we need the concept of asymptotic equality.

Definition 6.11 We write

$$f(x) = \Theta(g(x))$$

if there exist constants c, C_1, and C_2 such that for all $x > c$ we have

$$C_1 \cdot g(x) \leq |f(x)| \leq C_2 \cdot g(x).$$

We have already shown that a polynomial is asymptotically "less than or equal to" its main term; our first use of the big Theta notation is to show that a polynomial is asymptotically "equal to" its main term.

Theorem 6.12

Let $f(x) = a_k x^k + \cdots + a_0$. Then $f(x) = \Theta(x^k)$.

Proof To do the formal proof, we need to show that there exists a constant C and a constant c such that for every $x > c$, we have $|f(x)| \leq C \cdot g(x)$. Let $C = (k+1) \max |a_i|$. We have

$$\begin{aligned}
|f(x)| &= |x^k \cdot (a_n + a_{k-1}/x + a_{k-2}/x^2 \cdots + a_0/x^k)| \\
&\leq |x^k| \cdot (|a_n| + |a_{k-1}/x| + |a_{k-2}/x^2| \cdots + |a_0/x^k|) \\
&\leq \max |a_i| \cdot |x^k| \cdot (|1| + |1/x| + |1/x^2| \cdots + |1/x^k|).
\end{aligned}$$

Now if $x > 1$, we have

$$\begin{aligned}
|f(x)| &\leq \max |a_i| \cdot x^k \cdot (1 + 1 + 1 \cdots + 1) \\
&= \max |a_i| \cdot x^k \cdot (k+1) \\
&= C \cdot x^k.
\end{aligned}$$

Therefore $f(x) = O(x^k)$.

In the other direction, we need to show that there exists a constant C and a constant c such that for every $x > c$, we have $|f(x)| \geq C \cdot g(x)$. Let $C = \min |a_i|/k$. We have

$$\begin{aligned}
|f(x)| &= |x^k \cdot (a_n + a_{k-1}/x + a_{k-2}/x^2 \cdots + a_0/x^k)| \\
&\geq |x^k| \cdot (|a_n + a_{k-1}/x + a_{k-2}/x^2 \cdots| - |a_0/x^k|) \\
&\geq |x^k| \cdot (|a_n| - |a_{k-1}/x| - |a_{k-2}/x^2| \cdots - |a_0/x^k|) \\
&\geq \min |a_i| \cdot |x^k| \cdot (|1| - |1/x| - |1/x^2| \cdots - |1/x^k|).
\end{aligned}$$

Now if $x > k^2$, we have

$$\begin{aligned}
|f(x)| &\geq \min |a_i| \cdot x^k \cdot (1 - 1/k - 1/k^3 \cdots - 1/k^{2k-1}) \\
&\geq \min |a_i| \cdot x^k \cdot (1 - (k-1)/k) \\
&= \min |a_i| \cdot x^k/k \\
&= C \cdot x^k.
\end{aligned}$$

Therefore $f(x) = \Theta(x^k)$. □

6.3.3 Ignoring Fencepost Issues

Sometimes it can be tedious to make a sum come out to a function *exactly* of N; we go one step too far or one step too few and come up with an $N+1$ or an $N-1$. The next theorems are useful in allowing us to be a little bit sloppy about these fencepost conditions. For example, in sorting N items using the bubblesort from a previous chapter, two loops were used. The outer loop ran on subscript `i` through the first $N-1$ items and the inner loop ran from `i+1` through to the end. As another example, we note that a double loop from 0 through N takes $(N+1)^2$ iterations. The following theorem allows us to ignore the detail that we might have a polynomial with lead term a power of $N+1$ or $N-1$ and not of N.

Theorem 6.13

Let k be fixed and let $f(N) = (N+1)^k$ and $g(N) = (N-1)^k$. Then $f(N) = \Theta(N^k)$ and $g(N) = \Theta(N^k)$.

Proof Very crudely, we have for $N > 1$ that

$$(1/2)^k N^k = (N/2)^k < (N+1)^k < (2N)^k = 2^k N^k.$$

Since k is fixed, $(1/2)^k$ and 2^k are the constants needed for the $\Theta(\cdot)$.

A second version of a proof of this is also enlightening. We have

$$\begin{aligned} f(N) &= (N+1)^k \\ &= N^k + kN^{k-1} + \binom{k}{2} N^{k-2} + \cdots + \binom{k}{k-2} N^2 + kN^1 + 1 \end{aligned}$$

and now we can cite Theorem 6.6 to conclude that this polynomial is asymptotically exactly as large as its leading term. □

Theorem 6.14

Let i and k be fixed and let $f(N) = (N+i)^k$. Then $f(N) = \Theta(N^k)$.

We point out here that it is very important that the exponent k is a constant. That is, we think of k as two or three, for a doubly-nested or a triply-nested loop, say. If k is a variable, and worse yet a variable that depends on N, then the analysis is much different. The function N^N will be dealt with shortly, and is perhaps the worst function one ever has to deal with in computer science.

6.3.4 Basic Orders of Magnitude Revisited

In Section 6.2.2 we listed the common asymptotic functions that appear in computer science. In this section, we are going to do the analysis to show that the orders of magnitude are as we said they were.

In each of the instances from Section 6.2.2, we assume that the "work" to be done inside the loops is constant time. We will first deal with the question of powers of N and of powers of $\lg N$. The general theorem is as follows.

Theorem 6.15

Let $f_a(N) = N^a$ and $g_b(N) = (\lg N)^b$ for any positive real numbers a and b. Then

1. If $0 < a_1 < a_2$, we have $f_{a_1}(N) = o(f_{a_2}(N))$.
2. If $0 < b_1 < b_2$, we have $g_{b_1}(N) = o(g_{b_2}(N))$.
3. If $0 < a_1 < a_2$ and if b_1 and b_2 are nonnegative, we have $f_{a_1}(N) \cdot g_{b_1}(N) = o(f_{a_2}(N) \cdot g_{b_2}(N))$.
4. If $0 < b_1 < b_2$, we have $f_a(N) \cdot g_{b_1}(N) = o(f_a(N) \cdot g_{b_2}(N))$ for any nonnegative values of a.

Proof To prove part 1, we consider

$$\lim_{x\to\infty} \frac{|f_{a_1}(x)|}{|f_{a_2}(x)|} = \lim_{x\to\infty} \frac{N^{a_1}}{N^{a_2}} = \lim_{x\to\infty} \frac{1}{N^{a_2-a_1}}.$$

By assumption, $a_2 - a_1 > 0$. The denominator of the preceding expression thus goes to infinity, which means that the expression must go to zero, which is exactly what is required to be covered by the definition of little oh.

Part 2 is very similar. We have

$$\lim_{x\to\infty} \frac{|f_{b_1}(x)|}{|f_{b_2}(x)|} = \lim_{x\to\infty} \frac{(\lg N)^{b_1}}{(\lg N)^{b_2}} = \lim_{x\to\infty} \frac{1}{(\lg N)^{b_2-b_1}}.$$

Again, the denominator of the preceding expression goes to infinity, which means that the expression must go to zero, which is what is required to be covered by the definition of little oh.

To prove part 3, we note that

$$\lim_{x\to\infty} \frac{N^{a_1}(\lg N)^{b_1}}{N^{a_2}(\lg N)^{b_2}} = \lim_{x\to\infty} \frac{(\lg N)^{b_1-b_2}}{N^{a_1-a_2}}.$$

If we have $b_1 - b_2 < 0$, then the log term belongs in the denominator, which goes to infinity, and the limit is clearly zero. If we have $b_1 - b_2 > 0$, then we have

$$\lim_{x\to\infty} \frac{(\lg N)^b}{N^a}$$

with $a > 0$ and $b > 0$, and by applying L'Hôpital's rule once we get that this limit is zero.

Finally, proving part 4 is really the same as proving part 2 and canceling some powers of N at the beginning. □

We can now state a number of useful corollaries to Theorem 6.15.

Corollary 6.16

If $f(N) = \lg N$, then $f(N) = O(N^\epsilon)$ for any positive value of ϵ. In particular, we have then $f(N) = O(N^{1/2})$ and $f(N) = O(N)$.

Corollary 6.17

The restriction to exponent 1 in Corollary 6.16 is not necessary. In particular, if $f(N) = (\lg N)^a$ for any positive a, then $f(N) = o(N^\epsilon)$ for any positive value of ϵ, and then $f(N) = o(N^{1/2})$ and $f(N) = o(N)$.

Corollary 6.18

We can multiply by powers of N as we wish. In particular, if $f(N) = N \cdot (\lg N)^a$ for any positive a, then $f(N) = o(N^{1+\epsilon})$ for any positive value of ϵ, and then $f(N) = o(N^{3/2})$ and $f(N) = o(N^2)$.

Corollary 6.19

More generally, if $f(N) = N^k \cdot (\lg N)^a$ for any positive a and k, then $f(N) = o(N^{k+\epsilon})$ for any positive value of ϵ, and then $f(N) = o(N^{k+1/2})$ and $f(N) = o(N^{k+1})$.

These theorems and corollaries allow us to list a number of functions, each of which is little oh of the next going down the list.

- $(\lg N)^{1/2}$
- $\lg N$
- $(\lg N)^2$
- $N^{1/4}$
- $N^{1/2}$
- $N^{1/2} \lg N$
- $N^{1/2}(\lg N)^2$
- N
- $N \lg N$
- $N(\lg N)^2$
- $N^{3/2}$
- N^2
- $N^2 \lg N$
- N^3

and so forth. The power of N dominates, but if the powers of N are identical in two functions, then the next thing to look at is the power of $\lg N$. We shall see in the next section why this is usually enough for our purposes.

6.4 More Intuition — Common Asymptotics

By now the reader may well be wondering, and with some justification, whether all this machinery is necessary and what good it might bring to the design of algorithms and their implementation as programs. Fortunately, for most purposes in computer science we make use only of some basic asymptotics. Although we have discussed some of these practicalities on earlier pages, it is worth revisiting this topic.

We have already encountered an *algorithm that runs in logarithmic time*, namely the binary search of Chapter 3. The linear search runs in (you guessed it) *linear time.* A double loop that runs to completion in both subscripts will run in *quadratic time.* For example, consider the sort code from a previous chapter:

```
for(int i = 0; i < N-1; ++i)
{
  for(int j = i+1; j < N; ++j)
  {
    something
  }
}
```

In the first iteration of the outer loop, the inner loop runs on the $N - 1$ subscripts 1 through $N - 1$. In the second iteration of the outer loop, the inner loop runs on the $N-2$ subscripts 2 through $N-1$, and so on. The `something` code is thus executed

$$(N-1)+(N-2)+\cdots+1=\frac{(N)(N-1)}{2}=\frac{1}{2}(N^2-N)$$

times. Based on the theorems discussed earlier, we can assert that this is $O(N^2)$, or *quadratic time* because this is a quadratic polynomial in N.

For the most part in this course, we discuss a few logarithmic time algorithms like binary search, some algorithms like linear search that run in linear time, and some other algorithms like bubblesort that run in low-degree polynomial time. We will also learn that sorting cannot be done faster than time $O(N \lg N)$. Since $\lg N = o(N)$, we know that $N \lg N = o(N^2)$.

Finally, we must mention that some operations take place in *constant time*, which we write as $O(1)$ time. Operations that take place in constant time will require a fixed maximum number of execution steps regardless of the size of the data set. In the `something` code for the bubblesort in the example we need to fetch two records, the ith and the jth, compare the records, and then swap if they are out of order. Clearly, this `if` block requires at most a constant number of instructions to be executed, that constant being the cost of the record fetch plus the cost of the swap. In the worst case, we always swap, but this cost is the same regardless of the size of the loop.

1. Compute the address in memory of the ith index location and fetch the value into a CPU register.
2. Do the same for the jth index location.
3. Compare the two values. If the values are integers, this is one machine instruction.
4. Swap if necessary.
   - Store the ith record in a temporary location.
   - Copy the jth record to the ith record location.
   - Copy the temporary record to the jth record location.

None of these takes time that depends on the number of records in the entire array, so this entire operation takes time bounded by the worst case, which is still some fixed maximum number of instructions to be executed.

WARNING: Actually, this isn't quite true. If, for example, the index were a string, and were defined to be at most 30 characters long, say, then the worst-case cost in doing the comparison would be 30 (a fixed number) times the cost of comparing a single character. But if the index were allowed to be a string of some unbounded length, then the cost of the comparison of two strings could be unbounded in time. If we assume that all fields in a data record have some fixed maximum size, then we can assert that the comparison requires at worst some constant amount of work for each of some constant number of characters. In general, we need to make sure we have pushed down the analysis so that what we are counting are "atomic" operations with a fixed cost.

One can get an intuitive feel for algorithm analysis by looking at the likely cost of some specific programming constructs. If we assume that the interior `something` operation takes constant time (call this S), then the single loop

```
for(int i = 0; i < N-1; ++i)
{
  something
}
```

will obviously run in linear time ($O(N)$) because the work to be done is

$$N \cdot (\text{cost of } \texttt{something}).$$

Similarly, the loop

```
for(int i = 0; i < N-1; i = i+2)
{
  something
}
```

will run in the same $O(N)$ linear time even though it does only half as much work because "the constants out front don't matter." In this case, the constant is 1/2 because we are stepping by two in the loop.

However, if we assume that `something` has a cost that is logarithmic, as is the binary search, then clearly the loop will iterate N times a computation that has $O(\lg N)$ complexity, so the overall computation has complexity $O(N \lg N)$. For example, we might well have a set of nested loops

```
for(int i = 0; i < N; ++i)
{
  for(int j = 0; j < N-1; j = j+2)
  {
    for(int k = 0; k < N/3; ++k)
    {
      binary search on an (N/2)-size subset of the array
    }
  }
}
```

Our analysis of this would go as follows. First, the outer loop clearly executes N times. Next, the middle loop executes R times, where R is either $(N-1)/2$ if N is odd or $(N-2)/2$ if N is even. Third, the inner loop executes S times, where S is one of $N/3$, $(N-1)/3$, or $(N-2)/3$, depending on whether we have to throw away a remainder after dividing by 3. Finally, the inner computation takes $\lg(N/2)$ probes, and since this program segment would appear to be a search, the cost we are counting is the number of probes that are necessary to perform the search.

We thus know that our program segment will require

$$N \cdot R \cdot S \cdot (\lg N - 1)$$

steps, where $R = N/2 - a$ with $a = 1/2$ or $a = 1$, and $S = N/3 - b$, with $b = 0$, $b = 1/3$, or $b = 2/3$.

If we blast out this product, we get

$$N \cdot R \cdot S \cdot (\lg N - 1) = N \cdot (N/2 - a) \cdot (N/3 - b) \cdot (\lg N - 1).$$

If we combine all the results from this chapter, we can argue that the first three factors in the preceding expression are each $\Theta(N)$ and the last factor is $\Theta(\lg N)$, so the product is $\Theta(N^3 \lg N)$, which is the overall running time of the triple loop with its inner binary search.

From the point of view of looking at loops in code and coming up with an asymptotic analysis, we notice that we don't have to care that the second loop steps by two and not one and thus that there is a possible extra iteration depending on the parity of N. The contribution to the running time "is" $N/2$, which is $O(N)$. Similarly, the contribution of the inner loop "is" $O(N)$, even though it runs only up to $N/3$. And finally, the contribution of the binary search "is" $O(\lg N)$, even though it runs a search on $N/2$ items and not N items. In each of these three special cases, the adjustment to the basic N or $\lg N$ term leads only to lower-order terms in the eventual expression for the running time and thus do not affect the asymptotic running time.

As a final note, we observe that a more sophisticated look at execution time comes from considering a tree search for determining moves in a game such as chess. If we expect there to be *at least* N possible moves from any given position, and then at least N possible response moves from the opponent, and at least N countermoves from your side, and so on, then to examine move and response k levels deep will require at least N^k compute time. This is (although we won't do the math except in the next (starred) section) *exponential time*, worse than any polynomial of any fixed degree, and in general prohibitively expensive in time unless one can trim the search substantially. Most game-playing programs, for example, do not look at the entire set of move-response-countermove-. . . options but rather stop at some fixed depth, perhaps 8 to 10 moves down. More importantly, most game-playing programs will evaluate the "goodness" of a potential move at each step and then eliminate from consideration those moves whose evaluated goodness is significantly worse than the best. In this way the number of possible moves to be examined can be kept feasible, although this approach does make it difficult for a program to choose a move that only becomes obviously superior several moves beyond the current position.

*6.5 Exponential Orders of Magnitude

All our previous analysis has been on functions that were polynomials in N and $\lg N$. There are two "worse" complexity classes that need to be mentioned for the sake of completeness.

6.5.1 Exponential Orders of Magnitude

First, consider a set with N elements in it. From basic set theory we know that there are $M = 2^N$ possible subsets. If our computation required us to enumerate each subset, how long would it take to do this? This might happen, for example, if we were analyzing all the possible drug interactions that might occur for any patient being prescribed medication. If there were N possible drugs to be prescribed, there could potentially be $M = 2^N$ different sets of drugs that could be taken by a given patient.

The basic result is that 2^N is asymptotically larger than any polynomial in N and $\lg N$. An algorithm that is given N input items and that must enumerate over all possible subsets of the N items will take *exponential time* to complete.

Theorem 6.20

If $f(N)$ is a polynomial in N of any fixed degree k, then $f(N) = o(2^N)$.

Proof Consider

$$\lim_{x\to\infty} \frac{x^k}{2^x}.$$

This appears to be ∞/∞, so we apply L'Hôpital's rule successively to find that

$$\lim_{x\to\infty} \frac{x^k}{2^x} = \lim_{x\to\infty} \frac{kx^{k-1}}{(\ln 2)2^x} = \lim_{x\to\infty} \frac{k\cdot(k-1)x^{k-2}}{(\ln 2)^2 2^x} = \cdots = \lim_{x\to\infty} \frac{k!}{(\ln 2)^k 2^x} = 0.$$

□

Our second exponential complexity class is even larger than that of 2^N. Consider a computation like a naive program to solve something like the Jumble puzzle in the morning newspaper. In the Jumble puzzle we are provided with anagrams of five- or six-letter words and asked to produce the correct words by rearranging the letters. Given N input letters, there are $N!$ possible permutations of those input letters, and a naive program might generate all possible permutations and then just look up the putative word in a dictionary. Later on we will make use of permutations in considering the average case of a sorting algorithm: there are $N!$ different permutations of N data items, and if the items are all distinct then only one of these permutations is the correct sorted order of the data.

The number $N!$ of permutations on N items grows very quickly with N. Even without knowing the actual order of magnitude of $N!$, we can easily show that it is greater than a^N for any fixed positive value of a. In particular, $N!$ is asymptotically larger than 2^N.

Theorem 6.21

If $f(N) = a^N$ and $g(N) = N!$, then $f(N) = o(g(N))$.

Proof Consider the limit of the quotient:

$$\lim_{N\to\infty} \frac{a^N}{N!} = \lim_{N\to\infty} \frac{a \cdot \cdots \cdot a}{N(N-1)\cdots(2)(1)}$$

where the product in the numerator has exactly N factors. We can break up this expression as

$$\lim_{N\to\infty} \left(\frac{a \cdot \cdots \cdot a}{(b)\cdots(2)1}\right)\left(\frac{a \cdot \cdots \cdot a}{N(N-1)\cdots(b+1)}\right)$$

where we extend the product in the first fraction exactly to the point that $b \le a < b+1$, the numerator and denominator in the first fraction have b factors, and the numerator and denominator in the second fraction have $N-b$ factors.

We have fixed a from the beginning, which means that we have fixed the value of b and that the first fraction in the limit is a constant. Due to our choice of b, we know that $\frac{a}{b+1} < 1$ and thus that $\frac{a}{N-j} < 1$ for all the factors $\frac{a}{N-j}$ that make up the product in the second fraction. Not only do each of these factors go to zero in the limit, so the product will go to zero in the limit, but also we add yet more factors each less than one to the function whose limit we are taking. Clearly this limit is zero and $a^N = o(N!)$. □

We can actually get a better handle on the nature of exponential-time things by using *Stirling's formula*, which gives an exact value for $N!$ (provided we extend the definition of the word "exact" to allow for the e^{α_N} fudge factor in the expression).

$$N! = \sqrt{2\pi N}\left(\frac{N}{e}\right)^N e^{\alpha_N},$$

where

$$\frac{1}{12N+1} < \alpha_N < \frac{1}{12N}.$$

We observe that Stirling's formula, together with the asymptotic analysis that follows it, says that $N!$ is equal to a dominant $(N/e)^N$ term, times a $\sqrt{N}$ that is asymptotically smaller than $(N/e)^N$, times an asymptotically irrelevant term $\sqrt{2\pi}e^{\alpha_N}$ that tends to $\sqrt{2\pi}$ as N goes to infinity.

*6.6 Big Omega

In general, logarithmic time is the best that we can do for any serious algorithm, and even that can only be achieved after we spend more time in preparation. That is: we can achieve logarithmic search time only after having sorted the records, and the sorting will take more than logarithmic time. Indeed, it is clear that one cannot do anything serious on N data items without spending at least N time steps because without at least looking at each data item one has no information at all about those data items not viewed.

The big Oh and little oh notations allow for comparisons of functions that resemble an asymptotic "less than or equal" and an asymptotic "less than," respectively. The following definitions provide the asymptotic analogs of "greater than or equal" and of equality.

The two definitions of "greater than or equal" use the "big Omega" notation.

6.6.1 Traditional Big Omega (Hardy, about 1915)

Definition 6.22 We write

$$f(x) = \Omega(g(x))$$

if $f(x)$ is *not* $o(g(x))$, that is, if there exists a sequence $x_1, x_2, \ldots, x_n, \ldots$, tending to ∞, such that for any fixed constant C, there exists a constant c such that $x_i > c \implies |f(x_i)| \geq C \cdot g(x_i)$.

6.6.2 Knuth's Big Omega (Knuth, about 1975)

Definition 6.23 We write

$$f(x) = \Omega_K(g(x))$$

if for any fixed constant C there exists a constant c such that

$$x > c \implies |f(x)| \geq C \cdot g(x).$$

Notes:

- $\Omega_K(\cdot)$ is *stronger*; it requires *all* values to obey the $\geq$. Classic $\Omega(\cdot)$ requires only that a subsequence increasing to infinity violate the $\geq$.
- There can be confusion over the difference between the traditional definition of $\Omega(\cdot)$ and the modern revision by Knuth. The traditional definition will be used by most mathematicians, especially those in number theory and function theory, from where these concepts arose. Most computer scientists will not know about the traditional notation. The difference between the two can lead to some confusion. When you read a book or paper that uses the notation $\Omega(\cdot)$, you have to make sure you know which definition is being used.
- On the other hand, it turns out that the conflict between the two definitions is usually not an issue in the analysis of algorithms for the following reasons. Since we are using this kind of analysis for measuring work, our functions are usually increasing functions of N. More importantly, the function that we use in computer science is the function for the *worst-case behavior*. A mathematician looking at the function describing *any* insertionsort-like loop would have a function that could be as small as one comparison (if the list were sorted in ascending order and the new item was larger than the previous last and largest item) or as large as N comparisons (if the new item were smaller than anything already in the list and had to be pulled forward to the beginning). A mathematician analyzing the function for number of comparisons would have to account for this variation; the computer scientist would likely only be looking at the worst case, and maximum value, of the function.

Theorem 6.24

For any two functions $f(n)$ and $g(n)$, we have

$$f(n) = \Theta(g(n)) \iff f(n) = O(g(n)) \text{ and } f(n) = \Omega_K(g(n)).$$

6.7 What Do We Count?

In our warning in Section 6.4, we observed that counting the cost of comparing strings of a fixed maximum size is not the same as counting the cost of comparing strings of arbitrary length. In any analysis, we have to ensure that we get to a point where we are counting fixed, basic costs of whatever computation is being performed.

One might also ask where we stop in our list of basic complexity classes. In this case, the answer is that most of the common things that are done in computing don't seem to require more than N^3 time. Or perhaps it is the case that algorithms that are more complex than this are sufficiently complex that we naturally break them down into simpler algorithms. The most notable N^3 algorithm is probably matrix multiplication when it is done in the naive way. To multiply two $N \times N$ matrices to create an $N \times N$ product, we need to create N^2 entries in the product matrix. Each of these entries is the result of the dot product of two vectors of length N (row i dotted with column j to produce the entry at row i and column j in the product), so creating each of these entries requires N multiplications. (It also requires some additions, but in numerical mathematics the cost of a multiplication is usually large compared to the cost of an addition, so it is usually only the number of multiplications that is factored into the complexity of the algorithm.) Since each of N^2 entries requires N multiplications, a naive matrix multiplication takes N^3 multiplications and thus is $O(N^3)$. In scientific code, these are usually floating-point multiplications.

We have just mentioned that in numerical computation it is the number of floating-point multiplications that one counts to determine the complexity of an algorithm. Other algorithms will count different operations. For example, most sorting algorithms eventually reduce down to pulling two data items from memory, comparing the two values (or the values of their keys), and then exchanging their locations if they are out of order under the rules of the algorithm. For comparing sorting algorithms, then, we usually count the number of comparisons made. In each case the number of machine instructions is larger than one, because we must either fetch two operands, perform a multiplication, and put the product somewhere, or fetch two operands, perform a comparison, and then possibly put the operands back in exchanged order. In both cases we can view this as the basic unit of computation, with the complexity of the algorithm being the cost of doing these actions on data elements of size N.

6.8 Binary Divide and Conquer Is Optimal

We will close this chapter with one of the foundational principles of efficient computing, namely that an algorithm such as binary search is optimal with regard to the number of operations necessary to produce the desired result when presented with N items of data.

Binary search is an example of a *divide-and-conquer* algorithm. With each method call, we divide the problem space in half, rule out half of the possible space, and then attack the half that remains with another call to the same method. In general, a divide-and-conquer algorithm is going to be efficient; the following theorem provides an example of why this is so.

Theorem 6.25

Given a list L of N items in sorted order, binary search will determine whether a potential value x is in L in $O(\lg N)$ comparisons. Binary search is optimal for searching in the sense that if any other search method has $O(f(N))$ running time, then $\lg N$ is $O(f(N))$.

Proof What we need to show is that any search strategy must make at least $O(\lg N)$ comparisons. What we will show is that each comparison made in binary search is at least as "effective" as each comparison in any other search, and thus that no fewer comparisons than those needed for binary search can accomplish the search task.

We begin with an observation: it is impossible for a search algorithm to work correctly on all inputs unless a potential value x is compared against all N entries in the list L.

Clearly, if there is any element y in L that we do not compare to x, then we cannot determine whether or not $x = y$ and thus the algorithm cannot guarantee that it works correctly under all inputs. The algorithm must return an answer independent of the value of y, but both $y = x$ and $y \neq x$ are legal input data, so the algorithm cannot be right for all inputs.

It is necessary, therefore, that any search algorithm that actually works on all inputs must achieve the effect of at least N comparisons. What we now claim is that binary search achieves the effect of N comparisons by executing $O(\lg N)$ comparisons. This is exactly what we discussed when we first presented binary search. With our first comparison, we are comparing against not just one element (the element at the midpoint of the list) but half the elements in the list. If x is found in the first comparison to lie in the first half of the list, then we have effectively compared x to all $N/2$ entries in the upper half of the list because the "less-than" operator is transitive and the list is sorted. With our second comparison, we effectively compare against $N/4$ elements for the same reason. Because there are $\lg N$ summands on the right-hand side of the equation

$$N = N/2 + N/4 + N/8 + \cdots + 1, \tag{6.1}$$

we can conclude that we have effectively made the necessary N comparisons although in truth we have made only $\lg N$ comparisons.[3]

At this point, then, we can conclude that we need N comparisons in effect and that we can accomplish that task with binary search using only $O(\lg N)$ actual comparisons. To complete the proof we must show that no other search method can run with fewer actual comparisons.

What we will show is that with every actual comparison that is made in binary search, we are making at least as much progress toward answering the search question as can be made by any other algorithm making any single comparison. That is, we observe that every comparison performed in binary search eliminates half the items in the sorted list, and no other algorithm can ever eliminate more than that many items when it makes a single actual comparison.

Consider the sorted list of N items. If we compare a potential element x against some specific element in the list, then that comparison splits the list L into one subset L_1 of elements $< x$ and one subset L_2 of elements $> x$. If we compare against the element at subscript k, then these two subsets are of size k and $N - k$, respectively. Regardless of the values of x and k, there will be legal data input lists for which x is less than the kth element and for which x is greater than the kth element. In the worst case, then, we have made one comparison that has had the effect of $\min\{k, N-k\}$ comparisons and we have $\max\{k, N-k\}$ elements left in the list after one actual comparison. Because by choosing the midpoint in binary search the worst case is that we have $N/2$ elements, and by choosing any other subscript to test against we have $\max\{k, N-k\} \geq N/2$ remaining in the worst case, it is clear that the midpoint is the optimal choice for the first comparison. Comparisons after the first work in exactly the same way: with any actual comparison, we make at least as much progress with the midpoint choice of binary search than we can with any other choice, so we cannot do better overall than by performing binary search. □

Let's take a step back and think about this proof. In general, proving something is possible is much easier than proving something is impossible. To prove that binary search was better than *any* other approach, we had to show that nothing would work better, not just that the other methods we could think of wouldn't work any better. What we showed, then, was the following. First we determined the necessary cost of search under any circumstances, namely that the *effect* of N comparisons must be accomplished. Then we showed that binary search does what is necessary in its worst-case running time.

---

[3]We are going to ignore the issues of $<$ versus $\leq$ and of whether N is a perfect power of 2. If we really wanted to, we could be completely precise, but the precise proof will not offer any greater insight to the reader.

Then comes the more difficult part. In this case, what we were able to show was that the progress made by one unit of work done by binary search was at least as good at every stage of the computation as the progress made by one unit of work for any other algorithm. If no single comparison can make more progress than the progress made in binary search with the corresponding comparison, then clearly no aggregate of comparisons can make more progress than the aggregate of comparisons in binary search.

We will do a similar analysis in a later chapter on the minimal cost of sorting.

Finally, it is worth taking a look at ternary search instead of binary search. Namely, if divide and conquer into equal halves is effective, then why not a ternary instead of a binary search? If being able to discard half the array with each one comparison is good, then why wouldn't it be better to be able to discard two-thirds of the array each time? We know from the preceding theorem that this shouldn't be any better than binary search, but let's take a look at the specifics, which are enlightening.

First, we note that we can in fact with two comparisons determine which third of the array the potential entry x would fall in by testing x against the elements at locations $N/3$ and $2N/3$. If we keep going, then instead of Equation (6.1) with $\lg N$ summands, we have

$$N = 2N/3 + 2N/9 + 2N/27 + \cdots + 2, \tag{6.2}$$

with $\log_3 N$ summands. We can thus determine whether x is in the list with $2 \cdot \log_3 N$ comparisons. However, $2 \cdot \log_3 N = 2 \cdot \frac{\lg N}{\lg 3} \approx 1.26 \lg N$, so we are actually doing slightly more work than before. The decrease in the number of levels we have to search, from $\lg N$ to $\log_3 N$, is more than counterbalanced by the increased work at each level.

6.9 Summary

This chapter has been largely theoretical, but the principles developed here are crucially important for writing good code. For the most part, the mathematics necessary for determining the asymptotic efficiency of algorithms does not go beyond elementary calculus, primarily the application of L'Hôpital's rule for computing limits and the use of elementary combinatorics to count the number of iterations of certain loops.

There are several basic principles that make algorithm analysis easier by making it unnecessary to go back to first principles in order to do the analysis. These principles allow one, for example, to discard multiplicative constants and to discard all polynomial terms except the one of highest exponent, and thus simplify analysis.

By translating these principles into an ability to look at code fragments and immediately determine the number of iterations of a given set of loops, one can focus attention on writing efficient and clear code.

As part of our analysis, we have shown why binary divide and conquer is such a powerful computational technique that is usually optimal and thus a preferred underlying method for breaking down a problem into simpler and simpler steps.

6.10 Exercises

1. Prove using the definition of big Oh that if $f_1(x) = O(g_1(x))$ and $f_2(x) = O(g_2(x))$, then $f_1(x) + f_2(x) = O(g_1(x) + g_2(x))$.

2. Prove using the definition of big Oh that if $f_1(x) = O(g_1(x))$ and $f_2(x) = O(g_2(x))$, then $f_1(x) \cdot f_2(x) = O(g_1(x) \cdot g_2(x))$.

3. Prove the following:

(a) $(\lg N)^{100} = o(N^{1/100})$
(b) $(\lg N)^{100} = O(N^{1/100})$
(c) $N \lg N = o(N^{3/2})$
(d) $N \lg N = O(N^{3/2})$
(e) $N^2 \lg N = o(N^{2+1/8})$
(f) $N^2 \lg N = O(N^{2+1/8})$
(g) $(\lg N)^2 = o(N^\epsilon)$ for any $\epsilon > 0$
(h) $(\lg N)^2 = O(N^\epsilon)$ for any $\epsilon > 0$
(i) $2^N = o(3^N)$
(j) $2^N = O(3^N)$
(k) $\log_2 N = \Theta(\log_3 N)$

Note that the last three indicate that, although all logarithms are the same, all exponentials are not the same.

4. Prove the following:

(a) $x^{10} + x^5 + 1 = O(x^{10})$
(b) $-10^8 x^{10} + 10^{20} x^5 + 1 = O(x^{10})$
(c) $x^3 + 2x^2 + 3x + 4 = O(x^3)$
(d) $(x^2 + 7x + 1)^4 = O(x^8)$
(e) $1/x = O(1)$
(f) $(x + 1/x)^5 = O(x^5)$

***5.** Prove the following:

(a) $x + 2^x = O(2^x)$
(b) For any $a > 0$, we have $a^{2N} = O(N!)$.

6. In each of the following, assume that `myList` is an `ArrayList` of numbers that currently holds N items. Express your answers in big Oh notation in functions of N, indicate what it is that you are counting, and give a fragment of pseudocode that shows how you are producing the required result. You do not need to use the absolutely most efficient method for any of these computations;

you only need to show that you can analyze the method that you have chosen to use.

(a) What is the cost of computing the sum of all the entries in `myList`?
(b) What is the cost of computing the sum of the squares of all the entries in `myList`?
(c) What is the cost of listing all possible subsets of `myList`?
*(d) What is the cost of computing the sum of the numbers in each of all possible subsets of `myList`?

7. In each of the following, assume that `myArray` is an array of numbers of N rows and N columns. Express your answers in big Oh notation in functions of N, indicate what it is that you are counting, and give a fragment of pseudocode that shows how you are producing the required result. You do not need to use the absolutely most efficient method for any of these computations; you only need to show that you can analyze the method that you have chosen to use.

(a) What is the cost of computing the sum of all the entries in `myArray`?
(b) What is the cost of computing the sum of the squares of all the entries in `myArray`?
(c) What is the cost of computing the sum of all the entries on the main diagonal of `myArray`?
(d) What is the cost of listing, for each of the rows in the array, all possible subsets of the entries in each of the rows?
(e) What is the cost of finding, for each of the rows in the array, the minimum value in each of the rows?
(f) What is the cost of searching each row of the array for a given value and listing the rows that contain that value?

7 Stacks and Queues

Objectives

- An introduction to the concept of a stack and to at least two ways in which a stack can be implemented, including the `Stack` structure in the JCF
- An introduction to the concept of a queue and to at least two ways in which a queue can be implemented, including the `Queue` structure in the JCF
- An introduction to the use of a stack for processing such things as HTML or XML data that use explicit open–close tags for labeling data
- An introduction to the utility of the stack structure for implementing something like reverse Polish notation, in which the stack itself replaces explicit tags like HTML or XML or arithmetic operations and parentheses
- An introduction to the use of a queue for representing first-in-first-out processing structures that resemble checkout lines
- An introduction to the heap and the priority queue as mechanisms for maintaining a dynamic "next most important" data structure without requiring complete sorting of the data

Key Terms

arc	incomplete binary tree	queue
binary tree	max-heap	reverse Polish notation
child node	min-heap	root
complete binary tree	node	total order
deque	priority queue	tree
heap	push-down stack	

Introduction

The basic notion of a linked list uses the idea of a data item together with a link to "the next item." Two very useful data structures that are built on similar concepts are the *stack* and the *queue.* In both cases, although we could use an array or an `ArrayList` to implement the data structure, we will insist that the insertion and retrieval of data follow the "next item" protocol of a linked list rather than the random access by subscript of an array or `ArrayList`. At the end of this chapter, though, we will go back to the notion of an `ArrayList`-based structure to implement a *priority queue.*

It is important to think for a moment about the layers of concept and of implementation. In Chapter 4 we described a linked list data structure. We showed that the concept of a linked list, in and of itself, is a useful concept for a data structure, but we also showed how to implement a linked list using instances of nodes with the `DLL` class. In Chapter 3 we described the concept of a flat file, implemented it using an `ArrayList`, and mentioned that we could instead have used an array for the implementation.

Likewise in this and subsequent chapters, you should be careful to separate the *concept* of a given data structure from the means by which it is implemented. In the ancient days of computing, using programming languages whose most sophisticated inherent structure was an array of numbers, all data structure concepts had to be implemented as clever uses of arrays. Although this can in principle still be done, you should realize that this kind of programming can be error prone and tedious because the programmer's time is spent in details of subscripting, not in dealing with the bigger picture. Indeed, many of the features of modern programming languages, and much of the purpose of packages like the JCF, are specifically to eliminate dealing repeatedly with messy details, usually subscripting details, that are easy to think about but also easy to get wrong.

7.1 Stacks

A *stack*, sometimes also called a *push-down stack*, is a last-in-first-out (LIFO) data structure. Many napkin dispensers in restaurants or tray dispensers in cafeterias work as stacks. Napkins or trays are pushed into a spring-loaded dispenser through the same slot from which they are extracted. A Pez candy dispenser[1] functions in the same way.

The standard stack data structure is characterized by its two required methods, `push` and `pop`, and its one instance variable that is an attribute of the data structure,

[1]These were popular in the 1950s, then disappeared, and are now once again available.

a pointer called `top`. The `push` operation simply adds another item before the location pointed to by `top`, just like putting a tray at the top of the dispenser, and then adjusts the value of `top` so it now points to the new top item. The `pop` operation is the reverse; one removes the item pointed to by `top` and adjusts the variable to point to the new top item.

It is almost trivial, once one has written the code for a linked list, to implement the concept of a stack using that linked list, viewing the stack data structure as a linked list with the additional restriction that the additions and deletions are permitted only at the head node. This is done as follows.

We already have an instance variable that "is" the `top`, but we called it `head` in the case of a linked list. The `push` operation is exactly the same as the linked list's `addAtHead` method we previously implemented, so we need do no more than create a wrapper method called `push` that is a pass-through to `addAtHead`. The only slightly new method is `pop`, which we implement as a new method. We could have done this already as a linked list method and called it `deleteAtHead`, but we didn't need a method at that time that specifically deleted from a predefined location (namely, the head). We need that method now, and we will call it `pop`.

There are two auxiliary methods that we probably also ought to implement because we are virtually certain to find them convenient if we are going to write significant useful code using a stack. We should implement an `isEmpty` method that will tell us (surprise, surprise) if the stack is empty. This could be either a standalone method or a pass-through to an already-implemented `isEmpty` for the linked list. The other method is a `peek` at the top entry of the stack. The `peek` method would return the data item at the top of the stack but would not actually delete it. We don't actually have to have this. However, if our computation requires us first to *look* at the top data item and then *maybe* but not always pop it off and consume it, then not having a `peek` means that we have the extra hassle of popping the item, finding that we don't want to consume that data, and putting it back. We can avoid the put-back step by implementing `peek`.

The UML diagram for a `Stack` might look as simple as Figure 7.1.

Stack
+top:DLLNode
+Stack():void +isEmpty():boolean +peek():DLLNode +pop():DLLNode +push(DLLNode):void

FIGURE 7.1 ■ A UML diagram for a `Stack` class.

```
public boolean isEmpty()
{
  return 'isEmpty' of the underlying linked list
}
public Record peek()
{
  if(this.isEmpty)
  {
    return null;
  }
  else
  {
    Record rec = the 'head' record of the underlying linked list
    return rec;
  }
}

public Record pop(Record)
{
  if(this.isEmpty)
  {
    throw new StackPopException("tried to pop an empty stack");
  }
  else
  {
    Record rec = the 'head' record of the underlying linked list
    unlink the head record
    return rec;
  }
}

// CAVEAT: Note that we always assume we have enough memory to
//         add to the underlying linked list.  Runaway programs
//         will crash ungracefully.
public void push(Record)
{
  addAtHead(Record);
}
```

FIGURE 7.2 ■ Code stubs for a `Stack` class.

Stubs of code for the necessary methods with the `Record` class as the data payload would then look something like Figure 7.2, and with this as the conceptual framework, Figure 7.3 shows a stack in operation.

■ 7.1.1 Exception Handling

Just as with linked lists, we need to deal properly with the exceptions that can occur with the methods in Figure 7.1. The `isEmpty` cannot generate an exception because

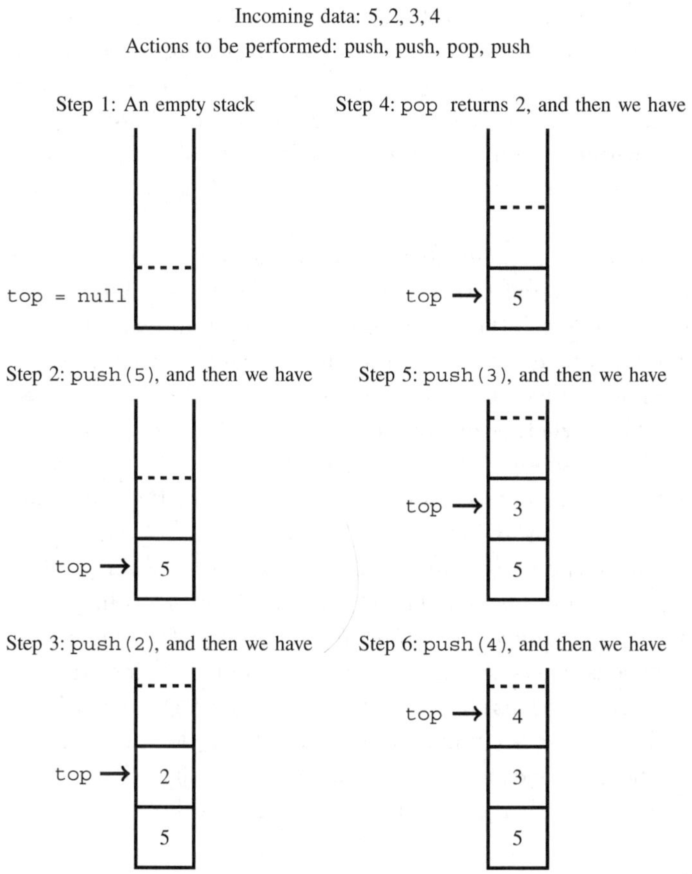

FIGURE 7.3 ■ Inserting elements into a stack.

it returns an `isEmpty` from the underlying linked list. Although in a truly sophisticated implementation one ought to check that sufficient memory exists to execute a `push`, we generally will not assume that we are running out of memory in this text.

The `peek` and the `push`, however, could cause problems. If we try to execute a `peek` on an empty list, we probably ought to return a `null` value and then require the user to check for that.

Most complicated is the `pop`; unlike a `peek` issued in error, which can be written just to return null data, the `pop` method is supposed to change the underlying data structure as well as return a data value. To ensure that we crash the program appropriately, we will issue an exception if we try to `pop` a stack that is already empty.

There are two schools of thought regarding exceptions like trying to `pop` from an already-empty stack. Viewing software as existing in hierarchical layers, the heart of the religious issue here is the question of which layer will handle the exceptional case.

What we have provided code for in Figure 7.2 is a data structure that generates an exception if an erroneous stack `pop` is issued. This will force programs to be written so as to execute correctly under all circumstances, and a program that issued a `pop` should never do so without first testing `isEmpty` to ensure that the `pop` won't crash the program. The test of `isEmpty` is a natural test in the layer of software that *uses* the stack data structure, and the exception is dealt with in the next layer down that *implements* the stack.

As an alternative, the layer that implements the stack could simply return a `null` value from an erroneous `pop` and require the programmer using the stack structure to check for nonnull data every time the `pop` is issued. If such a mechanism were used, the test for a valid `pop` would come after the method call to `pop` and would use a test for `null` instead of coming before the method call to `pop` and using a call to `isEmpty`. The test would be whether or not valid data had been returned. This would be advantangeous in one sense, in that the stack data structure was robust under erroneous use, but it can also be considered a dangerous practice. After all, why does the `isEmpty` method exist except to test for the presence of data in the stack? From a philosophical viewpoint, the call to `isEmpty` is a natural call regarding the state of the idealized version of a stack. The test for `null`, on the other hand, represents a test that involves the *implementation characteristics* of the stack.

Regardless of which religious tenets are adhered to, they should be adhered to; in a given program, one of the two versions should be used consistently and exclusively. Mistakes often happen when one does a mix and match of such styles, or when one person uses one version and a second person uses the other and they either don't communicate properly with each other or one has to rework the other's code.

■ 7.1.2 Stacks Using Nodes

A stack implemented using a linked list with nodes needs no further code to be developed except for the new `push` and `pop` methods. The `push` can be done simply as a method with a one-line body that wraps and thus renames the earlier `addAtHead` method. The `pop` requires a slight bit of new code; our `remove` methods for the linked list passed in the data payload to be searched for in a node and whose node was to be removed. In the case of the `pop`, we are specifying that the node (or rather, the data payload) first in position in the stack be removed, so there is no contextual search through the data structure.

For completeness, we must also include the `isEmpty` method and a `peek` method that returns the data at the top of the stack without actually `pop`ping the stack.

Done in this way, the linked list is more general than the stack because additions to and deletions from a linked list can nominally be made anywhere in the list, but the stack in contrast only permits changes at the top of a stack.

We emphasize yet again, because it is a very important point, that the concept of the stack should be separated from the implementation of the stack. As a concept, the stack exists as defined, say, in the UML diagram in Figure 7.1, and a user of the stack should be allowed to be blissfully ignorant of what lies beneath. The implementation of a stack is what we take up next.

7.1.3 Stacks Using Arrays

Implementing a stack using an array is straightforward, and indeed was the only method for implementing stacks using antique programming languages. There is the usual complication, in Java and in other languages, that an array must be preallocated with a fixed number of locations, so one does run the risk of overfilling the stack unless error-checking code is written.

More significantly, and contrary to what might seem the initial way in which a stack ought to be implemented, when using an array (or an `ArrayList`) one wants the `top` variable to point to the *last* array location that has been filled with data, not to the zeroth location. If one treats the zeroth location as the *bottom* of the stack, then no data needs to be moved when items are popped off. If one has a stack with subscripts 0 through 15 already used and `top` is 15, then one merely increments `top` to 16 and `push`es the item onto the stack by storing it in location 16. When this item is `pop`ped off the stack, the entry at location 16 is accessed and `top` is decremented back to 15. It isn't even necessary to get rid of the data in the location that is now one beyond `top`. Done the other way around, with `top` always pointing to location 0 in what might seem as the more natural way, then all data would have to be moved with every `push` and `pop` because all the rest of the data would have to be shifted down and back.

The same logic applies if one is using an `ArrayList` instead of an array. The code for the `push` method might well look as simple as the following, assuming that instance variables were properly declared in the class. This code checks for an out-of-space condition; if one were using an `ArrayList`, this checking would be done by the code at the next level down that implemented the `ArrayList`, and the programmer would not have to check this.

```
public void push(int newElement)
{
   if(top >= array.length)
   {
     throw an exception because we have no more space
   }
   ++top;
   array[top] = newElement;
}
```

A stack implemented with an array is shown in Figure 7.4.

Step 1: Empty stack
top = *

subscript	0	1	2	3	4	5	6	7	8	9
data	*	*	*	*	*	*	*	*	*	*

Step 2: `push(5)`, and then we have
top = 0

subscript	0	1	2	3	4	5	6	7	8	9
data	5	*	*	*	*	*	*	*	*	*

Step 3: `push(2)`, and then we have
top = 1

subscript	0	1	2	3	4	5	6	7	8	9
data	5	2	*	*	*	*	*	*	*	*

Step 4: `pop` returns 2, and then we have
top = 0

subscript	0	1	2	3	4	5	6	7	8	9
data	5	2	*	*	*	*	*	*	*	*

Step 5: `push(3)`, and then we have
top = 1

subscript	0	1	2	3	4	5	6	7	8	9
data	5	3	*	*	*	*	*	*	*	*

Step 6: `push(4)`, and then we have
top = 2

subscript	0	1	2	3	4	5	6	7	8	9
data	5	3	4	*	*	*	*	*	*	*

FIGURE 7.4 ■ A stack implemented with an array.

■ 7.1.4 Reverse Polish Arithmetic

One of the by-now classic uses for a stack is in the implementation of what is called *reverse Polish notation* (RPN) for evaluating algebraic expressions.[2] Unlike the standard notation for an expression, perhaps

$$4 +_a (2 \times_b 3) -_c ((5 +_d 7) \times_e 8)$$

[2]It is incumbent on anyone who writes a general-purpose book that uses this expression to point out that this has nothing to do with ethnic jokes. In fact, just the opposite is true; this notation is a tribute to the Polish mathematician Jan Łukasiewicz who pioneered the use of this representation.

that uses nested parentheses to group subexpressions, one can write the equivalent expression in RPN without needing parentheses. (We have labeled the operators with subscripts so we can distinguish, for example, the first plus sign subscripted a from the second plus sign subscripted d.) The preceding expression would become

$$4 \quad 2 \quad 3 \quad \times_b \quad +_a \quad 5 \quad 7 \quad +_d \quad 8 \quad \times_e \quad -_c.$$

This expression can be processed in the following way. We read the RPN expression left to right. If we have an operand, we push the operand onto the stack. If we have an operation, then (in our simplified version) we know we have a binary operation; we apply that operation to the first two operands popped off the stack and we push the result back onto the stack.

For our example, the processing is as follows.

1. Read the 4. Since it is an operand, we push it onto the stack, which now holds

$$top \rightarrow 4, \quad NULL.$$

2. Read the 2. Since it is an operand, we push it onto the stack, which now holds

$$top \rightarrow 2, \quad 4, \quad NULL.$$

3. Read the 3, and since it is an operand, push it onto the stack, which now holds

$$top \rightarrow 3, \quad 2, \quad 4, \quad NULL.$$

4. Read the $\times_b$. Since this is an operation, we pop two operands (3 and 2, in that order) off the stack, perform the multiplication to produce the product 6, and push the result onto the stack, which now holds

$$top \rightarrow 6, \quad 4, \quad NULL.$$

5. Read the $+_a$. Since this is an operation, we pop two operands (6 and 4, in that order) off the stack, perform the addition to produce the sum 10, and push the result onto the stack, which now holds

$$top \rightarrow 10 \quad NULL.$$

6. Read the operand 5 and push it onto the stack, which now holds

$$top \rightarrow 5, \quad 10, \quad NULL.$$

7. Read the operand 7 and push it onto the stack, which now holds

$$top \rightarrow 7, \quad 5, \quad 10, \quad NULL.$$

8. Read the operation $+_d$, pop two operands (7 and 5) off the stack, perform the addition, and push the result 12 onto the stack, which now holds

$$top \rightarrow 12, \quad 10 \quad NULL.$$

9. Read the operand 8 and push it onto the stack, which now holds

$$top \rightarrow 8, \quad 12, \quad 10, \quad NULL.$$

10. Read the operation $\times_e$, pop two operands (8 and 12) off the stack, perform the multiplication, and push the result 96 onto the stack, which now holds

$$top \rightarrow 96, \quad 10 \quad NULL.$$

11. Read the operation $-_c$, pop two operands (96 and 10) off the stack, perform the subtraction (and in this case we make sure to do the operation in the right order because subtraction is not commutative), and push the result -86 onto the stack, which now holds

$$top \rightarrow -86 \quad NULL.$$

The utility of RPN lies in the ability (which we have not shown completely) for expressions to be written unambiguously without parentheses, and for all arithmetic operations to be computable using a stack and operating on the two most recently pushed operands. With RPN, all references are to data that is only a constant distance away from "here," unlike with ordinary arithmetic expressions, in which one might have to parse a string of unknown length in order to find a closing parenthesis.

7.2 HTML/XML and Stacks

The use of a stack for handling RPN arithmetic is in essence an implied insertion of opening and closing parentheses to make well-formed algebraic expressions.

A very similar but more modern use for a stack would be to parse XML (eXtensible Markup Language) or similar input and to verify that the XML expressions are well formed. This has become an important part of handling documents on the Web and elsewhere because the use of XML has standardized the form in which documents are to be electronically stored.

An XML document might look like the text in Figure 7.5. An opening XML token in this simplified version consists of a single tag within angle brackets and has no spaces. A closing token has the same structure except that the character immediately following the opening angle bracket is a forward slash. (Those who have looked at real XML or HTML will note that other things are legal inside the angle

```
<book>
  <title> Data Structures Using Java </title>
  <bookinfo>
    <author>
      <forename> Duncan </forename>
      <surname> Buell </surname>
    </author>
    <author>
      <forename> Charles </forename>
      <surname> Dickens </surname>
    </author>
  </bookinfo>
[MORE INPUT FOLLOWS]
</book>
```

FIGURE 7.5 ■ A sample XML-like document.

brackets as modifiers to the initial tag. The attributes add complexity to the parsing of tags but don't really affect the idea of using a stack for this kind of processing, so we will concentrate only on the tag and ignore the possibility of attributes.)

To be valid under modern rules it is necessary that such a document have properly nested opening and closing tags, just exactly as one would nest parentheses in an algebraic expression. Thus, the opening `<book>` tag must eventually be closed with a `</book>` tag, and the two `<author> </author>` tags enclose author information for two authors inside the `<bookinfo> </bookinfo>` open–close structure. In general, to test that an XML expression is well formed is to test that at any given level of nesting, all tags that open a context at that level are closed at that level before the level itself is closed. For example, the display in Figure 7.6 is well formed, because `name`, `number`, and `office` are opened and then closed inside the `phonebook` level before another opening tag is encountered.

```
<phonebook>
  <name>
    John Smith
  </name>
  <number>
    555.1212
  </number>
  <office>
    3A73
  </office>
</phonebook>
```

FIGURE 7.6 ■ A well-formed XML document.

```
<phonebook>
  <name>
    John Smith
    <number>
      555.1212
  </name>
    </number>
  <office>
    3A73
  </office>
</phonebook>
```

FIGURE 7.7 ■ A badly formed XML document.

However, the display in Figure 7.7 is not well formed because `number` is opened inside the `name` level but not closed until *after* the `name` level has been closed. Although indentation is cosmetic for XML and not functional (white space is ignored), we have indented for readability, and one can easily see the nesting problem in the irregularity of the levels of indentation.

XML is in fact both more restrictive and less restrictive than are standard arithmetic expressions. One can write, as we did earlier,

$$4 +_a (2 \times_b 3) -_c ((5 +_d 7) \times_e 8)$$

using the same open and close parentheses symbols for grouping all expressions. This can lead to expressions that are syntactically correct but don't parse as intended if, for example, the writer has confused multiple nestings of "(" and ")". For this reason, we might see the preceding expression written as

$$4 +_a (2 \times_b 3) -_c ([5 +_d 7] \times_e 8),$$

which is easier for humans to read. XML is less restrictive than algebraic expressions in the sense that the writer can invent whatever `<thisTag> </thisTag>` pairs are desired, rather than using only the customary parentheses, brackets, and braces: "()," "[]," and "{}." On the other hand, by requiring the open–close nesting to be well defined with the unique open–close tags, XML is more restrictive than the conventions of algebra, which usually only counts the *number* of opening and closing parentheses. If you write an expression using only the standard parentheses, the rules of algebra say that a closing parenthesis closes whatever was most recently opened. One does not need a stack, then, to determine that an expression is well formed. A counter will do just fine. One increments the counter for an open parenthesis and decrements for a closing parenthesis, and need only check that the counter never goes below zero (which would indicate a close without a corresponding open) and that it does drop to zero at the end of the expression (indicating that the numbers of opening and closing parentheses are equal).

Just as with algebraic expressions, we can use a stack to handle the parsing of XML and to verify that the nesting of tags is correct. When we encounter an opening tag (that is, one with no slash), we `push` the tag onto the stack. When we encounter data with no angle brackets (and here we need to appeal to the fact that we are dealing with a simplified version of XML because in a real application there would have to be some sort of protocol for handling data that began with an open angle bracket), we also `push` that data onto the stack. When we encounter a *closing* tag, however (defined as beginning with "</" and with the appropriate protocol for trying to deal with data that might have these characters), we begin to `pop` the stack, treating all entries that are `popped` as data. If the first `popped` entry that is not data is a closing tag that matches up with an opening tag just `popped`, the XML is properly nested. If we encounter some other nondata tag first or if we never encounter the closing tag, then we have a case of improperly nested tags and invalid XML.

The processing of the XML in Figure 7.6 might go as follows.

1. Begin with an empty stack with the top at the top. We will be storing (*type*, *contents*) pairs and will load an initial (NULL, NULL) pair, so our stack begins as

   (NULL, NULL)

2. Read the first line and push onto the stack a (*type*, *contents*) pair that in this case is (*tag*, `phonebook`). The stack is now

   (tag, `phonebook`)
   (NULL, NULL)

3. Read the next line and push onto the stack a pair (*tag*, `name`). The stack is now

   (tag, `name`)
   (tag, `phonebook`)
   (NULL, NULL)

4. Read the next line and push onto the stack a pair (*data*, `John Smith`). The stack is now

   (data, `John Smith`)
   (tag, `name`)
   (tag, `phonebook`)
   (NULL, NULL)

5. Read the next line. Because this is a closing tag, we pop the stack and acquire the pair (*data*, `John Smith`). Because this is data, we consume the data and continue, which means that we pop the stack and acquire the pair (*tag*, `name`). This is the first nondata item we have popped, so we compare the contents

`name` against the closing tag contents that we read. This is also `name`, so the two match and we continue. The stack is now

(tag, `phonebook`)
(NULL, NULL)

6. We repeat steps 2 through 5 for the three lines of `number` and then for the three lines of `office`.
7. We read the closing tag `</phonebook>`. We pop the stack to get a tag with contents `phonebook` that matches the contents we just read. At this point we are out of both data and entries on the stack, so the XML expression is well formed.

Compare this with the processing of the XML in Figure 7.7 that might go as follows.

1. Read the first line and push onto the stack a (*type*, *contents*) pair that in this case is (*tag*, `phonebook`). The stack is now

   (tag, `phonebook`)
   (NULL, NULL)

2. Read the next line and push onto the stack a pair (*tag*, `name`). The stack is now

   (tag, `name`)
   (tag, `phonebook`)
   (NULL, NULL)

3. Read the next line and push onto the stack a pair (*data*, `John Smith`). The stack is now

   (data, `John Smith`)
   (tag, `name`)
   (tag, `phonebook`)
   (NULL, NULL)

4. Read the next line, which is `<number>`, and the following line, which is `<555.1212>`, and push them onto the stack. The stack is now

   (data, `555.1212`)
   (tag, `number`)
   (data, `John Smith`)
   (tag, `name`)
   (tag, `phonebook`)
   (NULL, NULL)

5. Read the next line, which is `</name>`. Since this is a closing tag, we pop the stack and acquire the pair (*data*, `555.1212`). Since this is data, we consume the

data and continue, which means that we pop the stack and acquire the pair (*tag*, `number`). This is the first nondata item we have popped, so we compare the contents `number` against the closing tag contents that we read. This is now comparing `number` against `name`, so we do not have a match. We know that the XML is not well formed, so we bail out with an appropriate exception message to the user.

The use of XML has become ubiquitous, so it is worthwhile for the reader to think about this example and to search the Web for further information. Common usage is for data to be stored as tagged XML, like the bibliographic data entry in Figure 7.5, with meaningful tag names. To make use of this data, the tagged XML data file is paired with a Document Type Definition (DTD) that "explains" which tags are legal and how to make use of them. There are many open-source and commercial packages that will read the data files and the corresponding DTD in order, for example, to present the data in a browser with formatting (type font and size, italics for book titles, etc.). For many years the standard example in a text for the use of a stack was reverse Polish notation, which was interesting but somewhat abstract. XML, in contrast, is very real throughout the computing industry, and versions or extensions of XML are found in many disciplines. Geographic information is encoded, for example, in KML, and a version of XML has been developed for text as part of the Text Encoding Initiative.

7.3 Queues

The stack is a LIFO data structure, with entries added and removed at one end of the stack. In contrast, a *queue* is a first-in-first-out (FIFO) structure that is similar to the way in which orders are managed in a fast-food restaurant or the way that normal checkout lines are managed in a retail store. Entries are added only at one end, called the `tail`, and are deleted only at the other end, called the `head`.

7.3.1 Queues Using Nodes

The simplest implementation (at least the conceptually simplest) of a queue is with a linked list in which data items are added to the structure only at the tail and removed from the list only at the head. Earlier in this chapter, we converted a linked list into a stack by wrapping the `addAtHead` method with code to create a `push` method, writing a specific method to unlink at the `head` and thus to serve as the `pop`, and adding (if they were not already there) the `isEmpty` and `peek` methods to simplify later programming tasks using the stack. Implementing a queue with a linked list underneath is an equally straightforward process, and the UML diagram for a `Queue` class could be as simple as that shown in Figure 7.8.

Queue
+head:DLLNode +tail:DLLNode
+Queue():void +dequeue():DLLNode +enqueue(DLLNode):void +isEmpty():boolean +peek():DLLNode

FIGURE 7.8 ■ The UML diagram for a `Queue` class.

Again, we encourage the reader to separate the traditional *concept* of a queue data structure from the *implementation* of a queue data structure. The concept of a queue is simple:

- Data items are added only at the tail.
- Data items are removed only at the head.
- The user is entitled to peek at the data item before removing it.
- A function exists to tell the user if there is nothing in the queue.

The UML diagram shows the queue as a concept. In implementation, we see that we can reuse code that has already been written, and nothing except a little wrapper code to rename methods is necessary. The `head` and the `tail` variables are identical to the variables of the same name in the underlying `DLL` class. Similar to the `push` for a stack, the `enqueue` method is just a wrapper that renames the method and passes through to what could be an `addBeforeTail` method. The `dequeue` can be code identical (again, except for wrapping a method to rename it) to the `pop` code of a stack and that is a specific version of an existing `unlink` method. The `isEmpty` and `peek` helper methods are the same as for the stack. If we treat an underlying linked list as the code that actually handles the data, the implementation for a queue is just another light layer of code that sits above the linked list.

As with linked lists in general and with stacks, in the case of a queue implemented using freestanding nodes, the issue of allocated space does not arise. We must check that we do not dequeue more nodes than we have enqueued (and we check this by calling `isEmpty`), but we can enqueue nodes essentially without worrying about space. If a program is overwhelmed by adding entries to a queue, then there will come a time when we run out of space and the *system* throws an out of space error, but this is a different kind of error. It would likely be caused in "finished" code by doing a supercomputer-sized application on a desktop or in the process of a programmer's testing because of a runaway loop. Or, perhaps, if one is using a queue to service Internet packet requests, then a denial-of-service attack will flood the server with packets and perhaps overload the available memory as the attacker probably intended. More "routine" use of memory for a queue, however, is unlikely to crash the system.

■ 7.3.2 Queues Using Arrays

A conceptual example of a queue in operation, using a linked list as the underlying structure, is shown in Figure 7.9.

Another conceptual view of a queue is as an array of potentially infinite length in one direction. Entries are added at the "right," and are removed from the "left," with the space between the **head** and **tail** pointers being the active window of the queue. A queue viewed as an array of infinite length, whose window of actively used

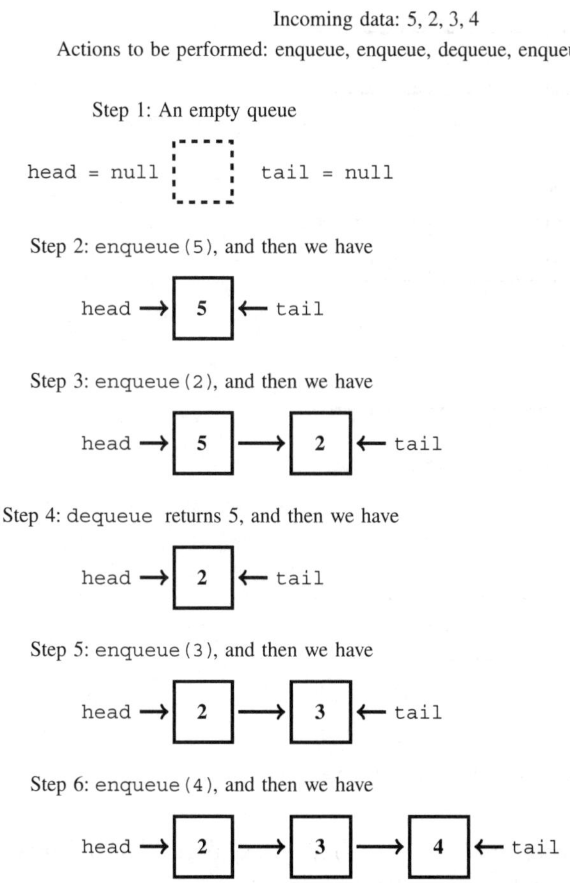

FIGURE 7.9 ■ A queue in operation.

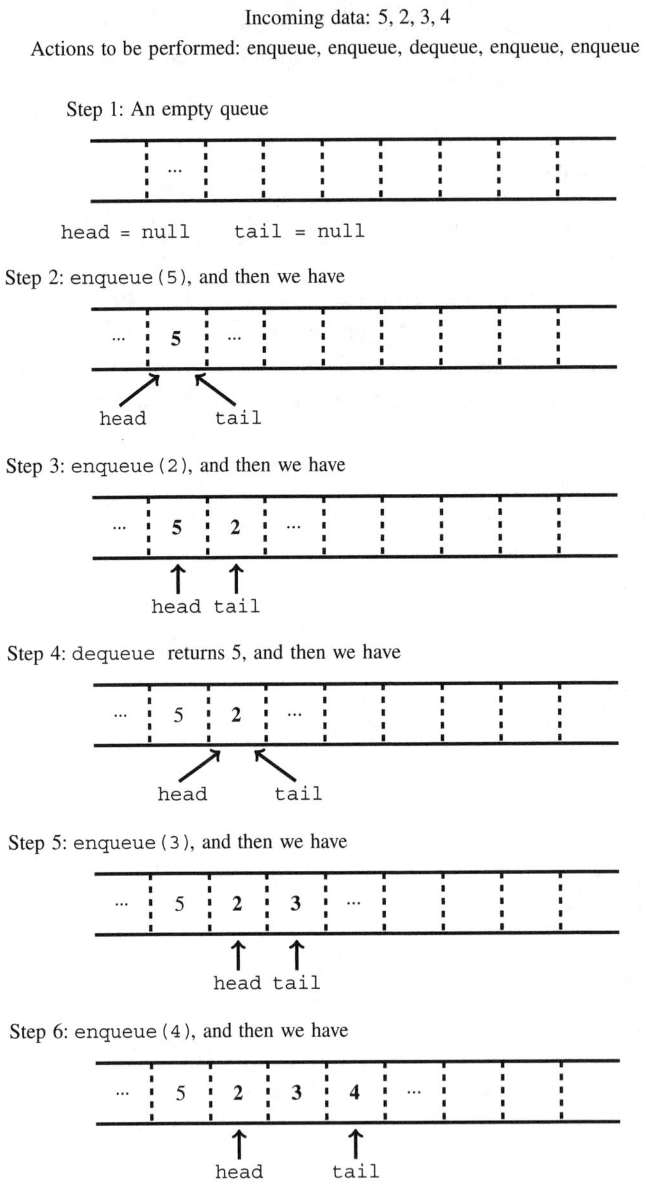

FIGURE 7.10 ■ A queue viewed as an array of infinite length.

locations shifts to the right, is shown in Figure 7.10. The in-use portion of the array simply moves off infinitely to the right as execution progresses.

Since objects of infinite size cannot be implemented in any computer, queues implemented using arrays have often used *circular* arrays that resemble the order ticket carousels in a restaurant. We preallocate an array of some fixed size, larger than we ever expect to need, and with `head` and `tail` pointers initially assigned as they would be if the array were of infinite length. Items are added to the queue at the tail, which "walks" around the circle, and are taken from the queue at the head.

Since an array in a computer cannot actually be set up as a circle, we must implement code to create the illusion of circularly organized space. Instead of using just the naive incrementing of the `top` pointer,

```
top = top + 1;
```

we make the subscripts wrap around using code similar to

```
top = (top + 1) % array.length;
```

As with any queue implementation, we must check that we do not remove any more elements than are in the queue (that is, that the `head` pointer does not walk beyond the `tail` pointer) and that we do not exceed the allocated space (that is, that the `tail` pointer does not walk beyond the `head` pointer).

A queue implemented as a circular array is shown in Figure 7.11. Except for the fact that we must test the size to ensure we have not run out of memory, and the

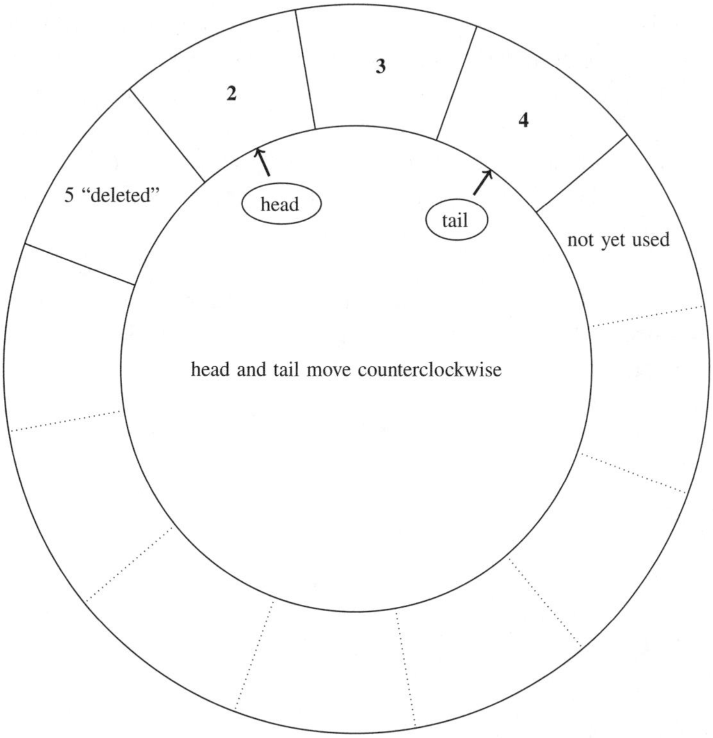

FIGURE 7.11 ■ A queue implemented as a circular array.

fact that our increment of head and tail subscripts works modulo `array.length`, this is really just the same thing as the (impossible) implementation that would use an infinite array.

7.4 The JCF Classes

7.4.1 The JCF Stack

We discussed in Chapter 5 the Java Collections Framework class `LinkedList`. Many of the data structures we discuss in this text are implemented in the JCF, and `Stack` and `Queue` are among them. It is worth looking at the differences between the JCF version of a stack and that shown in Figure 7.1. The JCF class has methods `empty`, `peek`, `pop`, `push`, and `search`.

The JCF `empty` method differs from our `isEmpty` only in the name. There is one school of thought in computing that argues that all boolean functions should begin with "is" to emphasize that their purpose is to answer a question. We have followed this style in this text, so reading a code fragment using our `isEmpty` method might look like the programmer is asking a question and the code resembles standard English, as shown in Figure 7.12. Although there may be no reason to believe that a casual reader would misunderstand the purpose of a method named `empty`, with the method name read as a verb and the purpose of the method being to empty the queue, we will stick with the "isX" convention for naming boolean methods like this one. All too often code is written that looks like that shown in Figure 7.13 and the `myQ.empty()` method was indeed a method that actually emptied a queue *and* returned a `boolean` value to say that the queue had been emptied. This kind of ambiguity should be avoided.

The `peek`, `pop`, and `push` methods have the same purpose as our methods of the same names. For completeness, we mention finally the `search` method, which returns the 1-based position of the object on the stack. This no doubt derives from the implementation heritage of the Java `Stack` as a subclass of `Vector`, an early version of `ArrayList`.

```
if(myQ.isEmpty())
{
  DO SOMETHING
}
else
{
  DO SOMETHING ELSE
}
```

FIGURE 7.12 ■ Code that reads like English.

```
if(myQ.empty())
{
  DO SOMETHING
}
else
{
  DO SOMETHING ELSE
}
```

FIGURE 7.13 ■ Code that could be ambiguous when read.

The primary difference between the JCF `Stack` and the stack as we have implemented it is that our methods explicitly refer to a stack of *nodes*, which we know contain data payloads. When our `pop` method executes, it returns a node, and we must issue yet one more method in order to return the data payload inside that node.

In contrast, the JCF versions of the structures are implemented with generics and iterators; the JCF `Stack` is constructed with a generic `E item` where we have used our `DLLNode node`. One could, of course, build a JCF-based stack by `Stack<DLLNode>`, and that would provide a structure that the programmer would view very much like that we have outlined with Figure 7.1. By building a JCF-based stack with `Stack<Record>`, the JCF is providing yet another layer of insulation between the concept of a stack and the implementation of a stack. The programmer sees a stack of data items, not a stack of nodes that each contain a data item. We discussed this earlier in Section 5.3.

On the other hand, if one wanted to implement a `Stack<DLLNode>` structure, the JCF stack would also work just fine, since it is implemented using generics and `DLLNode` is just as good an object as is `Record`. There are times when more than one access method is needed, so one can envision a situation in which nodes are pushed onto the stack but the nodes also permit some sort of "sideways" pointer to other nodes. (This kind of structure—a primary data structure with shortcuts or other pointers added that are not usually included in the primary structure—will show up later when we discuss trees.)

■ 7.4.2 The JCF `Queue`

The JCF `LinkedList` and `Stack` classes are easily recognizable as the same structures we have described in detail. What is likely harder for the inexperienced student to understand is the nature of the JCF `Queue`.

First off, we notice that `Queue`, per se, is not a class like `LinkedList` and `Stack` but instead is a Java interface. Unlike `LinkedList` and `Stack`, then, this requires a user-written class that implements `Queue` by including the methods required by `Queue`. These are at least moderately familiar, although they are different from what we have presented in Figure 7.8. Some of the reasons will be discussed momentarily; in brief, since the JCF `Queue` is not a finished product and a class by itself, but an interface intended to permit more general use of queue-like structures, there are more options required of the code that implements `Queue`.

Our class had methods `dequeue`, `enqueue`, `isEmpty`, and `peek`. The `Queue` interface requires that the programmer implement `add`, `element`, `offer`, `peek`, `poll`, and `remove`. All these methods have generic parameters similar to those of the `Stack` class. Since the parameters are defined by generics, it could be possible to pass a parameter of an invalid type or to pass a `NULL` parameter to a queue in which `NULL` was not a valid entry. All the `Queue` methods should throw exceptions for these kinds of actions.

In all instances, it is understood that the underlying structure that is implementing the `Queue` interface might be of fixed size (like a preallocated array), and thus all the `Queue` methods permit throwing exceptions or returning `false` if one is trying to add to an underlying structure that is already full.

The `isEmpty` method for `Queue` is present because it is inherited from the `java.util.Collection` interface. (Note that this method is named `isEmpty` and not just `empty`.)

Instead of an `enqueue` method, the `Queue` interface has two methods for adding data to the queue: `add` and `offer`. Both return a `boolean`. The difference between the two is that `add` returns `true` if the element can be added without overflowing the underlying storage but must throw an exception if the storage structure is already full. The `offer` method, in contrast, is preferred because although it will return `true` if the element is added to the queue, it will return `false` rather than throwing an exception if the element cannot be added due to capacity restrictions.

Instead of our `dequeue` method, the `Queue` interface has methods `poll` and `remove`. Both methods remove the element at the head of the queue and return the element. The `poll` and `remove` methods function analogously to `add` and `offer` in that `poll` returns `null` if the queue is empty, but the `remove` method simply throws an exception when the queue is empty.

Finally, instead of our single `peek` method, the `Queue` interface has methods `element` and `peek` that function in an analogous way to `poll` and `remove`. Both return the head element without deleting it if there is a valid head element; if the queue is empty and there is no element to return, `peek` returns `null` and `element` throws an exception.

Thus, `add`, `remove`, and `element` will throw exceptions if the storage limit is exceeded or the queue is empty, while `offer`, `poll`, and `peek` return either a `boolean` or `null`.

Another difference between using the interface and using the class is that type checking is done differently. When the `Stack` class is used in a program, an instance of a `Stack` is created with a line of code like `Stack<Record> myStack`, and all references to the `myStack` variable or to the `Stack` methods must conform to the requirement for parameters and returned values to be of type `Record`. This is something the compiler can check. There are no issues with space because the `Stack` class is assumed to take care of such things.

In contrast, the programmer must implement the `Queue` interface using some underlying data structure for storage. Since the interface is silent on the underlying storage structure, the programmer must be prepared to include code that checks for size constraints.

7.4.3 Stacks, Queues, and Deques

Perhaps the major difference between the JCF `Stack` class and the `Queue` interface is that the `Stack` is old, by Java standards, and adheres to traditional notions of what a stack ought to be, while the JCF `Queue` interface is actually much more general than what we have described as a queue in Section 7.3. The Java documentation describes a queue as "a collection designed for holding elements prior to processing" that typically but not necessarily orders elements in a FIFO fashion. The closest implemented JCF class to the traditional queue that we have described is the Java `ArrayDeque` class.

A *deque*, pronounced "deck," is a "double-ended queue," a list structure in which insertions and deletions can be made at either end but only at the ends. The JCF `ArrayDeque` class implements both the `Queue` interface and the `Deque` subinterface of `Queue`. As a JCF class, it subsumes `LinkedList` and `Stack` as well as provides a class that can be used as a queue. The penalty paid for using `ArrayDeque` is complexity; because the structure can be used as a double-ended queue, the `ArrayDeque` class has, for example, `addFirst` and `addLast` methods, as well as a queue `add` method that does the same thing as `addLast`. Similarly, the `offer`, `peek`, `poll`, and `remove` methods each occur in triplicate. The `addFirst` and `addLast` methods are required by the `Deque` interface, and the `add` method is required by the `Queue` interface.

Consistent with the Java documentation suggesting that `ArrayDeque` should be used instead of the older `Stack` class, the `ArrayDeque` class has the stack methods `pop` and `push`. Finally, the `ArrayDeque` class has methods for traversing the structure and dealing with entries that are not at the head or the tail. Taken together, the `ArrayDeque` is extremely useful, but the programmer who uses this class should probably exercise some self-discipline when using the methods. If it is intended that a stack be implemented, then only the base methods for a stack should be used. If a queue is intended, then only the base queue methods should be used. Otherwise, the resulting code could easily be misunderstood by a subsequent reader of the code.

7.5 Priority Queues

One of the major features of linked lists, stacks, and queues is that they accommodate dynamic data; that is, they provide structures that grow and shrink as data is added to them and taken from them.

The basic queue structure allows one to add data items onto the back end of a queue and to take them off the front, providing a first-in-first-out, or FIFO, processing order. Let us add another constraint: we want to be able to add items dynamically and to keep them ordered according to some priority value so that when we remove an item, the item we remove is always the item of highest priority in the current list. This scenario is similar to what needs to happen in an operating system as entries are added to the list of tasks to be performed and some new entries might have a higher priority than those already being executed.

A structure like this is called a *priority queue*. In this sort of queue, entries would always be added at the tail and always removed at the head, but the additional constraint is that some kind of ordering process occurs to ensure that the entry at the head is the entry of highest priority.

This structure can certainly be achieved with an ordinary queue with an insertionsort when items are added; when an item is added, we pull it forward in the queue until it is in its proper place in the sorted list. This method will work, but it will inherently take on average $O(N/2)$ steps, or linear time, to add an item and to recreate the state of being sorted. For a queue of active processes in an operating system, this would be excessively slow because a queue with an insertionsort does more work than is really needed.

The queue with an insertionsort keeps *all* the records in sorted order *all* the time. We have not asked for all the items to be sorted, only that the largest, or highest priority, item is at the head. What we would like to have is a mechanism that will

- efficiently (that is, faster than the linear time of a naive insertionsort[3]) rebuild the structure after the head is removed so that the next-highest-priority item is located at the head for the next removal; and
- efficiently (again, faster than linear time) insert a new entry into the structure so that the new structure, one larger than before, still has the property that the head is the item of highest priority.

7.5.1 The Heap

The structure that is commonly used for this purpose—that has as its head the item of highest priority and that allows the structure to be rebuilt in $O(\lg N)$ time

[3]You should remember that early on in this book we said that we would be dealing with ideas that would allow you to implement more sophisticated algorithms to replace the naive ones and to get improved performance as a result. This is one of those ideas.

and not $O(N)$ time—is the *heap*. The heap is more efficient than an insertionsort in large part because it does less work than an insertionsort. When an item is added in a list and an insertionsort is used to insert the item in its correct order, a *total order* is produced, with every element larger than all those farther down in the list. If our goal is only to be able to pull off the item with highest priority, we don't need a total order. Instead, we need only ensure that the item of highest priority is at the head. The priority queue maintains only this weaker property, and thus can be maintained with less work.

Consider an array of numbers `array[*]`. For convenience, because the algorithm is simpler to state, we shall consider the array to be indexed 1-up instead of the usual 0-up numbering of Java.[4] The array is said to *satisfy the max-heap property* and thus to be a *max-heap* if for all items `array[i]` indexed 1 to N we have

```
array[i] >= array[2*i]
```

and

```
array[i] >= array[2*i+1],
```

for all subscripts `i` for which the subscripts on the right-hand sides are valid for the given array length. (We could define a *min-heap* in the obvious analogous way.)

An example of an array with the max-heap property is given in Figure 7.14. Since it is not totally obvious that this is a heap just from glancing at subscripts and values, we also present, in Figure 7.15, a pictorial view of the same heap as a *tree* structure. In the tree representation, we have put the subscripts in brackets. (We will have a great deal more to say about trees later, including an entire chapter.)

This picture of the heap as a tree is clearly easier to understand than is the array in subscript order. We are going to be using tree structures extensively because they provide useful ways to visualize some important data structures. All trees are formed from *nodes* (the circles) and *arcs* (the lines). (An *arc* is also called an *edge* and we will use the two terms interchangeably.) Contrary to the usual way in which a tree is viewed, computer scientists usually write trees as in Figure 7.15 with the *root node* at the top (in this case, the node subscripted 1 and with value 104) and the rest of the tree hanging down from the root instead of growing up from the root. Nodes may have one or more *children*; these are the nodes immediately below a given node and connected to the given node by an arc. A tree for which no node has more than two children is called a *binary tree*. The tree in Figure 7.15 is a

[4]It can be argued that most of the time things are easier to express if one does indexing 0-up. In this case, however, indexing 1-up makes the subscript calculation much simpler. Indeed, one can probably justify just not using the subscript-0 data location and wasting that small amount of space in order to gain the benefits of the simpler arithmetic in the code.

Subscript	Value
1	104
2	93
3	76
4	17
5	82
6	65
7	71
8	13
9	2
10	71
11	69
12	63
13	61
14	70

FIGURE 7.14 ■ An example of an array that is a max-heap.

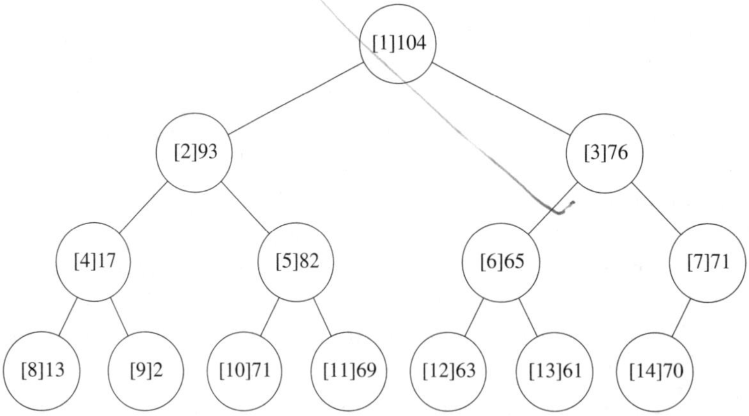

FIGURE 7.15 ■ A tree structure for a heap, with $[node]value$ entries.

binary tree. If the missing entry (that would be subscript 15) were there, it would be a *complete binary tree*; as it is, the tree is an *incomplete* binary tree.

Given the picture of the tree in Figure 7.15, and with the subscript labeling as indicated, the criterion for a tree to represent a max-heap is that the value at any given node is greater than or equal to the values at the child nodes.

In this case, 104 for subscript 1 is larger than the values 93 and 76 for subscripts 2 and 3, 93 for subscript 2 is larger than 17 or 82 at subscripts 4 and 5, and so forth. Since the value at each node in the tree is larger than the values of any of the children, the tree satisfies the heap property.

By the transitivity of "greater-than-or-equal to," and since the tree is a heap, we also know that 104 is the largest value in the entire structure, even though we do not know what the total sorted order of the array is.

Clearly, then, if we have an array that is organized as a max-heap, the largest value in the array is at subscript 1 in the root node of the tree.

To show that the heap provides a better structure for maintaining a priority queue than a queue with insertionsort, we must show that a priority queue can be created and maintained faster than by using an insertionsort. First we must know what we are comparing against. Given N records, an insertionsort will require $O(N^2)$ comparisons in order to create a sorted list. Although each entry could now be removed in sorted order, we want to consider a priority queue as a dynamic structure with new entries coming in as time progresses. Think of the queue of ready processes in an operating system; with every mouse click the user could be spawning new tasks to be added to the list of processes to be executed. Inserting these new processes would require on average $N/2$ further comparisons. A priority queue implemented as a sorted list with an insertionsort thus has a linear cost.

Since what we are doing is essentially a type of sorting, the unit of computation that we must count is the comparison of two entries. Instead of the linear time cost of an insertionsort-based method, we can prove two features of the priority queue implemented using a heap:

1. A priority queue of N items can be created from scratch in $O(N \lg N)$ comparisons.
2. Inserting one more item into a priority queue of N items can be done with $O(\lg N)$ comparisons in steady state.

There does exist an $O(N)$ algorithm for creating a heap (to be used in a priority queue or in some other application) from N data items. We will present instead an $O(N \lg N)$ algorithm that is simpler. Although it is nice to know that a faster algorithm exists for creating the heap, most uses of a priority queue will eventually require $O(N \lg N)$ comparisons anyway, so the benefit of the faster creation is lost in a real application. What is critically important for our use of a heap as a priority queue is that we have an algorithm to rebuild the heap in $O(\lg N)$ time after we extract the maximal element from the heap.

If we count the building of the heap as one-time work, as would be the case for an operating system's creating at boot time a queue of processes capable of being executed, then the priority queue implemented with a heap is a structure with an acceptable running time for maintaining a priority queue of data items.

7.5.2 Creating a Heap

Theorem 7.1

An array recs[i] of N numerical values can be converted into a heap in $O(N \lg N)$ time.

Proof Our proof is constructive: we present an algorithm that will create a heap from N data items and require $O(N \lg N)$ comparisons between values stored in nodes.

Given that we have loaded instances of data of Record type into an array of data records recs[*] indexed 1-up, we run the following loop

```
for(int i = 1; i < this.getNumElts(); ++i)
{
  this.fixHeapUp(i);
}
```

with the fixHeapUp method shown in Figure 7.16. If the length of the loop this.getNumElts() is N, and fixHeapUp runs (as we will claim) in $O(\lg N)$ time on an array of N items, then the running time of this code fragment is $O(N \lg N)$.

```
public void fixHeapUp(int insertSub)
{
  int parentSub;
  ProcessRecord insertRec;

  insertRec = this.theData.get(insertSub);
  parentSub = insertSub/2;
  while(1 < insertSub)
  {
    if(this.theData.get(parentSub).compareTo(insertRec) < 0)
    {
      this.swap(insertSub, parentSub);

      insertSub = parentSub;
      insertRec = this.theData.get(insertSub);
      parentSub = insertSub/2;
    }
    else
      break;
  }
} // public void fixHeapUp(int insertSub)
```

FIGURE 7.16 The fixHeapUp code.

We must now show that in any call to the `fixHeapUp` method in Figure 7.16, we make at most $\lg N$ comparisons. If there are N items in the list, then the value of `insertSub` is at most N in any given call. In the first comparison we compute `parentSub` as `insertSub/2`, and in the second comparison we assign that as the new running value of `insertSub`, and continue. With each comparison, then, we cut the value of `insertSub` in half until eventually we have `1 > insertSub` in the test in the `while` statement and we break out of the loop. Since we start with `insertSub` no larger than N, and we divide by 2 with each iteration and comparison, then in the worst case of any call to the `fixHeapUp` method we require at most $O(\lg N)$ comparisons. What the `fixHeapUp` method does is to bubble the entry at the "end" of the array (or `ArrayList`) into its proper position in a heap. □

We note that this method requires a comparison method `compareTo` that returns −1, 0, or 1 depending on whether the data in the `this` record is less than, equal to, or greater than the data value passed in as an argument. But we are accustomed to this as a standard method for nearly any data payload.

The reason for our original decision to subscript 1-up should be clear now from the tree representation of the heap and from the code in Figure 7.16. By subscripting 1-up we take advantage of the nature of integer division in Java (and most other languages) to get simpler, cleaner code. Certainly one could rewrite the property and the algorithm to run 0-up, but the convenience of integer division to get the subscript of the parent item would be lost.

We also note that this same `fixHeapUp` method easily allows for dynamic additions to the heap. If we add an item to the heap at the end of the array and then call `fixHeapUp`, the element will percolate up to its proper location in the heap, taking at most $O(\lg N)$ comparisons in the process.

An example of converting into a heap an initially random array, viewed as a binary tree structure, is presented in Figures 7.17–7.19. In each step the colored values are compared and then swapped if they are out of order and the nodes in the array that are included in the current heap are outlined in bold. Our outer loop runs from array subscript 1 up through subscript N.

7.5.3 Maintaining the Heap

The `fixHeapUp` method takes $\lg N$ time, and when applied to an array of N items, converts in $O(N \lg N)$ time an array into an array that can also be read as a heap using the subscripting in Figure 7.14. This in itself would not be all that useful. What is useful is the following little bit of almost-magic that allows us to use the heap as a priority queue as a dynamic data structure. It takes $O(N \lg N)$ time to create the heap *ab initio* for N nodes or data items; after that, in steady state, we can remove the maximum value (the value of highest priority), add a new data item, and recreate the heap in only $O(\lg N)$ comparisons.

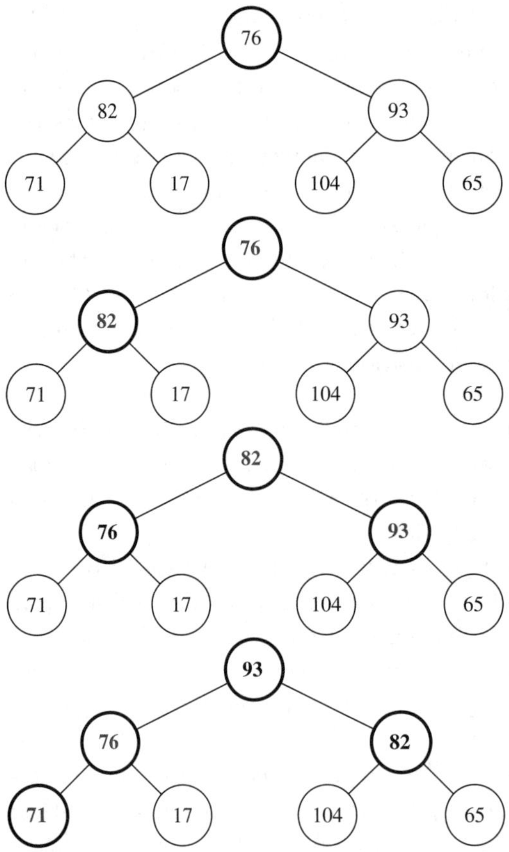

FIGURE 7.17 ■ Building a heap from an array, part 1.

■ **Theorem 7.2**

The root node of the heap contains the element whose data payload has the maximal value of the entire array, and we can remove that element and recreate the heap structure in $O(\lg N)$ time.

Proof Let us assume that we have first created a heap. We now extract the maximal value in the entire array. This leaves a vacancy at the root, and our array ought to be one shorter than the array we started with. We accommodate this by moving the *last* element, originally stored at location N but in steady state stored at location `array.length-1`, into the root node. This element is probably out of place, but we

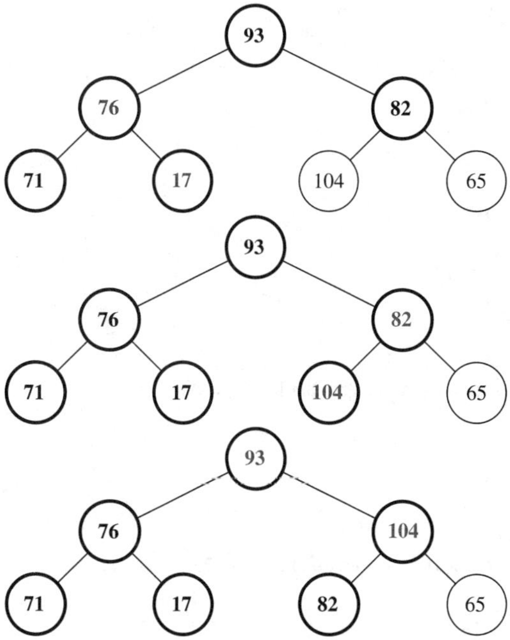

FIGURE 7.18 ■ Building a heap from an array, part 2.

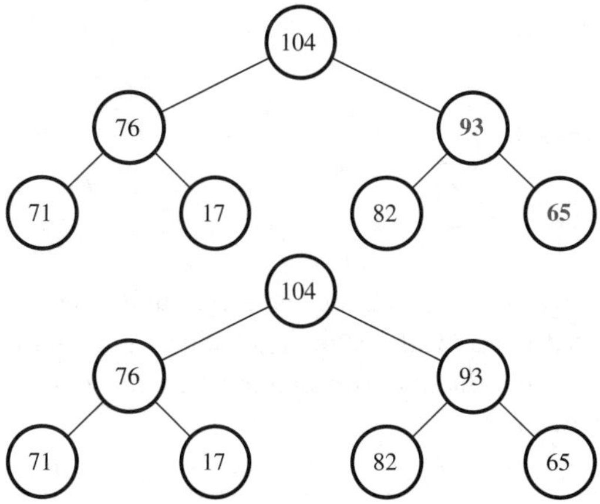

FIGURE 7.19 ■ Building a heap from an array, part 3.

can now run `fixHeapDown` (Figure 7.20) to push that element down into its proper place in the new array. The `fixHeapDown` method also takes the same $O(\lg N)$ time as does `fixHeapUp` and differs from `fixHeapUp` mostly in that it takes two comparisons at each level and not one. In `fixHeapUp`, if the left child, say, is larger

```
public void fixHeapDown(int insertSub)
{
  int largerChild, leftChild, rightChild;

  leftChild = 2*insertSub;
  rightChild = 2*insertSub + 1;

  while(this.getSize() > leftChild)
  {
    largerChild = leftChild;
    if(this.getSize() > rightChild)
    {
      if(this.theData.get(leftChild).
                compareTo(this.theData.get(rightChild)) < 0)
      {
        largerChild = rightChild;
      }
    }
    if(this.theData.get(insertSub).
              compareTo(this.theData.get(largerChild)) < 0)
    {
      this.swap(insertSub, largerChild);
      insertSub = largerChild;
      leftChild = 2*insertSub;
      rightChild = 2*insertSub + 1;
    }
    else
      break;
  }
} // public void fixHeapDown(int insertSub)
```

FIGURE 7.20 ■ The `fixHeapDown` code.

than the parent, then it must also be larger than its sibling the right child because we had started with a heap to begin with. In **fixHeapDown**, we must make sure to put the largest of the three elements (parent and two children) in the parent location in order to maintain the heap property. □

■ 7.6 Summary

We have in this chapter introduced the concept of a stack and presented multiple ways in which a stack can be implemented. This includes the use of the built-in Java **Stack** construct. We have similarly introduced the concept of a queue together with ways in which a queue can be implemented. This includes the Java `Queue` construct, which implements much more than the basic version of a queue as we have presented it.

As examples, we have looked at the processing of HTML or XML data, which has explicit open–close tags that label the data lying between the tags. With the explosion of data and applications on the Web, stack processing of data tagged with a markup language has become a significant basic feature of much of modern computing.

We also looked at reverse Polish notation. In processing RPN, the stack structure makes the explicit tags of a markup language unnecessary. Although not so common any more, many computers were originally built physically as stack-based machines.

Finally we presented the priority queue, used everywhere for keeping track of dynamic task data for which "the most important" task must be processed next. The priority queue, implemented with a heap, is one of the key data structures due to its simplicity and efficiency for handling such computational problems.

7.7 Exercises

1. Finish the implementation of a stack by packaging up the existing linked list code and finishing off the methods from the UML diagram in Figure 7.1 and the code stubs in Figure 7.2.
2. Implement a queue, following the lead of Figure 7.8 and the code of the previous exercise.
3. Improve the code of one or both of the previous exercises to use generics instead of the `Record` class as the data payload.
4. Implement a stack or a queue using the `LinkedList` structure from the Java Collections Framework.
5. Use your stack code from the first exercise and write a class that will parse an XML file to determine whether or not it is well formed.
6. Use the JCF `Stack` class and write a class that will parse an XML file to determine whether or not it is well formed.
7. Rewrite either of your XML-parsing programs to process the XML tag–data pairs as a separate class.
8. Use any stack code and write a class that will parse arithmetic expressions in RPN and evaluate them.
9. Use the JCF `ArrayDeque` class and write a class that implements a stack to parse an XML file to determine whether or not it is well formed. You should use only the methods in Figure 7.1.

10. Implement a `myQueue` class as described in the text by wrapping the `ArrayDeque` class and its methods so that the public methods of `myQueue` are named as in Figure 7.8 but call the methods from `ArrayDeque`.
11. Finish off the implementation of a priority queue. Read in a collection of random numbers (25 or so, which will be enough for you to notice patterns and will also guarantee that you get the not-power-of-two fencepost problems handled properly). Then extract the elements in priority order, rebuilding the heap each time. What have you been able to do with this? (We will do more on this in Chapter 11.)

8 Recursion

Objectives

- An introduction to the concept of recursion
- Examples of recursively defined functions, such as factorials, the Fibonacci sequence, the "$3n + 1$ function," and the Ackermann function
- Use of recursion in program code, including binary divide-and-conquer algorithms
- Recursion for computing permutations and combinations
- Recursion for gaming and search tree computation
- Dealing with memory use in recursion

Key Terms

$3n + 1$ problem	context	recursive
Ackermann function	Fibonacci sequence	Syracuse problem
binary search	heuristic	
Collatz problem	objective function	

Introduction

The concept of recursion is central to computer science. A standard way to solve a complex problem is to break it down into smaller problems and then to solve the complex problem by solving the smaller problems. In essence, recursion is a variation on this common approach, a variation in which the smaller problems are in fact just smaller versions of the original problems. Most modern programming languages, including Java, support recursion and, although the specifics of implementation may differ from one language to the next, the concepts used in recursion are independent of the programming language.

8.1 Factorials and Fibonacci Numbers

A *recursive* algorithm, function, or program is one that calls, that is, invokes, itself. Two of the classic examples of functions that can (or should) be defined recursively are the Fibonacci sequence and the factorial function.

The *Fibonacci sequence* of integers is

$$1, 1, 2, 3, 5, 8, 13, 21, 34, 55, \ldots$$

The nth Fibonacci number F_n is defined by

$$F_n = F_{n-1} + F_{n-2}$$

subject to the base conditions

$$F_1 = 1, \quad F_0 = 1.$$

We are more familiar with the *factorial function* $N!$. This can be written in a nonrecursive way as

$$N! = N \cdot (N-1) \cdot \cdots \cdot (2) \cdot 1$$

or it can be written as

$$N! = N \cdot (N-1)!$$

subject to the base condition

$$0! = 1.$$

Recursion is often the best way to describe a computation. In the case of the Fibonacci sequence, there is a closed form solution that can be worked out algebraically, but the recursive formula is conceptually much clearer.

In both cases, and in defining functions recursively, there are two parts to the definition.

- First, we define what is in effect the steady-state function, such as

  $$N! = N \cdot (N-1)!.$$

  In this part of the definition, we define the function for parameter N in terms of the function when given smaller input parameters ($N-1$ in the case of factorial and both $N-1$ and $N-2$ in the case of the Fibonacci sequence).
- Second (and this is the part most often omitted in error or incorrectly specified), we define the base condition that allows us to know when to stop the recursion. For the factorial function, this is the base condition that $0! = 1$. The factorial function is a single-step recursion, so we need one base condition. Since the Fibonacci sequence is defined as two-step recursion, we need to specify the base case for both 0 and 1.

Note that we could produce (almost) the same sequence by starting with any two consecutive values as our base case for the Fibonacci sequence. For example, if we define $F(0) = 0$ and $F(1) = 1$, we get the sequence $0, 1, 1, 2, 3, 5, 8, 13, 21, 34, \ldots$, but if we define the base cases $F(0) = 3$ and $F(1) = 5$, we get the sequence $3, 5, 8, 13, 21, 34, \ldots$, which is the same sequence except that it skips the initial values. We can also produce Fibonacci-like sequences by applying the same recursion but with different base cases. For example, with $F(0) = 2$ and $F(1) = 1$, we get the sequence $2, 1, 3, 4, 7, 11, 18, 29, 47, \ldots$. This is called the *Lucas sequence*, after the French mathematician Edouard Lucas. In general, such sequences are called *linear second order recurrences*, with "linear" meaning that the $F(N)$ terms appear in the recurrence as polynomial terms to the first degree and "second order" referring to the fact that we need two consecutive values in the base case in order to define the sequence uniquely.

8.2 The Collatz Problem

The Fibonacci sequence is a well-behaved sequence that is quite naturally defined recursively, although it is also possible to work the algebra through to a closed form for Fibonacci numbers. In both the factorial and the Fibonacci sequence, computation of $N!$ or of $F(N)$ is a deterministic process. To compute $N!$ recursively requires exactly N function calls, each of which operates on successively smaller parameter values. Computing $F(N)$ recursively is slightly more complicated but still deterministic. One can show that

$$F(N) = \frac{1}{\sqrt{5}}\left[\left(\frac{1+\sqrt{5}}{2}\right)^N - \left(\frac{1-\sqrt{5}}{2}\right)^N\right].$$

We won't prove this, not because it is hard (it's only high school algebra) but because it is off the topic of this book.

A different function that is also defined recursively but whose computation is not (yet) known to be a deterministic process is the function for the *Collatz problem*, also called the *$3n + 1$ problem* or the *Syracuse problem*. We define a function that can be iterated as follows.

$$\begin{aligned} C(n) &= 3n+1 && \text{if } n \text{ is odd} \\ &= n/2 && \text{if } n \text{ is even.} \end{aligned}$$

Unlike most recursive functions, in which we know the behavior of the function involved, this particular function happens to be the study of some open questions in research. For all values of n for which $C(n)$ has ever been computed, the function eventually iterates down to the value 1. However, it has never been proved that iteration of this function always results eventually in 1, nor has there ever been a really good result on how many iterations are necessary before 1 is reached. Powers of 2 clearly iterate down to 1 immediately. On the other hand, $C(27)$ takes 111 steps to reach 1, and the high-water marks for $n < 10^8$ and for $n < 10^9$ are 63,728,127 and 670,617,279, respectively. Although no real use has been found for this mathematical curiosity, it remains an interesting example of a function that is very easy to define, and defined recursively, but which as yet cannot be completely analyzed and cannot be described except recursively.

8.3 Greatest Common Divisor

Yet another mathematical function that has a computationally simple formulation using recursion is the *greatest common divisor*, or *gcd*. The greatest common divisor of two integers n and m is the largest positive integer g such that both n/g and m/g are integers. We write $g = \gcd(m, n)$. The simplest algorithm for calculating the gcd is the *Euclidean algorithm.* The description of the Euclidean algorithm in Euclid's *Elements* is perhaps the earliest written description in history of an algorithm as we know it, and although there are slightly more sophisticated ways to compute the gcd, the standard method using the Euclidean algorithm has been virtually unchanged for more than two millennia.

Euclid's algorithm relies on two simple theorems that we will not prove.

Lemma 8.1
Given positive integers m and n, we can write $m = q \cdot n + r$, with q and r positive integers and r satisfying $0 \leq r < n$.

Lemma 8.2
Given positive integers m and n, with $m = q \cdot n + r$ as in Lemma 8.1, then $\gcd(m, n) = \gcd(r, n)$.

Computationally, we recognize q in the preceding lemmas as due to the rules of integer division in Java, `m/n`, and we recognize r as `m % n`. This means that we can define the gcd recursively (ignoring error conditions) as

$$\gcd(m, n) = \gcd(n, m\%n)$$

and we are guaranteed that with the second call to the gcd function the second argument is smaller than the first argument, and with succeeding calls the arguments are continually getting smaller. Because the arguments are getting smaller with each recursive call, the recursion must eventually terminate. A Java method for the gcd follows. The first lines of this method ensure that it works for positive and negative integers (the convention is that the gcd is always positive, even of two negative integers) and that we do not inadvertently call the method with a zero second argument. If the first argument m is zero, the gcd is n. If both arguments are zero, then technically the gcd should be infinity, which we indicate symbolically (there is no integer infinity in Java, so the value returned by calling the method with two zero arguments would have to be defined by convention). We use as the base case the point at which the remainder n is zero, at which point we return the other argument m.

```
public int gcd(int m, int n)
{
  m = Math.abs(m);
  n = Math.abs(n);
  if(0 == n)
  {
    if(0 == m)
    {
      return INFINITY;
    }
    else
    {
      return m;
    }
  }
  else if(0 == (m % n))
  {
    return n;
  }
  else
  {
    return gcd(n, m % n);
  }
}
```

8.4 The Ackermann Function

Another function that is defined recursively, and which *does have* a history in computer science, is the *Ackermann function*. There are in fact several variants of the original Ackermann function, which was used as an example in the early days of computability theory, but the one most commonly known in computer science is defined as a recursion on two variables as shown in Figure 8.1.

$$\begin{aligned} A(m,n) &= n+1 && \text{if } m=0 \\ &= A(m-1,1) && \text{if } m>0 \text{ and } n=0 \\ &= A(m-1, A(m,n-1)) && \text{if } m>0 \text{ and } n>0 \end{aligned}$$

FIGURE 8.1 ■ The formulas defining the Ackermann function.

The real study of the Ackermann function is limited to the theory of computing, but the function is a common example in introductory texts in computer science. It is a function that is very easy to specify and write a program for, but it grows very rapidly even for small values of m and n. The code required is very simple, but only the very smallest values can be computed because there is no nonrecursive definition of the function and yet a recursive program will run out of memory for all but the smallest inputs. Indeed, $A(3,3)$ requires more than 3000 method invocations before returning the value 61, and $A(4,2)$ is an integer nearly 20,000 decimals in length.

8.5 Binary Divide-and-Conquer Algorithms

We can also define in a recursive way a divide-and-conquer algorithm for *binary search*. In our earlier definition of binary search, we compared the key to be searched for with the midpoint element in an array, determining whether the item would be found in the first half or the second half of the array, and then we repeated the process. Our iterative (and thus nonrecursive) program was essentially the following.

```
set lower and upper subscript bounds
while(lower < upper)
{
  midpoint = (lower + upper)/2
  compare the search key K against the midpoint
  if(f(lower) < f(midpoint) < K < f(upper))
  {
    lower = midpoint
  }
  else if(f(lower) < K < f(midpoint) < f(upper))
  {
    upper = midpoint
  }
}
```

This is a common way to write a method that works iteratively but which also can be converted to a recursive version. In this iterative version, we shift pointers inside a loop. Done as a recursive computation, we could use the following pseudocode, where we write

```
a[beginning_subscript ... ending_subscript]
```

to indicate the subarray of an array `a[.]` from subscripts `beginning_subscript` inclusively through `ending_subscript`.

```
public int binary_search(array_to_be_searched)
{
  if(array length is 1)
  {
    compare the search key K against the single element
    set return_value if a match
  }
  else
  {
    midpoint = (lower + upper)/2
    if(K < f(midpoint))
    {
      array_to_be_searched = array_to_be_searched[1 ... midpoint]
    }
    else if(f(midpoint) < K)
    {
      array_to_be_searched = array_to_be_searched[midpoint ... end]
    }
    call binary_search(array_to_be_searched)
  }
  return return_value
}
```

In the recursive version, rather than shifting pointers into the array (or `ArrayList`), we package up the appropriate lower half or upper half of the array and then call the same method with that half of the array as the parameter. Since the array length is cut in half each time, we know that an array of length N can be searched with at most $\lg N$ calls to the method.

8.6 Permutations and Combinations

The factorial, Fibonacci, and gcd functions are standard functions used in explaining recursion, but they don't come up much in practical computing problems.

Similarly, the Collatz problem is fascinating (because it is so simple and yet so little progress has been made in answering the question of whether it always terminates with a 1), but this problem is really a problem in pure mathematics. The Ackermann function similarly, although it has been useful in theoretical computer science, is not something that has found its way into practical issues central to computation in the real world.

In contrast, a computation that does come up in the real world, and that can and should be defined recursively if possible, is the generation of the *permutations* or *combinations* of a list of items. A rank-ordering of preferences of N items, for example, can occur in $N!$ ways because any of the possible rank orderings could occur. It frequently happens in specifying requirements for a computation that one must generate permutations and combinations of options if only in order to test that one's software works for all possible sets of input values.

One puzzle-level problem that when attacked naively is a permutation problem is the Jumble puzzle from the newspaper, in which readers are given anagrams of five- and six-letter words and asked to come up with the English words made up of those letters. Given the letters "celos," for example, one would be expected to come up with the word "close."

A naive method for solving the Jumble puzzle is to generate all the permutations of the list of letters, that is, all the five-letter (or six-letter) rearrangements of the given letters used without replacement. These putative words could then be looked up (using binary search of course) in a dictionary of English words. The naive solution to the Jumble puzzle is to treat the letters as a mathematical set of N letters. We start with a "word" `word` initialized to the null string and then call a permutation-generation method, passing in the set of letters and the current value of `word`.

The method runs a loop over all N possible starting letters. In each iteration of this loop we pick one letter from the set, assign that letter as the next letter in the word by concatenating the letter onto the current value of `word`, remove the chosen letter from the set, and then recursively call the method, passing in as parameters the new set (one smaller than before) and the new partially constructed `word`, one letter longer than before. The base case occurs when there are no more letters in the set, at which point we return `word` as constructed.

The recursive process for generating the permutations is shown in Figure 8.2, where we generate all possible permutations from the list of three letters $\{e, h, t\}$. In the first step, we choose a first letter, e, add the e to the partial permutation we have created, remove e from the list of unused letters, and call the method recursively. The method chooses a letter (the second letter), choosing the first entry in the list, h, adding it to the partial permutation, deleting the h from the list of unused letters, and calling the method recursively. The third letter is now chosen, and we have the three-letter word made up of the three letters in their original sequence order 123.

Action	Partial	Unused	Numerical Permutation
choose first letter	e	h t	
choose second letter	e h	t	
choose third letter	e h t		123
put back third letter	e h	t	
put back second letter	e	h t	
choose second letter	e t	h	
choose third letter	e t h		132
put back third letter	e t	h	
put back second letter	e	h t	
put back first letter		e h t	
choose first letter	h	e t	
choose second letter	h e	t	
choose third letter	h e t		213
put back third letter	h e	t	
put back second letter	h	e t	
choose second letter	h t	e	
choose third letter	h t e		231
put back third letter	h t	e	
put back second letter	h	e t	
put back first letter		e h t	
choose first letter	t	e h	
choose second letter	t e	h	
choose third letter	t e h		312
put back third letter	t e	h	
put back second letter	t	e h	
choose second letter	t h	e	
choose third letter	t h e		321
put back third letter	t h	e	
put back second letter	t	e h	
put back first letter		e h t	

FIGURE 8.2 ■ Generating permutations recursively.

At this point, when the method is called we have no more choices to make, and we must return from the recursion, putting letters back, until we reach a point when we can choose again. This only happens after we put back the second letter, h, and can now choose as our second letter the t that we did not choose the first time through.

And so forth. Note that we must maintain the context of where we are in the recursion. For example, when we get to the second time we choose a second letter, we need to know to choose the t and not to choose the h again.

Generating permutations is an important process, but it is also a computationally expensive process because there are $N!$ permutations on N distinct letters. We can choose the first letter of our word in N ways. We have $N-1$ letters remaining, so we can choose a second letter in sequence in $N-1$ ways. We remove the second letter from our set, so we now have $N-2$ ways to choose a third letter, and so on. For a set with N letters, then, we can come up with $N!$ possible permutations. Since this grows multiplicatively with N, we can very quickly exhaust the computational power of even a supercomputer. A number as simple as 20! is already more than 100 times greater than the number of nanoseconds in a year. Current CPU speeds are measured in small gigahertz values. Executing instructions at a 1GHz clock speed is the same as executing instructions at one per nanosecond. If our computer ran at 1GHz and could generate permutations at one permutation per instruction (this is clearly impossible, but it puts us into a rough ballpark of computation cost), we would need about 100 computers running for a year just to enumerate the possible permutations on 20 letters. If one had a situation in which all 20! permutations were possible, then clearly a brute force exhaustion would likely be infeasible, but it frequently happens that exhaustion over smaller sizes is needed.

The code for a recursive generation of permutations is shown in Figure 8.3. We have chosen in this method not to actually do anything with the permutations except to generate them and print them out. In reality, there is no clear action that would be taken with a list of permutations. If the goal is simply solving the Jumble puzzle, then one will be given only five- and six-letter input sets, and there will be only 120 or 720 lines of output, which is manageable but tedious. In a more serious application, though, in which one might be generating permutations of 20 inputs, there are too many results to be printed out or displayed for human reading. What we do with the permutations at the point where this method prints them out will depend, then, on the application. In this case, for demonstration purposes, we can just print them out and verify that we get the right number and that the output lines are, as they should be, all distinct.

8.7 Gaming and Searching Applications

Another significant use of recursion is in game and search applications.

Consider, for example, a program for chess. At any given point in the game, a program playing White will know the status of the board and pieces and will have some numerical goodness values for the overall status of both White and Black. In theory, then, the program would consider every possible move that White could

```
/*********************************************************************
 * Method to generate the permutations of the <code>letters</code>.
 * A) If no more letters, we are done, and we print the permutation.
 * B) Else run a loop on i on the letters in the current list.
 *   1a) Copy the current list as passed in to a new current list
 *       to be passed recursively to this method.
 *   1b) Get the i-th letter in the new list.
 *   1c) Add the i-th letter to the end of the current perm.
 *   1d) Remove the i-th letter from the new list.
 *   2)  Call this method recursively, passing in the current perm
 *       and the new list of unused letters.
 *   3)  When the program returns from the recursion, take
 *       off the last letter of the current perm in preparation for the
 *       next iteration in the loop on i.
**/
  public void generatePermutations(ArrayList<String> thePerm,
                                   ArrayList<String> currentLtrs)
  {
    String letter = "";
    if(0 == currentLtrs.size())
      System.out.printf("%s%n", thePerm);
    else
    {
      for(int i = 0; i < currentLtrs.size(); ++i)
      {
        ArrayList<String> newLtrs = new ArrayList<String>(currentLtrs);
        letter = currentLtrs.get(i);
        thePerm.add(letter);
        newLtrs.remove(i);
        generatePermutations(thePerm, newLtrs);
        thePerm.remove(thePerm.size()-1);
      }
    }
  }
```

FIGURE 8.3 ■ Permutation generation for the Jumble puzzle.

make, and every possible response that Black could make, and would recompute the goodness value of the board position for White. A basic principle of game programs, looking only at one move and one response, is that the most sensible move for White is the move that maximizes White's goodness value after Black's *best* response.

In practice, such game-playing programs are really search programs trying to optimize what is known as an *objective function* (the goodness value), and they rarely stop after one move and response. A practical chess-playing program would search down several move-and-response levels before coming up with a current best move. The natural way to write such a program is via recursion. The method is passed the state of the board, the player (White or Black), and the value of the objective function, and it will loop through possible moves, calling itself recursively.

A somewhat different kind of recursive search would be that of a program to look for Sudoku solutions. In the case of chess or other board games, the complexity of game play and the number of options require one to come up with a goodness function that measures the quality of the board status. In the case of Sudoku, one would be much more likely to make a choice for a square to fill, verify that such a choice is valid, and call the method recursively. Most of the time the recursive descent would end when there is no valid choice to be made, and the program would back up and try a different choice. In many ways, this is really just a variation on a permutation-generating program. If one views the Sudoku tableau as having 81 squares to fill with the integers 1 through 9, and thus a total of 9^{81} possible solutions to test, the rules of Sudoku simply stipulate that large chunks of the solution space are illegal and need not be explored further.

8.8 Implementation Issues

Naive generation of all possible solutions, whether it be of a simple Jumble puzzle, all possible grids in a Sudoku puzzle, or for some more serious purpose, is part of a time-honored tradition of BFI computing (Brute Force and Ignorance). Asymptotically we know that we cannot apply BFI to a permutation problem of any serious size because the number of permutations on N items is $N!$ and this grows exponentially fast. Similarly, we cannot explore all possible moves in a chess game or any other game of similar complexity because there are just too many possibilities. We can expect as one of the implementation issues that the search will progress only "some number" of levels down.

There are many times in computation when we don't have any *theory* that will help us in the computation and must therefore rely on a *heuristic*. A heuristic is a notion that somehow "ought" to be true or seems like a reasonable way to trim away unlikely candidates. Suppose we are given a set of letters and told that the letters are an anagram of exactly one English word. If in our naive search we come upon an intermediate possible word that starts out "syz," we could apply a heuristic that it is unlikely that an English word exists with this letter sequence and do an early abort of our descent down the recursion. This would run the risk of missing a word that might exist (namely, "syzygy"), but it would allow us to prune away segments of an otherwise exponentially large search space and thus shorten the search.

A very important issue that comes up in using recursion is that memory space is taken up with every recursive call to the method. Every time any method is called, some memory is allocated for the *context* of that method when in a state of execution. The context contains the variables allocated as well as scratch space the compiler will have felt was necessary, space for the actual executable code in some cases, and pointers to the program that called the method and to methods called by the current method. Although memory space is not usually an issue with small programs, it is possible through recursion to use up all the space by doing too many recursive method calls. In the Collatz problem, for example, the "current" integer N not only shrinks by division by 2 but also grows when the $N \leftarrow 3N + 1$ part of the method is called. Because the behavior of this function is still not known, we do not know how many recursive calls will be needed before we get to the expected end result of 1, and there are pathological bad cases that will need so many recursive calls that available memory space is exceeded.

A more common memory problem with recursive methods is that we would need to pass a data array in to the method each time. We do this in our permutation method of Figure 8.3; not only do we pass a copy of the current permutation, we also, with each method invocation, create a new instance of `newLtrs`. In the case of permutations, the depth of our recursion is known (depth N for the N-letter inputs) and the maximum size of the variables passed in is known and small (two `ArrayLists` of length no more than N), so we know that we will never need space for more than N^2 data items. Given that the time complexity of generating permutations is $N!$, it is highly likely that we will run out of patience for computing the $N!$ permutations long before we run out of the N^2 space for this program as it executes.

Although we probably won't have to worry about memory when doing a 15-deep recursion on 15 items to generate permutations, the same is not necessarily true for binary search in a very large array. The naive version of our recursive search program requires us to package up half of the input array and pass that down to the next level of recursion. Even if we had the memory (and memory is, after all, fairly cheap these days), it's a colossal imbalance of processing time to do this. In binary search, our "computational" cost is one arithmetic step to compute the subscript for the midpoint, one lookup in the array of the element at the midpoint, and one comparison. It doesn't seem to make sense to move thousands or perhaps millions of elements into and out of arrays for each invocation of a method that has only three simple computational steps.

One way to avoid memory copying in searching is with a hybrid of the naive recursive search and the iterative search using pointers. If we declare the array to be searched as an array in the class but not passed as a parameter to the method that conducts the search, then we can pass lower and upper endpoints only, replacing the `while` loop with a method that recursively calls itself until the searched-for element is found or determined not to be present.

The simplistic solution for memory-efficient binary search does not really work in the case of permutation generation. In binary search, the data values under consideration are contiguous in an array. In the case of a permutation-like computation, the set of values to be dealt with at any level changes, and the values are not contiguous in the original array; values already used in the partial permutation show up as holes in the original list of elements.

One solution to this is shown in Figure 8.4.

```
/*********************************************************************
 * Instance variables for this class.
**/
  private ArrayList<Boolean> used;
  private ArrayList<String> letters;
  private ArrayList<String> thePerm;

  ...

/*********************************************************************
 * Permutation generating method
**/
  public void generatePermutations(int lettersLeft)
  {
    String letter = "";
    if(0 == lettersLeft)
    {
      System.out.printf("the permutation is %s%n", thePerm);
    }
    else
    {
      for(int i = 0; i < this.letters.size(); ++i)
      {
        if(false == used.get(i))
        {
          letter = letters.get(i);
          thePerm.add(letter);
          this.used.set(i,true);
          --lettersLeft;
          generatePermutations(lettersLeft);
          thePerm.remove(thePerm.size()-1);
          this.used.set(i,false);
          ++lettersLeft;
        }
      }
    }
  }
```

FIGURE 8.4 ■ Permutation generation without copying the array.

We create as an instance variable of the class the set of letters, `letters`, from which permutations are to be generated, and we declare as an instance variable of the class a `boolean` array `used` to indicate which elements of the `letters` array have already been used. We lose in computational efficiency in that we must now iterate over the entire array `letters` and then skip over those that have already been used, where in the previous version our set of current letters kept getting smaller. We gain, however, in not having to perform a deep copy of arrays and to pass those arrays as parameters. We also must take care to set and reset `used` before and after the calls to the recursive method and to add and remove the new letter from the running partial permutation as we progress through the computation. In this version, we also have a counter that drops to zero when all the letters have been used. In the previous version, we knew we had reached the base case of the recursion when the set of letters passed in was empty. In order to make the same determination in the code in Figure 8.4, we would need to run a loop and determine that all the letters had been used. This extra loop for every recursive call of the method seems excessive, and it can be avoided by using a `lettersLeft` counter.

In general, then, we have a common theme recurring. A simple recursive approach is possible, for which we pay in resource utilization in exchange for programming simplicity. A better use of resources can be made at the expense of some greater complexity in the programming, and the right choice of which approach to take will depend in part on the details of the computation that is needed.

8.9 Summary

We have introduced recursion, with examples including the factorial function, the Fibonacci sequence, the "$3n + 1$ function," and the Ackermann function.

We have shown how to implement recursion in program code, taking special care to distinguish computations in which memory space for recursive function calls will be problematic and computations for which memory usage is unlikely to be a problem.

Recursion is used extensively in game programs and in search trees, and binary divide-and-conquer algorithms are often implemented recursively.

Finally, among the most common uses for recursion are in computing and in enumerating permutations and combinations.

8.10 Exercises

1. Write a complete program for computing the factorial function using recursion. Test it thoroughly, and include in your documentation of the method for the function a comment about the range of values that can be computed without error. Include a variable that will allow you to keep track of the number of method calls to the recursive method.

2. Write a complete program for computing Fibonacci numbers using recursion. Test it thoroughly, and include in your documentation of the method for the function a comment about the range of values that can be computed without error. Include a variable that will allow you to keep track of the number of method calls to the recursive method.
3. Write a complete program for verifying the Collatz conjecture that the function eventually reaches 1 for any input N. Test your program thoroughly to find the pathological worst cases in a range of integer inputs, and include in your documentation of the method for the function a comment about the range of values that can be computed without error. Include a variable that will allow you to keep track of the number of method calls to the recursive method. Since recursive calls take memory, the number of such method calls could be different on different machines and configurations before system errors occur. A user reading and using your code should be given insight into how to test the limits of the local execution environment.
4. Write a complete program for computing the Ackermann function using recursion. Test this as discussed in the previous exercises.
5. Rewrite any of the preceding programs using `long` variables instead of `int` variables, and compare the difference.
6. Rewrite any of the preceding programs using the Java `BigInteger` class instead of `int` variables, and compare the difference. What you should see is that arithmetic precision is no longer an issue, but running time is increased and it is now easier to run out of memory.
7. You are probably familiar with Sudoku puzzles. Consider the microversion of Sudoku given here, with integers running 1 through 4 and arranged in 2×2 blocks. The rule is that the digits 1 through 4 must appear exactly once in each row, in each column, and in each 2×2 subblock of the tableau.

1	2	3	4
3	4	1	2
2	1	4	3
4	3	2	1

Write a recursive program that will find all the legal configurations of a puzzle of this size. You will probably want to think first about how to handle the determination of which entries might be legal in a given location. The naive, computationally more expensive but easier to program approach would be to recalculate the list of legal values for each location. A more polished approach would be to keep `used` lists of the illegal values, but that would require more programming. Heeding the admonition "make it right before you make it better" might be the smart thing to do for this assignment.

8. It is not hard to become convinced that if you have one legal configuration of the micro-Sudoku in the previous exercise, then another legal configuration can be found by applying a permutation on the digits. That is, the permutation $1 \rightarrow 3$, $2 \rightarrow 4$, $3 \rightarrow 2$, $4 \rightarrow 1$ converts the preceding legal tableau into the following legal tableau.

3	4	2	1
2	1	3	4
4	3	1	2
1	2	4	3

Write a program that will apply the permutations on four symbols to the first legal configuration in order to generate 23 more legal configurations.

9. Implement a binary search dictionary lookup program. There are a number of lists of English words available from the Web without copyright. Download one and use it as the source data to create a lookup program using recursive binary search. Do not pass the arrays as parameters. Rather, as suggested in Section 8.8, pass pointers to the left and right endpoints in the search in the recursive call to the method.

10. Finish the creation of a Jumble-puzzle-solving program by combining permutation generation (using recursion) with dictionary lookup. Be sure to test your code on words that have the same letters but form more than one word depending on the order, such as "form" and "from" or "close" and "socle."

9 A First Look at Graphs

Objectives

- An introduction to the formal definitions of graph theory, including the concepts of trees
- A discussion of examples of graphs in real-world computing situations
- An introduction to the concepts of local and global properties of graphs and how the difference is relevant to computing
- A description of transitive closure in graphs
- An introduction to the idea of greedy algorithms

Key Terms

adjacent node	greedy algorithm	relation
arc	incident node	subgraph
clique	length	transitive closure
connected component	multigraph	transitive relation
connected graph	node	tree
cycle	node degree	undirected graph
directed graph	node indegree	unweighted graph
edge	node outdegree	vertex
forest of trees	path	weighted graph
graph	primary key	

Introduction

A tree is a special kind of graph, so in order to discuss trees in the next chapter, we must first cover some definitions about graphs. Most of these definitions are merely formalizations of intuitively obvious concepts.

More generally, we will begin in this chapter to deal with data organization that is no longer strictly linear. Linked lists, stacks, and queues are (at least in their naive forms) linear structures. In dealing with graphs and trees, we will have two-dimensional or higher-dimensional structures to look at and organize.

9.1 Formal Notions of a Graph

Formally, a *graph* G is a pair $G = (V, E)$ comprising a set $V = \{v_i\}$ of *nodes* (sometimes also called *vertices*, whose singular is *vertex*) and a set $E = \{e_k = <v_i, v_j>\}$ of *edges* (sometimes also called *arcs*), with each edge being a pair of nodes. If an edge $e_k = <v_i, v_j>$ exists, we say that node v_i is *connected* to node v_j and that the edge e_k is *incident* to node v_i and node v_j. If there is an edge $e_k = <v_i, v_j>$ from a node v_i to a node v_j, then we say that the two nodes are *adjacent*. We will use the terms "vertex" and "node" and the terms "edge" and "arc" interchangeably.

The notion of a graph is the formalization of a common notion of points connected with lines. A standard layout of streets in a city is a graph, with the nodes being the intersections and the streets being the edges. Graphs can be either *directed* or *undirected*. Intuitively, if some of the streets in a grid are one-way streets, then we have a directed graph because the ability to traverse the graph from a node v_i to a node v_j along an edge $e_{ij} = <v_i, v_j>$ requires that the edge be an *ordered pair*. The edge $e_{ji} = <v_j, v_i>$ would point in the other direction. Mathematically, it is conventional to view edges in an undirected graph as mathematical sets without order on the elements. The edge $e_{ij} = \{v_i, v_j\}$ is thus identical to edge $e_{ji} = \{v_j, v_i\}$ and we count this as "one" edge. In a directed graph, we view the edges as ordered pairs and not just as sets.

Usually, unless we specifically say that we are referring to a *multigraph*, we will assume that at most one edge can exist between any two nodes in an undirected graph, or at most one edge in either direction in a directed graph.

A *subgraph* of a graph $G = (V, E)$ is another graph $G' = (V', E')$ for which $V' \subset V$ and $E' \subset E$ and the edges in E' only connect nodes in V'. That is, a subgraph is exactly what one would think it is: a subset of the nodes, together with some subset of the edges that join nodes in the subset.

A *path* in a graph is a sequence of edges that connect tail to head

$$\begin{aligned} e_0 &= <v_{i_0}, v_{i_1}>, \\ e_1 &= <v_{i_1}, v_{i_2}>, \\ e_2 &= <v_{i_2}, v_{i_3}>, \\ \ldots, \\ e_{n-1} &= <v_{i_{n-1}}, v_{i_n}> \end{aligned}$$

from an origin vertex v_{i_0} to a destination vertex v_{i_n}.

We would refer to such a path as being of *length* n because it contains n edges. (Remember this: We count the number n of edges, not the number $n+1$ of vertices connected by the edges.)

A *cycle* in a graph is a path for which the beginning and the ending node are the same.

In an undirected graph, the number of edges incident to a particular node is the *degree*. In a directed graph, we need to consider both the *indegree* and the *outdegree* because these will normally be different; their definitions are obvious.

A graph is said to be *connected* if there is a path between any pair of nodes in the graph. (The path must be a directed path in a directed graph.) Even if a graph is not connected, it will still have connected components. A *connected component* in a graph is a subgraph of the nodes that is a connected graph and is maximal with respect to being a connected subgraph. The maximality property means that any node that is reachable by a path from any node in the component is already in the component.

Although the mathematical definition of a connected component is a global and setwise definition of maximality, the operational definition of a connected component is much more algorithmic and intuitive. Beginning with a single node as a subgraph, we add the edges incident on that node, and then the "other" nodes for those edges, and recursively repeat this process. Clearly each of the subgraphs we get is connected, and when we can no longer add new nodes by following edges incident on nodes in the subgraph, we will have satisfied the maximality property and will have a connected component. We note that if C is the connected component containing any node v, then C is also the (unique) connected component containing any other node v' in C.

Finally, we mention that there are both *weighted* and *unweighted* graphs. In an unweighted graph, we know only that an edge exists that connects two nodes. In a weighted graph, we are permitted to assign a weight to each edge. This is often either a capacity or a distance function representing either the flow capacity between two nodes (think bandwidth between Internet nodes) or distance (think miles between airports). Clearly, the data structures to represent weighted graphs will require more complexity because they will store more information, and there is no free lunch. We will discuss both kinds of graphs later in this book.

9.2 Examples of Graphs

We present in Figure 9.1 some examples of graphs and in Figure 9.2 some examples of multigraphs (to show the difference). Each of the graphs in these two figures is

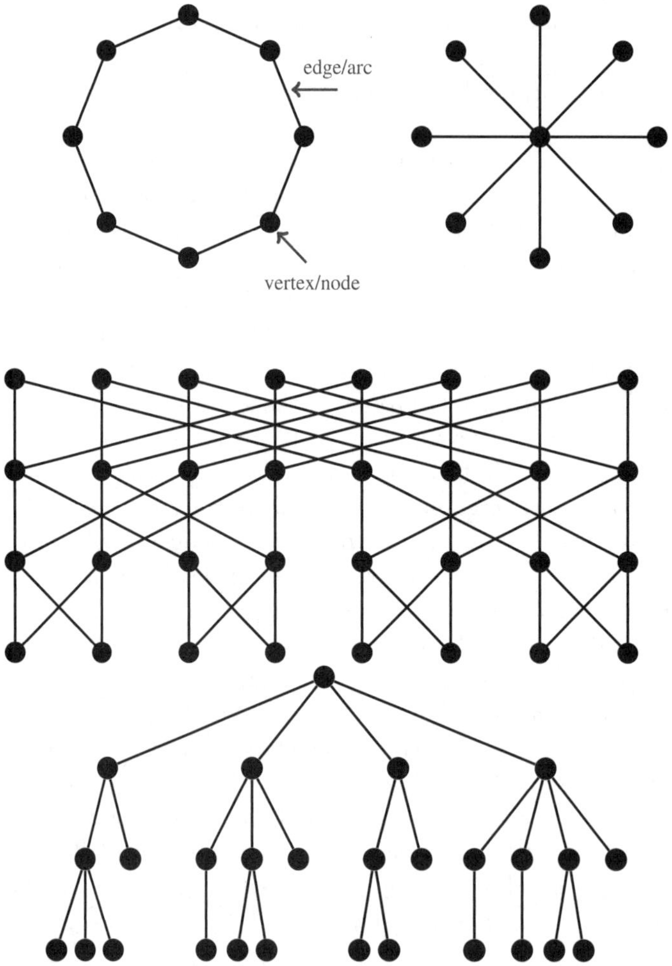

FIGURE 9.1 Examples of graphs.

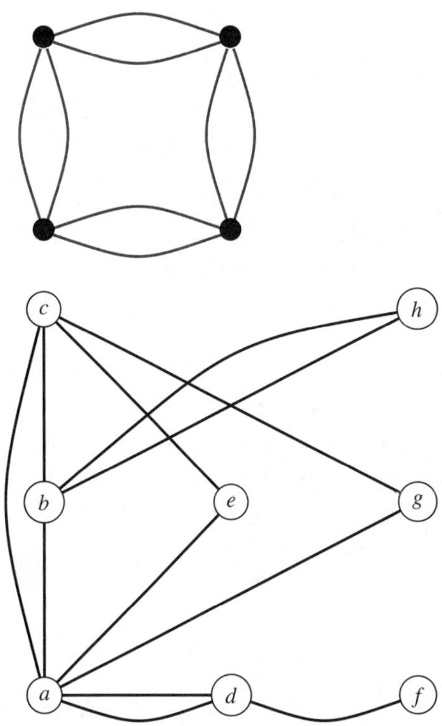

FIGURE 9.2 ■ Examples of multigraphs.

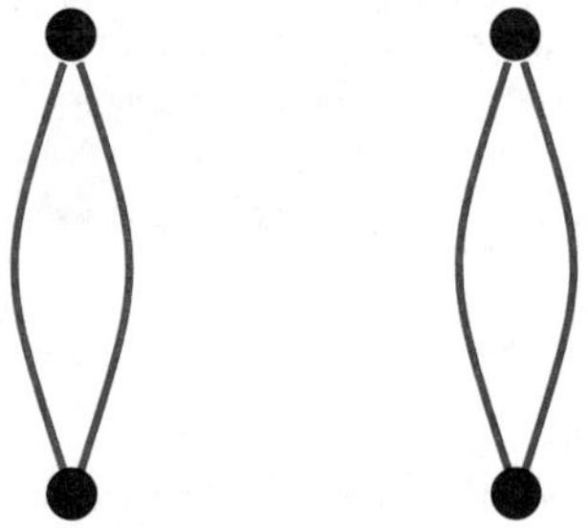

FIGURE 9.3 ■ An example of a disconnected graph.

connected, which is to say that each possesses only one connected component. The graph in Figure 9.3 is still one graph, but it is a graph with two distinct connected components.

Other useful examples of graphs include the following.

EXAMPLE 9.1

The Internet graph, whose nodes are the individual machines connected to the net (or the IP address numbers) and whose edges are the physical (or wireless) connections from one machine to another, is one such example. Formally, it might be difficult to pin down exactly what constituted the graph, due to wireless devices that come and go, dynamic IP address generation, etc. Intuitively, though, we can probably all agree that the basic notion of a graph is applicable. In the case of the Internet graph, we are interested both in the existence of connections from one node to the next and in the bandwidth between nodes, so for many purposes this will be a weighted graph.

EXAMPLE 9.2

In an institution that requires high security, it is likely that an internal network would exist in addition to the institution's network that is connected to the Internet itself. Thus, although "the Internet" per se is probably a connected graph, the graph of all the world's networked computers almost certainly includes multiple connected components.

EXAMPLE 9.3

The interlocking networks of friends on a social network like Facebook form a graph, with individuals as nodes and the "friend" links as edges. If one believes the "six degrees of separation" notion that everyone is connected to everyone else through no more than six links, then this graph would be a connected graph. In reality, the graph is probably not connected. As with the Internet graph, social network graphs often have the property that many small sets of nodes might each have many connections among them (such as two groups of students on two different university campuses) and then only a few links might connect these highly connected subsets. Understanding these graphs is a subject of intense study by researchers in many different disciplines.

EXAMPLE 9.4

Street maps are obvious graphs, as mentioned previously. Because most cities have some one-way streets, maps are usually directed graphs. Again, these are graphs that could be considered as unweighted if one were only interested in connectivity, but usually there is a weighting, even if unconscious, that users assume. When traveling from one city to the next, for example, we often go somewhat out of our way to get to a major highway. In a graph of this sort, it could even be the case that the edge weights vary with time; commute times in cities can depend heavily on the time of day.

EXAMPLE 9.5

A *tree* is a graph that is connected but has no cycles. Chapter 10 is entirely devoted to trees and the data structures and algorithms for working with trees. One standard form of tree is an evolutionary tree of species descended from a common ancestor as shown in Figure 9.4. These are often constructed bottom-up because we do not have DNA data of extinct species. Rather, we start with a set of isolated nodes for existing organisms for which we have the DNA. The computation then works backward in time, assuming standard rates of evolution, mutating the isolated-node DNA until common ancestors are found, and repeating the process. In the first few steps, what will be produced is a *forest of trees*, a set of disconnected graphs each of which is a tree. Eventually the forest will resolve itself into a single tree when all the nodes are eventually connected to a common ancestor far enough back in time. For example, including human, chimp, dog, and wolf as isolated nodes, we will link human to chimp and dog to wolf early on to create two trees that are not (yet) connected, and then only later in the process, earlier in evolutionary time, link the ancestor of human–chimp to the ancestor of dog–wolf and eventually to the ancestor of earthworm. This particular computation is enormously expensive in CPU time because the number of possible trees grows exponentially with the number of leaf nodes. The number of possible unrooted trees with N leaf nodes is $(N-5)(N-7)\cdots(3)$, a function that grows exponentially and makes an exhaustive search completely impossible. For 5, 10, 15, and 20 leaf nodes, for example, the number of trees that would need to be searched naively is 15, 2,027,025, 7.9×10^{12}, and 2.2×10^{20}, respectively.

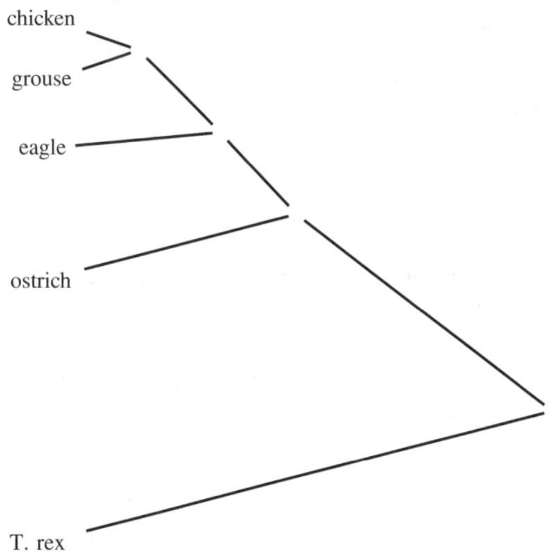

FIGURE 9.4 ■ A possible evolutionary tree.

EXAMPLE 9.6

A thesaurus is a collection of terms and the synonyms for those terms. This would form a graph, with the words as nodes and the existence of synonymity as an edge between words. Just as with evolutionary trees, we might well want to extend the notion of a graph to allow for a weight on each edge to indicate the degree of synonymity or to indicate a more hierarchical connection between words. For example, *feline* and *cat* might have a high degree of synonymity, while *cat*, *dog*, *horse*, and *goat* might be linked to *mammal* but have a low edge weight as true synonyms of each other.

9.3 Transitive Closure

9.3.1 Facebook Graphs

Before leaving this initial discussion of graphs in general and moving on to a treatment of trees, which are a special kind of graph, we comment on the idea of *transitive closure*. Let's start with a graph that consists only of your personal Facebook page. Now follow the "friend" links to the pages of the people you have friended, and add those links and pages to the graph. Then follow the friend links of *those* people to add new links and pages to the graph. Keep going until there are no new people to be added. What you will have done is compute the transitive closure of the "friend" relation on Facebook, and the graph you will have produced is the connected component of Facebook to which you belong.

This is an enormously important concept in computer science. It is becoming even more important as the mass of data builds up around the world, so it's worth taking a few pages to think about the concept more generally.

9.3.2 Theory

For the general definition of transitive closure, we go back to the more abstract definition of a mathematical relation: a *relation* on a set $S = \{e_i\}$ is a subset of $S \times S$, that is, a set of ordered pairs $R = \{(e_i, e_j) : e_i, e_j \in S\}$. For example, the relation "less than" on the set $S = \{1, 3, 5, 7\}$ consists in formal mathematics of the set of pairs $R = \{(1, 3), (1, 5), (1, 7), (3, 5), (3, 7), (5, 7)\}$. We normally think of "less than" as a *transitive relation* because $a < b$ and $b < c$ means that $a < c$. What that means in the definition of relations as sets is that if the pair (a, b) is in the relation and if the pair (b, c) is in the relation, then the pair (a, c) is also in the relation.

In general, if we have a set of elements $S = \{e_i\}$ and a binary relation R, then the *transitive closure* is the smallest relation R' containing R such that R' is a transitive relation.

In an undirected graph $G = (V, E)$ with a set V of vertices and a set E of edges, what this means is the following, just as in the previous example: Create a subgraph

H_0 of G consisting of one vertex $g \in G$, so that initially $H_0 = \{\{g\}, \emptyset\}$. Now create a new subgraph H_1 by adding to H_0 all the arcs extending outward from g and all the nodes that are connected by these arcs. In creating H_1 from H_0 we have applied the "an edge exists" relation once.

Now let us apply the "an edge exists" relation again, as if we were calling a method recursively. We create a new subgraph H_2 by adding to H_1 all the edges extending outward from all the vertices in H_1 and all the vertices connected by those edges.

And we repeat. Indeed, we repeat this operation until the resulting graph is closed under the operation of adding edges and vertices, that is, until there are no more new edges and vertices added under this operation. The repetition of the "an edge exists" operation is the application of transitivity, and closure occurs when we run out of new things to add, hence the term transitive closure.

For a tiny example, consider the graph in Figure 9.5, which is a simplified version of one of the graphs from Figure 9.2. We begin with vertex a, so $H_0 = \{\{a\}, \emptyset\}$. Since a is connected to vertices c and e, we add those two vertices and those two edges to H_0 to create H_1 as shown in Figures 9.6 and 9.7. In the next application of the "an edge exists" relation, we cannot add any more vertices from a, but we can add b and g, which are connected to c, and we can for the sake of completeness add the redundant edge from c to e. This gives us H_2 as shown. Finally, we can add h and the edge from b to h to create H_3. At this point we are done. We have computed the transitive closure that begins with the vertex a. This subgraph is the connected component containing a, and it does not intersect the second connected component that contains nodes d and f. (It is also the connected component containing b, or any other of the vertices in the component.)

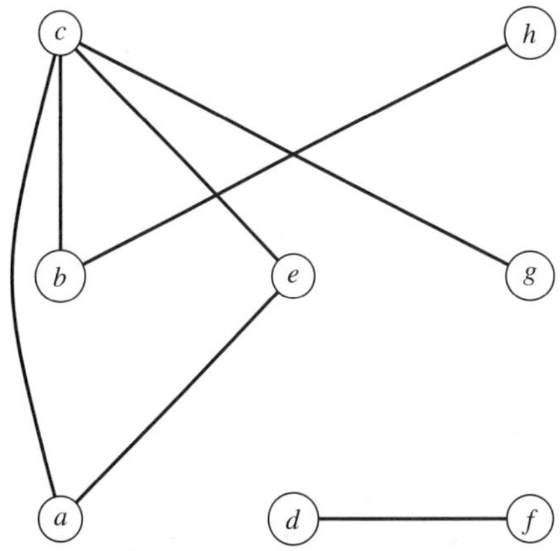

FIGURE 9.5 ■ Finding the transitive closure of "connected to" in a graph.

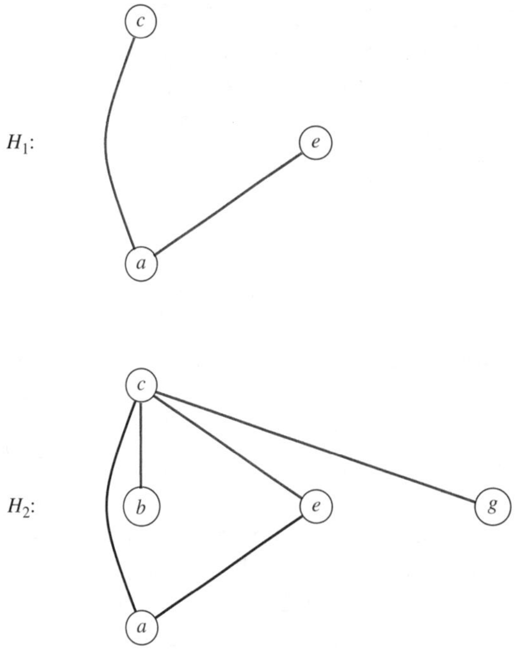

FIGURE 9.6 ■ Transitive closure, part 1.

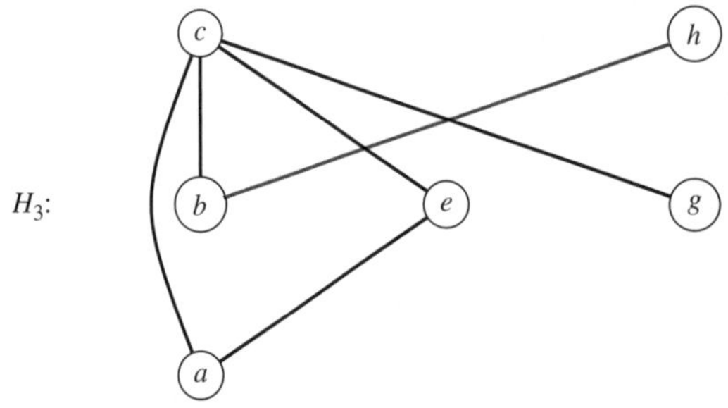

FIGURE 9.7 ■ Transitive closure, part 2.

■ 9.3.3 Applications in Computing

This concept of transitive closure is enormously important in computing because we frequently have data that can be viewed as a graph, and the computational problem is that we have only local information about a node and its nearest neighbors, but what we need to determine is a global property of the graph.

For example, the common assumption of "six degrees of separation" is that the transitive closure of "people I know" is the entire universe. Leaving aside the question of whether this is in fact true or whether the original experiment by Milgram was done wrong, consider the computational and data storage issues associated with storing the transitive closure. Even assuming that I might know, by transitive closure, all six billion people on the planet, it is unreasonable for me to include in my local address book the contact information for all these people. It is even more unreasonable for everyone to store everyone else's contact information; that would be an enormous duplication of information with very little payoff.

It is similarly both infeasible and unreasonable for every Internet node to keep track of every other Internet node. Although all nodes on the net are connected by a path to all other nodes, the Internet is not an "everyone directly connected to everyone" network. Instead, the goal with each hop is to route traffic through main routers to a location closer to the destination than before. The number of main routers is much smaller than the number of destinations, and the detail information about the final destination will not be kept in any of the hub routers except those close to the destination.

In both the previous examples, we have edges that are clearly determined by yes–no conditions: I do or don't know a given person; the router either is or is not closer in an Internet sense to the final destination. In many cases, we have a graph that describes connections that are not yes–no connections. Consider a thesaurus of words. A dog is clearly a mammal, and a mammal is an animal, and an animal is a living thing. Pond scum is a plant, and plants are living things, so clearly in some thesaurus-oriented sense there ought to be a link between *dog* and *pond scum*. But should this link have the same "weight" in a thesaurus as the link from *dog* to *wolf*, say? Probably not; although some relationship path of similarity should probably exist, in any practical application one would almost certainly want a link of similarity to be greater between *dog* and *wolf* than between *dog* and *pond scum*. The problem in building software, though, is that it is hard in practice to determine mathematical functions that will realistically attenuate this relationship of similarity.

These are three examples of situations in computation in which

- the underlying real-world structure can be represented as a graph;
- for reasons of feasibility or reasonability, we can store in any given node only local information about the nearest neighbors of that node; and
- we will need to know global properties about the graph, like its connected components.

In order to determine the global properties, we will need to balance the storage of local information with the computational cost of traversing the network to compute the global properties on the fly when we need them.

9.4 Local–Global Questions

The final sentence in the preceding section is worth expanding upon. In the past, courses on computer literacy or data processing would distinguish between *data* and *information.* Data comprised just the mass of records, whether they be accounting records, address records, photographs, bibliographic card catalog entries, or whatever. Information was what was produced when that data was organized so that it could be accessed and used efficiently. The most obvious organization of data into information comes from sorting records—address books alphabetically by name, accounting records perhaps by transaction date, and so on. In traditional organizations of data into information in databases, there usually must be what is referred to as a *primary key* that will be the principal organization given to the data. Phone books have the name as the primary key; small accounting systems may use transaction date.

What is important to notice in dealing with many graphs is that there is no obvious primary key, no obvious way to "sort" the graph so as to present it in a linear fashion. Consider the graph in Figure 9.8. We have given labels a through h to the nodes, but that ordering is essentially arbitrary. Even if we could identify a "start" node, what if the other nodes were the drop-off points for a FedEx delivery and the arc lengths represented costs in time, gasoline, and distance? How might we determine the cheapest complete route for the delivery truck?

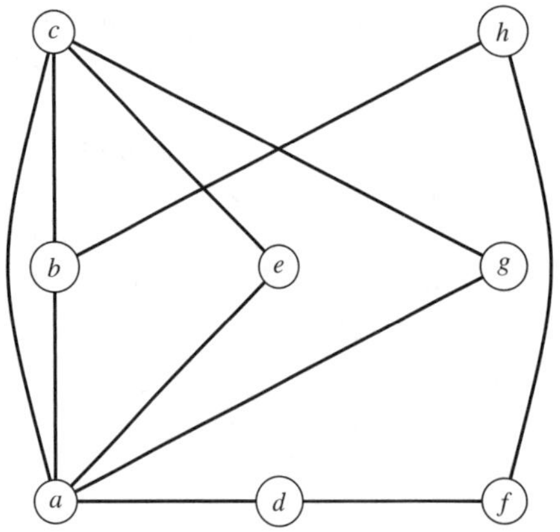

FIGURE 9.8 ■ Local versus global properties.

What this illustrates is a local–global problem that is common in computing. As a program executes, each node is an instance of a class and stores the local information of the other nodes to which it is connected, but each node is an independent instance. If what we want is a global property of the graph, like the transitive closure of the Facebook friends or the shortest delivery route, then it is necessary for us to crawl the graph in some way in order to turn our local information at each node into global information.

This problem becomes even more acute when one thinks about Internet nodes and searches. It is not all that difficult to determine that a given web page contains or does not contain keywords in a search. This is information local to a given web page. What has made the best search engines successful is their ability to compare the relevance of a given web page against the relevance of other web pages to produce a global ranking of pages by relevance. What is even more remarkable is that this global ranking can be done on data that is as dynamic as web pages, with content changing and pages appearing and disappearing all the time.

9.5 Greedy Algorithms

Now is as good a time as any to mention the concept of a *greedy algorithm.* Greedy algorithms are characterized by the idea that at any stage of the computation when a choice is to be made one takes the "greedy," intuitively obvious, hopeful choice of whatever looks to be best at the time. Greedy algorithms are the ultimate in using local properties only and not looking ahead to see what the global properties might be.

For example, consider the problem of constructing a path of minimal weight from one node in a graph to some other node. The greedy approach would be to choose as a first edge in the path the edge of minimal weight from the originating node, and then to progress recursively from there. In the graph in Figure 9.9, for example, the greedy approach to finding a path from A to D would be first to take the edge to node B because the local cost of A to B is 1 and the cost of A to C is much higher at 100. At the next step, however, the fact that this was a bad first choice becomes evident.

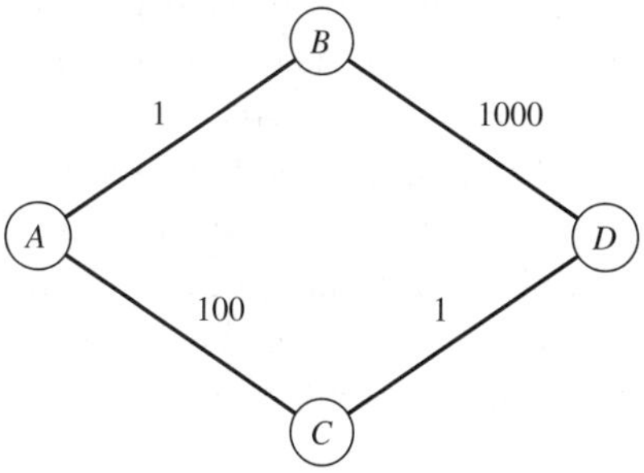

FIGURE 9.9 ■ A sample graph with capacities on the edges.

Game-playing programs must be careful to avoid using greedy algorithms for exactly these kinds of reasons. There is a term for a move in a game that looks like the move from A to B—it's called a "trap"! If your opponent makes you an offer that looks too good to be true, it's probably the case that further down the path there's a catch to the offer. The quality of a chess-playing program, for example, is heavily dependent on the number of moves and responses that can be tested and for which a goodness-of-move function can be computed. A program that used a greedy algorithm and looked only one level deep would be unlikely to play very well.

On the other hand, greedy algorithms with an appropriate randomization can be used to balance load. If an Internet router is trying to determine to which next router to send a packet, it may have a list of "closer" routers to which that packet could be sent and that would constitute "progress" toward the eventual destination. A purely greedy algorithm would select the first such router in a list and send on the packet. To balance the load over time, it might generate a random choice among the different routers that were equally close. A three-dimensional problem for which a greedy algorithm is often applied is the bin-packing problem. If the goal is to pack a set of several smaller boxes of varying sizes into a larger box, the greedy approach would be to insert the largest box first, because that is the hardest one to accommodate, and to progress through the packing in decreasing order of size.

We note that the term "algorithm" isn't perfectly applied here. The greedy algorithm is in fact an algorithm if we restrict the meaning to be: choose the locally best option at each stage of the computational process. That is in fact an "algorithm" because it presents a deterministic process. As a process for solving the original problem, however, this is not an algorithm but is instead only a heuristic. Much of the time[1] a greedy algorithm will not in fact solve the original problem or generate the optimal solution to the original problem. It is entirely possible, for example, in the bin-packing problem, that a precise placement of a subset of boxes is necessary in order to fit all the smaller boxes into the larger one. For minimizing costs for a path in a graph, it is easy to envision a graph such as that in Figure 9.9 for which the greedy first choice (node A to node B) does not lead to the best path from A to D.

Because greedy algorithms often do not produce an optimal solution but are often the only algorithm that might run in an acceptable time, there is a separate subdiscipline of algorithmics that analyzes the extent to which a greedy algorithm produces the desired outcome. In the case of shortest paths, a theoretical analysis might say, for example, that a greedy algorithm always produced a path no worse than 25 percent longer than the optimal path. In the bin-packing problem, the result might be that one could always fit in at least all but two of the boxes. If the desired outcome cannot be guaranteed, it is often useful to know how close we can come to the original goal.

---

[1] perhaps most of the time?

9.6 Summary

Much of this chapter has been an introduction to graphs by means of defining the jargon used to describe the graph. The concept of a graph is really a formalization of intuitive concepts; since the use of graphs is ubiquitous in computing, it is necessary to have established a standard set of terms so that nothing is misunderstood. We will have later chapters on graphs as well as on trees, which are special kinds of graphs.

One issue that is important to understand is the difference between an existential definition, which is often the definition used in mathematics, and an algorithmic definition, specifying the process by which the term being defined is constructed. An example of this is that of a connected component. From the point of view of computer science, the mathematical definition is unsatisfying because it uses a property (maximality) that is hard to test. The algorithmic definition, using the recursive computation of the transitive closure of connectedness, is more relevant to computer science because it results in the appropriate property being satisfied but is something that can be written up into a program.

As part of the introduction to graphs we have discussed the issue of local properties and global properties and the concept of transitive closure. These are both important because an algorithmic computation through a global search space in a graph is usually infeasible due to size and thus greedy approaches using local properties are often the only recourse.

9.7 Exercises

1. Assume the population of the world to be six billion people. Assume the "six degrees of separation" concept is correct, so that only six arcs of friendship are needed to reach from any one person to any other person on the planet, and assume everyone has exactly the same number of friends. What is the minimal number of friends that we each must have in order that six arcs take us from anyone to anyone else?
2. Computing the minimal number of friends requires us to assume that none of our friends knows any of our other friends, which is almost certainly not true. Now assume that each of our friends knows exactly one person whom we do not know, and that this relationship is true for everyone else. What is the minimal number of friends we must have in order for six arcs to cross the planet?
3. A *clique* is a graph on n nodes such that every node is connected to every other node. Your Facebook page would be part of a clique if you had exactly $n-1$ friends (you plus $n-1$ makes n nodes), and if each of your friends has

exactly you and the same other $n - 2$ friends of yours as friends. How many arcs of friendship would there be in a clique like this of n nodes?

4. Graphs as used in computer science are often representations of communication patterns or communication paths. What is the length of the longest path in the graph in Figure 9.8?

5. Consider the graph in Figure 9.10, which might resemble a small piece of a local area network. If every node in the left star (labeled a_i) wants to send a message to node b_3, and sending a message takes one time unit for each hop on the communication graph, what is the minimum time necessary for sending these messages?

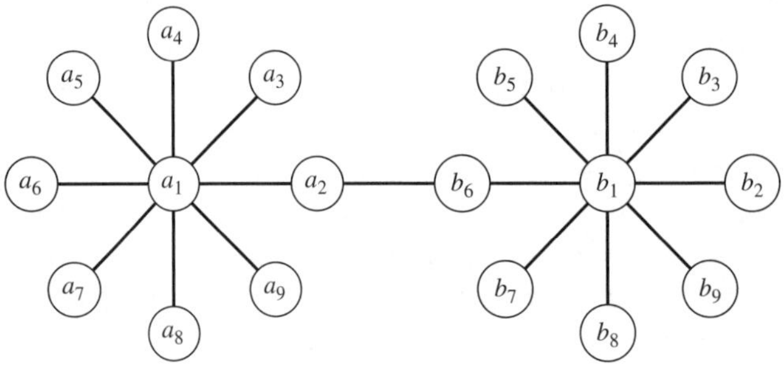

FIGURE 9.10 ■ A graph of two hubs connected together.

6. Consider the graph in Figure 9.11, where the node labelings are coordinates in the (x, y) plane. Show that the average distance from any given node to the other three nodes in the graph is $2n$. Now consider the graph in Figure 9.12, with the two blue nodes inserted. Show that by choosing $k = n/\sqrt{5}$, the average

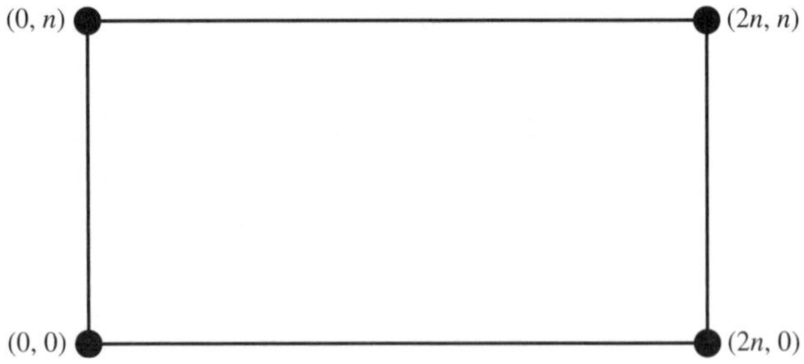

FIGURE 9.11 ■ A graph before adding nodes.

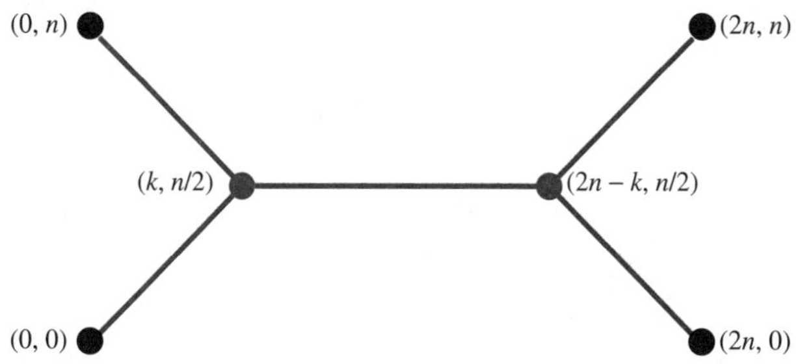

FIGURE 9.12 ■ A graph after adding nodes.

distance from one node to the other nodes is reduced to $2n - \frac{4}{3}\frac{n}{\sqrt{5}}$. If the coordinate locations represent real locations (Seattle, San Diego, New York, and Miami, for example), what does this say about the wisdom of opening up intermediate distribution offices in Denver and St. Louis?

10 Trees

Objectives

- An introduction to rooted and unrooted trees
- An introduction to spanning trees
- Code and data structures for representing trees
- Code and data structures for representing binary trees
- The heap structure as a tree structure
- Preorder, postorder, and inorder traversal of a tree

Key Terms

ancestor of a node	embarrassingly parallel	load balancing
balanced tree	greatest common divisor	max-heap
binary tree	heap	min-heap
breadth-first search	heap property	objective function
breadth-first traversal	height-balanced	parent
bush factor	height of a binary tree	postorder traversal
children	height of a node	preorder traversal
complete binary tree	inorder traversal	right child
complete ternary tree	interior node	root
decision tree	leaf node	spanning tree
depth-first search	left child	tree
depth-first traversal	level of a tree	tree traversal
depth of a node	level traversal	unrooted tree

Introduction

In the previous chapter, we covered the basic notion of a graph and the formal definitions needed to discuss graphs in a precise way. We will cover general graphs in a later chapter. This chapter, however, is devoted to a special kind of graph called a tree because organizing data and information into trees is ubiquitous in computing. You have already used trees any time you have used a modern computer, and now we will discuss how to create and use trees in programs.

10.1 Trees

There are many equivalent definitions of a tree. We will define a *tree* to be a connected graph with n nodes and $n - 1$ edges. We will equivalently use the definition that a tree is a connected graph with no cycles. We will leave the proof that these two definitions are equivalent as an exercise.

Perhaps the most obvious tree is a family tree of one's parents, grandparents, and so forth (assuming no incest or other unusual circumstances). Each person has two biological parents, who are distinct nodes in the tree. Each parent has two parents, who are distinct, and so forth.

As defined here, a tree is not viewed as a "directional" object. However, if we were to think of an evolutionary tree from a common ancestor, we would probably view the common ancestor at "the top" and the descendants hanging "down" from the top. Conversely, if we were thinking of our own descent from parents, grandparents, etc., we would probably place the *root* of the tree (ourself) at the bottom and extend our ancestors upward back in time. Note that there are many examples of *unrooted trees* that have no obvious focal point. Figure 10.1 is a general tree with no identifiable root. Figure 10.2 is a less general tree, with an identifiable root at the top of the figure and the *children* of each node hanging down from the *parent* node. Continuing the analogy with a family tree, for any node v, we refer to any parent, grandparent, great-grandparent, etc., node as an *ancestor* node.

We refer in a tree to the nodes with only one edge incident upon them as *leaf nodes*. Whether the tree is displayed in a directional manner, like a family tree, or without direction or root, the notion of a leaf is obvious. If one is traversing the tree by using the edges to move from one node to another, then once one comes to a leaf, there is no place to go except to return along the edge just traversed to the node from which one just came. A node that is not a leaf node is referred to as an *interior node*. In the tree in Figure 10.1, nodes a, c, h, and i are leaf nodes and the rest are interior nodes.

As you might imagine, dealing computationally with unrooted trees is more complicated than dealing with rooted trees. There is, for example, no obvious starting

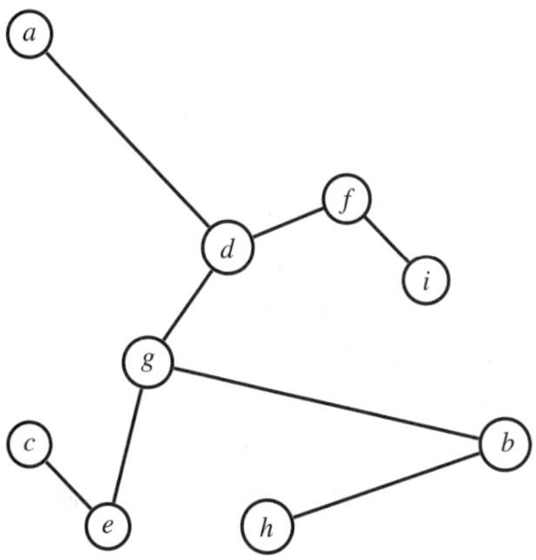

FIGURE 10.1 ■ A general unrooted tree.

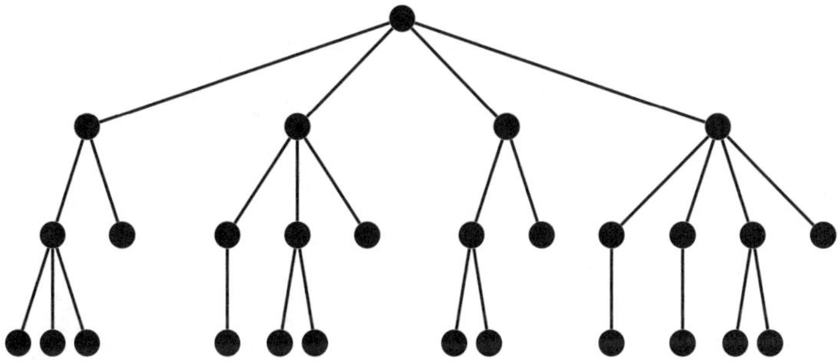

FIGURE 10.2 ■ A general rooted tree.

point from which to traverse an unrooted tree, nor is it obvious how we might use the intuitive two-dimensional layout of the tree to our advantage. In contrast, most tree algorithms make heavy use of the concept of the root of the tree. In a game-playing program, for example, the root represents the starting point of the game, the first level "down" the choices of opening moves, the next level "down" the choices of responses to the opening moves, and so forth. Further, we can make heavy use of the two-dimensional layout with the idea of progressing "down" from the root and of working "left" to "right."

Given a rooted tree such as in Figure 10.2 (which we have already seen in Figure 9.1), the *height* and *depth* of a particular node in the tree are defined as follows. The depth of a node v is the number of edges between v and the root of the tree, that is, the number of ancestors of v, not including the node v itself. Given that a tree is a graph with no cycles, there is only one path from any given node to the root, and the depth of a node is the length of that path. We can also define this recursively: the depth of the root is 0, and the depth of a nonroot node is 1 plus the depth of the node's parent.

The depth of a node is the measurement of its distance from the root. The height of a node is the distance in the opposite direction, that is, the distance to the farthest leaf node. We must be a little more careful, however, in defining the height than in defining the depth because not all trees are balanced. A tree is *balanced* if no leaf node is "much farther" away from the root than any other leaf node. As should be obvious, this isn't a precise definition due to the vague nature of the "much farther" part. Clearly, the tree in Figure 10.3 should be viewed as not being balanced, and the tree in Figure 10.4 should be viewed as being balanced. In most contexts, however, we would also consider the trees in Figure 10.5 both to be balanced and for many (but not all) purposes equivalent.

In general, as we shall see later in this chapter and in Chapter 12, we want our trees to be balanced because processing on balanced trees is more efficient.

FIGURE 10.3 ■ An unbalanced tree.

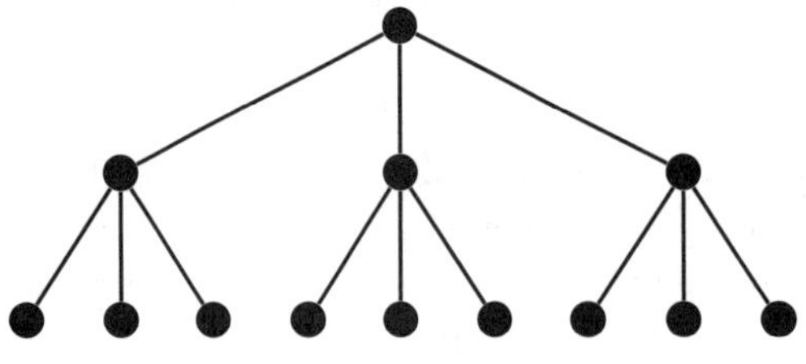

FIGURE 10.4 ■ A balanced tree.

Thus: The height of a leaf node is 0, and the height of a nonleaf node v is 1 plus the *maximum* of the heights of all the children of v. This is illustrated in Figure 10.6.

Finally, we will refer to all the nodes of depth n as *level* n of that tree.

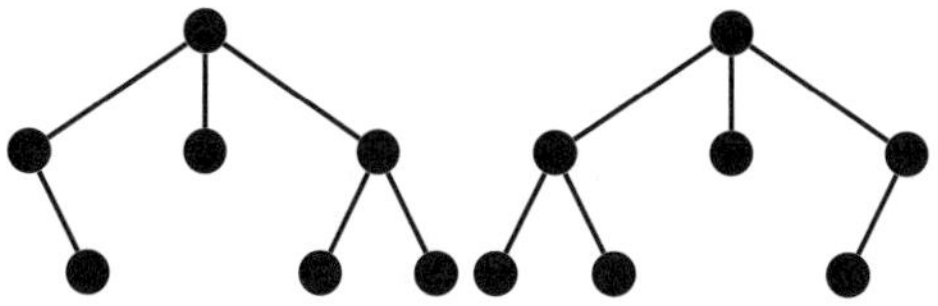

FIGURE 10.5 ■ Equally balanced trees?

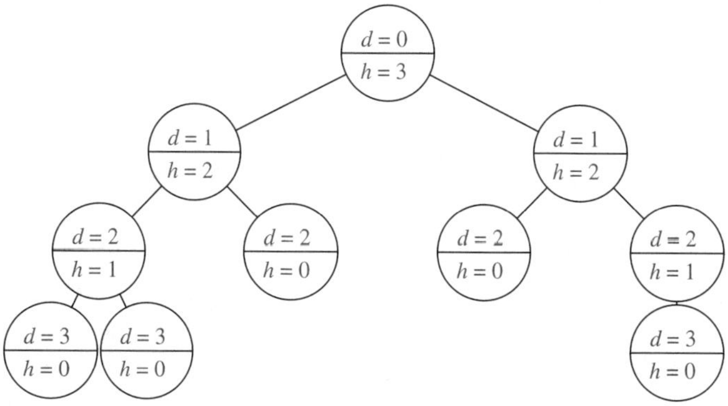

FIGURE 10.6 ■ Depths and heights.

■ 10.2 Spanning Trees

A common problem in computing is to compute a *spanning tree* for a more general graph. Given a general graph, a spanning tree would be a tree that includes all the nodes in the graph and a subset of the edges that connect the nodes into a tree. Just as a phone tree allows an organization like a political action committee to reach all its members by having members call members who then in turn call more members, a spanning tree is often constructed when it is necessary to create a communications backbone that would reach all the nodes in a graph. This is an increasingly important computation in setting up networks of wireless devices. Such devices change position relative to each other and relative to the fixed communications towers through which they communicate, so efficiently establishing networks for what amounts to a conference call among mobile devices has become an important problem to solve.

Figure 10.7 shows a spanning tree with dashed edges indicating the spanning tree and colored edges indicating other edges in the graph. We will discuss algorithms for spanning trees in Chapter 13.

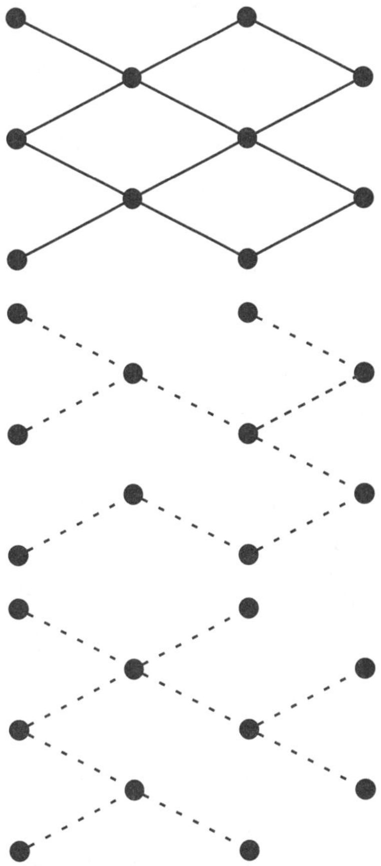

FIGURE 10.7 ■ Two spanning trees (dashed) for the same graph.

■ 10.3 Data Structures for Trees

One can easily implement a tree using almost the same code as one uses for a linked list. Indeed, most of the structures in this text follow the hierarchy of a data structure class, which contains instances of a node class in the structure with each node class containing a data payload. The primary changes, from one structure to the next, in the node class are in the connections from one node to the next that implement the data structure one level higher up.

In the case of linked lists to implement linked lists, stacks, and queues, the nodes have a `next` and a `previous` pointer. With a node in a tree, there will be a `parent` pointer that points "up" and some number of `children` pointers that will point "down." The complication that arises in dealing with trees is that a tree is a

```
public class TreeNode
{
  private TreeNode parent;
  private ArrayList<TreeNode> children;
  private DataPayload data;

// constructors
// accessors
// mutators
// other methods

} // public class TreeNode
```

FIGURE 10.8 ■ A code stub for a tree node.

TreeNode
-parent:TreeNode -children:ArrayList<TreeNode> -dataPayload:Record
+ accessors

FIGURE 10.9 ■ UML diagram for a tree node.

two-dimensional object, not a one-dimensional object like an array or `ArrayList`. Also, since the number of children of any given node is variable, we need a variable-length structure like an `ArrayList` or a linked list in which to store the pointers to the children. A `TreeNode` in Java might therefore have a stub that looks like Figure 10.8 and a UML diagram that looks like Figure 10.9. This is really only a very slightly different structure from the node for a linked list, stack, or queue. Instead of a `previous` node, we have a `parent` node. Instead of a single `next` node for a given node, we have zero or more children nodes that hang down from a given node and can be stored in an `ArrayList`. Since an `ArrayList` imposes a natural order (the subscripting) on its entries, we would naturally think of the sequential ordering of child nodes in the `ArrayList` as being the same as our graphical layout of the tree on paper, as indicated in Figure 10.10. In traversing a linked list, we used `next` and `previous` to make a linear traversal. If we want to make a similar traversal of all the nodes in a tree, we will now have to run a loop over the list of `children` entries in the `ArrayList`.

Clearly, if we wanted to, we could use the `Iterator` concept to implement a structure that hides the `TreeNode` from the programmer. This will, of course, be harder to do with a tree than with a stack or queue because the notion of the "next" item is no longer unique.

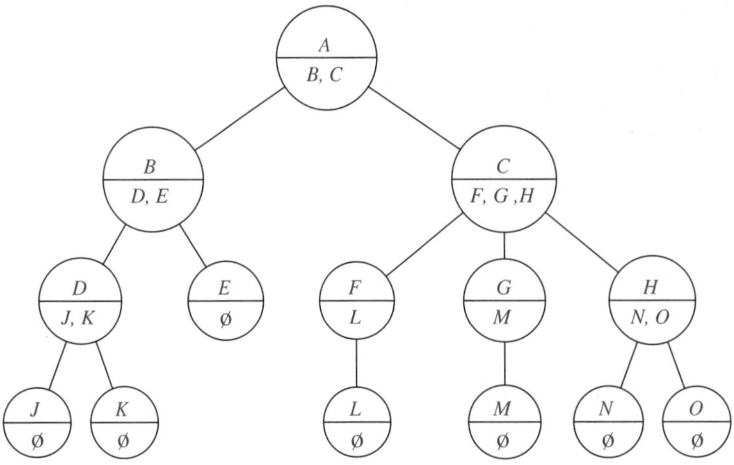

FIGURE 10.10 ■ Node labels (top) and `ArrayList` children (bottom).

10.4 Binary Trees

In many situations a general tree is needed because one cannot control or specify in advance the number of children for any given node.[1] However, there are many situations in which the program design or the algorithm can be imposed upon the data, and in many of these situations what is needed is a *binary tree*, a tree in which each node has at most two children.

We have already seen binary trees appear in (at least) two different contexts—the heap structure for a priority queue and the binary decision structure of binary search.

A particular use of binary trees comes in these two situations—when the tree structure is used for adding the ability to search or sort some data or the binary tree is either explicit or implicit as part of a divide-and-conquer algorithm. Since we have at most two children, we can refer explicitly to the *left child* and the *right child* of a given node, with left and right determined by the visual placement of the nodes when the tree is displayed in standard position as in Figure 10.11.

Almost invariably, if we are referring to a tree as a binary tree, we will retain the right-child or left-child layout even if one of the two nodes is missing. That is, even if we have missing nodes, we will display the tree as in Figure 10.12 rather than as in Figure 10.10 with the single nodes dropping straight down from the parent. For some binary trees, such as the binary search trees we will discuss in Chapter 12, the left-ness or right-ness has meaning, so maintaining the missing node as a missing right node or a missing left node is required.

[1] For example, if this is a family tree and the children really are children.

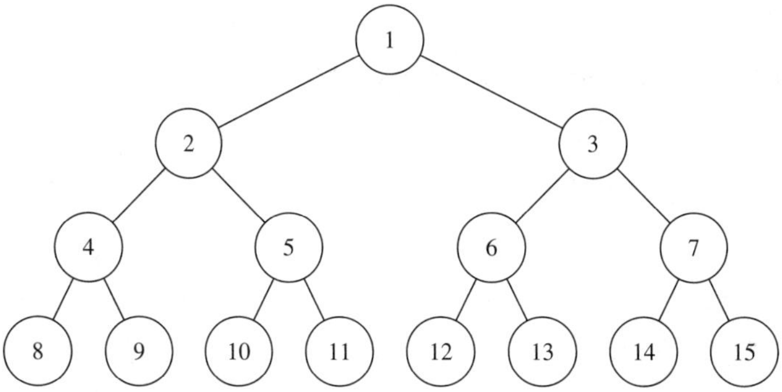

FIGURE 10.11 ■ A binary tree.

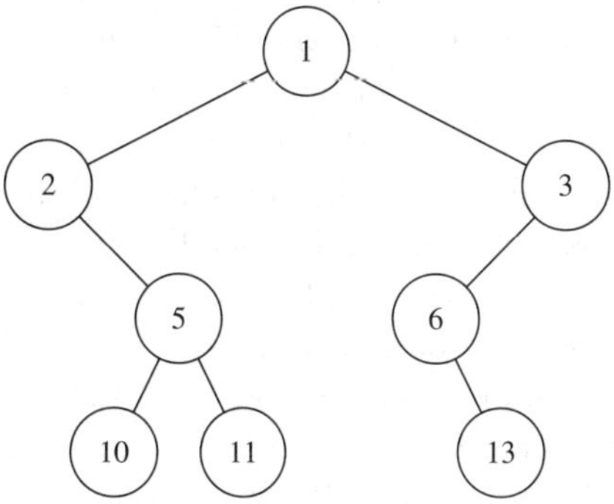

FIGURE 10.12 ■ A binary tree with missing nodes.

We call a binary tree *complete* if every interior node has exactly two children. As one can easily see, a complete binary tree with n *levels* will have exactly $2^n - 1$ nodes and 2^{n-1} leaf nodes. We define the *height* of a binary tree to be the maximum distance from the root of the tree to any leaf. In some instances we will relax slightly the definition of complete binary tree to allow for a partial row of leaf nodes, provided that the partial row of leaves is the "bottom" row and that the "missing" nodes are all at the right-hand edge of this bottom row, just as we specified earlier in the case of a heap for a priority queue. If the purpose of calling a tree "complete" is to refer to the fact that there are no holes in the display, then clearly there is more justification for calling the tree in Figure 10.16 complete than there is for the tree in Figure 10.12, which clearly has holes in the middle.

■ 10.4.1 Implementing Binary Trees with Nodes

To implement a binary tree we can use a program stub like the code in Figure 10.13 for the nodes in the tree; the fixed nature of one parent and two children (one or

```
public class BinaryTreeNode
{
  private BinaryTreeNode parent, leftChild, rightChild;
  private DataPayload data;

// constructors
// accessors
// mutators
// other methods

} // public class BinaryTreeNode
```

FIGURE 10.13 ■ A code stub for a binary tree node.

both of which may be `NULL`) make this look very much like the node for a linked list. All the complications that arise from the possibility of a variable number of children disappear, and we do not need the variable-length `ArrayList` of a general tree. One might also wish to include an instance variable `sibling` that points to the `rightChild` of the parent if one is a `leftChild` and to the `leftChild` of the parent if one is a `rightChild`. Knowing who the sibling is can be useful (as in the heap discussed later), but in a minimalist implementation of a binary tree a node might not know whether it is the right or the left child of its parent.

A word about programming style is relevant here. In developing code for a general tree, we have almost no choice but to use an `ArrayList` to store the children of a node because we don't know how many children, if any, will exist. Processing of children nodes will probably take place in subscript order in the `ArrayList` because the natural way to deal with an `ArrayList` is with a simple loop. With a binary tree, we have the option of explicitly labeling child nodes as either left or right. Although this can make the code easier to read (because the text of the code will specifically say "left" or "right"), it can also lead to duplication of code segments, which could lead to errors. It also means that general-purpose tree code will be much different from binary tree code. A middle ground might be to use the general-purpose tree code with an `ArrayList` for storing children but to build into that code additional safeguards to ensure that no node mistakenly is assigned more than two children. Since the `ArrayList` would likely be processed in subscript order, the code documentation should point out that the abstract subscript order $(0, 1)$ should match up as `(left_child, right_child)`, and this can be facilitated by defining `final` constants `LEFT_CHILD = 0` and `RIGHT_CHILD = 1` to ensure that the code has no magic numbers. To Einstein is attributed the statement, "Make everything as simple as possible, but not simpler." In writing code, there is always the need to find a middle ground between explicit code that is very readable but can be buggy because it is overly verbose and general-purpose code that is smaller but less readable because it is less explicit, and thus can be buggy because it requires more concentration to ensure correctness. Your mileage may vary. If circumstances permit, it is often better to write the explicit version first to get the output correct and then to write the general-purpose version. In that way, when you write the general-purpose version with more abstraction and chance for error, you will have correct results to use for diagnosing the errors.

10.4.2 Implementing Binary Trees with Arrays

In implementing a general tree, we have no way *a priori* to determine a sequence number for a given node because the number of child nodes is variable. This is an example of the local–global information issue we commented on in the previous chapter; we cannot look locally at a given node in a tree and determine a proper sequence number for that node without looking globally at the rest of the tree. For example, viewing the tree in Figure 10.14 as a general tree, we can look globally to determine that the three nodes on the bottom level should be numbered 4, 5, and 6, but it requires global information and some sort of indexing scheme to be able to point definitively to a specific node as the child of some other specific node. Consider the tree in Figure 10.14 with nodes labeled as array subscripts working top to bottom and left to right. If we were to store the nodes in an array or `ArrayList` of nodes, we would need an auxiliary index array such as

$$\texttt{index} = [1, 4, NULL, 5, NULL, NULL, NULL]$$

to indicate that the children of the root node (which is subscript 0) begin at subscript 1, the children of the node at subscript 1 begin at subscript 4, and so forth. If our only means for chasing down the paths of a tree were to run through the array of nodes, we would also need to determine the number of children for any node. For example, we would be able to determine that the child nodes of the root begin at $\texttt{index}[0] = 1$ and end at $\texttt{index}[1] - 1 = 3$.

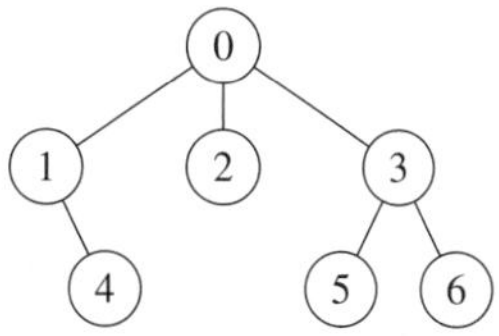

FIGURE 10.14 ■ A hard-to-subscript tree?

In contrast to this situation with general trees, we can with binary trees establish a *fixed* subscripting mechanism using an array (or an `ArrayList`). This is exactly what we did for the heap in Chapter 7.

The complete binary tree in Figure 10.11 has been deliberately subscripted 1-up instead of 0-up so as to map the nodes into a linear array with the subscripts matching up cleanly. In Java, which subscripts 0-up, an implementor would have to adjust subscripts accordingly or else just decide to waste the zeroth storage location but gain the advantage of code that was easier to read.

With this choice of subscripting, the *left child* of the node at subscript i will be the node that has subscript $2i$, and the *right child* of the node at subscript i will be the node that has subscript $2i + 1$, as can be seen by comparing the table in Figure 10.15 against the tree in Figure 10.11. Level k in such a tree will have nodes subscripted 2^k through $2^k - 1$, which is clearly easier to work with than it would be with 0-up subscripting and nodes at level k having subscripts $2^k - 1$ through $2^k - 2$.

Subscript	Tree Level	Node
1	0	v_1
2	1	v_2
3	1	v_3
4	2	v_4
5	2	v_5
6	2	v_6
7	2	v_7
8	3	v_8
9	3	v_9
10	3	v_{10}
11	3	v_{11}
12	3	v_{12}
13	3	v_{13}
14	3	v_{14}
15	3	v_{15}

FIGURE 10.15 ■ Mapping a binary tree into an array.

Of course, we can implement any tree with a fixed maximum on the number of child nodes using exactly this subscripting algorithm for array subscripts. However, the potential benefit from using an array diminishes if a large number of the array locations wind up not being filled. Only if a tree is reasonably complete will the advantage of the array with simple subscripting and access to nodes overcome the added cost of memory space that is allocated but not used.

10.5 The Heap

Most of the time, the algorithmic and implementation issues involved in turning an idea into program code are relatively straightforward, often being simply the commonsense conclusion from looking at the problem in the right way. As we saw in Chapter 7, though, one structure that appears to add some almost-magical extra value is the *heap*. We have already seen a heap used for a priority queue in Chapter 7, and we will use the heap in Chapter 11 to implement the *heapsort*. Some of what is presented here has already been presented in Chapter 7. That's OK—this is a concept so important that it is worth explaining it in two different ways.

Let's repeat the definition but this time in the terminology of trees. A binary tree whose nodes carry data payloads that have comparable numerical values is said to *satisfy the heap property* if for all nodes other than the root we have

```
thisNode.getValue() <= thisNode.getParent().getValue()
```

that is, if the data payload value stored at any given node is less than or equal to the payload value stored at the parent node. A binary tree that is complete except possibly for missing nodes on the right-hand edge of the lowest level, and all of whose nodes satisfy the heap property, is called a *heap*. Figure 10.16 shows a complete binary tree that is a heap.

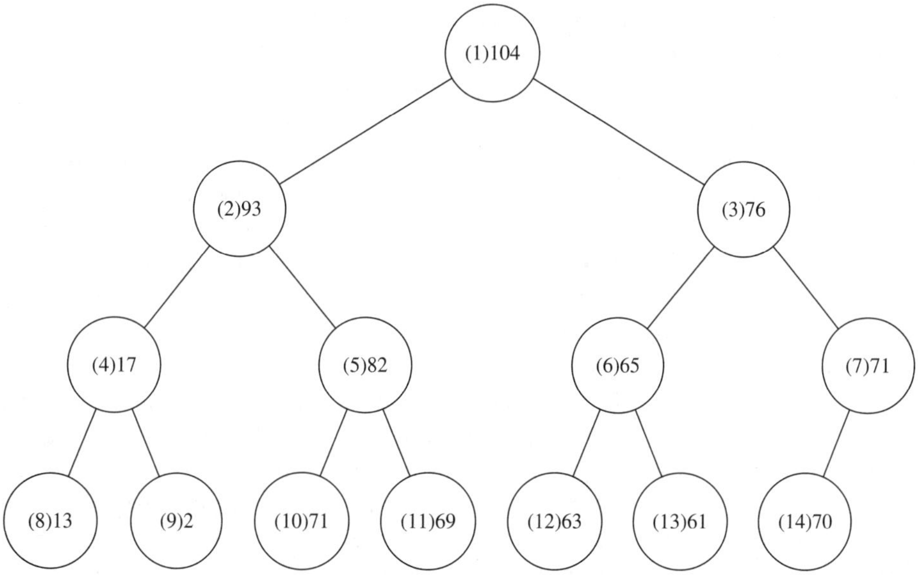

FIGURE 10.16 A heap.

We note that in a heap,[2] whose data payload values are nonincreasing from the root "down" to any leaf node, the maximum value (which need not be unique) would be stored as the payload in the root.

The power of the heap as a data structure comes in large part from Theorems 7.1 and 7.2. The first asserts that we can create a heap in $O(N \lg N)$ time, and the second asserts that we can add or delete an item and then rebuild the heap in $O(\lg N)$ time.

10.6 Traversing a Tree

The basic notion of a tree is ubiquitous in computer science because it is such a useful concept. In many instances, such as with a priority queue, the two-dimensional structure of a tree can be used as added information to a one-dimensional array and thus be used to maintain at low cost a structure from which the minimum (or maximum) entry needs to be extracted and then replaced.

Equally important is the concept of *traversing* a tree. One canonical example of tree traversal comes in thinking of a game-solving program for a puzzle such as Sudoku. We start with a set of open squares and some rules about whether or not a given number can be placed in one of those open squares. Starting at a dummy root node (the starting position), we can choose a large number of possible first moves. For each of those, there is another large set of possible moves, each of which must take into account the fact that our first move also limited the ability to make certain second moves by taking out of consideration moves that would reuse the number of our first choice in that row, column, or subsquare.

Looked at in this way, what we have for a given Sudoku puzzle is a *decision tree* of the possible moves: "If X is our first move, then we have a different set of possible second moves, and we choose move Y from among the possible choices. This provides us with a set of possible third moves, from which we choose Z. . . ." If we have a properly formulated puzzle, there will be some decision tree that leads to a unique solution. That is, if we were to lay out the entire tree graphically, then a particular choice that was legal at level n but that could not be completed to a legal solution would have no children at level $n + 1$.

Such decision trees are commonplace both in life and in computer science. Given the decisions we make, the options open after a given decision are changed, leading to a set of options for the second decision. If we are to analyze properly what the tree looks like, then we need to know how to *traverse* the tree, that is, to visit all the nodes of the tree in some predefined order. In what follows, all traversal methods except for inorder traversal make sense for any tree. Inorder traversal makes sense only for binary trees. And although any tree can be traversed, a complete binary

[2]Actually, this is a *max-heap* because we insist that the data value for the parent is *greater than* that of the child. This property forces the overall maximum value to be in the root node of the tree. If we reversed the inequality, we would have a *min-heap*.

tree is used as our canonical example. For preorder and postorder traversal of general trees, one should do the obvious generalization in the algorithms that follow: replace the "recursively visit the left subtree... recursively visit the right subtree" instruction with "recursively visit subtrees from left to right."

We will use the complete binary tree with labels that was presented in Figure 10.11.

Algorithmically, the *preorder traversal*, *postorder traversal*, and *inorder traversal* are done as follows:

```
Preorder traversal:
  visit the root
  recursively visit the left subtree
  recursively visit the right subtree

Postorder traversal:
  recursively visit the left subtree
  recursively visit the right subtree
  visit the root

Inorder traversal:
  recursively visit the left subtree
  visit the root
  recursively visit the right subtree
```

If we execute a preorder traversal of the tree in Figure 10.11, we will visit the nodes in the sequence shown in Figure 10.17.

$$1, 2, 4, 8, 9, 5, 10, 11, 3, 6, 12, 13, 7, 14, 15$$

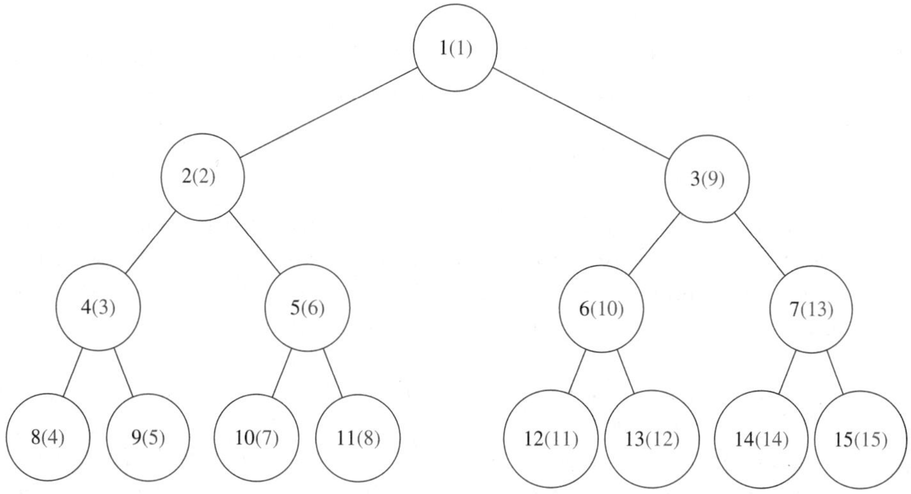

FIGURE 10.17 ■ Preorder traversal of a binary tree.

If we execute a postorder traversal of the tree in Figure 10.11, we will visit the nodes in the sequence shown in Figure 10.18.

$$8, 9, 4, 10, 11, 5, 2, 12, 13, 6, 14, 15, 7, 3, 1$$

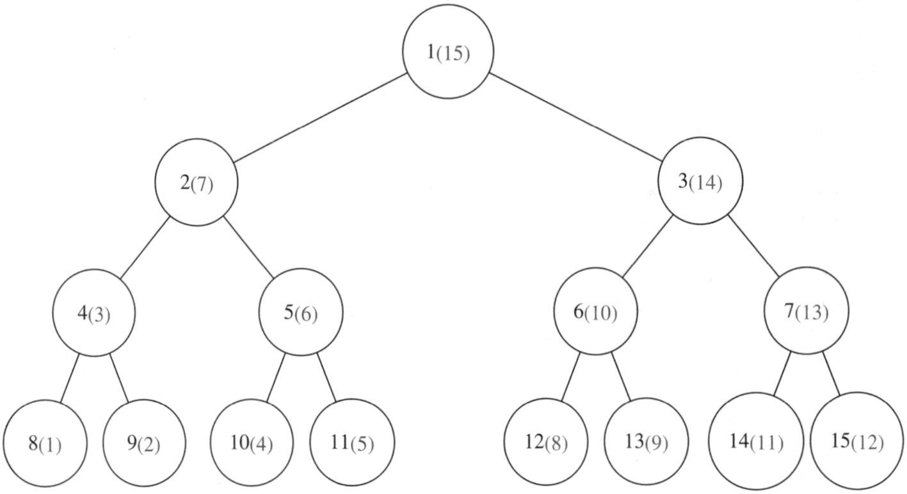

FIGURE 10.18 ■ Postorder traversal of a binary tree.

If we execute an inorder traversal of the tree in Figure 10.11, we will visit the nodes in the sequence shown in Figure 10.19.

$$8, 4, 9, 2, 10, 5, 11, 1, 12, 6, 13, 3, 14, 7, 15$$

You have in fact seen these traversals before but perhaps not with the formality of these names. Consider an arithmetic expression, such as

$$5 + (3 + 2 + 1) * (6 + 7) + 26/2.$$

Although the usual MDAS (My Dear Aunt Sally) rules for performing Multiplication and Division before Addition and Subtraction would apply here, the rules usually applied in algebra are not the left-to-right rules used by most compilers, so we will insert extra parentheses to be completely unambiguous:

$$\{5 + [(3 + 2 + 1) * (6 + 7)] + (26/2)\}.$$

This expression can now be written as a tree as shown in Figure 10.20 and the evaluation of the expression, inside out and left to right, is exactly the postorder

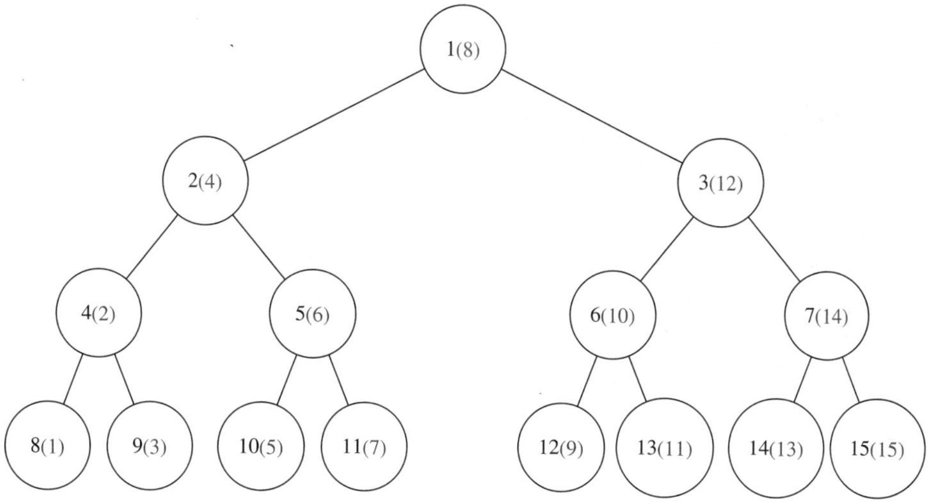

FIGURE 10.19 ■ Inorder traversal of a binary tree.

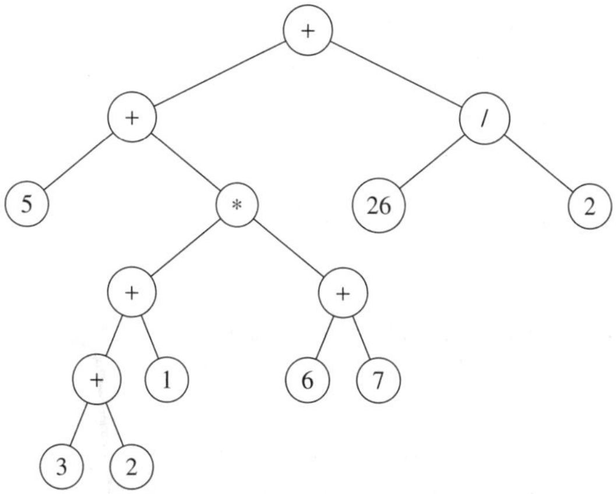

FIGURE 10.20 ■ An arithmetic expression tree.

traversal of the tree, especially if we view the evaluation of the expression in the same way we looked at stack processing in Chapter 7. Processing is essentially inside out: we visit the 5 node first and then must progress down the right child path to the leaves containing 3 and 2. Having visited both children and collected the arithmetic arguments in doing the visit, we can visit their parent, the +, and add $3 + 2$ to get 5. We then visit the right child to pick up the 1, and then the root (again a +) to add $5 + 1$ to get 6. And so forth. Some of the successive stages of the

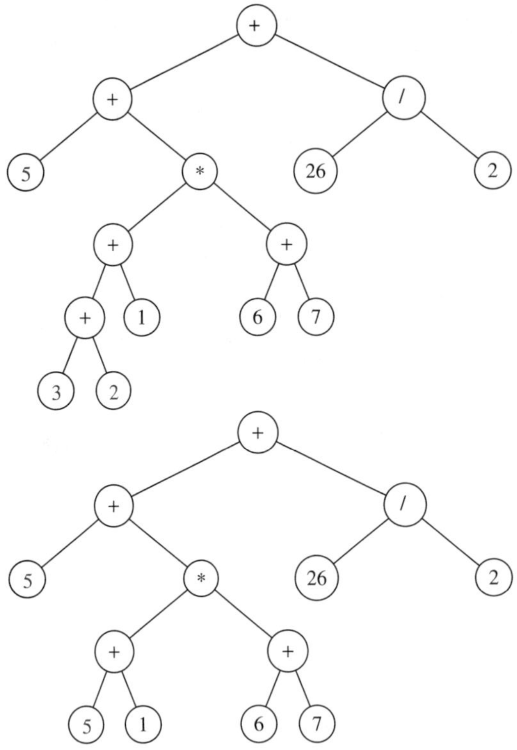

FIGURE 10.21 ■ Postorder processing of an arithmetic expression tree, part 1.

postorder processing are shown in Figures 10.21–10.23. (Not all the individual visits are shown in order to save some space, and we don't run the processing through to the final result.)

In covering the use of a stack in Chapter 7, we discussed XML or HTML tree structures, which very closely resemble arithmetic expressions. In fact, there are extensive standards for laying out web pages and XML documents as trees so that standard software packages can process the trees. One of these standards is the DOM, or Document Object Model, and there are standard packages in many programming languages (including Java) that will read web pages and XML documents, create a tree much as we have created trees for arithmetic expressions or XML, and provide methods for navigating the tree and processing the document. It should be clear that if the XML tree structure were analogous to Figure 10.20, then the processing of the XML would be analogous to evaluating an algebraic expression.

We will see in Chapter 12 a use for inorder traversal of a tree.

We presented postorder processing as one version of the use of a stack for processing algebraic expressions or nested markups in a markup language like HTML or XML. Somewhat similar examples of preorder processing can be found. We

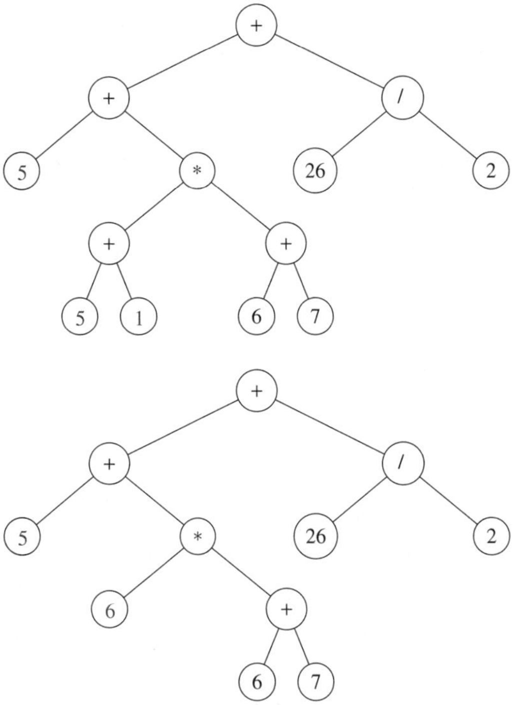

FIGURE 10.22 ■ Postorder processing of an arithmetic expression tree, part 2.

described the *greatest common divisor* function back in Chapter 8. We can also define a recursive gcd function as follows.

```
int gcd(int a, int b)
{
  if(a == b)
    return a;
  else if(a < b)
    return gcd(a, b-a);
  else if(a > b)
    return gcd(a-b, b);
}
```

This definition and method rely on the (easy to prove) fact that

$$\gcd(a, b) = \gcd(a, b - a) = \gcd(a - b, b),$$

with suitable special cases for negative integers, zero, and such. In Scheme, which is a variant of LISP,[3] both of which are languages used for many years now in

[3] Both "Lisp" and "LISP" seem to be in common usage. What is true for both is that the acronym could possibly stand for "Lots of Irritating Single Parentheses"; counting up the right number of nested parentheses has always been difficult.

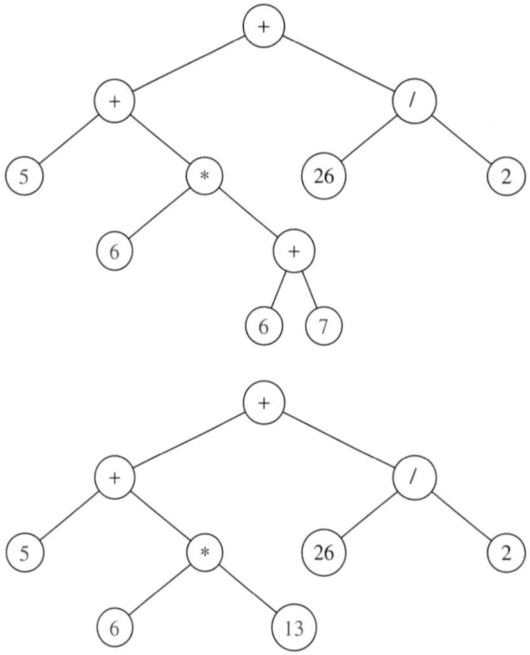

FIGURE 10.23 ■ Postorder processing of an arithmetic expression tree, part 3.

artificial intelligence and compiler writing, the greatest common divisor function can be written as follows.

```
(define gcd
  (lambda (a b)
    (cond ((= a b) a)
          ((> a b) (gcd (- a b) b))
          (else (gcd (- b a) a)))))
```

The Scheme language is intended to be parsed in a preorder fashion. The `define` keyword becomes the root of the tree, the `gcd` name of the function is the left child of the root, and the function itself is the subtree whose root is the right child, beginning with the keyword `lambda`. Then `lambda` is the root of a subtree with the parameters `a b` as the left child and the rest of the expression as the right child. Even if you don't know Scheme (and you probably don't, which is perfectly OK until you take the programming languages course later in the curriculum), it's possible to see that keywords (or function names or operators) like `gcd` are followed by two arguments, both of which could be entire subtrees. All this is entirely analogous to the postorder processing of algebraic expressions; the real difference is that with algebraic expressions and a stack one waits for an operator to appear and then applies that operator to the top two arguments on the stack. With algebraic expressions, it is easy to think inside out, in a postorder fashion. With LISP or Scheme, the intent is that one thinks top-down, with a preorder mindset.

10.6.1 Breadth-First and Depth-First Traversal

There are two other traversal methods for trees (or more generally for graphs). A *depth-first traversal* is essentially the same as an inorder traversal. The order in which nodes are visited is the same (left subtree, root, right subtree), but a depth-first traversal is used in many instances as part of a *depth-first search*, which will be discussed in the next chapter. There are two variations of depth-first search that come immediately to mind if the tree represents, for example, a game strategy.

First, we might probe paths of game moves, starting with the leftmost unexplored path, all the way to the end of the game to determine whether or not that path was a winning strategy. In the case of a naive Sudoku solver, with each level being a specific square to fill in and each node branching out to nine possible choices for that square, we would encounter a very large number of search "crash" conditions for illegal choices, and the entire tree below the node giving the crash would be pruned away; we wouldn't actually have to probe all the way to the end of the game. One can imagine that this would be a simple program to write because it would be a recursive call to a method that ran a couple of loops, and also that it would be very inefficient because a large number of the paths would be illegal. The program would spend most of its time in worthless looping and testing of possibilities already shown to be illegal. We note that in this kind of search the interior nodes don't really have a part to play. Unlike the tree in Figure 10.20, in which the interior nodes were the operations to be performed on the data in the child nodes, in this kind of search the interior nodes contain no information other than "more work to do" or "all subpaths already examined."

The other kind of depth-first search tree is exemplified by a game such as chess. In chess, there are too many possible moves to be able to explore any path all the way to the end, but we also have, based on the knowledge of experts, a way to quantify the "goodness" of any given board position. If we were to consider one move on our part and then one response by the opponent, we could calculate the board's "goodness" for each move and response, and the purpose of our tree search would be to choose our move so as to maximize the goodness. The goodness (or badness, depending on one's point of view) function is referred to in this kind of search as an *objective function* to be minimized or maximized depending on the details.

The naive depth-first search, then, would probe down as many levels as was feasible (competition chess games are timed, after all), compute the objective function for the leaves at that level, and then minimize or maximize the objective function as needed by applying a min or max function in the interior nodes of the tree.

In a *breadth-first traversal*, also called a *level traversal*, the nodes of the tree in Figure 10.11 are visited in order

$$1, 2, 3, 4, 5, 6, 7, 8, 9, 10, 11, 12, 13, 14, 15$$

that is to say, all the nodes of level 0, followed by all the nodes of level 1, all the nodes of level 2, and so forth. In a complete binary tree, especially one that is stored in an array or `ArrayList` with subscripts, breadth-first traversal is relatively simple because there is a static assignment of nodes to subscripts as in Figure 10.15. For a general tree, however, or one that is maintained simply as nodes with links to parents and children, there isn't enough information to allow one to conveniently perform breadth-first search. For example, we have no way to determine the breadth-first successor to node 9 in Figure 10.11 without knowing more about the position of node 9 in the overall tree. The same is true of nodes 5 and 11. Think back to our comments about local information and global information: in order to process breadth first, we need more information about depth and position. A further complication arises if we have a dynamic tree with additions and deletions occurring. Let's assume that we include in a tree node the links going right and left that would make the nodes at a given level into a doubly-linked list. If we now allow a node (say node 5) to be deleted, we must now adjust the doubly-linked lists at the level of node 5 and at the levels of all its children. Although this may be entirely appropriate in some situations, it also starts looking like a complication for which some other data structure might be more appropriate.

10.6.2 Traversal on Parallel Computers

It frequently happens that tree traversal is a computationally expensive proposition because game trees can be very large. In any serious game, such as chess or go, the total number of possible move-and-response paths is huge, making an exhaustive search impossible. Even for something as simple as Sudoku, it can be prohibitively expensive in CPU time to pursue a naive search through trial and error. Because searching in decision trees is an important application but is computationally expensive, it is often done on parallel computers, in part because searching on a decision tree is an *embarrassingly parallel* process. A problem is referred to as embarrassingly parallel if it is absolutely trivial to sketch out an approach for doing independent parts of the computation in parallel with each other.[4]

Consider a totally naive program for Sudoku. There are 81 total squares, and in a medium-difficult puzzle there might be about 31 of these filled in. Since each square

[4]It is commonplace at this point for those in parallel computing to point out that they are not at all embarrassed to work on problems that are embarrassingly parallel.

could be filled in with one of the digits 1 through 9, there are $9^{50} \approx 5.15 \cdot 10^{47}$ possible solutions that could each be checked in parallel, since each of these is completely independent of one another. We have naively a 9-ary tree of 50 levels representing the possible decision trees toward a solution to the puzzle. We start at the root of the decision tree, choose an empty square S_{ij}, and farm out the work to nine different processors P_1 through P_9. Each processor P_k will check whether k is a legal value in square S_{ij}; if so, it will assign k to the square and recursively farm out the test for the next square to nine more processors.

We obviously aren't going to solve the Sudoku puzzle this way. First, in even the largest supercomputers we have perhaps 10^5 processors, not 10^{47}, so we are clearly not going to be able to use a different processor to test each possible solution. Second, spawning a parallel process to test a solution almost certainly takes a lot more work than does the simple test of whether the possible solution actually works, so using one processor for one test incurs an enormous waste in overhead. Finally, it is obvious that huge parts of the game tree don't have to be explored—for every value that fails to be possibly valid in the choice at the first level, 1/9 of the entire tree can be pruned away. If we don't take this into account in assigning processors to tests, we will waste processors by having them sit idle.

What invariably happens in doing a search through a tree on parallel processors is as much art as it is science, and it is to perform a hybrid of breadth-first and depth-first search, with the parallel processors self-scheduling their work off a task queue. The task queue in steady state will be a partial puzzle board and a list of "some number" of "the next" squares to be tested. If a single processor can reasonably handle exhausting the 9^6 possibilities of a complete search through six levels, then the value of "some number" will be set to 6. In steady state, then, each processor will pull a task off the task queue and will conduct a six-level depth-first exhaustive search. Every partial board for which six new squares can be assigned values will become a new task appended to the task queue. The processor will then take another task off the top of the task queue and continue. Locally, on each processor, a depth-first exhaustion of the tree is performed. Globally, if all the tasks were to take exactly the same amount of time, then the parallel assignment of tasks to a block of processors would resemble a breadth-first search. We would be assigning a block of processors to a horizontal set of nodes or tasks at a given level every time, thus progressing across the level in blocks.

The "art" in this kind of computation involves ensuring *load balancing* so that an individual task is an efficient computation and the cost of spawning processes and managing tasks is small compared to the cost of computing depth-first chunks of the tree. If the "some number" of levels is too small, we waste processor time in startup and shutdown activities. If the number of levels is too large, we run the risk of having an inefficient local computation (more tests often means more memory used) and insufficient parallelism. The "science" is generally just the general principles; the art comes from knowing detailed costs for the machine on which the computation will be performed.

10.7 Summary

We have introduced rooted and unrooted trees and the notion of a spanning tree. Trees are important computational structures, and they can be implemented in any of several ways, although most general tree structures would be implemented in Java using an `ArrayList` to store pointers to the child nodes for any given node.

Binary trees are trees that have at most two children for any given node. Since binary trees often correspond to binary divide-and-conquer algorithms, binary trees are often implemented explicitly instead of with the more general code and data structures.

Another use of a binary tree is to implement a heap.

Finally, we have presented preorder, postorder, and inorder traversals of a tree. These are the common traversal methods, and each of these is used for specific important purposes.

10.8 Exercises

1. Show that the two definitions of a tree are equivalent. That is, show that
   (a) If a graph on n nodes is connected and has $n-1$ edges, then it has no cycles.
   (b) If a graph on n nodes is connected and has no cycles, then it has $n-1$ edges.
2. Identify the leaf nodes and the interior nodes on the graphs in Figures 10.1, 10.2, 10.3, 10.4, and 10.5.
3. (a) Show that a complete binary tree with levels 0 through m has exactly 2^i nodes at each level i, $0 \leq i < m$, exactly $2^{m+1}-1$ total nodes, exactly 2^m leaf nodes, and exactly $2^m - 1$ interior nodes.
   (b) A *complete ternary tree* is a tree in which every interior node has exactly three children. Show that a complete ternary tree with levels 0 through m has exactly 3^m nodes at each level i, $0 \leq i < m$, exactly $\frac{3^{m+1}-1}{2}$ total nodes, exactly 3^m leaf nodes, and exactly $\frac{3^m-1}{2}$ interior nodes.
   (c) Develop the general formulas for a complete n-ary tree for any n.
4. Give the preorder, postorder, and inorder traversals of the tree in Figure 10.20.

5. Give the preorder, postorder, and inorder traversals of the following tree.

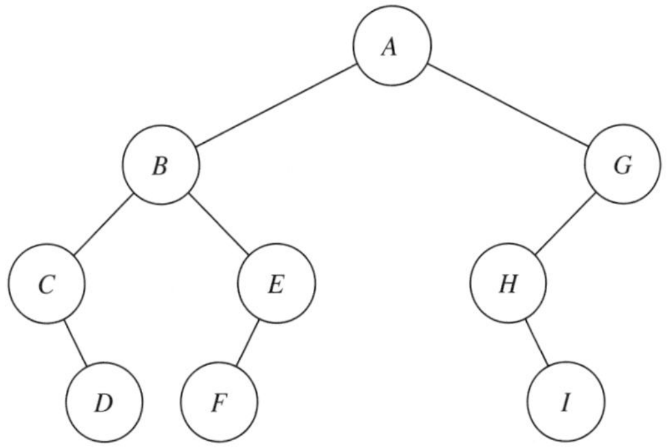

6. Implement a tree in code and use it to process the XML in Figure 7.5.

7. Implement a binary tree in code using an `ArrayList` and the standard subscripting for a binary tree done as a list. Use it to process the arithmetic expression in Figure 10.20. If you convert the expression into the explicit list of nodes and subscripts, you can concentrate on the tree traversal and evaluation of the expression rather than on parsing the expression. The input file can be found on the website at `go.jblearning.com/Buell`.

8. Implement a binary tree in code with explicit left and right child nodes. Use it to process the arithmetic expression of Figure 10.20 just as in Exercise 7.

9. Add a method to any of your tree codes to compute the minimum, maximum, and average depth of the leaf nodes in the tree.

10. Add a method to any of your tree codes to determine if the tree is height-balanced. A tree is said to be *height-balanced* if the maximum and minimum distance from any node v to any leaf node below v differ by at most 1. Your method should be recursive because this definition is inherently recursive.

11. Add a method to any of your general tree codes to compute the minimum, maximum, and average bush factor of a node. The *bush factor* is the number of children emanating from a given node in the tree.

12. Given a general tree without a root, such as the following, show all possible trees that can be constructed from the original tree by adding one more leaf node. Write a method that will generate from an arbitrary tree all the augmentations obtained by adding one leaf node.

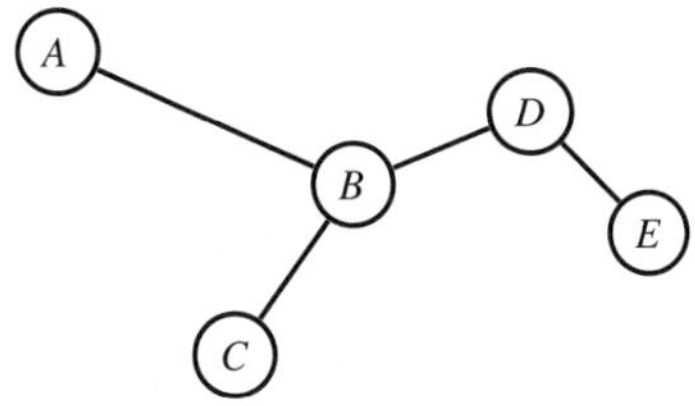

11 Sorting

Objectives

- The concept and implementation of standard sorting algorithms—bubblesort, heapsort, insertionsort, mergesort, and quicksort
- Analysis of the worst-case running times of the standard sorting algorithms
- Analysis of the average-case running times of the standard sorting algorithms
- The difference between worst-case and average-case running times of algorithms and how to perform an average-case analysis
- Practical considerations of sorting: auxiliary space, disk, the extent to which the input data is already sorted, multilevel sorting, and stability
- The lower bound on sorting by comparisons
- * Sorting on a distributed memory parallel computer

Key Terms

average-case running time	in-place algorithm	quicksort
best-case running time	insertionsort	shared memory parallel computer
bubblesort	key	stable sort
bucketsort	mergesort	worst-case running time
distributed memory parallel computer	out-of-place algorithm	
	pivot element	

Introduction

It has been asserted by Knuth that perhaps a third of all CPU cycles are spent in sorting data. This is a huge fraction, but the problem of sorting data comes up in many circumstances when it might not be so obvious that sorting was important. Sorting and searching go hand in hand (indeed, Volume 3 of *The Art of Computer Programming* by Knuth bears *Sorting and Searching* as the title), and creating and maintaining sorted lists, or searchable trees like a priority queue with a heap or a binary search tree, is enormously important. For example, when a Java program is compiled, the compiler must do a lookup every time a symbol or variable name appears. Every time Google does a search, it must process index files. We have already seen that in the absence of some means for creating a sorted or searchable list, the time needed to find a single record among N records is, on average, $O(N/2)$, which is expensive. With binary search on a sorted or indexed file, as in our `FlatFile` example, or with a binary search tree, that cost can be reduced to $O(\lg N)$. With a heap used as a priority queue, we can extract the most important entry and then rebuild the heap structure in $O(\lg N)$ time.

As is customary, we will refer to sorting *keys* under the assumption that our data record, which might be an entire student transcript, is to be sorted based on the value of some key, like the student's ID number. Although it sometimes happens that there is an assigned key for a record, like an ID number or a Social Security number, it is often the case that the key is constructed from data in the record. For example, one might try to construct as unambiguous a key as possible from last name, first name, and middle name (probably in that order) when sorting an address book. This involves some art rather than science, and perhaps also some rules for deciding how to alphabetize. We will gloss over somewhat the process of creating the key and simply assume that keys can be created based on a set of rules. Our interest is in how to use the keys in sorting algorithms.

11.1 Worst-Case, Best-Case, and Average-Case

In this chapter we will, for the first time, explore more deeply the issue of *worst-case running time* versus *average-case running time* and *best-case running time.* For the purpose of doing asymptotic analysis, we always concentrate on the worst-case running time, and we would like to discover algorithms that are fast even in the worst case. However, as we shall see with *quicksort*, an algorithm that has a good average-case behavior might be preferable if its implementation takes advantage of other factors beyond simple asymptotics. The usual goal, after all, is to sort, not to prove theorems about how one might sort.

Under some circumstances we might also look at the best-case behavior of an algorithm. We can't write code as if we are going to encounter the best case in practice, but we can learn sometimes from best-case behavior. For example, there are some sorting algorithms that are fixed-cost algorithms, taking always the same length of time regardless of the nature of the input data. Some algorithms, though, are much more effective on almost-sorted data than they are on random data. The algorithm chosen to sort a large file that is known to be nearly sorted to begin with will probably be different from the algorithm chosen to sort a file of data about which we know nothing.

11.2 Bubblesort

The simple version of code for a *bubblesort*, as used in the `IndexedFlatFile` example, is given in Figure 11.1.

```
public void bubblesort()
{
  for(int length = this.getSize(); length > 1; --length)
  {
    for(int i = 0; i < length-1; ++i)
    {
      if(record[i] > record[i+1])
      {
        CODE TO SWAP record[i] WITH record[i+1]
      }
    }
  }
}
```

FIGURE 11.1 ■ Code fragment for a bubblesort.

As should be clear by now, this is an $O(N^2)$ computation. The outer loop iterates $N-1$ times. In the first iteration of the outer loop, the inner loop iterates $N-2$ times. In the next outer iteration, the inner loop iterates $N-3$ times, and so forth. This is a total of

$$(N-1)+(N-2)+\cdots+1=\frac{(N-1)N}{2}=O(N^2)$$

iterations of the inner loop code to compare and perhaps swap two records based on comparing the values of their keys.

This algorithm works because in each iteration of the outer loop we exchange pairs, bubbling the largest element down the list into the current "last" position, and by the time we have finished the ith iteration, the element in the ith location from the end is the ith largest of all elements. With each outer loop iteration, then, we fix only one more element into its proper place.

11.3 Insertionsort

An *insertionsort* is not asymptotically better than a bubblesort, but it can be better in practice under some circumstances. The insertionsort from Chapter 4 is given in Figure 11.2.

```
public void insertionsort()
{
  for(int i = 1; i <= n; ++i)
  {
    insertSub = i;
    for(int j = insertSub-1; j >= 0; --j)
    {
      if(key[insertSub] > key[j])
      {
        CODE TO SWAP record[insertSub] WITH record[j]
        insertSub = j;
      }
      else
        break;
    }
  }
}
```

FIGURE 11.2 ■ Code fragment for an insertionsort.

This is really very similar to a bubblesort, in that we are fixing only one entry into position with each iteration of the outer loop. In the first iteration, we compare key 1 with key 0 and swap if the two records are out of order. After this first iteration, the records at subscripts 0 and 1 are in the proper order. In the second iteration, we "pull" record 2 forward through records 1 and 0 (if necessary) and swap if necessary so that when we finish this iteration, the three records at subscripts 0 through 2 will be in the proper order. In the worst case, then, when the records are presented in exactly reverse sorted order, this requires

$$1 + 2 + \cdots + (N-1) = \frac{(N-1)N}{2} = O(N^2)$$

comparisons.

In the *best case*, however, insertionsort could run in linear time. If the records are presented in correct sorted order, then we will test the new value against the last of the old values. These two will be in the correct order already, so we know that the entire list with the new value included is in the correct order, and we break out of the loop with every iteration after only one comparison.

In the average case of insertionsort, we have to progress halfway through the current list with every iteration, so we only cut a factor of $\frac{1}{2}$ off the worst-case total comparison count, and that's still $O(N^2)$ comparisons.

Finally, we point out that insertionsort as presented here runs an outer loop on subarrays of lengths $2, 3, \ldots$, and in the inner loop pulls the last entry in the subarray forward until it drops into place. Our code actually does a swap of two entries if they are out of place. This isn't necessary; if we save off the entry we are trying to position, we can avoid half the stores into the array by simply moving the one that is out of place down one location, and then eventually just dropping the entry to be positioned into its correct location. Whether this will actually save any time will depend on how the computer actually does the storing back into memory. Although a program that reads a data item can't progress until it has that data item, a program that stores a data item can continue if the lower-level code and hardware of the machine carry out the store in the background.

11.4 Improving Bubblesort

In both the bubblesort and insertionsort presented here, the effect of the outer loop is to move exactly one element into its proper position with every iteration. We seize upon the one element to be placed into position and compare and exchange only with that element. In the case of bubblesort, the element is the "current largest" (or smallest); in the case of insertionsort, the element is the new element at the end of the list. We also saw that insertionsort could run in linear time, but bubblesort as described previously will always take worst-case time.

There are variations of these sorts that still have worst-case $O(N^2)$ running time but could finish much faster.

In an improved version of bubblesort, we keep track of whether there have been any swaps in a given outer loop. If there have been no swaps, then there were no pairs of elements out of place, which means that the list is sorted. The code for this version could look like Figure 11.3. After the ith iteration of the outer loop, we know that the element at position $i+1$ (and all subsequent elements) are in the correct locations. However, in this variation we compare all adjacent elements and swap any pairs that are out of order, and we keep track of whether any swaps in the current inner iteration have been necessary. If there have been no swaps in the inner iteration, then there were no pairs out of order and we can exit early.

```
public void bubblesort()
{
  boolean didSwap = true;
  length = this.getSize();
  while(didSwap)
  {
    didSwap = false;
    for(int i = 0; i < length-1; ++i)
    {
      if(record[i] > record[i+1])
      {
        CODE TO SWAP record[i] WITH record[i+1]
        didSwap = true;
      }
    }
    --length;
  }
}
```

FIGURE 11.3 ■ Code fragment for an improved bubblesort.

■ 11.5 Heapsort

We will learn later, in Section 11.12.1, that any sort that is done with comparisons, and indeed any sort of a large number of data records, cannot be accomplished in fewer than $O(N \lg N)$ comparisons in the worst case. The heapsort is one of a small number of sorts that is guaranteed to run in exactly $O(N \lg N)$ comparisons for the worst case and the average case, so it is a sort that is guaranteed to run in the asymptotically best possible time. Algorithmically, heapsort is accomplished with the following algorithm. On an array of N records,

```
// Run code to build a max-heap

for (i = N; i > 0; --i)
{
  Exchange the root data item with the item at location i
  Run fixHeapDown(*) on the root of the tree/heap/array
}
```

What this does is the following. After building the max-heap, the largest value in the array is stored at the root. We exchange this largest value with the value stored at location N, so the maximal value is now at location N. We shorten the array by one so that this maximal value will never be looked at again, and then we recreate the heap structure using `fixHeapDown()` to push the new value stored at the root (and that used to be at location N) down into its proper place. After this step, the second-largest value in the entire array, which is the largest value in the newly shortened array, is now stored at the root. We exchange this with the value at location $N-1$, shorten the array again, and rebuild the heap.

We have N items to extract from the root and place at the end of the array, and for each of these extractions, we pay $O(\lg N)$ comparisons to rebuild the heap. Thus the entire process requires, for extracting the values in sorted order, $O(N \lg N)$ comparisons. We combine this with the $O(N \lg N)$ running time for creating the heap in the first place to get an overall running time of $O(N \lg N)$.

(Remember also that we said back in Chapter 7 that there was an $O(N)$ algorithm to build the heap from scratch. One of the reasons we weren't so worried about the $O(N \lg N)$ cost is that the heapsort takes $O(N \lg N)$ time to sort after having built the heap, so we couldn't get an asymptotically better sort even if we did build the heap in $O(N)$ time.)

11.6 Worst-Case, Best-Case, and Average-Case (Again)

Determining best-case, average-case, and worst-case running times is important for sorting because sorting is important. It is also important because there are a number of situations in which we know that data will be partly sorted or that data will have specific characteristics, so if we can exploit what we know about the data we can have algorithms that run faster than worst case. In the case of insertionsort, for example, we have $O(N)$ best case if the data is already sorted correctly, but $O(N^2)$ average-case and worst-case running times. Similarly, our variant of bubblesort, in which we keep track of the number of swaps that have been necessary, and if there are no swaps we can terminate early, provides a best-case $O(N)$ running time on a list that is already sorted. But for both insertionsort and bubblesort, if the data are sorted in exactly backward order, we have to pull every new entry all the way to the beginning of the array or push every entry to the end. Unfortunately, the average case is no better asymptotically than the worst case: If the data are randomly presented to the insertionsort, then on average we save only half the worst-case time because on average we have to move an entry halfway into the list before it can be placed in its proper location.

In the case of heapsort, the best-case, worst-case, and average-case running times are all $O(N \lg N)$, making it at least a totally predictable algorithm to implement.

Quicksort, on the other hand, to be presented later in the chapter, has become the de facto standard sorting method because, although its worst-case time is $O(N^2)$, its average-case running time is $O(N \lg N)$ and its operating characteristics make it highly suited for a variety of standard computing platforms. Further, the constant out in front of the big Oh seems, based on experimentation, to be better than that of heapsort. Our own tables and graph in Figures 11.5–11.7 bear out this fact.

One feature of sorting that makes it somewhat easier to analyze the algorithms is that we know exactly what the possible data inputs are. Given three data items a, b, c to be sorted, they can be presented to the sort in exactly $6 = 3!$ possible permutations (orderings): *abc*, *acb*, *bac*, *bca*, *cab*, *cba*. With four data items, there are $4! = 24$ possible permutations:

$$\begin{gathered} abcd, abdc, acbd, acdb, adbc, adcb, \\ bacd, badc, bcad, bcda, bdac, bdca, \\ cabd, cadb, cbad, cbda, cdab, cdba, \\ dabc, dacb, dbac, dbca, dcab, dcba. \end{gathered}$$

And so forth. If we have N data values, then we can have $N!$ possible permutations of those data values, as is easily seen: We can choose the first value in N ways. For the second value, we have $N-1$ unused values, and we can thus choose the second value to be any of these. For the third value, we have $N-2$ choices, and so forth. All these choices are independent, so the number of possibilities is the product of the number of individual choices, and we have

$$N \times (N-1) \times \cdots 2 \times 1 = N!$$

total possibilities. As stated in Chapter 6, we can use Stirling's formula to get an approximation for the number of possible different permutations as data inputs. This approximation has $(N/e)^N$ as its main term, and grows faster than an ordinary exponential function e^N.

For examining the average-case behavior of an algorithm, the symmetry inherent in the set of possible permutations helps to make analysis possible. For every instance of insertionsort, for example, in which the new element to be inserted is smaller than all the existing elements, and thus needs to be pulled all the way to the front, there is a corresponding permutation in which the new element is larger than all the existing elements and will only need to be compared against the element at the end. These pairs of input permutations will be mutually exclusive and will exhaust the possible inputs. In this instance, then, the average case can be found as the average of best case and worst case.

The fact that the possible inputs to a sorting algorithm include all possible permutations also makes harder our analysis and choice of algorithm, partly because the number of permutations grows rapidly and partly because having all possible inputs as legal means that we have no *a priori* information that we can use to our advantage.

Unless we have additional knowledge of what the data will look like, we will not be able to assume anything except the worst case for input data in analyzing worst-case running time, and therefore we have to prepare for the worst. If, however, we have reason to believe that the data do not appear in entirely random order, then it is conceivable that a less-than-optimal sorting algorithm might still be appropriate. If, for example, one has an array of N records already sorted, and it is necessary to add only another m records, then an insertionsort will run in only $m \cdot N$ time. If m is much smaller than N, this may not actually be so bad. If the situation is that a very large file needs to be updated only occasionally, then the insertion of new records with an insertionsort is likely to be preferable to even a good sorting algorithm if the "good" algorithm would require resorting a large and almost-sorted file.

11.7 Mergesort

Mergesort is a divide-and-conquer algorithm that requires $2N$ space in order to sort N records but completes a sort in $O(N \lg N)$ time. The $2N$ space includes the original N-sized space to hold the array to be sorted, but the downside of mergesort is that it cannot be done *in place* but must be done *out of place* using auxiliary space equal to the size of the original data. This need for extra space is in significant contrast to bubblesort, insertionsort, heapsort, and quicksort, each of which requires only one extra storage location (as temporary space for the swap) beyond the space for the original data array.

Mergesort can be described top-down or bottom-up. Either way, the motivation for mergesort comes from the following steady state merge operation. Given a *sorted* array `A` of length N and a sorted array `B` of length N, we create the sorted array of length $2N$ containing all the elements of arrays `A` and `B` with the pseudocode in Figure 11.4 (this isn't correct Java, but the intent of the pseudocode should be obvious and we want to emphasize the array lengths).

What this code fragment does is the following. We have a pointer into the array `A`, a pointer into the array `B`, and a pointer into the array `C`, each of which is initialized to point to the beginning of the arrays.

We now repeat:

- If the value pointed to in the `A` array is smaller than the value pointed to in the `B` array, then we copy the value from the `A` array, bump the `A` pointer by one, and bump the `C` pointer by one.
- If the value pointed to in the `B` array is the smaller, then we copy that value into `C` and bump the pointers for `B` and `C` instead of those for `A` and `C`.

As long as we have data in both arrays, we copy the smaller of the two values into the result array `C`, and thus in general merge the two sorted arrays into one sorted array. At some point we run out of one or the other of `A` or `B`. If it happens that the

```
public int[2*N] merge(int[N] A, int[N] B)
{
  int[2*N] C;

  ASubscript = 0;
  BSubscript = 0;
  CSubscript = 0;
  while((ASubscript < N) && (BSubscript < N))
  {
    if(A[ASubscript] <= B[BSubscript]
    {
      C[CSubscript] = A[ASubscript];
      ++ASubscript;
    }
    else
    {
      C[CSubscript] = B[BSubscript];
      ++BSubscript;
    }
    ++CSubscript;
  }
// Note that only one of the following two loops actually executes
  while(ASubscript < N)
  {
    C[CSubscript] = A[ASubscript];
    ++ASubscript;
    ++CSubscript;
  }

  while(BSubscript < N)
  {
    C[CSubscript] = B[BSubscript];
    ++BSubscript;
    ++CSubscript;
  }
}
```

FIGURE 11.4 ■ Pseudocode for a merge.

B array still contains data, then all the keys remaining in B are larger than any of the keys in A, and since they are in sorted order already, we can simply copy them in place into the result array. If it happens that the A array still contains data, we do the corresponding copy from A.

We note three basic facts about this central operation.

- First, the question of equal keys doesn't affect anything. If there are equal keys, then we can (unless there are other conditions imposed) choose entries from either array without affecting the fact that the eventual array is in sorted order.

- Second, there is no way to avoid using extra storage space. In the best case, we are interleaving entries from `A` and `B`, and we would need only fixed extra storage. But in the worst case, all the entries of one array (say `A`) are smaller than all the entries of `B` and thus we have to copy all of `A` into `C` and then copy all of `B`. The only way to do this is by having space in the result array for both subarrays.
- Finally, this merge runs in linear time. With two arrays of length N, we can perform the merge in worst-case $2N$ comparisons (in the case of perfectly interleaved data).

The mergesort algorithm can be viewed either top-down as a recursive algorithm or bottom-up as an algorithm that creates with each phase a sorted list of $2N$ items by merging two lists of N items each. It is perhaps better understood in the bottom-up form.

Consider an array of 2^n items arranged as 2^{n-1} pairs of data items. For example, if $n = 4$, we would have 16 items in all that could be arranged as 8 pairs as shown here.

1	3
7	4
0	8
2	1
9	2
8	3
9	8
7	8

In the first pass, we use one comparison per pair, eight times over, to sort the eight pairs into proper order. (This is in fact the same algorithmic step as the merge phases later on, but it's a degenerate merge when we have only two items.)

1	3
4	7
0	8
1	2
2	9
3	8
8	9
7	8

We now apply the preceding merge operation on the four pairs of pairs.

1	3	→	1 3 4 7
4	7	↗	
0	8	→	0 1 2 8
1	2	↗	
2	9	→	2 3 8 9
3	8	↗	
8	9	→	7 8 8 9
7	8	↗	

We now have four quadruples, which we can merge into pairs.

1	3	4	7	→	0 1 1 2 3 4 7 8
0	1	2	8	↗	
2	3	8	9	→	2 3 7 8 8 8 9 9
7	8	8	9	↗	

Finally, we merge the pair of arrays of length 8.

0	1	1	2	3	4	7	8	→	0 1 1 2 2 3 3 4 7 7 8 8 8 8 9 9
2	3	7	8	8	8	9	9	↗	

We have described mergesort from the bottom up, which is arguably the more intuitive approach. If we were to code this, the outer loop of the program would look something like the following.

```
// N = 2^n items to be sorted
for(int phase = 1; phase <= n; ++phase)
{
//  merge the 2^(n-phase) pairs of arrays of length 2^phase
}
```

Note that the code inside the loop requires $O(N)$ comparisons. Our earlier example merge code would perform a merge of two N-long arrays in $2N$ comparisons. Indeed we can merge *all* the pairs of arrays in time equal to the total length. If we are merging pairs of arrays of length 8 into arrays of length 16, for example, our loop would look something like the following.

```
pointer1 = 0
pointer2 = 8
while((pointer1 < N) and (pointer2 < N))
{
  merge entries at 0,1,...,7 and entries at 8,9,...15
  store the merged set as entries 0,1,...,15

  pointer1 = pointer1 + 8
  pointer2 = pointer2 + 8
}
```

Note that we are walking through the array exactly once, even though we are using a merge loop nested inside the `while` loop.

Writing a mergesort bottom up like this is not especially difficult, but it is slightly tedious. The subscripting is a bit complicated and we must get the subscripting exactly correct. Mergesort can often be written recursively, and the recursive version is slightly less complicated. In either case, the critical factor becomes the fact that extra storage is necessary. Done wrong, a program would need additional storage with *every* new phase of the sort. (Think back to the extra storage in the Jumble puzzle code.) Done right, mergesort would be written to ping-pong from one data array to another, taking data from array X in phase 1 and storing the result in array Y, then taking data from array Y in phase 2 and storing the result in array X, and so forth. If one were to implement mergesort recursively, one would absolutely *not* want to implement the code as in Figure 11.4 that passed in data arrays as parameters but would rather have the data arrays stored outside the method and pointers (subscripts) passed as parameters to the method.

11.7.1 Analysis of Mergesort

The easiest way to analyze mergesort is to look at the bottom-up algorithm. For simplicity, we consider the problem of sorting $N = 2^n$ items. In the first merge phase, we use $O(N)$ comparisons to put 2^{n-1} pairs into sorted order. In the second merge phase, we use $O(N)$ comparisons to merge 2^{n-2} quadruples into sorted order. In the third merge phase, we use $O(N)$ comparisons to merge 2^{n-3} octuples into sorted order. This continues until the entire list is sorted. If $N = 2^n$, we will need to continue for $n = \lg N$ phases in order to sort the entire list, which means that overall we will be doing $O(Nn) = O(N \lg N)$ comparisons.

11.7.2 Disk-Based Sorting

We would be derelict in our duty if we did not make one final observation with regard to mergesort. As will be taught in computer architecture and operating systems courses (at least), modern computers are built so as to maximize the appearance of an ideal computer to the user and to minimize for the user the complexity of the physical device. This is done in part by trying to match what *can* be done efficiently on the hardware with the choice of what *could* be wanted by the user. Since the cost of physically moving a read head on a disk to a particular location on a disk is high, compared with the cost of actually doing the read of data, streaming N sequential items off a disk into memory is much faster than searching for and accessing N specific items located randomly throughout a file. One slow positioning followed by N fast reads takes much less time than N slow positionings each followed by a single N fast read.

If the data to be sorted are on disk instead of in memory (and this will be the case for extremely large files to be sorted), there will be a huge advantage in implementation for a sorting algorithm that can take advantage of streaming data from a disk, and in this regard, mergesort excels. The mergesort algorithm streams data sequentially from two source locations (files), performs simple (and thus fast) comparisons, and then streams the result data back to the disk to be stored (in sequential order). Its execution characteristics thus match the characteristics of the underlying hardware. Although this doesn't show up in asymptotic analysis (except in the constant out front), it can make a huge difference in practice.

11.8 Quicksort

We now come to the last of the sort methods we will examine, which has become the de facto standard as the best compromise between worst-case asymptotics, average-case asymptotics, and execution characteristics on extant machines.

To understand the notion of *quicksort*, we recall one aspect of each of two previous sorting algorithms. First, we recall the recursive nature of mergesort when run on an array of $N = 2^n$ data items: by splitting the sorting problem in half for each phase, we run $n = \lg N$ phases. Each phase k comprises 2^{n-k} subsorts, each of which is done on 2^k data items, and each phase requires $N = 2^n = 2^k \cdot 2^{n-k}$ comparisons and exactly one traversal of the entire data set. This gives us a running time of $N \lg N$, which is good (we will see in a moment that it's the best we can do). The negative feature of mergesort is the need to do the merge using extra storage space. Quicksort accomplishes this recursive sorting without needing extra space.

On the other side, we remember that both bubblesort and insertionsort fixed, in a single iteration of the outer loop, one element in the array into its proper place. Since only one element is properly positioned with each outer iteration, and such a positioning takes N comparisons, these sorts run in N^2 time.

In contrast, what we will be able to accomplish with quicksort is to fix one element in phase 1, then two elements in phase 2 (one in each of the two half-arrays passed recursively to the sort), then four elements in phase 3 (one in each of the quarter-arrays), and so forth. If we can do this, then in $n = \lg N$ phases, each of which fixes k elements, we will be able to fix

$$1 + 2 + 2^2 + \cdots + 2^{n-1} = 2^n - 1 = N - 1$$

elements. Fudging N and $N - 1$ for convenience, this means we will have an $O(N \lg N)$ algorithm, with $\lg N$ phases, each of which takes N time.

The Achilles heel of quicksort, when it comes to worst-case asymptotics, is that we cannot guarantee that our recursive breakdown of the array will divide the array into equal halves at each step. If we are lucky, and we get roughly equal halves, then we will run $\lg N$ recursive phases just as with mergesort, and on average we will get the behavior we need for an efficient algorithm. Each of the recursive phases of quicksort will run in $O(N)$ time. In the worst case, however, it is possible that when we split a subarray of length m into two "halves," we will in fact have one "half" of a single element and the other half containing $m - 1$ elements. If this happens with every phase, then we will have N phases and not $\lg N$ phases, and the total running time will be $O(N^2)$. Referring to the previous paragraph, in this worst case we will not be fixing *multiple* elements into their proper location but in fact fixing only a single new element with each phase.

11.8.1 The Quicksort Algorithm

The basic quicksort algorithm is as follows.

1. We choose a *pivot element* whose key is k. This can be any element in the array, but most implementations will choose either the first or the last element.
2. We divide the full array into three subarrays: subarray A contains the elements whose keys are less than k; subarray B contains the elements whose keys are equal to k; and subarray C contains the elements whose keys are greater than k.
3. We recursively sort subarrays A and C, and return the elements of A, B, and C in that order.

In general, dealing with the case of equal keys adds a certain complexity but no further understanding to the problem of sorting, and we will assume in our examples that all keys are distinct.

11.8.1.1 Quicksort—the Magic

Clearly, if we can divide the array into equal subarrays in every phase, then we would have $\lg N$ phases in the computation. If each phase were to take N steps, the running time would be $N \lg N$. The crucial issue is then the choice of the pivot element. A good choice splits the array in half; a bad choice might leave either subarray A or C empty with all the elements in the other subarray.

Let's assume for the moment that we have a magical algorithm for choosing a pivot element. We must still show how to perform each phase of the array-splitting of step 1 in linear time so as to hope for $N \lg N$ overall running time, and we must show how to perform this splitting so as to do better than mergesort by not requiring extra space. Consider the following array.

97	11	90	81	34	40	65	72	51	23	57

We choose to pivot on the last element 57, and we set up pointers at the beginning of the array and at the penultimate entry of the array.

↓									↓	
97	11	90	81	34	40	65	72	51	23	**57**

We now move forward from the right pointer. As long as the entry pointed to by the right pointer is larger than the pivot, we keep moving the right pointer to the left and checking again. In this case, $23 < 57$ so we switch to moving the left pointer. We test and immediately determine that $57 < 97$, so our left pointer and our right pointer are pointing to elements that are in the wrong half of the array. We exchange these two values.

↓									↓	
97	11	90	81	34	40	65	72	51	23	**57**
↓									↓	
23	11	90	81	34	40	65	72	51	97	**57**

We now move the right pointer once and find that $51 < 57$, so we stop moving the right pointer and switch again to the left pointer. We find that 11 is in the correct subarray, move the left pointer once, and find that 90 is not in the correct subarray.

↓								↓		
23	11	90	81	34	40	65	72	51	97	**57**
	↓							↓		
23	11	90	81	34	40	65	72	51	97	**57**
		↓						↓		
23	11	90	81	34	40	65	72	51	97	**57**

We exchange 90 and 51 and continue, moving first the right and then the left pointer until we encounter entries in the wrong locations and then exchanging.

		↓						↓		
23	11	51	81	34	40	65	72	90	97	**57**

		↓					↓			
23	11	51	81	34	40	65	72	90	97	**57**

		↓				↓				
23	11	51	81	34	40	65	72	90	97	**57**

		↓			↓					
23	11	51	81	34	40	65	72	90	97	**57**

			↓		↓					
23	11	51	81	34	40	65	72	90	97	**57**

			↓		↓					
23	11	51	40	34	81	65	72	90	97	**57**

			↓	↓						
23	11	51	40	34	81	65	72	90	97	**57**

				↓↓						
23	11	51	40	34	81	65	72	90	97	**57**

We now exchange the pivot element with the first element of the "larger-than" array. The pivot is now in its proper location and we have two subarrays that we hope are of roughly equal size.

(23 11 51 40 34) **57** (65 72 90 97 81)

We make the recursive calls to sort the subarrays.

↓			↓							
(23	11	51	40	**34**)	57	(65	72	90	97	81)

↓		↓								
(23	11	51	40	**34**)	57	(65	72	90	97	81)

↓	↓									
(23	11	51	40	**34**)	57	(65	72	90	97	81)

	↓↓									
(23	11	51	40	**34**)	57	(65	72	90	97	81)

	↓↓									
(23	11	**34**	40	51)	57	(65	72	90	97	81)
						↓			↓	
(23	11)	34	(40	51)	57	(65	72	90	97	**81**)
						↓		↓		
(23	11)	34	(40	51)	57	(65	72	90	97	**81**)
						↓	↓			
(23	11)	34	(40	51)	57	(65	72	90	97	**81**)
							↓↓			
(23	11)	34	(40	51)	57	(65	72	90	97	**81**)
							↓↓			
(23	11)	34	(40	51)	57	(65	72	**81**	97	90)
(23	11)	34	(40	51)	57	(65	72)	81	(97	90)

At this point, as with mergesort, we have recursed down to subarrays of length two, and we can simply compare and exchange. The array has been sorted.

(11 23) 34 (40 51) 57 (65 72) 81 (90 97)

This was an example created to be a best-case example. We split 11 elements into a pivot and two 5-element subarrays, and each subarray was further split into a pivot and two 2-element subarrays.

What allows us to get a linear time for the array-splitting, however, is that we have traversed the entire array only once for each splitting phase of the algorithm. We move pointers and compare elements once in each subarray, and all the subarrays are nonoverlapping, so we never actually look at any particular element more than once. This gives us worst-case linear time for each phase.

To see how a worst-case quicksort would execute, consider the following sorted array.

1 2 3 4 5 6 7 8 9 10 **11**

When we start moving pointers in the first phase, we find that the pivot element is larger than the rest of the array, and one of our two subarrays is empty. After the first phase, we have produced the unsatisfying tableau

(1 2 3 4 5 6 7 8 9 10) **11** ().

In the next phase, this continues to be true. If we choose 10, the last element, as our pivot, then after the entire second phase we have

$$(1 \quad 2 \quad 3 \quad 4 \quad 5 \quad 6 \quad 7 \quad 8 \quad 9) \quad \mathbf{10}() \quad 11.$$

After the third phase we have

$$(1 \quad 2 \quad 3 \quad 4 \quad 5 \quad 6 \quad 7 \quad 8) \quad \mathbf{9}() \quad 10 \quad 11$$

and so on. Since we are fixing only one element per phase into its proper location, we will need nine phases (assuming that when only two elements remain we can do a comparison and return).

The difference between the best-case $O(N \lg N)$ and worst-case $O(N^2)$ running times clearly lies in our choice of the pivot element. What we would like to have is an oracle that would tell us which element chosen as pivot would split the array in half, but if we were that good at predicting the future, we'd be working on Wall Street instead of learning how to write programs and design algorithms. There are variations of quicksort that work to mitigate the performance degradation from pathologically bad input data by choosing a better pivot element. For example, instead of choosing the last element in the array every time, one could sample three values from throughout the array and take the middle as the pivoting value. In the case of already-sorted data, a random sample would be more likely to return a better pivot; if we did this in the preceding array, we would get a pivot value of 6 for the first phase, which would be clearly superior. On the other hand, for *any* such sampling scheme, there will be *some* pathological worst case, so no pivot choice method will be able to overcome the fact that quicksort has $O(N^2)$ running time when presented with the worst case of data input for that choice.

11.8.2 Average-Case Running Time for Quicksort

The proof of the following important theorem is beyond the scope of this book, but the statement of the theorem is not.

Theorem 11.1

The average-case running time of quicksort is $O(N \lg N)$.

We will show later in this chapter that no sorting algorithm that sorts by making comparisons can sort asymptotically faster than $O(N \lg N)$. That result coupled with this one is tremendously important. Together we thus know that although the worst-case behavior of quicksort is as bad as the "naive" bubblesort and insertionsort, the quicksort algorithm actually does as well as any algorithm could possibly do when presented with a random set of input data.

We will also discuss later why quicksort is a preferred sort in terms of using the physical hardware efficiently. It is the efficient use of hardware plus the best-possible average-case running time that make quicksort the standard sorting algorithm in most implementations.

11.9 Sorting Without Comparisons

All the sorting methods we have just described require comparisons. Under normal circumstances, this is what we count when we consider the asymptotics for sorting data. It is possible, though, under certain very restricted circumstances, to be able to sort without comparisons. For example, if we happen to know that all the keys have values in the range 1 through 100, we can sort the records using a *bucketsort*.

In such a bucketsort, we would set up 100 buckets of variable size, and instead of comparing keys, we would simply look at the key value and store the record in the appropriate bucket for that key.

Dealing with duplicate keys in a bucketsort requires further knowledge of what is actually going on. In some cases, we don't care whether there is one element or many with a given key, because we need only know that *some* element occurred with that key. For such an application, we need only keep a boolean value in the array.

For other applications, we might be able to assume that all records with the same key are identical. If we are sorting mail by zip code for a particular metropolitan area so as to get bulk mail discounts, then this is a safe assumption because we would probably be physically sorting mail into actual bins. Even if it is not a physical sort, it may well be the case that it does not matter in which order records with the same key value are stored. If it does matter, then it might still be the case that the number of elements with the same key is small and we could use a linked list with an insertionsort to store the elements in each bucket.

Unfortunately, this kind of sort is usually not possible because it requires that we know in advance all the possible values and that we be able to set up a bucket of arbitrary size for each possible key value. In the cases when it can be used, it runs in linear time $O(N)$ because we need only look at the record once and place it in the correct bucket.

For the most part, though, we will be looking at sorting algorithms that require comparisons, and in our asymptotic analysis we will measure the quality of an algorithm by counting the number of comparisons.

11.10 Experimental Results

In Volume 3 of *The Art of Computer Programming*, Knuth presents empirical data on the performance of various sorting algorithms as he had implemented them. We have done our own simple implementations of bubblesort, insertionsort, heapsort, and mergesort in Java, and have counted the number of comparisons and the number of swaps when run on data arrays of lengths 127, 511, 2,047, 8,191, 32,767, and 113,071. We generated "reasonably random"[1] arrays of these lengths of integers less than 99,991 (the largest prime smaller than 100,000).

The raw data from these tests are presented in Figure 11.5. We show the number of comparisons made and the number of swaps for each of the four sorting methods on our six (ostensibly) random data sets.

	Bubblesort		Insertionsort	
Data	Comps	Swaps	Comps	Swaps
127	8,001	4,024	4,146	4,024
511	130,305	64,184	64,690	64,184
2,047	2,094,081	1,058,276	1,060,314	1,058,276
8,191	33,542,145	16,804,307	16,812,488	16,804,307
32,767	536,821,761	268,317,072	268,349,824	268,317,072
131,071	8,589,737,985	4,054,936,240	4,296,967,076	4,296,836,017

	Heapsort		Quicksort	
Data	Comps	Swaps	Comps	Swaps
127	1,423	836	930	215
511	7,826	4,416	4,883	1,100
2,047	39,431	21,707	24,596	5,430
8,191	190,910	103,572	121,762	25,365
32,767	894,810	479,714	594,064	116,024
131,071	4,103,982	2,181,680	2,665,459	523,552

FIGURE 11.5 Raw counts of comparisons and swaps.

We have theorems that claim that the worst-case running times for these four sorts are $O(N^2)$ and $O(N \lg N)$. If our "random" data produced running times like

[1] Our generation method would almost certainly not hold up under a rigorous test of randomnicity, but we believe it is sufficient for this illustrative purpose.

	Bubblesort/N^2		Insertionsort/N^2	
Data	Comps	Swaps	Comps	Swaps
127	0.496	0.249	0.257	0.249
511	0.499	0.246	0.248	0.246
2,047	0.500	0.253	0.253	0.253
8,191	0.500	0.250	0.251	0.250
32,767	0.500	0.250	0.250	0.250
131,071	0.500	0.236	0.250	0.250

	Heapsort/($N \lg N$)		Quicksort/($N \lg N$)	
Data	Comps	Swaps	Comps	Swaps
127	1.601	0.941	1.046	0.242
511	1.702	0.960	1.062	0.239
2,047	1.751	0.964	1.092	0.241
8,191	1.793	0.973	1.143	0.238
32,767	1.821	0.976	1.209	0.236
131,071	1.842	0.979	1.196	0.235

FIGURE 11.6 ■ Normalized counts of comparisons and swaps.

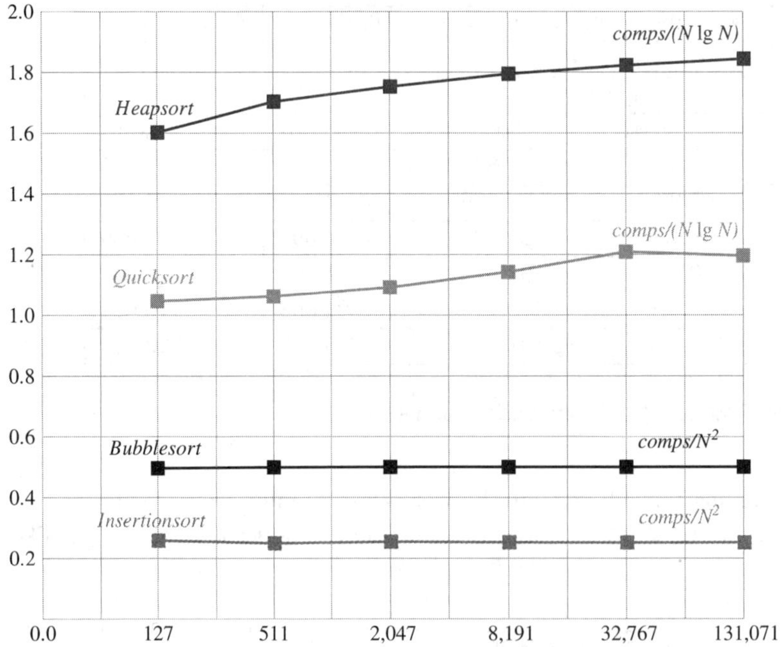

FIGURE 11.7 ■ Comparison counts for the four sorting algorithms.

this, then we would have some reason to believe (but not a proof) that perhaps these are not just worst-case running times but also average-case running times.

In fact, that's exactly what we see. In Figure 11.6 we divide these counts by N^2 and by $N \lg N$ as appropriate so as to estimate the constant C in the asymptotic estimate. The data of Figure 11.6 is graphed in Figure 11.7. It is reassuring to notice that as the data size increases, the "constant" is in fact reasonably constant, although there is some upward creep in both heapsort and quicksort. Our earlier estimate was that heapsort as we implemented it would require $2N \lg N$ comparisons, so we would expect the constant to stabilize at no larger than 2.0.

One obvious observation is that quicksort is indeed faster than heapsort on this (allegedly) random data. In addition to the implementation advantage that quicksort has, it would appear that on random data it also has an asymptotic advantage as well. If we accept the truth of Theorem 11.1, we should not be surprised at the graph for quicksort, but it's nonetheless reassuring to have observations fit the theory.

11.11 Auxiliary Space and Implementation Issues

When analyzing a sorting algorithm, the most prominent issue is the asymptotic running time. In theory, this is the most important aspect of a choice of sorting methods. Asymptotic running time, however, is not the only criterion to be considered. Indeed, if one is actually going to be sorting data,[2] then all of the real-world considerations and characteristics of the problem to be solved must be brought into the discussion. The U.S. Internal Revenue Service, for example, has a very different problem when sorting some 200 million tax records that live on disk than does an Internet server that has to take in packets in real time and sort all the packets for a particular transmission in order to deliver them to the eventual recipient. We don't expect the IRS to be sorting constantly, but when it does it will sort a large number of items. The packet server, in contrast, is sorting a small number of items, but it's doing a new sort on a new message all the time.

Further, data that is known to be almost sorted *a priori* should probably be sorted differently from data about which nothing is known. Data to be sorted on a large mainframe might well be sorted differently from data on a desktop or laptop. Unless one is an algorithmist or theoretical computer scientist, the goal in implementing a sorting algorithm is probably to be able to sort data, and the real world, however messy, must intrude.

[2] As opposed to proving theorems about how one *might* sort data

11.11.1 Space Considerations

The first implementation issue to be considered is whether extra space is needed for the sorting algorithm. In the case of bubblesort, insertionsort, heapsort, and quicksort, no extra space is needed other than the one extra location necessary for temporary storage in doing a swap of two records. The array in which the data are stored at the beginning of the sort is the array in which the data are stored at the end.

In the case of mergesort, extra space is required, and the amount of extra space is $O(N)$, equal to the size of the original array. On the one hand, this is a major burden on mergesort if all the data must be kept in memory. On the other hand, mergesort is the one sorting algorithm, of the several we have discussed, that is highly suitable for disk-to-disk sorting of very large files. One characteristic of mergesort that is highly desirable for this purpose is that all the data are accessed in a purely sequential way. Two (large) files are brought in from disk sequentially for comparisons and the result array is written exactly in sequence to the output file. Since a disk is at its best when streaming data to the processor, this match between best use of the hardware and the needs of the sorting algorithm make mergesort a favorite for large-file sorts. This is in sharp contrast to heapsort, whose access pattern goes all over the array, pulling up entries n, $2n$, and $2n + 1$ that will be located in very different places on disk. Even quicksort is likely to perform poorly in a disk-to-disk implementation because it requires accessing and then rewriting (or not) at specific locations that may or may not be contiguous on disk.

11.11.2 Memory

Of the three $O(N \lg N)$ sorting algorithms we have discussed—mergesort, heapsort, and quicksort—we can generally decide that mergesort is not the best general-purpose sort because it requires $O(N)$ extra space. Between heapsort with guaranteed $O(N \lg N)$ running time and quicksort that is only guaranteed on average to run in $O(N \lg N)$ time, it is somewhat surprising at first that quicksort has become the standard sort found in software libraries, but that is in fact true.

Part of the reason for quicksort's success is that the memory access patterns for quicksort are far superior than those for heapsort given the constraints of standard computer architectures. We normally only care about the running time of sorts when we have large arrays to sort, so we assume, in dealing with real-world constraints, that substantial memory space is needed for our array. The feature of quicksort that makes it superior to heapsort for general applications is that quicksort usually runs largely in cache, not in main memory.

Cache, which these days is usually on the processor chip, is a smaller, intermediate memory space between the processor's registers and logic units and the RAM that lives elsewhere on the motherboard. For various reasons including the fact that cache is actually on the processor chip, access to cache is much faster than access to main memory. This comes at a price in real dollars, though, and while many desktops are configured with some number of gigabytes of RAM, cache is still measured in megabytes, with as much as 8 MB showing up only in current high-end processors. For the most part below the level that any programmer can control (even in assembly language), the processor loads blocks of data from the main memory RAM into the cache either as the data is requested or in anticipation of requests for the data. As long as the processor's requests for data can be met with values from cache instead of main memory, execution is faster.

It is here, with respect to cache, that heapsort's memory access patterns work against the algorithm. Records accessed at subscripts n, $2n$, and $2n + 1$ are likely to be in different blocks of memory for large values of n, so they are unlikely to be in cache because they are only accessed once every so often. In contrast, quicksort accesses sequential locations in the array with its moving pointers, and it rapidly recurses down to working on subarrays that will fit in cache. Once the subarray fits entirely in cache, all the processing can be done by moving data in cache, not in main memory, with a concomitant increase in speed.

■ 11.11.3 Multilevel Sorts

It is not uncommon for a large general-purpose sort to be implemented as a multilevel sort with more than one sorting method. Although a mergesort is effective on large files, its effectiveness is greater in the later phases when merging large, sorted arrays than in the early phases. One might well implement a sort of large data by first bringing into memory blocks of data in as large a block as would fit conveniently and efficiently, sorting that data in memory with a quicksort, and then writing that block of data back out to disk. By doing this subsorting in memory, one gets the advantage of a (faster) memory-based sort on blocks of data as large as can be managed, and one can follow this with a disk-to-disk merge of the large blocks of sorted data.

We will see a variation of this idea later in this chapter when we discuss sorting on parallel computers.

■ 11.11.4 Stability

A final consideration for sorting data is that some sorting methods are *stable* and some are not stable. A sort is *stable* if two records that have the same key end up being stored in the sorted array in the same order in which they are presented in the original array. If record i precedes record j in the original array, and if both records have the same key, then record i should still precede record j when the array is eventually sorted. Stability of sorting algorithms is important, for example, when one is adding new data to an already sorted list or when one is sorting on multiple keys. If one is sorting on last name and is adding data to an existing list, one usually wants the new data simply inserted where it ought to go in the augmented list. It could be especially annoying to find that the original list of last name "Smith" entries came out in a different order from what they had been before just because a new "Smith" entry was added.

Not all sorts are stable. Heapsort, for example, is pretty much guaranteed not to be stable. Bubblesort and insertionsort are stable provided one gets the "less-than" and "less-than-or-equal" comparisons done properly. In the preceding implementation, two records are swapped if the key of one is *greater than* the key of the other. If the keys are equal, the records are not swapped, so records of equal key end up being stored in their original order, and the sort is stable. If one wrote the sort comparison as `if(key[i] >= key[j])`, the records would still end up sorted, but the sort would not be stable.

Quicksort is stable in the same way that bubblesort and insertionsort are stable, that is, provided one takes care not to force the exchange of records with equal keys. In all three instances we are moving records only because they are out of order, and we do not move records that are locally in the correct order.

11.12 The Asymptotics of Sorting

We have seen three sorting algorithms that run in $O(N \lg N)$ time. What we will now prove is that this is asymptotically the fastest possible running time for any sorting algorithm that sorts by comparing keys. This is a very important result. If the asymptotic running time of heapsort, mergesort, and quicksort (and any other sort we can come up with that has this running time) is as good as is possible, then the best we can do is to improve the constant out front and to improve the implementation; no further theoretical improvement is possible. As we have seen from Figures 11.5 and 11.6, quicksort appears to have a better constant than heapsort, at least on our experimental data. As we have discussed previously, it also has better characteristics when implemented on modern computers. Any algorithm that would replace quicksort as the standard would have to have an $O(N \lg N)$ running time and a better constant on observed execution instances or better implementation characteristics.

11.12.1 Lower Bounds on Sorting

What we are going to prove in the next few pages is a *lower bound* on the cost of sorting by comparisons. That lower bound will be $O(N \lg N)$. Since that is the worst-case running time for heapsort and mergesort, we can conclude that no sorting algorithm that uses comparisons will be asymptotically faster than either of these. If one algorithm is to be faster than another, it will be either because the constant out front is smaller (remember Figure 6.1) or because the algorithm just happens to be better suited to the way certain computers (possibly most computers) are constructed.

Consider an algorithm to sort three elements $\{a, b, c\}$ by comparison of keys as a decision tree, as in Figure 11.8. What we are going to do is show that there is a lower bound on the number of comparisons needed to sort by comparisons. Specifically, we will show that no comparison-based sort can possibly sort all possible input permutations in fewer than $O(N \lg N)$ comparisons.

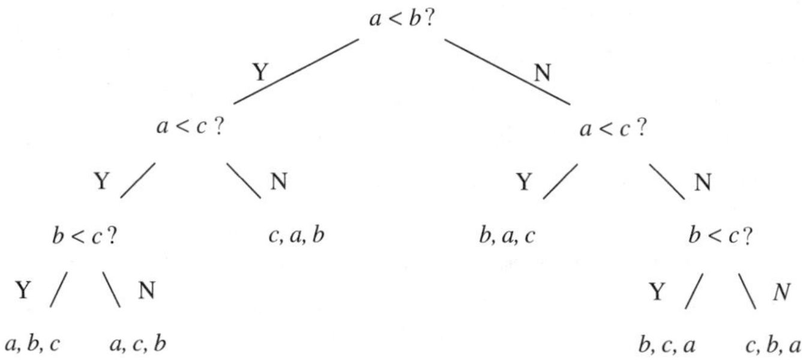

FIGURE 11.8 ■ A decision tree.

What we have in the decision tree is a tree of comparisons to be applied in order going down from the root, so that after the sequence of comparisons down any given path, we know that the leaf provides the order of the input data.

For example, for three inputs $\{a, b, c\}$, with the six possible ways in which those values could appear in sorted order, we could first compare a against b. If a is less than b, then we have one of the three orders $a < b < c$, $a < c < b$, or $c < a < b$. And that's all we know after that one comparison. If we next compare a against c, and find that a is in fact less than c, we can exclude the case $c < a < b$ and we know we have one of the two possibilities $a < b < c$ or $a < c < b$. A third comparison of b against c is necessary to resolve this uncertainty.

If we can prove a lower bound for sorting using decision trees, then clearly the number of levels in the tree is that lower bound because each level corresponds to one comparison. We point out that there are many decision trees, all of which result in being able to uniquely identify which correct sorted order is found in the data. If we are to prove a lower bound, we have to show that *no* decision tree has fewer than some minimum number of levels.

Let's just hammer away with what we know:

- There are $N!$ total permutations of N elements, so a decision tree for sorting N elements must have at least $N!$ leaves. If we don't have a path from the root (the first comparison) down to every possible input permutation, then we can't actually sort.

- For a binary tree of k leaves and height h, we have $k \leq 2^h$, that is, $h \geq \lg k$.
- Thus a decision tree with $N!$ leaves must have height at least $\lceil \lg(N!) \rceil$.
- The lower bound for number of comparisons is the lower bound for the height of the decision tree.
- So the lower bound for sorting by comparing keys is $\lceil \lg(N!) \rceil$.

It may take a moment to understand why this guarantees a lower bound and not just a lower bound for this instance or this representation of the problem. We have chosen to compare a with b in the top level, and then made other choices as well. If we chose to compare a with c at the top level, we could produce a decision tree that was merely the result of exchanging b for c throughout the tree. Any other decision tree is merely the result of permuting the input of the three elements a, b, and c, not a change to the algorithm itself.

Next, we can observe that all these comparisons are necessary. With each comparison, we have a set of possible permutations for either of the two outcomes of the comparison. If we take the right path for the first two levels, we know that a is not less than b and that a is not less than c. We have at this point no information as to the relative position of b and c. Both $b \leq c \leq a$ and $c \leq b \leq a$ are possible, and since this is a sorting algorithm, any possible ordering of the three inputs is a possible input to the algorithm. Unless and until we compare b against c, we cannot determine which of the two remaining possibilities is correct. Unless we have a decision tree with at least as many leaves as there are possible input possibilities, we will not have a path of decisions that will uniquely identify each of the possible inputs.

11.12.2 A Proof of Lower Bounds

We now know that it takes at least $O(\lg(N!))$ comparisons to sort N items. The question is, exactly how big is $\lg(N!)$? The answer, at least for today's purposes, comes from Stirling's formula that we introduced in Chapter 6.

Theorem 11.2

Sorting N items by comparisons takes at least $O(N \lg N)$ comparisons.

Proof By what we have just done in the preceding section, what we need to show is that

$$\lg(N!) = O(N \lg N).$$

From Stirling's formula we have

$$N! = \sqrt{2\pi N}\left(\frac{N}{e}\right)^N e^{\alpha_N}.$$

This means that

$$\begin{aligned}
\lg(N!) &= \frac{1}{2}(1 + \lg\pi + \lg N) + N(\lg N - \lg e) + \alpha_N \lg e \\
&= N\lg N - N\lg e + \frac{1}{2}(1 + \lg\pi + \lg N) + \alpha_N \lg e \\
&\geq N\lg N - N\lg e \\
&\geq \frac{1}{2}N\lg N \qquad \text{(for large } N\text{)} \\
&= O(N\lg N)
\end{aligned}$$

comparisons are needed to sort N items for large N. The first line becomes the second line by simply rearranging terms; the second line becomes the third because we are throwing away terms that are known to be positive; and the final inequality holds because we know that $N\lg e = o(N\lg N)$, so for large N we have $N\lg e \leq \frac{N\lg N}{2}$, and the inequality holds. Sorting cannot be done in fewer than $O(N\lg N)$ comparisons. □

11.12.3 Lower Bounds for the Average Case

We have shown that the lower bound for sorting is $O(N\lg N)$ by showing that in the worst case the maximal path down a decision tree has a path of length at least $\lg(N!)$. We can actually prove something somewhat stronger, which is that the *average* path length down the decision tree must be at least of length $\lg(N!)$. What we can conclude from this is that we don't have pathological worst cases that might be few and far between. Quite the contrary, if we have best cases that take less time, it is the best cases that are exceptional and few and far between.

Consider the general decision tree for sorting N items. The tree has $N!$ leaves, so the average path length from the root to a leaf is

$$\frac{\text{sum of all path lengths to leaves}}{N!}.$$

We start with a lemma about the numerator.

Lemma 11.3

The sum of all path lengths to leaves is minimized when the tree is completely balanced.

Proof If we disconnect any subtree from a balanced binary tree and move that subtree so as to connect it somewhere else in a binary tree, we necessarily have increased the sum of the path lengths. □

We can now prove the theorem.

Theorem 11.4

The average case of any sort by comparison of keys is at least

$$\lg(N!)$$

comparisons.

Proof The minimal sum of all path lengths to trees is

$$(N!) \cdot (\lg(N!))$$

so the average path length is bounded below by $\lg(N!)$. □

Thus, sorting either in the worst case or in the average case takes at least $O(N \lg N)$ comparisons. What this means is that we cannot improve upon sorting methods such as heapsort and mergesort in the worst case, and we cannot improve upon heapsort, mergesort, or quicksort in the average case.

*11.13 Sorting in Parallel

We will close this chapter with a section on parallel computing, specifically on how to sort on a distributed memory parallel machine. The canonical version of a *distributed memory parallel computer* is a collection of standard computers connected by as fast an interconnect as one can afford. This is the model of computation adopted by the very common Beowulf cluster computers. Each node is an independent computer and can only access its own memory locations. If processor A wants to get data stored in the memory of processor B, for example, then A must send a message to B requesting data, and B must respond by sending back the data in another message. This makes the communication of data the bottleneck to efficient computation because the overhead of sending a message across a slow connection (possibly just Ethernet) is very large when compared with the cost of accessing a memory location local to the computer.

In a cluster computer, a head node computer farms out identical tasks to a collection of compute nodes, each of which is an independent computer. The compute nodes process for as long as they can using the data they have available to them locally. At some point in the computation, the compute nodes will probably have to exchange data. In the cheapest version of a Beowulf cluster, the interconnect would be simply an Ethernet connection; although faster interconnects exist, they are still much slower than is a simple memory reference local to the computer itself.

Invariably, it is this communication of data from one processor to another that is the bottleneck that slows down the parallel computation. In the worst-case scenario, if one processor is collecting data from all the other processors, then the incoming data flood will overwhelm the bandwidth. Ideally, when we have to exchange data, we would like to arrange things so that all processors are sending and receiving equal amounts of data because this will distribute the data equally across the communication paths.

We note that the other kind of parallel computer is a *shared memory parallel computer* in which all processors have access to all memory locations in the machine. Clearly, this is a more powerful model of computation because it eliminates the need for moving large quantities of data from one machine to another. However, this power comes at a price—it is not unreasonable for the switch between processors and memory to be the most expensive single part of the computer. It just isn't very easy to have lots of processors all with the ability to access huge amounts of memory at the very high speeds and very fine granularity of loading and storing entries in memory.

The contrast between the two different kinds of parallel computer is made very clear when considering how to sort. Let's consider what happens when we use four processors labeled P_0 through P_3 to sort 32 integers, and assume that the data is initially distributed as shown in Figure 11.9. Remember that computation by a

P_0	P_1	P_2	P_3
25	27	26	3
29	4	24	5
7	8	19	9
2	1	2	2
10	3	12	13
15	14	5	4
18	21	20	3
22	30	28	31

FIGURE 11.9 ■ Initial configuration of data for a parallel sort.

processor on its own memory locations is fast, but communication of data from one processor to another is slow.

The first step in the parallel sorting process is for each processor to sort its own data, using whatever is the fastest sort for that processor. (Probably this is a quicksort.) This results in the data shown in Figure 11.10.

P_0	P_1	P_2	P_3
2	1	2	2
7	3	5	3
10	4	12	3
15	8	19	4
18	14	20	5
22	21	24	9
25	27	26	13
29	30	28	31

FIGURE 11.10 ■ Data after the local sort.

Now the problem is to extract the sorted lists from the processors and merge them together to create a single completely sorted list. So far, our computation has resembled a mergesort, and if this were a single processor doing a mergesort on disk, we would just continue with the merge. But the rules are different with parallel machines, especially with Beowulf clusters. The overhead cost of the head node's sending messages to P_0 and P_1, say, asking for the top two elements and merging the two, is very high. If we are going to send messages and move data, we want to move blocks of data; we absolutely do *not* want to pull off entries from each processor one at a time. Further, if the head node is performing a merge from P_0 and P_1, then P_2 and P_3 are sitting idle, and we don't want half of the machine doing nothing; we want all processors working in parallel as much as possible. Note that if we had a truly shared memory machine, then this would be a simple task even in parallel; although there can be some contention in the lower levels of the hardware by having multiple processors reading from the same hardware memory banks, there is nothing algorithmic that prevents all processors in a shared memory computer from reading different locations in memory simultaneously.

The solution is as follows. Given that we have $n = 4$ processors, we let each processor select the $n - 1 = 3$ breakpoint elements that break up local memory into four pieces. In Figure 11.11, we read the boldface numbers to mean, for example, that entries for processor P_2 that are less than or equal to 5 are in the first quarter, entries greater than 5 but less than or equal to 19 are in the second quarter, and so forth.

P_0	P_1	P_2	P_3
2	1	2	2
7	**3**	**5**	**3**
10	4	12	3
15	**8**	**19**	**4**
18	14	20	5
22	**21**	**24**	**9**
25	27	26	13
29	30	28	31

FIGURE 11.11 ■ Data after determining local breakpoints.

Each processor now sends its samples to the head node, so the head node has the data in Figure 11.12.

7	15	22	3	8	21	5	19	24	3	4	9

FIGURE 11.12 ■ Head node sample data before sorting.

The head node now sorts these sampled values, and then it splits its sample data into four quarters, as indicated by the bold entries in Figure 11.13.

3	3	**4**	5	7	**8**	9	15	**19**	21	22	24

FIGURE 11.13 ■ Head node sample data after sorting.

The head node now broadcasts the boldface sample values (4, 8, and 19) to all processors. Each processor now sends all entries less than or equal to 4 to processor P_0, all entries greater than 4 but less than or equal to 8 to processor P_1, all entries greater than 8 but less than or equal to 19 to processor P_2, and all entries greater than 19 to processor P_3. This results in the situation illustrated in Figure 11.14. In this tableau we have listed the "local" data first and then the entries that would have been received in processor subscript order, but this is arbitrary, since we cannot usually rely on a cluster computer to send data in predictable ways. For example, for P_3, the entry 31 comes from the processor locally, the entries 22, 25, and 29 come from P_0, the entries 21, 27, and 30 come from P_1, and the entries 20, 24, 26, and 28 come from P_2.

Now, each processor sorts its own data locally, using whatever is its fastest sorting algorithm, to produce the final tableau in Figure 11.15.

P_0	P_1	P_2	P_3
2	8	12	31
1	7	19	22
3	5	10	25
4	5	15	29
2		18	21
2		14	27
3		9	30
3		13	20
4			24
			26
			28

FIGURE 11.14 ■ Data after the global sends.

P_0	P_1	P_2	P_0
1	5	9	20
2	5	10	21
2	7	12	22
2	8	13	24
3		14	25
3		15	26
3		18	27
4		19	28
4			29
			30
			31

FIGURE 11.15 ■ Final tableau of data.

We can now stream the data in sorted order to the head node in processor subscript order.

■ 11.13.1 Analysis

Let's step back a moment and think about what we have done, what will make this algorithm work, and why this is a better approach than other ideas for sorting on distributed memory computers.

First, we have been able to use the parallelism of the computer. Except for the time spent by the head node in sorting the samples, all the processors were working and were working in parallel. That's a good thing.

Second, the time spent by the head node in sorting, when the other processors are sitting idle, is probably relatively short. Each of n processors sends $n - 1$ values to the head node. For a 1024-processor machine (which is large but not huge), this results in the head node's having to sort about a million items. Given that each compute node probably had gigabytes of storage, each local node was probably sorting much more than a million items, so the head node's sort is small by comparison.

The third consideration is the data movement. If there were n processors, then each processor had to send nearly all its data to other processors, so in essence we were moving all the data exactly once. But we were moving all the data simultaneously to all the other processors. We can't do much about the fact that the overall network might have been bandwidth limited, but we didn't create any hot spots by moving all the data on a single wire to a single machine.

Finally, let's think about whether this actually works in practice. If the data get distributed randomly to the various processors, then each processor's data will be similar. This means the breakpoints sent to the head node will be similar. When the head node sorts to produce a set of global breakpoints, these breakpoints sent back to the local processors will be fairly similar to what the local processors already had. This means that we will in fact be sending about $1/n$th of the data to each of the other processors, thus balancing the load on the network. There will be some imbalance in the size (look again at Figure 11.15, in which P_1 is underloaded and P_3 is overloaded), but it ought not to be too bad if the data are essentially randomly distributed.

Contrast this with the worst-case situation (at least for the load balancing of the data movement) in which the data are already sorted when they get distributed to the local processors, but the distribution is in reverse order. If the original configuration, for example, is as in Figure 11.16, then each processor winds up having to send all its data to a single other processor, and there is no real balancing of the load.

P_0	P_1	P_2	P_3
25	17	9	1
26	18	10	2
27	19	11	3
28	20	12	4
29	21	13	5
30	22	14	6
31	23	15	7
32	24	16	8

FIGURE 11.16 ■ Worst-case parallel sort tableau.

In general, sorting is the worst possible kind of computation to be done on a parallel machine. No matter where we initially place a data element on a local processor, there is some input data set that would require the element eventually to wind up at any other processor. In many parallel computations in physics, for example, there is a known locality of reference. Seattle's weather, for example, has little effect on Miami, so one can safely task one processor with computing Seattle weather and one with computing Miami weather and not expect there to be much data movement between the two. But in sorting, all possible configurations could happen, This makes controlling the worst case of data movement the primary problem for a cluster computation.

As a general rule, the methodology used in this parallel sorting algorithm is the norm for cluster computing. If we cannot *a priori* force data and computation to be localized, then we rely on statistics to try to balance the load. If we suspect that our data might already be partially sorted, then we would not choose to pivot in a quicksort on the last element in the array but would instead do a quick sampling of the array to pick a value we hope would be closer to the middle. Similarly, we sample locally in this parallel sort and then sort the samples, in hopes of producing global breakpoints that will break the entire data set into equal-sized chunks. If we cannot rely on deterministic predictions of what the data will look like, then we must rely on statistical analysis and hope for reasonably random inputs.

11.14 Summary

We have in this chapter provided a thorough introduction to the standard sorting algorithms of bubblesort, heapsort, insertionsort, mergesort, and quicksort. We have done both a worst-case running time analysis and an average-case running time analysis of these algorithms, and discussed the nature of average-case analysis compared to the (usually easier) worst-case analysis.

Having done an asymptotic analysis, we have gone further to consider the practical aspects of sorting, such as the use of auxiliary space, disk-based sorting for very large data sets, the extent to which the input data is already sorted, multilevel sorting, and stability. These considerations often affect the choice of a sorting algorithm other than the theoretically best algorithm. Indeed, the common use of quicksort as the default algorithm is not because its worst-case running time is optimal, but because its average-case running time is $O(N \lg N)$, the pathological cases seem very rare, and it can be implemented more efficiently on modern computers than the worst-case asymptotically better heapsort algorithm.

Finally, in a starred section, we have discussed sorting on a distributed memory parallel computer. This is an example of the use of the assumption of statistically random data in an algorithm that can be shown to be efficient if that assumption holds.

11.15 Exercises

1. Given the following sequence of integers, show the first three levels of the mergesort from the bottom up (that is, first comparing adjacent pairs).

$$33, 55, 2, 19, 92, 18, 45, 74, 88, 27, 51, 6, 91, 22, 44, 13$$

2. If we choose the *last* element in the (sub)array as the pivot element, show the first two complete phases of quicksort. The first phase should use the last element as the pivot and result in two subarrays. The second phase should use the last element in each subarray as the pivot and result in four subarrays.

$$33, 55, 2, 19, 92, 18, 45, 74, 88, 27, 51, 6, 91, 22, 44, 13$$

3. Repeat the previous exercise but choose the first element as the pivot instead of the last.
4. In the best possible case, what is the minimum number of comparisons necessary in order to determine the proper order of n integers?

   What does this tell you about the minimum distance from the root to a leaf in a decision tree for sorting?
5. Consider the possible input sequence of data items:

```
Freshman Tyrone
Sophomore Tyrone
Freshman Amanda
Sophomore Amanda
```

   We would like this to be sorted first by class, then by name, so our desired output is

```
Freshman Amanda
Freshman Tyrone
Sophomore Amanda
Sophomore Tyrone
```

   We have said that our bubblesort as written is stable with the strict "greater than" of Figure 11.1, and we have said that stability of sorting is important when one is doing a multilevel sort first on one key, then on a second key. With the strict $>$, we pull the *first* occurrence of the least value to the top; if we wrote $\geq$ instead of $>$, we would pull the *last* occurrence of the least value to the top.

Trace the execution of a bubblesort with $\geq$ replacing the $>$, sorting first on class (freshman is lower, of course) and then alphabetically on name. Demonstrate that we don't get a stable sort by showing that we don't get what we want as the output.

(In the case of bubblesort, we write $>$ more naturally because there is no reason to do the extra work of an exchange for an equal key. In the case of heapsort, for example, it is not at all obvious how we might be able to force stability.)

6. In the preceding problem, we sorted first on class and then on name. Some people might have argued that it would be easier to concatenate class and name and do a single sort.

   Under what circumstances might this not be such a simple thing to do or perhaps not a desirable thing to do? (Hint: think Java, object-oriented programming, reusable code, etc.)

7. The table in Figure 11.6 suggests that our insertionsort takes about $0.25N^2$ comparisons and our quicksort takes about $1.1N \lg N$ comparisons for small N. If we accept these constants as the actual values, how large does N have to be for quicksort to take fewer comparisons? Given that quicksort is a more complicated program, does this suggest that we should switch to insertionsort when the subarrays in quicksort get sufficiently small?

8. Implement a complete mergesort from the bottom up. Include with your sorted output a counter of the number of comparisons.

9. Implement a complete mergesort recursively from the top down. Include with your sorted output a counter of the number of comparisons.

10. Implement a complete quicksort as a recursive computation. Make sure that you do *not* create new arrays and thus waste memory but rather are working on subscripts pointing into an array that is declared as an instance variable for the class. Include with your sorted output a counter of the number of comparisons and compare this to Figure 11.6.

11. Implement quicksort, but this time, if the subarray is of length at least 9, sample the first element, the last element, and the middle element, and choose the middle value as the pivot. Count the comparisons and see if you do any better than either your previous implementation or Figure 11.6. (Don't worry too much about rounding up or down for the pivot or about rounding up or down to get the middle subscript. Statistically this shouldn't matter, although you might see if it does on the sample data you use.)

12. Implement a sort on an `ArrayList` of `Record` instances (from Figure 3.1) that will allow you to sort either by name, by course being taught, or by office

number. The office number is formatted with the leading character as the floor number, the second as the building wing, and then the room number, and you want to sort by floor, then by wing, then by number. Use an interface to allow a comparison method to accept as parameters both a `Record` value and a constant to direct which field is to be used for sorting.

12 Searching

Objectives

- An introduction to binary search trees
- An introduction to hash functions and hash tables
- A brief introduction to random number generation
- An introduction to Java Collections Framework structures supporting search: `List`, `Map`, `Set`, `HashSet`, `TreeMap`, `TreeSet`, and `HashMap`

Key Terms

associative search	document nonrepudiation	JCF
binary search tree	hash collision	map
content-addressable search	hash function	mixed-linear-congruential
document authentication	hash table load factor	probe
document integrity	index	pseudorandom number

Introduction

Much of this course and text have been about the efficient storage and retrieval of data. The interest in linked lists, queues, stacks, and trees is largely because each of these offers a different way to organize data. Each in turn has its own ways for the data to be retrieved from storage. In this chapter, we will focus more specifically on the process of searching for a data item in one of various storage structures that have been specifically designed to make searching easier.

12.1 Associative Matching

In an ideal world, we would perform a search as an *associative* or *content-addressable search*. That is, we would ask for "the record for J. Random Student" and the full record for Ms. Student would instantly appear. We would have the key ("J. Random Student") uniquely associated with the full record, and be able to pull up the record by specifying the key. As mentioned in the earlier discussion on linear and binary search, we measure the efficiency of the search process by the number of *probes* necessary to retrieve the record in question. In an ideal world, we would want to be able to retrieve a record with only a single probe for "the record for J. Random Student."

In the real world, things don't work as pure associative search. In a naive lookup of data in an array of records, we would run the obvious `for` loop on subscripts, pull up the records one at a time, and compare each key in turn to the key for whose record we are searching, as in the following code fragment.

```
for(int i = 0; i < number_of_records; ++i)
{
  if(key(record_at_subscript_i) == the_key_we_are_looking_for)
  {
    return record_at_subscript_i
  }
}
```

Two problems exist with this kind of search. First, this requires that we write a loop to walk through the array. That is not in itself a difficult task, but it is a task that is prone to error. What we really want is to be able to look up a record based on a key, but most of the programming deals with subscripts, fencepost considerations, and such; these are contributions of complexity for no algorithmic gain. This complexity can be mitigated somewhat by the use of iterators; proper use of an iterator allows us to walk through the data directly, rather than through the subscripts that then provide us access to the data.

The second reason this is not a good approach for searching is that it requires linear time. If the key that is being searched for exists in the array of length N, it will be found on average after having compared keys at $N/2$ subscripts. If the key is not present, we have to search all the way to the end, thus taking N probes to find that the key is not in the list. In the case that our records have been sorted, of course, we can do a binary search in $O(\lg N)$ time, but the initial sort will cost us $O(N \lg N)$ comparisons (and a probe is essentially the same thing as a comparison).

We discuss in this chapter techniques for searching that will perform a lookup in either constant time or logarithmic time, depending on the circumstances of the search. Creating a pure associative search is essentially not possible; at some level it will always be the case that one must access records and compare keys. Our goal, though, is to accomplish most searches on lists of length N with a logarithmic number (that is, $O(\lg N)$) of probes.

12.2 Indexing for Search

We have already seen, in Chapter 3 on flat files, the first approach for improving a search. If we create an *index* for the file of records, that is, a *sorted* array of keys for the file, then we can perform a search of N records in guaranteed $O(\lg N)$ time by using binary search. That guarantee of logarithmic time comes at a price, namely the $O(N \lg N)$ time that is required to perform the initial sort. And if the file is dynamic and requires constant sorting (probably with an insertionsort if the file is large but the number of additions is small), then there is an ongoing linear-time cost for insertion in order to maintain the guaranteed $O(\lg N)$ search time.

12.3 Binary Search Trees

In general, although a complete sort on the data would give us perfect information and guarantee a log time for a search, this information would come at a cost we could not afford. Further, it is often the case that we need a *dynamic* data structure and that we can settle for "reasonably fast" search on data that enters and leaves the structure. This implies that we will use a heuristic that will work well with reasonably random input data but that may well have poor performance if the input data is truly pathologically bad. This is entirely similar to the quicksort that works well in the average case or on random data but that is $O(N^2)$ on data that is already sorted and for which a deterministic choice is made for the pivot.

In an earlier section, we discussed the heap and the ability to use a heap for creating a priority queue for which the highest priority item was the root of the tree. When this item was removed from the tree, the heap that implemented the priority queue could be rebuilt in logarithmic time. This was the first example in which we imposed an additional second dimension of structure on what might otherwise be viewed as a linear array of records.

In a binary search tree (BST), we impose slightly more structure on the array. A *binary search tree* is a binary tree whose nodes hold key values for which the following two properties hold.

1. For any given node v, the key values for all nodes in the left subtree of v are less than or equal to the value of the key for v.
2. For any given node v, the key values for all nodes in the right subtree of v are greater than or equal to the value of the key for v.

We can choose to disallow equality of keys or not, depending on the application. In order to simplify the discussion, we will not worry about duplicate keys in our examples. The asymptotics don't change, so taking care of the question of duplicate keys adds complexity for no real purpose.

With a heap, we can guarantee $O(\lg N)$ time for insertion and for rebuilding the heap after removing the top element. With the binary search tree, we cannot guarantee this running time for all cases, but we can expect it on data that is sufficiently "random," so for most instances of real data the BST or a close relative is a good compromise.

An example of a binary search tree is given in Figure 12.1.

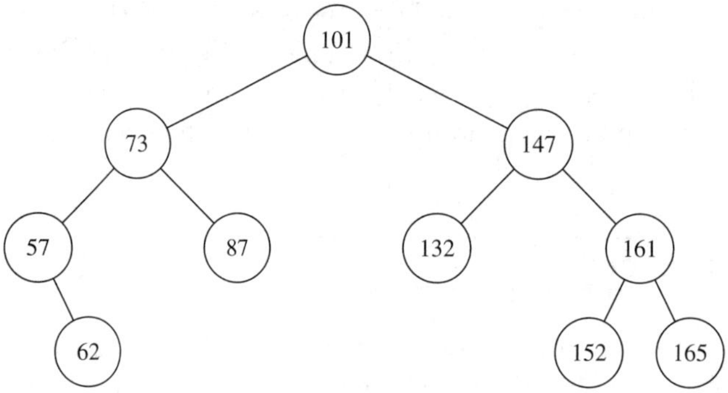

FIGURE 12.1 ■ Example of a binary search tree.

By now, even the casual reader should expect us to say something like the following: we will get the best performance if the tree is balanced or nearly balanced because we can then store the maximum number of entries ($N = 2^n$) when measured against the depth ($n = \lg N$) of the tree. It should not be surprising, then, to realize that the tree given in Figure 12.2 is an example of the degenerate worst case of a binary search tree. If the tree is strung out in a line like this, then searching the tree takes the same linear time as does searching a linked list. This is even worse than if we had an array because we don't have direct access to locations at subscripts; as with a linked list, we must traverse the tree from node to node one link at a time.

If we have a binary search tree already constructed, and if the tree is a reasonably complete and balanced binary tree, then we can search the tree in logarithmic time with the pseudocode algorithm in Figure 12.3.

■ 12.3.1 Inorder Traversal and Binary Search Trees

Back in Chapter 10 we promised to give an example of an inorder traversal of a tree. Now is the time to make good on that promise. If we look at the binary search

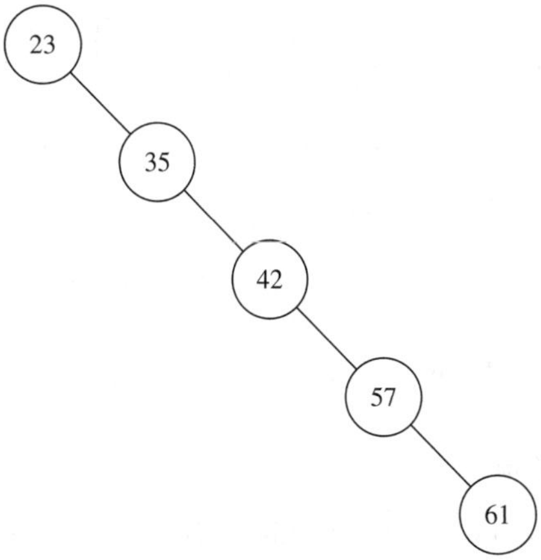

FIGURE 12.2 ■ Example of a worst-case binary search tree.

```
binarytreesearch(Key key)
{
  Node returnNode = null

  if(!tree_is_empty())
  {
    v = tree_root
    while(null != v)
    {
      if(key == v.getKey())
      {
        returnNode = v
        break
      }
      else if(key < v.getKey())
      {
        v = v.getLeftChild()
      }
      else if(key > v.getKey())
      {
        v = v.getRightChild()
      }
    }
  }

  return returnNode
}
```

FIGURE 12.3 ■ Pseudocode for a binary search tree.

tree in Figure 12.1, and we choose to traverse the tree in inorder order,[1] taking care to traverse missing nodes, we get the following sequence.

$$missing\quad 57\quad 62\quad 73\quad missing\quad 87\quad missing\quad 101$$
$$missing\quad 132\quad missing\quad 147\quad 152\quad 161\quad 165$$

That is, the inorder traversal reads off the entries in the binary search tree in order. This would allow us, for example, to write a search tree to disk for a checkpoint and then read it back into a BST without actually having to rebuild the BST.

12.3.2 Building a Binary Search Tree

There are two distinct instances in which we might want to build a binary search tree. In the first instance, if we had a list of sorted data, such as

Subscript	1	2	3	4	5	6	7	8	9	10	11	12	13	14	15
Data	1	13	19	21	23	28	31	35	39	45	49	53	57	59	61

then we would want our binary search tree to be a structural representation of what binary search on the array would look like, namely the tree in Figure 12.4.

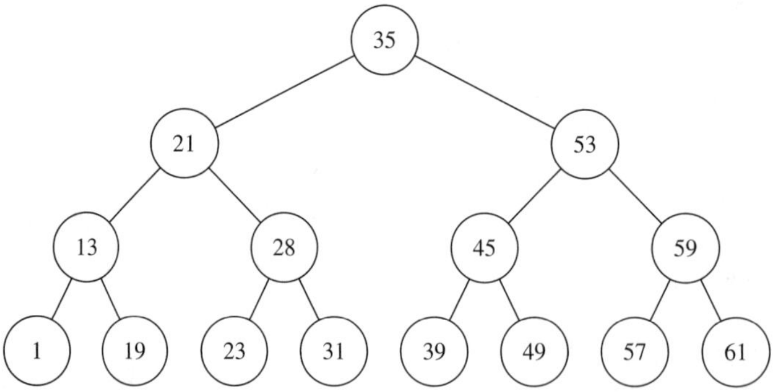

FIGURE 12.4 ■ A binary search tree created from a sorted list.

The mapping of subscripts to tree nodes is exactly that of an inorder traversal. The BST provides us with no more information about searching this list than we would get from the original array paired with a method for binary search.

[1] That's an expression your high school English teacher would probably have marked you down for using.

Most of the time, however, we will not start with a sorted list but will be receiving data that comes in dynamically and needs to be organized on the fly into a search tree. If, for example, we were presented with a stream of data such as

$$23, 35, 42, 57, 61$$

and required to create a BST from that stream of data, we would get the worst-case tree shown in Figure 12.2. The first value we would see is 23, which would become the value at the root. When the second value 35 came in, we would position it to the right of the root, since $35 > 23$. The third value of 42 is also larger than the 23 at the root, so we would descend to the right. Since $42 > 35$, we would store the 42 in a node to the right of 35. And so forth.

Contrast this with the tree we would build dynamically from the input sequence

$$101, 147, 161, 132, 73, 87, 152, 57, 62, 165.$$

This is one of a large number of input sequences that would result in the same BST as in Figure 12.1. The first few subtrees created as the input stream is processed are shown in Figure 12.5.

We begin with the first element, 101, as a single root node. The second element, 147, is placed to the right. The third element, 161, is placed to the right of the root, and then to the right of 147. The fourth element, 132, is placed to the right of the root but to the left of 147. Then the fifth element, 73, is placed to the left of the root, and so on. If the data arrives in a reasonably random order, then the search tree will be reasonably balanced as we build it because we will be moving left or right in a reasonably random order.

12.4 Sophisticated Search Trees

It should be clear that a balanced binary search tree is going to be the most efficient data structure for performing searches. It is the structure of the BST that permits searches in $O(\lg N)$ time. We can view this as follows. With the first comparison at the root, we move right or left down the tree and eliminate half the entries as being either too large or too small. With the next comparison, we move right or left and eliminate half of what remains. Continuing on, we reach a decision in $O(\lg N)$ comparisons because we cut the size of the data to be examined in half with each comparison.

The key to the success of the BST, then, is to be able to guarantee to eliminate half the remaining data with each comparison. If the tree is balanced, the search

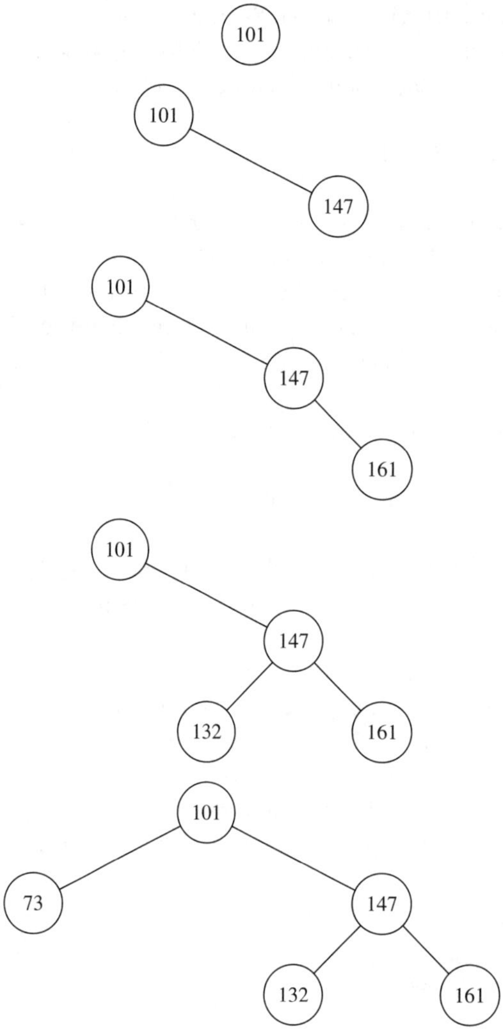

FIGURE 12.5 ■ A dynamically created binary search tree.

of the tree is a true divide-and-conquer computation. If the tree is badly balanced, this won't be true, and we will have pathologically bad cases (such as Figure 12.2) that are entirely analogous to the bad cases with the quicksort.

With dynamic data, we can never guarantee that we will not be presented with what would be pathologically bad cases, and there are a number of sophisticated algorithms for balancing trees that are used as search trees. In each case, the goal of the more complex algorithm is to balance the tree and convert what would be a long chain such as in Figure 12.2 that is "rooted" at one end into a balanced tree rooted at a node that is more in the middle. Although we will not go into detail on the more sophisticated balancing algorithms,[2] we will indicate the flavor of tree balancing with the following observation. If we look at the tree in Figure 12.2, we can recognize by eye that a more efficient tree can be constructed by "rotating" the 57 node up and the 42 node down to create the tree in Figure 12.6. In general, this is what tree balancing is—rotating subtrees so as to turn a three-node linear sequence into a parent node with two children.

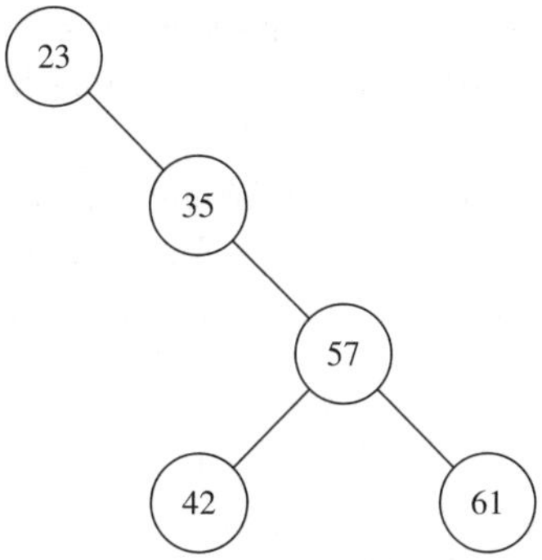

FIGURE 12.6 ■ The search tree in Figure 12.2 after one rotation.

■ 12.5 Hashing

With an indexed file, we can achieve guaranteed $O(\lg N)$ search time for an array of N data records but at the cost of $O(N \lg N)$ time in sorting the array and the additional cost of maintaining a sorted array as data records are inserted and deleted. With a binary search tree, we *probably* can get $O(\lg N)$ search time without the cost of sorting and maintaining a sorted array, but we cannot *guarantee* the $O(\lg N)$ search time because pathologically bad data arrangements could exist.

An alternative to a search tree or to an index is the use of a *hash function.* A hash function is a mathematical mapping from the value of a key to a subscript in an array (or similar data structure) with the expectation that the hash values $h(key)$ will provide a reasonably random scattering of the data entries across the array in which the records will be stored. The storage array addressed by a hash function is called a *hash table.*

For example, we could implement a hash function on Social Security numbers as follows. Let us assume that we need to store 25,000 student transcript records based

[2]This is lovely material, but it's really more advanced than is necessary for a course at this level.

on SSN. Since the SSN is a nine-digit number, we would not want to allocate space for a billion ($= 10^9$) records, since that is a lot of space and we would only use about 1 location in 10,000 if all we had were 25,000 records. Instead, we allocate an array of 100,000 records and we look for a hash function that will map a nine-digit SSN into a five-digit subscript to be used as the array subscript. Because SSNs are assigned with regional leading digits, they are likely to cluster if we simply chop off the first digits. (Words in a language like English exhibit similar clusterings: the words "machine," "machining," "machinery," "machination," "machinist," etc., all have "machin" as a stem; the words "machination," "organization," "implementation," "cogitation," etc., all end in the same five-character sequence "ation".) A good hash function will remove such clusterings.

Although there are now somewhat more sophisticated methods for generating pseudorandom numbers,[3] one method that has been in widespread use for decades is the *mixed-linear-congruential* pseudorandom number generator that computes from an integer n a mapped pseudorandom number $f(n)$ as

$$f(n) = (A \cdot n + B) \pmod{p}$$

where p is a prime, A is a well-chosen *multiplier*, and B is a well-chosen *addend.* For our student records system, we might choose $p = 99{,}991$ as the largest prime smaller than 100,000, allocate an array of 99,991 spaces (and not 100,000), choose $A = 32{,}939$ and $B = 8{,}443$, and compute for each student transcript a subscript

$$s = (A \cdot SSN + B) \ \% \ 99991$$

and store that student's transcript in storage location s in the array.

What a good hash function now permits is *single probe, constant time* access to a record. We no longer have to search even $O(\lg N)$ steps through a tree to find the key and retrieve the record. Given the key (SSN), we apply the hash function (a simple, constant time process) to compute the subscript s, and then we can go directly to location s in our array with a single probe to get the data record we want. In a perfect world, with a perfect hash function, this would be a true associative search.

In reality, although this is close to what we can achieve, there is no free lunch and there are some complications with any hashing scheme. Although we can find good hash functions, there are no perfect hash functions, and we must be prepared for *hash collisions.* A hash collision occurs when, for example, different input SSNs would map under the hash function to the same output value s. Since the whole

[3]We will distinguish "random" from "pseudorandom" later in this chapter.

purpose of using a hash function is to map a large key space down into a smaller storage space (nine-digit SSNs, for example, into 99,991 locations), we are virtually guaranteed to have some collisions. In our example, any two SSNs that differed by 99,991, such as 123-45-6789 and 123-55-6780, would hash down to the same value.

In the real and imperfect world, the simplest way of dealing with hash collisions is to store the key along with the data record and, when collisions occur, to store the record whose key caused the collision in the next open storage location in the array. When we apply the hash function to a key, we first compare the key with the stored key at location s. If this is not a match, then we test the key at location $s + 1$, then at $s + 2$, and so forth. With a good hash function, most of our retrievals will take place with a single probe, a small number will require a second probe, an even smaller number will require a third probe, and so forth. And importantly, with a good hash function, even keys that cluster like stems of words, phone numbers from the same exchange, or such will scatter across the array space in a reasonably random way. (For example, we would *not* want to take the first three digits of a telephone number because that would cluster all the numbers with the same exchange.)

Crucial to getting a good hash is that the *load factor* not be too large. The load factor is the number of entries to be stored divided by the total number of possible storage locations. In our example, storing 25,000 student records in an array of length 99,991 would give us a load factor of just over 0.25. Clearly, if one is storing N hashed entries in an array that is only N long, one needs an almost-perfect hash function to avoid lots of linear searching after a collision. The larger the array, the more room there is for a less-than-perfect hash function, but of course the larger array will use space that may be at a premium.

Another metaphysical view of a hash function is that it's an approximation of a bucketsort. In a bucketsort, we simply look at the key and stuff the data item into the appropriate bucket. This is fast but requires that we have a bucket for any possible key value. What a hash function provides is a simple function, computed from the key, that almost always and almost uniquely provides a bucket in which to stuff the data.

12.6 Random Numbers and Hash Functions: A Brief Digression

12.6.1 Random Numbers

The use of pseudorandom number generators for hashing and of specific hashing functions has been studied extensively in the literature. Some guidelines for choosing A and B can be found in Knuth. Other guidelines come from the National

Institute of Standards and Technology (NIST), a division of the U.S. Department of Commerce.

We have promised to distinguish *random* numbers from *pseudorandom* numbers. It is actually very hard to define what is meant by a "random" number because that would imply that we had knowledge that a generating process was in fact truly random. It is easier to define what a sequence of *pseudorandom numbers* is: a sequence of numbers is said to be pseudorandom if it passes an accepted set of tests that would be passed by truly random numbers. For example, a sequence of one million integers each less than 100,000 should contain about 10 instances of every such integer, but we cannot specify that it must contain exactly 10 instances of every integer or else the sequence would be deterministic and not random. There should also be no statistical correlation between the nth integer in the sequence and the $(n+1)$st; the sequence $2, 4, 6, 8, \ldots$ of even integers would clearly fail such a test and is clearly not random. The scientists who do research in random numbers must, if they come up with a new function they wish to claim is a better generator of pseudorandom numbers, show that the sequences generated by their function pass the statistical tests available from NIST, or else no one will use that function for pseudorandom numbers.

Although scientists often talk about needing random numbers, it is usually the case that what is really needed are pseudorandom numbers, not truly random numbers. If the sequence is truly random, then with every execution of the function a different sequence will appear, and testing programs becomes much more difficult. Unless we are running a lottery,[4] we probably want a sequence of pseudorandom numbers that has the statistical characteristics of truly random numbers but that is deterministic, so if we run the program twice we will get the same results and can verify that code is working as expected.

Finally, for a pseudorandom number generator like the mixed-linear-congruential method mentioned earlier to provide good sequences, we would like the sequence to be of maximal length (in our example, this is 99,990, since zero is excluded for technical reasons), and we would like it to be "hard" in some statistical sense to predict the next value from the current value. (The values are supposed to be pseudorandom, after all.)

One characteristic of the integers modulo prime numbers is that most reasonably random choices of functions[5] that operate with prime numbers generate good sequences. One can prove fairly easily that for prime numbers p, there are always multipliers m for which the sequence m, m^2, m^3, $m^4, \ldots$, all taken modulo p, has maximal length $p-1$. Proving that more complicated functions still provide

---

[4] and the British lottery was said at one time to have used a cosmic ray sampler to get truly random winning numbers

[5] for some definition of the terms "most," "reasonably," and "random"

reasonable randomness is a little harder but still the subject of an elementary course in number theory. A final advantage of using this theory is that the function for computing random numbers isn't hard, requiring only ordinary multiplication and modular reduction.

12.6.2 Cryptographic Hash Functions

Our use here of random numbers and hash functions is for efficient storage and retrieval of data. What NIST has provided regarding random numbers also includes a set of statistical standards for random numbers to be used in cryptographic applications. Hashing passwords, or encrypting passwords, has been standard practice for decades. Instead of storing a file with actual passwords, the passwords are encrypted and the encrypted version is stored. When a password is entered by a user logging in, the password as entered is encrypted and the encrypted version is compared against what is stored.

Similar techniques are increasingly important for electronic commerce because authentication of electronic documents and signatures is required in a paperless world. We would like to know, when we receive an official document electronically, that the document has *integrity* and has not been altered while in transit on the Internet. We would also like to know that the sender is the *authentic* sender he or she claims to be; this is usually accomplished with a public key cryptographic mechanism. And we would like the document to possess *nonrepudiation*, that is, that the sender cannot later claim not to have sent the document.

Critical to most of this for electronic commerce (as well as for good password protection in an operating system) is that the hash functions cannot be run backward, that is, that it is very hard to produce an input value that hashes down to a specific hash value. We would like it to be difficult, for example, for an attacker to be able to read the encrypted or hashed password for a user and then to produce *some input password*, which doesn't have to be the one the user uses, that encrypts or hashes down to the value stored on disk. An attacker who could accomplish this would be able to forge a login. Someone who was able to forge such a hash value for a digital signature would be able to intercept an electronic document in transit, replace it with a document of her choice, and then create the hash value retained by the sender. The sender in this case would have no way to deny having sent the forged document.

12.6.3 Random Numbers in Java

We have digressed somewhat into a discussion of random number generation. Unless one is involved in computations for which a high degree of reliability is needed on the statistics of the random numbers, it is sufficient to call the functions that are built into most major programming languages. Running the lottery would require for legal purposes a demonstration that the numbers that were generated and used passed statistical tests for randomnicity. Running some large-scale scientific computations might require so many random numbers, or might require random numbers generated in parallel, that the built-in functions cannot be used. But for the most part, the Java `Random` class can be used. There is also a function `Math.random` in the `Math` class that provides a simple wrapper for the `Random` class. The online documentation for `Random` states that the sequence of numbers is generated by a linear congruential method (the terms "linear," "mixed-linear," and "mixed congruential" all seem to be in common use). One version of the Java documentation provides the method shown in Figure 12.7 to generate the next pseudorandom number from the previous or current value.

```
synchronized protected int next(int bits) {
      seed = (seed * 0x5DEECE66DL + 0xBL) & ((1L << 48) - 1);
      return (int)(seed >>> (48 - bits));
}
```

FIGURE 12.7 ■ The Java random number method.

We note that this involves multiplying by hexadecimal `0x5DEECE66DL`, adding in hex `B` (decimal 11), and extracting the rightmost 48 bits. The method has as an input parameter the number of bits b of pseudorandom number to produce, and it returns the rightmost b bits of the 48-bit string produced in the previous line of code.

■ 12.7 The Java Collections Framework

At some point in a data structures course like this any sensible student ought to start asking the question "If this material is so basic to computer science, then surely someone must have programmed these structures already. Why are we learning how to program the structures instead of learning how to use the programs that have already been done by professionals, tested, and shown to be free of bugs?"

In fact, there is a set of standard structures called the *Java Collections Framework* that is used in storing and retrieving data. The JCF has several interfaces that are highly useful: the `Set`, `List`, and `Queue` interfaces that are actually part of the `Collection` interface, and the `Map` interface that is technically not actually a `Collection` but which ought to be discussed along with the others.

Strictly speaking, a `Collection` represents a group of objects known as its *elements*. From the Java tutorial[6] we find that the `Collection` interface is defined as in Figure 12.8.

[6] `http://download.oracle.com/javase/tutorial/collections/index.html`

```
public interface Collection<E> extends Iterable<E>
{
  // Basic operations
  int size();
  boolean isEmpty();
  boolean contains(Object element);
  boolean add(E element);          //optional
  boolean remove(Object element); //optional
  Iterator<E> iterator();

  // Bulk operations
  boolean containsAll(Collection<?> c);
  boolean addAll(Collection<? extends E> c); //optional
  boolean removeAll(Collection<?> c);        //optional
  boolean retainAll(Collection<?> c);        //optional
  void clear();                              //optional

  // Array operations
  Object[] toArray();
  <T> T[] toArray(T[] a);
}
```

FIGURE 12.8 ■ Basic methods of the `Collection` interface.

We will get to the `Iterator` later in this chapter. Except for that, the meaning of the methods in the interface should be obvious even if the precise syntax of the Java is not obvious.

The `Set` interface, which has the `Collection` interface as a superinterface, defines a structure that is modeled after the mathematical concept of a set. There are two properties of a set that are specifically useful in dealing with the representation of a set in a computer. First, duplicate entries are not allowed—if one adds the element a to a set $S = \{a, b, c\}$, then the set is still just $S = \{a, b, c\}$. Second, the elements in a set are unordered, so the following are all the same set:

$$S = \{a, b, c\} = \{a, c, b\} = \{b, a, c\} = \{b, c, a\} = \{c, a, b\} = \{c, b, a\}.$$

In contemplating why and how one would implement the concept of a true mathematical set in a program, one should think of the programming complications inherent in what would be the naive implementation using an array. If one stores the elements of a set in an array, then unless one sorts the entries, adding an element requires a search through the entire array to ensure that the element is not already in the array because any ordering is a valid ordering. But if one does choose to sort, then one has to pay the price for sorting the array and then maintaining the array in sorted order. Finally, if the array is to be sorted, insertions and deletions require moving elements in the array. Although it should be clear that it isn't fundamentally difficult to program a class that would implement a mathematical set, it should be obvious that the details might be hard to get completely correct. For this reason, it's nice that Java already has a `Set` interface that has been implemented in several classes as part of the JCF.

The `Set` interface is given in Figure 12.9.

```
public interface Set<E> extends Collection<E>
{
  // Basic operations
  int size();
  boolean isEmpty();
  boolean contains(Object element);
  boolean add(E element);         //optional
  boolean remove(Object element); //optional
  Iterator<E> iterator();

  // Bulk operations
  boolean containsAll(Collection<?> c);
  boolean addAll(Collection<? extends E> c); //optional
  boolean removeAll(Collection<?> c);        //optional
  boolean retainAll(Collection<?> c);        //optional
  void clear();                              //optional

  // Array Operations
  Object[] toArray();
  <T> T[] toArray(T[] a);
}
```

FIGURE 12.9 ■ The `Set` interface.

The `List` interface is given in Figure 12.10.

We have already used the `List` interface as it is implemented in the `ArrayList` structure. As mentioned earlier, the `ArrayList` has all the properties of a one-dimensional array but also has the convenience of dynamic addition and removal of entries and differs from an array in that it does not need to have the number of entries specified *a priori*.

A second `List` structure that can be very useful is the `LinkedList` interface that implements (yes, you guessed it) a linked list. We discussed this back in Chapters 4 and 5. We also mentioned the `Queue` interface.

What we have not discussed yet is the `Map` interface, given in Figure 12.11.

The `Map` interface implements what in computer science is referred to as a *map* structure. A `Map` resembles a mathematical function mapping a domain to a range and maps key values to data (i.e., record) values. The most recent notorious use

```
public interface List<E> extends Collection<E>
{
  // Positional access
  E get(int index);
  E set(int index, E element);    //optional
  boolean add(E element);         //optional
  void add(int index, E element); //optional
  E remove(int index);            //optional
  boolean addAll(int index,
    Collection<? extends E> c);   //optional

  // Search
  int indexOf(Object o);
  int lastIndexOf(Object o);

  // Iteration
  ListIterator<E> listIterator();
  ListIterator<E> listIterator(int index);

  // Range-view
  List<E> subList(int from, int to);
}
```

FIGURE 12.10 ■ The `List` interface.

of the map concept is in the Google "map-reduce" that is close to an associative lookup.

12.8 The Java `HashSet`

Earlier in this chapter we discussed the concept of a hash table. The built-in implementation of a hash table in Java is the `HashSet`. The Java `HashSet` class permits one to implement a set with a hash function for (probable) constant time access to the set. (The documentation says that constant time access is guaranteed but uses the necessary weasel-wording that the hash function must disperse the data elements across the various buckets.)

We note that the `HashSet` allows for storing the *existence* of a key in the set but not the storing of the key itself for retrieving a record. That is, the methods of `HashSet` allow one to add and remove elements, test whether an element is already in the `HashSet`, test for an empty structure, and such. What is *not* possible is to store a value; to accomplish this will require the `TreeMap`, to be discussed later.

We also note the `iterator` method that returns a list of the keys in the `HashSet` but not in any particular order. This is consistent with the idea that a hash function

```
public interface Map<K,V>
{
  // Basic operations
  V put(K key, V value);
  V get(Object key);
  V remove(Object key);
  boolean containsKey(Object key);
  boolean containsValue(Object value);
  int size();
  boolean isEmpty();

  // Bulk operations
  void putAll(Map<? extends K, ? extends V> m);
  void clear();

  // Collection Views
  public Set<K> keySet();
  public Collection<V> values();
  public Set<Map.Entry<K,V>> entrySet();

  // Interface for entrySet elements
  public interface Entry {
    K getKey();
    V getValue();
    V setValue(V value);
  }
}
```

FIGURE 12.11 ■ The `Map` interface.

should be easy to compute but hard to invert; given a data element, or key, then computing the hash function and adding the element to the set is easy. Going backward from the hashed value to the original data element is hard, and thus we should expect the iterator to return the entries in the set in the order of the hashed value of the key, not the order of the key itself.

■ 12.8.1 A Spell-Checking Program

A spell-checking program is an interesting use of a hash table, interesting in part because it will not necessarily be perfect in catching spelling errors. To implement a spell-checker, we start with a dictionary. Because we know that the load factor in a hash table is important, we go to the Web and find several dictionaries there, all of which have between about 80,000 and 130,000 English words, so we take that as the size of the dictionary of properly spelled words. Since $2^{17} = 131{,}072$, we use this as the upper bound on the number of words to be able to spell correctly, and we plan to allocate about eight times that much space (2^{20}, about a million) so as to have about a $1/8$th loading of the hash table.

We assume that our array of length 2^{20} is zeroed (or set to a boolean `false`), and we now read the dictionary and hash the legitimate words into array subscripts, storing a 1 (or a boolean `true`) for the 100,000 or so words in the dictionary.

Now, if we read some other document, breaking the document into tokens that are taken to be words, we can hash the words into our array. If the hash turns up a boolean `false`, then we know that the word is not in our dictionary, and thus may well be misspelled. If the word hashes to a boolean `true`, then either it is spelled correctly, corresponding to a word in our dictionary, or else it is a new word that happens to collide with a word in the dictionary when the hash function is applied.

With a reasonable hash function and a small loading on the array, we won't have many collisions, and the spell-checker will be reasonably good. If space and processing permit, and if high accuracy is necessary, we could implement a second such array with a different hash function. If each function admits, say, a 1 in 1,000 chance of missing a misspelled word due to hash collisions, then two such arrays, done independently, would have a 1 in 1,000,000 chance of missing a misspelled word because the probabilities multiply for independent tests. We know that this will detect misspelled words. We don't know that this will detect *all possible* misspelled words, but the probability of an error can be made arbitrarily small by using multiple hash functions and hash tables.

12.9 The Java TreeMap

The Java `HashSet` allows us to implement a hash table with little or no fuss and to rely on the built-in methods to get the details correct. To implement a binary search tree, what we want from the JCF is the `TreeMap`, which allows us to store a data record using a key and then to retrieve that data record quickly based on the key. The documentation for `TreeMap` begins by stating that the underlying structure is a "Red–Black tree." Earlier in this chapter we mentioned that sophisticated search trees exist that are improvements to binary search trees and that improvements involve automatic balancing of the tree to ensure a balanced binary tree and thus a good worst-case behavior. A Red–Black tree is one of these sophisticated binary search trees; although it is rather complicated in its details, it is in a very real sense similar to what we have already discussed—a BST with some additional features.

Just as an `ArrayList` is declared with something like

```
ArrayList<String> myList;
```

that would declare a variable `myList` to be an `ArrayList` of `Strings`, a `TreeMap` variable would be declared with something like

```
TreeMap<Integer, Record> myTreeMap;
```

that would use an `Integer` variable as a key and would store for each key value an instance of a `Record` variable. Just as with an `ArrayList`, a `TreeMap` makes extensive use of generics.

A simple example of `TreeMap` is shown in the following code fragment.

```
theMap = new TreeMap<Integer, String>();
while(inFile.hasNext())
{
  theKey = inFile.nextInt();
  theString = inFile.next();
  theMap.put(theKey, theString);
}

for(Integer key: theMap.keySet())
{
  System.out.printf("Key='%d' String='%s'%n",
                    key, theMap.get(key));
}
```

In this, we declare an instance of `TreeMap` with `Integer` values as the keys and a `String` value as the payload for the mapping. The `put` method stores the payload with the associated key (in the Red–Black tree that is the underlying storage structure). To list all the elements in the structure, in key-sorted order, we can use the iterator of the second loop in this example, and then the `get` method retrieves the payload given the key value.

In addition to the `get`, `put`, and `keySet` methods shown in the code here, there are `containsKey` and `containsValue` methods that return `boolean` values in answer to the "equals" question about keys and values, and a `remove` method that (surprise, surprise) removes values at a key location. In addition, there are a number of methods that help in traversing the map by producing the keys immediately preceding or succeeding a possible key, or the entire initial or trailing segments of the map up to a given key or following a given key. For example, the `higherKey` and `higherEntry` methods take a key as the parameter and return either the key or the key-value mapping, respectively, for the least key that is strictly greater than the parameter, or else `null`.

■ 12.9.1 A Digression on Documentation

As a point of metaphysics, one should note that although this class implements (we are told) a Red–Black tree, none of the tree structure details are exposed to the user of the class. There are no methods to descend the left child branch of the tree, for example; all the methods deal simply with the data of key and value. There is a lesson here about Java documentation, your own documentation, and software design in general.

You, the user and programmer, can read in the Java documentation that `TreeMap` implements a Red–Black tree that provides guaranteed lg N access time for the primary methods, and the documentation cites the source for the algorithms used (in this case, one of the very standard references on algorithms). You, the programmer, have to trust that the underlying implementation has been done properly, just as those who use your code will have to trust that your code is a correct implementation. You also know, because you have read this book or taken this course, that the "guaranteed" efficient execution might depend on some assumptions about either the data or the methods involved.

Reading on in the documentation, there are disclaimers about what is necessary in order to ensure that the hoped-for efficient execution time of `TreeMap` is in fact observed and about how the class ought to be used. All documentation for code should contain such disclaimers. You, the programmer, are providing a black box for a subsequent user (in this case, the `TreeMap` class that implements a fast-access map). In addition to stating in the documentation what the black box *does* provide, you need also to include the caveats so a user will not misuse your black box through ignorance. To leave out mention of the kind of tree implemented is to leave the user in the dark, and to leave out mention of the source of the algorithms is to leave the reader guessing as to what to expect.

12.10 The Java TreeSet, HashMap, and LinkedList

In addition to the `ArrayList`, `HashSet`, and `TreeMap`, there are also other structures in the Java Collections Framework. These include the `TreeSet`, `HashMap`, and `LinkedList`.

One can summarize the capabilities of the set and map structures as follows.

- The `HashSet` allows one to store a record of the *existence* of a given key, with single probe (constant time) access, but does not allow one to retrieve the keys in sorted order.
- The `HashMap` is a map in that it stores a record, not just the existence of a key for that record, with single probe (constant time) access, but does not allow one to retrieve the records in sorted order by key.
- The `TreeMap` is a map that stores a record retrievable by key in sorted order by keys. Access is guaranteed to be in logarithmic time, as one would expect from a balanced tree.

- The `TreeSet` is a set that stores the existence of keys, and the keys can be retrieved in sorted order. Unlike the `HashSet`, which uses a hash function, the `TreeSet` stores existence of keys in a tree structure. Access is guaranteed to be in logarithmic time, as one would expect from a properly done balanced tree.
- Finally, the `LinkedList` structure is a `List` structure, similar to the `ArrayList`, but one that implements the insertion, deletion, and traversal mechanisms necessary for a doubly-linked list.

12.11 Summary

One of the primary uses for computing in the modern world is to search a data collection for a given record based on a key value. It is efficient search, after all, that has made Google the company that it is today. A linear search is easy to program and hopelessly inefficient for large collections of data. The key to efficient search is to organize the data so that the number of probes is logarithmic in the number of items of data. This leads to the immediate conclusion that a balanced binary tree is the optimal storage structure for data that must be searched repeatedly. We have discussed the construction of binary search trees from static and from dynamic data. We have also covered the topic of hash functions, which can be more efficient than search trees under certain circumstances. The study of hash functions prompted a digression on how to generate pseudorandom numbers.

Finally, we covered the JCF classes and interfaces that provide professionally-written and thoroughly-tested structures to aid in search and retrieval. Although it is always a good idea to know what goes on inside the classes provided in Java or any other programming language, because that knowledge permits one to correctly choose which structure to use in a given instance, it is not necessary to reinvent the wheel and write all these structures from scratch.

12.12 Exercises

1. You have 2^{30} sorted records to be searched with a binary search. Assume that your binary search takes $1.5 \lg N$ time to search a list of N records. (That is, assume that the constant is 1.5 for this $O(\lg N)$ algorithm.) Assume that you can arrange your data in blocks of size 2^m, so that you have 2^{30-m} blocks. You can choose to search the entire array with one search, or you can choose to search first for the block number and then for the record in the relevant block. Does it matter which option you choose?

2. You have two lists of records, and your problem is to find all instances in list A of the records that occur in list B. Give an efficient algorithm for doing this along with the running time for the algorithm.
3. The integers 1009, 2003, 4001, 8191, 16001, and 65537 are all prime. Assume that you use 43 as your initial value (the "seed") in a pseudorandom number generator. Write a program to find values of A and B that will generate maximum cycles, which would be of lengths 1008, 2002, 4000, 8190, 16000, and 65536.
4. Complete the implementation of a binary search tree. Write your code, for test purposes, to count the number of tree nodes visited in conducting a search. Conduct two experiments, one after loading the search tree from a sorted list and the other after loading the search tree from a list in "random" order. Verify that the number of nodes visited is in each case what the theory says it should be. (That is, linear for a worst-case situation and logarithmic for the random case.)
5. After writing your binary search tree code, add the method for inorder traversal of the tree and for reading and writing from an array into the tree or from the tree to an output array on disk.
6. Set up a hash table of length 100,000. Use the Java `Random` class and reduce the result modulo 100,000. Generate a list of 10,000 additional random numbers and load them into the hash table, keeping track of the number of hash collisions. Increase the count from 10,000 to 20,000, then 30,000, 40,000, and 50,000, and keep track of the total number of probes necessary in order to store the new entries.
7. Write a spell-checking program. Pull down one of the open-source dictionaries from the Web for the hash table, and then check that you can distinguish the properly spelled words from the misspelled words from another list of words submitted to your program.
8. Rework the `FlatFile` code to use a `TreeMap` instead of an `ArrayList` and thus make it easy to store and retrieve `Record` data. Note that this makes it unnecessary to have a sort method or a search method.

13 Graphs

Objectives

- A review of terms and concepts in graph theory
- The adjacency matrix representation of a graph
- The sparse matrix representation of a graph
- Breadth-first search/traversal in a graph
- Depth-first search/traversal in a graph
- An introduction to *NP*-completeness as the measure of complexity of a problem
- Easy and hard problems in computations on graphs

Key Terms

adjacency matrix
arc
Boolean satisfiability
clique
connected component
connected graph
cycle
density of a matrix
Dijkstra's algorithm
directed graph
edge
edge weight
Eulerian cycle
Eulerian path
graph
Hamiltonian cycle
Hamiltonian path
incident
maximal clique
multigraph
node
node indegree
node outdegree
NP-complete problem
path
shortest path
simple path
spanning tree
sparse graph
sparse matrix
Traveling Salesman Problem
undirected graph
vertex

Introduction

In earlier chapters we covered the basic definitions used to discuss graphs and then the special case of trees, which are graphs that have no cycles. General graphs are much more complicated objects to deal with in a computer. We know, for example, that any traversal of a tree will eventually reach a dead end in a leaf node. This just isn't true with graphs that have cycles, though—unlike the finite process that is tree traversal, following a path through a general graph could be open-ended and involve infinite loops on cycles unless we are careful. This makes it harder to write programs to work with graphs and very much harder either to analyze graphs or to determine their structure.

13.1 Graphs and Applications

We have already introduced the notion of a *graph* as a pair $G = (V, E)$ comprising a set $V = \{v_i\}$ of *nodes* (a node is sometimes also called a *vertex*), and a set $E = \{e_k = <v_i, v_j>\}$ of *edges* (sometimes also called *arcs*), with each edge being a pair of nodes. If an edge $e_k = <v_i, v_j>$ exists, we say that node v_i is *connected* to node v_j and that the edge e_k is *incident* to node v_i and node v_j.

Graphs can be *directed* or *undirected.* depending upon whether we assign a direction, as with a one-way street, to the edges. If a graph has even one edge (A, B) that must be interpreted as *from node A to node B*, then the graph is directed. We have also noted that there can exist graphs as well as *multigraphs* in which more than one edge joins two nodes.

Many of the issues surrounding graphs have to do with such problems as finding a *path* from one node to another, with the ability to find a *shortest path* between nodes; the ability to find a *cycle* outward from a node, traversing through a graph, and returning to itself; and the ability to find the *connected components* of a graph. If the edges have *edge weights* assigned to them, perhaps representing a flow capacity, then the problems posed often become problems not of the existence of a path between nodes but of determining the path with the maximum capacity.

As we have already discussed in Chapter 9, in the world of computing, there are a number of problems that can be referred to as local–global problems on a graph. In finding a path from one node to another, say, our information may well be confined locally to only the information about the current node and about the connections from that node to its immediately adjacent neighbors. In sending an email message across campus, for example, we may have more than one path that can be taken. From our lab computer, however, we may be keeping statistics about traffic for the first hop from our local computer to an immediate neighbor, but we probably will not know that the line from the second hop in a certain direction is jammed because someone has downloaded a virus.

In other instances, *we*[1] may have knowledge that would guide a search, but a computer program would not *a priori* have that knowledge. In scheduling a trip from Columbia, South Carolina to Eugene, Oregon, for example, the smart traveler knows that the better routes will lead through major airports (Atlanta, Charlotte, San Francisco, Portland), but the naive computer program might enumerate all possible paths from Columbia to somewhere in one hop, then all possible paths from there to somewhere else, and so forth. In the first place, this leads to a combinatorial explosion in the number of possibilities, so the search would not likely be fast. In the second place, such a naive search would ignore the realities of the capacity weights that would distinguish freeways and side roads, trunk lines in the phone system or the electric power grid, hub-to-hub connections in the air traffic system or the Internet, or similar considerations.

As an example, consider the graph in Figure 13.1. If the edge weights represent costs, and the problem to be solved is that of finding a minimal-cost path from A to D, then the need to expand from local to global awareness is obvious. If we apply the greedy algorithm and look only one hop away, then we would choose to move first from A to B. That this is a mistake is evident when we are now forced to take the only edge from B to D at a larger total cost than if we had paid a higher price in the first step by going from A to C.

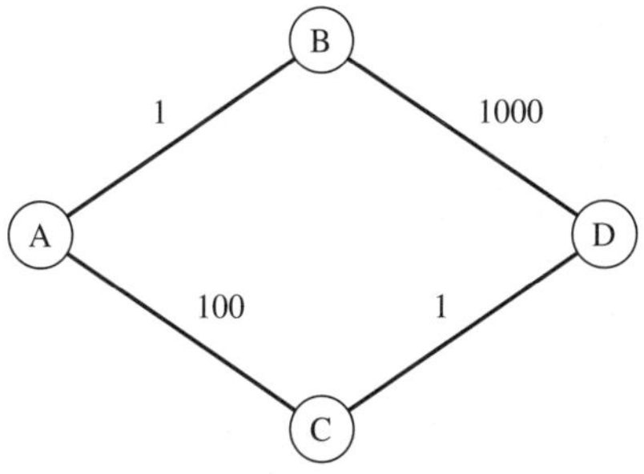

FIGURE 13.1 ■ A sample graph with capacities on the edges.

■ 13.2 Adjacency Matrices and Linked Lists

A further complication in graph problems is simply the use of space. We will see shortly that there are two basic data structures for storing the information about a graph. In one structure, we store information about every *possible* edge, even if the edge does not exist. In the other structure, we store information only about the

[1]the primates with big brains and opposable thumbs

edges that happen to exist. The former method takes very little storage for each possible edge but is an inefficient method if most edges do not in fact exist, and it is hugely impractical if the graph is as large, say, as the entire Internet graph. The latter method takes more storage for each edge, but if the number of actual edges is small compared to the number of possible edges, then it can be more efficient.

13.2.1 Adjacency Matrices

The simplest data structure for storing the representation of a graph is an *adjacency matrix*, a matrix being simply a two-dimensional tableau of numbers. In the case of a graph with N vertices $V = \{v_i : i = 1, \ldots, N\}$, we would want a matrix of N rows and N columns. In the location for row i, column j, we would put a 0 if there were no edge from vertex v_i to vertex v_j, and a 1 if there were such a vertex. (In Java, we might be tempted to use a `boolean` array instead of an `int` array. This would be entirely an issue of space and usage. It is true that we are storing a yes–no condition, so a `boolean` value might be more appropriate and space-saving than an `int`, but there are algorithm instances in dealing with graphs in which one wants to use the matrix entries as actual numbers.)

For example, the graph in Figure 13.2 would have as its adjacency matrix the tableau in Figure 13.3.

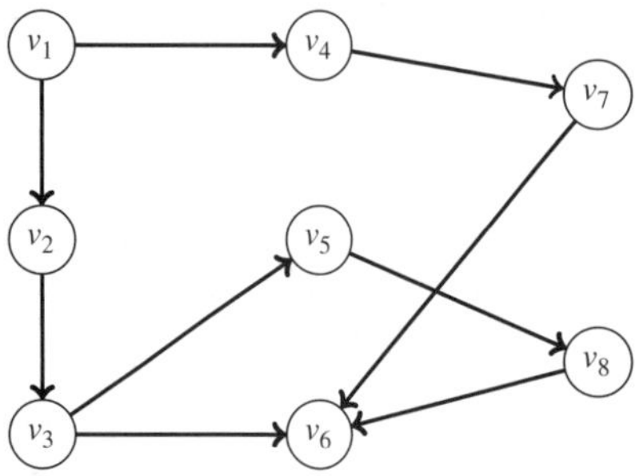

FIGURE 13.2 ■ A sample directed graph.

In this example, we have deliberately chosen a directed graph, for which the adjacency matrix is *not* symmetric, and we have a 1 for row i, column j, if there is a directed edge from v_i to v_j. If the graph were undirected, then the adjacency matrix would be symmetric, and if there was a 1 in row i, column j, then there would also be a 1 in row j, column i. If we dropped the directions from the edges in the graph in Figure 13.2, the adjacency matrix would simply be the symmetric completion of the matrix in Figure 13.4. In this matrix, we have indicated in color the entries produced when the graph is changed from directed to undirected.

	v_1	v_2	v_3	v_4	v_5	v_6	v_7	v_8
v_1	0	1	0	1	0	0	0	0
v_2	0	0	1	0	0	0	0	0
v_3	0	0	0	0	1	1	0	0
v_4	0	0	0	0	0	0	1	0
v_5	0	0	0	0	0	0	0	1
v_6	0	0	0	0	0	0	0	0
v_7	0	0	0	0	0	1	0	0
v_8	0	0	0	0	0	1	0	0

FIGURE 13.3 ■ The adjacency matrix for Figure 13.2.

	v_1	v_2	v_3	v_4	v_5	v_6	v_7	v_8
v_1	0	1	0	1	0	0	0	0
v_2	1	0	1	0	0	0	0	0
v_3	0	1	0	0	1	1	0	0
v_4	1	0	0	0	0	0	1	0
v_5	0	0	1	0	0	0	0	1
v_6	0	0	1	0	0	0	1	1
v_7	0	0	0	1	0	1	0	0
v_8	0	0	0	0	1	1	0	0

FIGURE 13.4 ■ The adjacency matrix for the undirected version of Figure 13.2.

As a structure for representing a graph, the adjacency matrix has some major advantages as well as disadvantages.

One advantage is that the code required to "do X for all edges leading out from vertex V" is easy—it's a simple loop over the row for X, with a test for the 1 value and execution of the code for Y in all cases in which the test comes up true. It is very often necessary to know the *indegree* or the *outdegree*. Both can easily be computed by running across a row or down a column and counting the number of ones. A matrix has the advantage of being a simple two-dimensional array, and there is little in computing that is simpler than just running loops on such an array.

Another major advantage of the array data structure is that retrieval of the 1 or 0 that indicates the presence or absence of an edge is the simple indexing `a[i][j]` into the adjacency matrix. We get random access into the array, so with one lookup we can tell if there is an arc from one vertex to another.

The primary disadvantages of the adjacency matrix for representing a graph come from the storage and processing requirements for a *sparse graph*. In a graph such as in Figure 13.2, there are $8 \times 8 = 64$ entries, of which only 9 are nonzero. Nonetheless, we store entries for all 64 possible edges, so we wind up having to store

55 zero entries. In a very sparsely connected graph, we might expect $O(N)$ edges connecting N nodes. In this case, we would need to store $N^2 - N$ zeros and only N ones. As the graph and the matrix got larger, the *density* (the fraction of nonzeros) would decrease. This can be very wasteful.

Indeed, it can probably be argued that for the most part the larger the graph, the more likely it is to be sparse. Whether the graph is the connectivity graph of the Internet, a street map in a city, or the connections of people in a city or on Facebook who know each other, it just seems that connecting everything to everything is hard and doesn't come up very often. Just as it is physically impossible to have too many streets coming into one intersection in a city, it also seems that the larger the group of people one looks at on Facebook, for example, the less likely it will be that, say, 80 percent of them will all know each other.

The other disadvantage of the adjacency matrix is that in the case of very sparsely connected graphs, although the code for traversing a row to find all the edges connected to a given vertex is easy to write, it is also computationally wasteful to perform the "do X for all edges leading out from vertex V." If most of the entries are 0, then most of the CPU time is spent in accessing the entry for column j in a given row i, testing and finding that X is not to be performed, and going on to test for yet another possibility that happens not to be present.

We could mitigate some, but not all, of the wasted time by having a separate storage location for each row and for each column that would hold the number of nonzero entries, that is, the number of edges, for that particular row or column. This would make it unnecessary to process a row or column that had no nonzero entries and would also allow us to stop our loop when we had processed all the nonzeros rather than having to continue to the end of the row or column.

In summary: the adjacency matrix is easy to code, but it is wasteful in both time and space if the graph is very sparsely connected.

13.2.2 Sparse Graphs and Sparse Matrices

We will frequently use the term *sparse graph* or *sparse matrix*, but we won't actually quantify what it means to be sparse. There are specific algorithms for working with sparse graphs or sparse matrices; these algorithms take advantage of the fact that most entries in the adjacency matrix are zero. The usual "definition" of "sparse" will be recursive: a matrix (or graph) is considered sparse if the techniques for dealing with sparse matrices or graphs efficiently happen to be efficient on that particular matrix or graph.

13.2.3 Linked Lists for Sparse Graphs

The techniques used for sparse graphs still rely on the adjacency matrix, but they use data structures and algorithms specifically designed to be more efficient in time and space on matrices with low density, that is, relatively few nonzeros. The techniques used for sparse matrices invariably deal only with those entries that have to be there—the edges that actually exist between nodes—rather than with the edges that could exist. Instead of storing an adjacency matrix of both "connected" and "not connected" information on all nodes, we store only the information that indicates where the edges really do exist. In the case of the directed graph in Figure 13.2, we could represent the very sparse matrix in Figure 13.3 using an array of linked lists. If we think of the array as running down the column of nodes, then each entry in the array would be a linked list of the column (nodes) for which an edge existed. Each entry in the linked list would contain as the data payload the node number (column number) and a link to the next nonzero. This could be shown as in Figure 13.5.

v_1	$\rightarrow$	2	$\rightarrow$	4	$\rightarrow$	null
v_2	$\rightarrow$	3	$\rightarrow$	null		
v_3	$\rightarrow$	5	$\rightarrow$	6	$\rightarrow$	null
v_4	$\rightarrow$	7	$\rightarrow$	null		
v_5	$\rightarrow$	8	$\rightarrow$	null		
v_6	$\rightarrow$	null				
v_7	$\rightarrow$	6	$\rightarrow$	null		
v_8	$\rightarrow$	6	$\rightarrow$	null		

FIGURE 13.5 ■ The linked-list representation for the directed graph in Figure 13.2.

The array of linked lists in Figure 13.5 is the simplest and most naive way in which to store a sparse graph for later processing. It is also rather inflexible, and it doesn't have all the information we might need for processing on the graph.

What we have stored are the lists of edges leading out from a given node. If our computational need is to traverse the graph from a node to nodes to which it is connected, this might be a sufficient representation. This is a very cumbersome representation, however, if we need to find all the edges leading *into* a particular node. For example, to determine that node v_6 has edges leading in from nodes v_3, v_7, and v_8, we would have to traverse the entire array, node by node, and then for each node traverse the linked list for that node until we have either found the edge or walked past v_6. This is both complicated and expensive.

A more complete representation for a graph would be to have each nonzero entry itself be a node in *two* doubly-linked lists, one going across each row and one going down each column. A data structure for a sparse matrix would include at least the conceptual view in Figure 13.6 and at least the structure shown in the UML diagram in Figure 13.7. The `DLL2D` class for a two-dimensional doubly-linked list would replicate the ordinary variables and methods for a DLL but would require the ability to traverse the list, to add, and to delete in both left–right and up–down directions. The node structure of a sparse node, labeled *SN* in Figure 13.6 and shown in Figure 13.8, again merely replicates the usual DLL node requirements in both directions. We have written the UML with distinct methods for row and column processing. The code could also be written with only one next and one previous method but with a parameter to indicate the direction. In either case, a goal ought to be to eliminate as much as possible the duplication of code fragments.

Note that for this application, where the purpose of the matrix is to indicate the existence of edges between nodes, there is no need for a data payload. The data payload in the array form is simply a 1 or a 0. In this represention, nodes are present

	Col Head 1 ↓	Col Head 2 ↓	Col Head 3 ↓	Col Head 4 ↓	Col Head 5 ↓	Col Head 6 ↓	Col Head 7 ↓	Col Head 8 ↓	
Row Head 1 →		*SN*		*SN*					← Row Tail 1
Row Head 2 →			*SN*						← Row Tail 2
Row Head 3 →					*SN*	*SN*			← Row Tail 3
Row Head 4 →							*SN*		← Row Tail 4
Row Head 5 →								*SN*	← Row Tail 5
Row Head 6 →									← Row Tail 6
Row Head 7 →						*SN*			← Row Tail 7
Row Head 8 →						*SN*			← Row Tail 8
	↑ Col Tail 1	↑ Col Tail 2	↑ Col Tail 3	↑ Col Tail 4	↑ Col Tail 5	↑ Col Tail 6	↑ Col Tail 7	↑ Col Tail 8	

FIGURE 13.6 ■ The conceptual two-dimensional sparse matrix for Figure 13.2.

SparseMatrix
-columnList:ArrayList<DLL2D>
-rowList:ArrayList<DLL2D>
+SparseMatrix():void

FIGURE 13.7 ■ A partial UML diagram for a `SparseMatrix` class.

SparseNode
-nextColumn:SparseNode -nextRow:SparseNode -previousColumn:SparseNode -previousRow:SparseNode
+SparseNode():void +getNextColumn():SparseNode +getNextRow():SparseNode +getPreviousColumn():SparseNode +getPreviousRow():SparseNode +setNextColumn(SparseNode):void +setNextRow(SparseNode):void +setPreviousColumn(SparseNode):void +setPreviousRow(SparseNode):void

FIGURE 13.8 ■ A partial UML diagram for a `SparseNode` in a sparse matrix.

where the value would be 1, and they are absent wherever a 0 would have occurred, so the existence of a node is sufficient to represent the existence of an edge.

This representation allows us to process "forward" from any node v to any node to which v is connected by an edge by going across the rows, or "backward" into any node w from the nodes connected to w by going down the columns.

Provided the matrix is sparse enough, what we gain in the sparse matrix–linked list implementation of a graph representation is more efficient use of both space and time. If the fraction of nonzeros is small enough, then the extra storage cost of storing a linked list, or several linked lists, is less than the cost of storing a very large number of zero entries. And for sparsely connected graphs, the cost of traversing the list of edges for a given node is proportional to the number of edges, not proportional to the number of nodes in the graph. We know, with such a representation, that we are handling information only for the edges that do exist, not for all the edges that could exist. On the other hand, it is also undeniable that the cost in complexity of code is higher for the linked list representation than the dense adjacency matrix representation.

In general, though, the matrix must be quite sparse to be better stored as a linked list than a matrix. If storage is a real problem, we could compact the 0 or 1 value into a single bit and store 32 such entries in a single 32-bit word.

In the full-blown sparse representation in Figures 13.6–13.8, there is a great deal of information in addition to the actual linked list entries in the matrix. We need an array of doubly-linked lists of the nonzero row entries and we need an array of doubly-linked lists of the nonzero column entries. For every nonzero entry in the matrix, we would thus need a link forward and backward in the row and a link up and down in the column to the next and previous nonzeros. If these links are addresses in memory, they are probably 32 bits or even 64 bits in length. The data payload for each entry in the linked lists is likely to be two `int` values for the row and column subscript, so we would need at least six 32-bit values (forward, backward, up, down, row, column), or 192 total bits, to store 1 bit of information. (Remember, the existence of a nonzero in the matrix can be done with a single bit set to 1!) In order for this to pay off in terms of space, we would need an edge density of fewer than 1 in 192. For most small graphs, the adjacency matrix is almost certainly a better bet, but for truly large graphs, the linked list is probably necessary because the number of entries in a matrix grows as the product of the number of rows and columns.

13.2.4 A Middle Ground, Somewhat Helped by Java

It is sometimes true that most of the processing on a graph will be done on the rows of the adjacency matrix, with only some of the processing done on the columns. If we view an entry in the (i, j) position as indicating an edge *from* vertex i *to* vertex j, for example, and our processing is generally done from a vertex to the vertices connected to it, then most of our processing will be done on rows, from row i (corresponding to vertex i) to the vertices to which it is connected. We could reach a compromise in storage and in complexity, then, by using a Java `ArrayList` structure as a middle ground. An array of `ArrayLists` for the rows would permit efficient row processing without some of the overhead of traversing linked lists of nodes. Walking down a column could be done by a logarithmic-time binary search on the `ArrayList` for each row. In this case, we could use the subscripting capability of the `ArrayList` to facilitate lookups in a given row, while still benefiting from the space and time characteristics of the dynamically sized `ArrayList` structure that would store only the nonzero locations.

Such a scheme would simplify programming at the level of the graph program. Underneath, however, there would be the additional (and hidden) overhead of the implementation of the `ArrayList` itself, but unless space and time became truly crucial priorities for a very, very large graph, this would simplify programming at the level of the graph program.

13.3 Breadth-First and Depth-First Search

We have already mentioned depth-first search (DFS) and breadth-first search (BFS) in the context of trees. In the case of DFS or BFS on trees, we can use the intuitive view of a tree as a two-dimensional object laid out before us together with the normal representation of a tree node that has a list of children to provide us the order in which to process nodes on the tree. Further, the fact that a tree is a graph with no cycles means that any path from the root will end in a leaf.

Depth-first and breadth-first searching is also important in graph traversals but is somewhat more complicated in the case of general graphs because cycles might exist. Fortunately, it is only slightly more complicated. To perform DFS on the graph in Figure 13.9, we might start at vertex A. We can pick any path from A, but we will process in the order in which we have labeled the vertices, so our first move will be to vertex B, as indicated in Figure 13.10. Importantly, as we traverse the graph, we will mark the nodes we have visited in the past (in color), just as we are indicating the current node by filling the circle in color. We can continue in a greedy fashion from A to B to C, until we get to node D. At this point, there are no edges from D that go anywhere except to node A, which we have already visited and marked. At this point we have to back up (and the reader should immediately realize this is best done as a recursive search, so that "backing up" is just bumping up one level in the recursion stack), first to node C and then to node B.

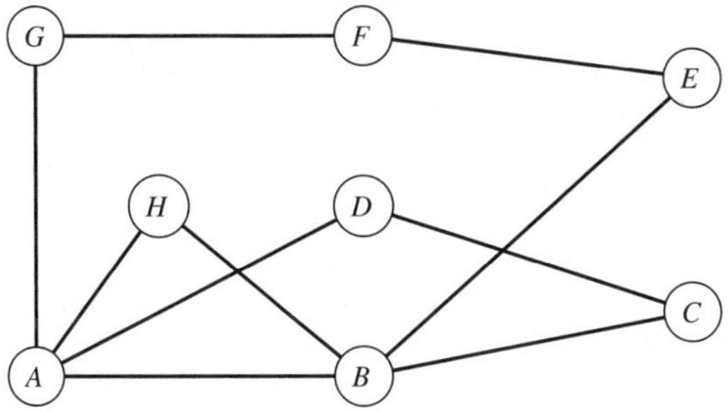

FIGURE 13.9 ■ An undirected graph for depth-first search.

At node B, we find there is an edge leading to an unmarked node E, so we take it, and continue.

A pseudocode fragment for recursive DFS thus looks like the following.

```
void DFS(Vertex v)
{
  visit 'v' and mark 'v' as visited
  for each edge 'e' leading from 'v' to a vertex 'w'
  {
    if 'w' has not been visited
    {
      DFS(w)
    }
  }
}
```

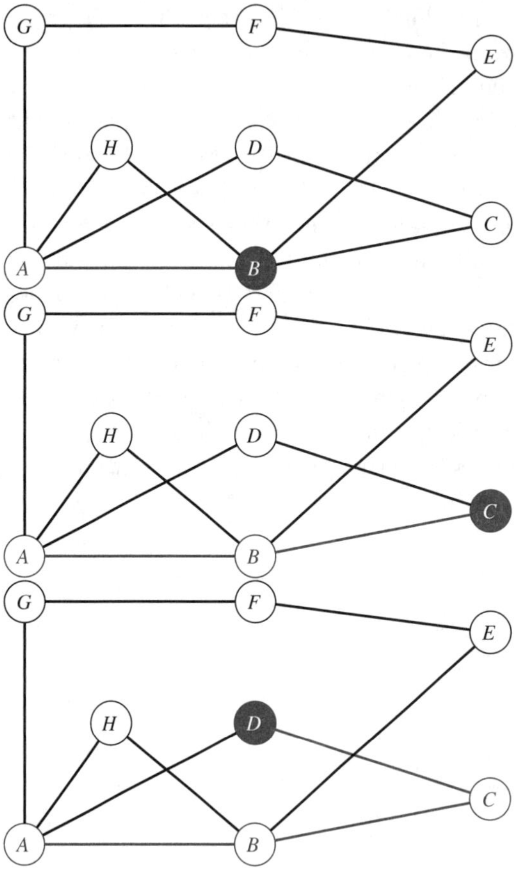

FIGURE 13.10 ■ Depth-first search, part 1.

Depth-first search is thus something that can be accomplished with a reasonably simple algorithm; the only aspect that is not totally naive is that we must remember to mark vertices so we don't get caught in loops. DFS on the graph in Figure 13.9 thus proceeds as in Figures 13.10–13.12. We assume that the ordering of edges leading out from a given node is in the alphabetical sequence of the node labels. For example, we assume that the edges leading out from node A are stored in order as the edges leading to nodes B, D, and then H.

The DFS processing proceeds as follows.

- Visit A and mark it as having been visited.
- The edges from A are in order the edges leading to nodes B, D, and H. This is depth-first search, so we take the edge to node B.

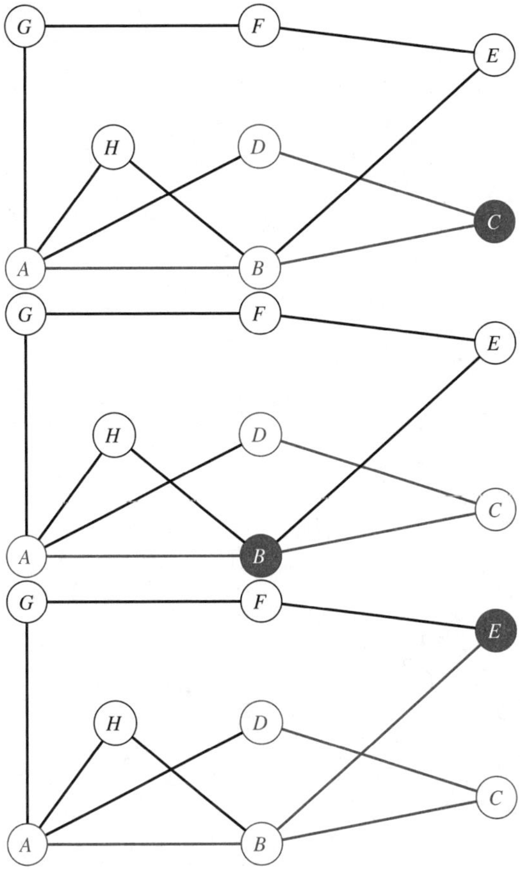

FIGURE 13.11 ■ Depth-first search, part 2.

- We visit B and mark it as having been visited. Since the edges from B are in order the edges leading to nodes C and E, and this is depth-first search, we take the edge to node C.
- We visit C and mark it as having been visited. Since the edges from C are in order the edges leading to nodes B and D, and this is depth-first search, and we have visited node B already, we take the edge to node D.
- The only edges from node D are the edge back to C and the edge back to A, both of which we have visited. We are done with this part of the depth-first probing, so we back out and return to C and then go back to B.
- From B the next edge to be taken is to node E, so we take that edge.
- From E the only edge to be taken is to node F, so we mark E as having been visited and we take the edge to F.

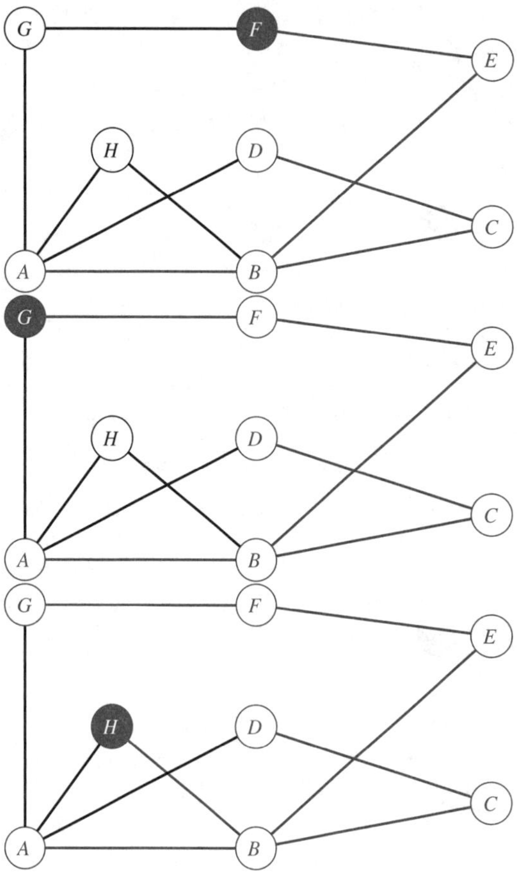

FIGURE 13.12 ■ Depth-first search, part 3.

- From F there is only one edge to an unvisited node (G), so we mark F as having been visited and we take the edge to G.
- From G there is no edge to an unvisited node, so we back up recursively, to F, then to E, then to B.
- From B there is one more edge to an unvisited node (H), so we take the edge, visit H, and then back up to B and then A, at which point we are done.

Breadth-first search is only slightly more complicated. In BFS we sweep across the edges from a given node. But instead of having the recursion stack to keep our place, as in DFS, we use a queue to list the nodes that we have not yet processed. Returning to the example in Figure 13.9, BFS can be done as follows (and shown in Figures 13.13–13.15), again using our node labeling to reflect how we would have stored the nodes in a linked list or adjacency matrix.

- We visit node A, mark it as visited, and insert A onto the queue, which is now $Q = <A>$.
- We take A from the head of the queue.
- We detect that edges exist from A to B, D, G, and H in that order. We visit these nodes and insert them on the queue, which is now $Q = <B, D, G, H>$.
- We take B from the head of the queue. We detect that edges exist to C, E, and H in that order. We visit C and E and insert them on the queue, which is now $Q = <D, G, H, C, E>$. When we come upon H, we notice that it has already

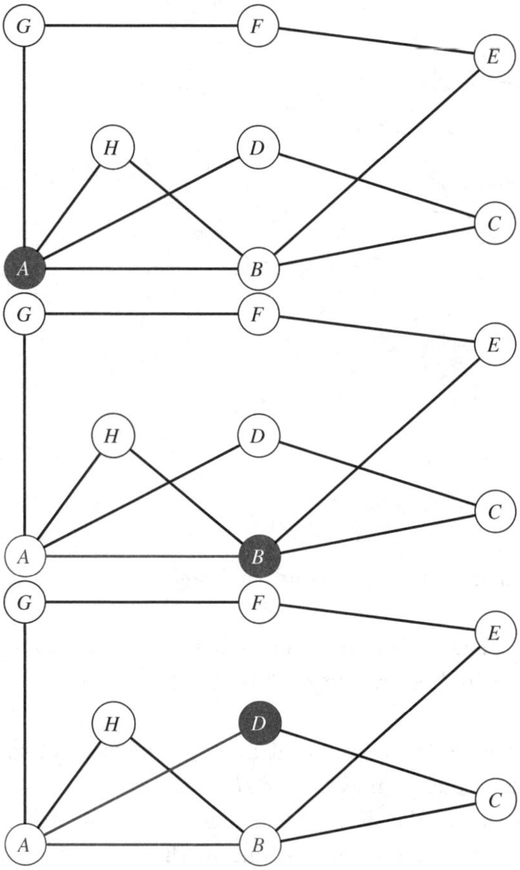

FIGURE 13.13 ■ Breadth-first search, part 1.

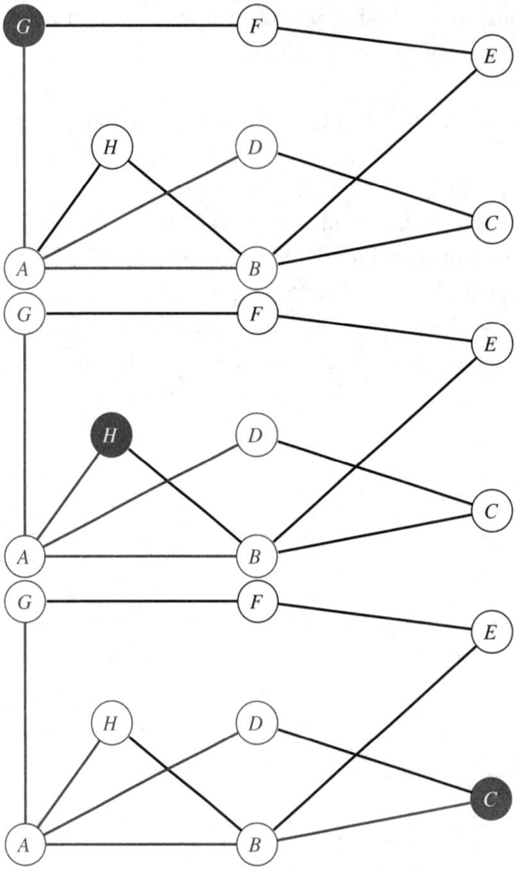

FIGURE 13.14 ■ Breadth-first search, part 2.

been visited, so we do not mark it as visited a second time and do not put it on the queue.

- We take D from the head of the queue. We detect that edges exist only to A and C, both of which have been visited, so we do nothing further. The queue is now $Q = <G, H, C, E>$.
- We take G from the head of the queue. We notice that an edge exists to F, so we visit F and add it to the queue, which is now $Q = <H, C, E, F>$.
- We take H from the head of the queue. We detect that edges exist only to A and B, both of which have been visited, so we do nothing further. The queue is now $Q = <C, E, F>$.
- We take in succession C, E, and F from the queue, processing the edges to find that no unvisited nodes exist, and thus we add nothing to the queue.

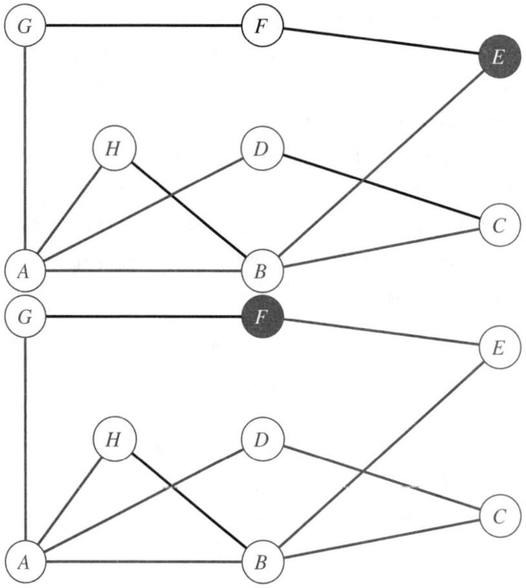

FIGURE 13.15 ■ Breadth-first search, part 3.

The BFS algorithm terminates when the queue is drained. In pseudocode, the method would be as follows.

```
void BFS(Vertex v)
{
  visit 'v' and mark 'v' as visited
  add 'v' to the queue

  while the queue is not empty
  {
    extract the head node 'w'
    for each edge 'e' leading from 'w' to a vertex 'x'
    {
      if 'x' has not been visited
      {
        visit 'x' and mark 'x' as visited
        add 'x' to the queue
      }
    }
  }
}
```

Both DFS and BFS can be accomplished with relatively simple algorithms. These are also reasonably fast algorithms. We have referred to the processing activity done at a given node as "visiting" the node (this processing might, for something like a chess-playing program, involve computing the goodness of the board position). We have to visit each node at least once in order to do the processing. What we would like to do is minimize the number of times we *examine* a node, that is, the number of times we pass through the node. The first time we examine the node, find it to be unvisited, and then visit is necessary. The subsequent examinations are overhead in the graph traversal and are what we would like to minimize.

Theorem 13.1

The BFS and DFS algorithms perform node examinations $O(|E|)$ times, where $|E|$ is the cardinality of the set E of edges in the graph.

Proof Consider how DFS works on a given node v. Once we visit v, we then call DFS recursively once for every outgoing edge from v. This means that we must also return from the recursive method call once for every outgoing edge. For any given node, then, we examine that node once for each outgoing edge, so the total number of examinations performed is $O(|E|)$.

BFS is somewhat similar (which is why we have these two together as one theorem and not two). For each outgoing edge from a given node, we examine the node at the other end of the edge, and either add the node to the queue or not. But once we have used that edge, we do not return to it, just as we do not return to an edge in depth-first search. Again, the total number of times we examine nodes is $O(|E|)$.

We note that we cannot do better than $O(|E|)$ for either BFS or DFS. Almost by definition, any tree is a worst-case example. Since a tree can be defined as a graph with n nodes and $n-1$ edges, and since following an edge can only add one new node to the list of visited nodes for either search method, the only way to visit all the nodes of a tree is to follow all the edges in the tree. □

13.4 Graph Problems

A very large number of computing applications can be reduced to problems on graphs or the use of graph algorithms, and the study of graphs as a subdiscipline of mathematics has a long history. Graph theory is one of those branches of mathematics in which it is possible to pose problems that are easy to state and to understand but hard to solve. Although most of the solutions to these problems are beyond the scope of this book, the statement of the problems is not. We present these topics here because students would be well-served, when an application requires the solution of a problem in graph theory, to know that it is a problem in graph theory. If the solution is easy, then even undergraduates should be able to write the program for the solution. For the hard problems, knowing the solution is hard means knowing that a naive approach may not be too much worse than a sophisticated approach.

13.4.1 *NP*-Completeness

One of the interesting, and curious, things about graphs and problems on graphs is that some problems are quite simple, and some apparently similar problems can be very difficult. Another characteristic of problems on graphs is that the proofs of theorems, and the demonstration that algorithms perform as they are claimed to perform, can be almost completely obvious once one presents the information in exactly the right way. This can make it somewhat hard to keep track of what is easy and what is not so easy.

Although a real study of computational complexity is beyond the scope of this book, it is not unreasonable, especially when talking about graphs, to introduce the concept of an *NP-complete problem.* To do that we first have to describe "problems that are in *P*."

13.4.1.1 The Class *P*

A problem is said to be in the class *P* if an algorithm exists that runs in polynomial time $p(N)$ in the input size N of the problem and that solves the problem for any inputs. This requires us to be somewhat more specific about what is meant by the "input size" of the problem.

For example, we claim that addition of two b-bit integers can be done in fewer than $p(b) = 2b$ boolean operations on bits. If we line up the bits for the standard addition algorithm, we have b pairs of bits. For each pair, we have one addition of 2 bits, plus possibly one more addition of 2 bits in order to add in the carry from the previous bit addition. Playing it safe, this is at most $2b$ bit operations. Since the input size of the addition problem is $2b$ bits, this means we can add two such integers in a polynomial number of operations ($O(b)$) relative to the number of input bits ($2b$).

When we represent a graph problem for complexity analysis, we need to ensure that we can represent the problem in a polynomial number of bits relative to some controlling basic property of the graph. This is usually the number of nodes in the graph. If we have N nodes, we have at most N^2 edges for an undirected graph or twice that many for a directed graph, assuming that we have a graph with no repeated edges and not a multigraph. An edge consists of two integers (node numbers), so we can present a graph to an algorithm using no more than $N + 2N^2$

integers, each of which is less than or equal to N. Since an integer of this size requires no more than $\lg N$ bits for its representation, we can represent the graph using no more than

$$(N + 2N^2) \cdot \lg N < (N^2 + 2N^3)$$

total bits. This is a polynomial in the number of nodes.

The upshot of all this is that when we look at graph problems, we are going to be looking at running times in terms of the number of nodes in the graph. For asymptotic purposes, that is the base characteristic of the graph.

13.4.1.2 The Class *NP*

The class P consists of problems for which we have an algorithm to find a solution for the problem that runs in polynomial time in the input representation. The class NP is the set of problems for which we can check a putative solution in polynomial time. Perhaps the easiest such problem to describe is that of *Boolean satisfiability*, which is often abbreviated "SAT." Given a Boolean expression (such as you would write for an `if` statement in Java) consisting of variables, *AND*, *OR*, *NOT*, and parentheses, is there an assignment of `true` and `false` to the variables that will make the entire expression evaluate to `true`? For example, the expression

$$(a\ OR\ b\ OR\ c)\ AND\ (b\ OR\ c)$$

has a satisfying assignment of $a =$ `false`, $b =$ `true`, $c =$ `false`. It should be clear that we can test a putative solution in time that is linear in the number of input symbols (and thus in polynomial time) because that's exactly what we would do by using a stack to evaluate the expression. Testing a possible solution to the SAT problem can be done in polynomial time, so SAT is in class NP.

This example also shows us where the hard part of complexity theory is. With n variables in a SAT expression, there are 2^n possible assignments of `true` and `false` that could be the solution. But as we have seen in Theorem 6.20, 2^n is genuinely bigger than any polynomial. If we have no algorithm that is fundamentally better than trial and error for a problem whose possible solution set is growing exponentially in size, then the problem will not be known to be in class P.

13.4.1.3 *NP*-Completeness

The class P contains all the problems for which we have found polynomial-time algorithms for their solution. The class NP contains the problems for which we can check a putative solution in polynomial time. A problem is said to be *NP-complete* if it is in the class NP and if any other problem in the class NP can be reduced to it in polynomial time. The Boolean satisfiability problem described earlier, and the Hamiltonian cycle problem, to be mentioned shortly, are both in *NP*. They are also *NP*-complete problems because there is a way to transform, in a polynomial number of operations, an instance of SAT into an instance of the Hamiltonian cycle problem, and conversely.

The list of *NP*-complete problems is essentially the list of the toughest open problems in all of algorithms and theoretical computer science. Almost certainly the biggest open problem in all of computer science is the question of whether the class *P* is the same as the class *NP*. As of this writing, the Clay Mathematics Institute is offering a million-dollar prize for answering the question: Is *P* equal to *NP* or not?

We saw earlier that the hard nut to crack in SAT is the exponential growth in the possible number of assignments of `true` and `false` to the variables.

In graph problems, the hard nut to crack is often the combinatorially explosive number of paths. The classic graph problem is the Traveling Salesman Problem: Given a set of cities, with distances known between them, in what sequence should a traveling salesman visit the cities in order to travel a minimal number of miles? The combinatorial explosion comes from the factorial growth of the number of permutations. If we have N cities, the first choice is free, but then we have $N-1$ choices for our first city to visit, then $N-2$ for the second city, and so forth. There are thus $(N-1)!$ possible sequences of cities to visit. Since factorials grow faster than polynomially (see Theorem 6.21), we have the same situation as with SAT: if we can't do better than trial and error, we can't get polynomial time.

13.4.2 Eulerian Cycles

One of the classic problems in mathematics, dating back to the original invention of graph theory by the eighteenth century Swiss mathematician Leonhard Euler, is that of finding an Eulerian cycle in a graph. An *Eulerian path or cycle* is a path or cycle that visits each edge exactly once.

This is one of the easy problems.

Theorem 13.2

A graph $G = (V, E)$ has an Eulerian cycle if and only if the graph is connected and every node has even degree.

Proof First, it is clear that if the graph is not connected, then no Eulerian path can exist because a path must stay confined to one connected component in a graph.

So let's assume that we have a connected graph. Pick any vertex v_1 as the starting point for a path, and pick any edge from v_1 to some vertex v_2. Take that edge.

When we arrive at v_2, we will have used an odd number of edges (namely one) of the edges incident to v_2, so there is some edge that leaves v_2 that we can follow, and we take that edge. We have now used an even number of edges incident on v_2. If we go back to v_1, then we will have used an even number of edges incident on v_1. If we go to a new node v_3, we will have used only one edge incident to it, so there must be another edge leading away.

We continue in this way. At some point we will complete a cycle, and the cycle will use an even number of edges from any node. If there are no more edges in the graph, we are done. If there are any edges left over, then we can pick up the path from a node with remaining edges and continue. Since the graph is connected, we are actually forming a path, even though we might have to move from our base vertex v_1 to some other vertex after exhausting the edges at v_1. Since all nodes have an even number of edges, we cannot run out of edges except by forming cycles. □

13.4.3 Connected Components

A second easy problem is that of finding the connected components of a graph. The connected component of you on Facebook, for example, is the transitive closure of your friends, and their friends, and their friends, and so forth.

Finding the connected components of a graph is not one of the hard problems. Indeed, starting from any node, either breadth-first search or depth-first search will find the connected component for that node. We can view breadth-first search, for example, as a greedy algorithm: starting at any given node, connect to the nodes adjacent to the starting point and include these in the component. For each node that is now in the component, perform the same process, and continue this recursively. When there are no more nodes to connect, we are done. If we have exhausted the set of nodes, the graph is connected and has only one component. If there are any nodes not yet visited, then they must lie in some other component. We can start with one of those nodes and find its component, and continue. Since this is breadth-first search, the running time is no worse than the number of edges in the graph.

13.4.4 Spanning Trees

There are a number of problems involving graphs in which it is necessary to create a *spanning tree* for the graph. We defined a spanning tree back in Chapter 9—it is a subgraph of a graph that is a tree (and thus has no cycles) and that contains all the nodes in the original graph. One instance in which a spanning tree might be necessary is in a dynamic communications environment. A collection of mobile communications devices might need to set up a conference call link among all the devices in the set. If each device is connected to a single fixed tower, then a spanning tree would be needed among the fixed towers in order to link all the devices together.

Finding a spanning tree is another of the easy problems. Look, for example, at the colored-edge tree of depth-first search in Figure 13.10. In doing DFS, we must reach all nodes in the connected component, and by not visiting nodes already visited we are in fact creating a tree structure of the nodes that we do visit.

13.4.5 Shortest Path

One of the standard graph problems is that of finding the shortest path between two nodes in the graph. We recall that a *path* is a sequence of edges that connect nodes. By convention, we will insist that a path has at least one edge, and for the most part we are concerned with *simple* paths for which each node in the path is distinct.

If the nodes were cities on a map and the edge weights were distances between cities, then the shortest path problem is in fact the problem of finding the shortest path between two cities on the map.

The best known and simplest of the shortest-path algorithms is *Dijkstra's algorithm*, discovered by Edsger Dijkstra, which runs in $O(|V|^2)$ time. The details of this algorithm are beyond the scope of this book.

13.4.6 Hamiltonian Cycles

An Eulerian path or cycle is a path or cycle that uses each edge in a graph. A *Hamiltonian path (or cycle)* is a path (or cycle) that visits each *node* exactly once (with the additional criterion that a Hamiltonian cycle must return to the originating node when it traverses the last edge). The general problem of determining whether a graph has a Hamiltonian cycle is *NP*-complete.

13.4.7 Traveling Salesman Problem

The *Traveling Salesman Problem*, or TSP, is one of the celebrated graph problems and is a problem that is known to be "*NP*-hard." The graph consists of a set of cities as nodes and the distances between every pair of cities as edge weights, with all edges considered possible. The problem is to find the path from a given node that traverses every node in the graph with the minimum total distance traveled.

In its simplest and purest form, this is a problem that is posed on an undirected graph that is a *complete* graph, that is, a graph in which an edge exists between any pair of vertices. Even in this abstract form, as a problem of finding the Hamiltonian cycle of minimal weight, the problem has applications. There are even more applications that are restricted versions of the TSP. Because this is such an important problem, there is an extensive theory of how to "almost" solve TSP, with the "almost" being quantified as "with some high probability, a Hamiltonian cycle can be found with weight that is within some small fraction of being minimal."

13.4.8 Cliques

A *clique* in a graph $G = (V, E)$ is a subgraph $G' = (V', E')$, with $V' \subset V$ and with $E' \subset E$, such that for every pair of vertices in V', there exists an edge in E' connecting those vertices. An example of a clique is indicated by the colored nodes and edges in Figure 13.16.

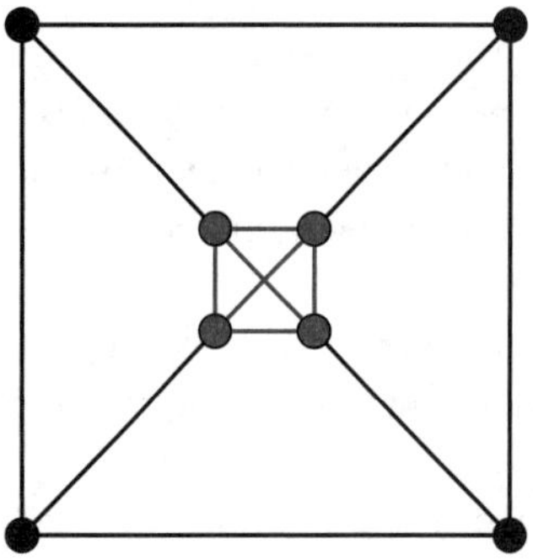

FIGURE 13.16 ■ An example (in color) of a clique.

The *maximal clique* problem is the problem of finding a clique of maximal size in a given graph. In real-world terms, this could be phrased as: find the largest subset of people on Facebook all of whom have friended each other in pairs. One might also have this in a communications setting: find the largest subset of computers in a network all of which are connected in pairs by a high-speed connection; this could be useful because communication through this subset of computers could replace communication through a single hub (that might fail).

Unfortunately, the clique problem is also *NP*-complete.

13.5 Summary

We have reviewed the basic concepts of graph theory, which includes and extends the use of trees in computation. We have covered the adjacency matrix and the sparse matrix representation for a graph. Adjacency matrices are simple to use but can be expensive for large and sparse graphs. For these graphs, the sparse notation should be used.

Although we have only touched on the subject of computational complexity, we have briefly discussed several problems in graph theory that arise in doing computations. Some of these have easy solutions, but for many of these problems there is simply no solution that runs in time polynomial in the size of the problem.

13.6 Exercises

Many of the algorithms associated with graph problems are complicated and their details are beyond the scope of this book. Nonetheless, it is worthwhile in the modern age of cheap, fast computers to run naive programs and notice that some problems scale up badly. For some of these problems, the naive approach will work only on small graphs, and it is worth seeing how the running time scales with the size of the problem.

1. Find the cliques, find a spanning tree, and list the nodes visited in order in a depth-first and a breadth-first search of the following graphs. In your searches, start with node a.

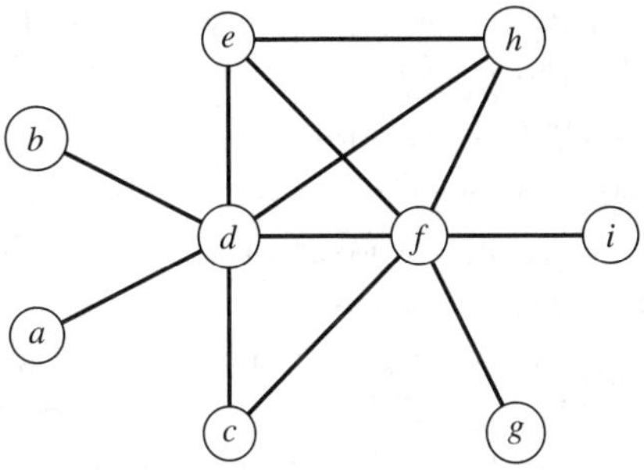

(a)

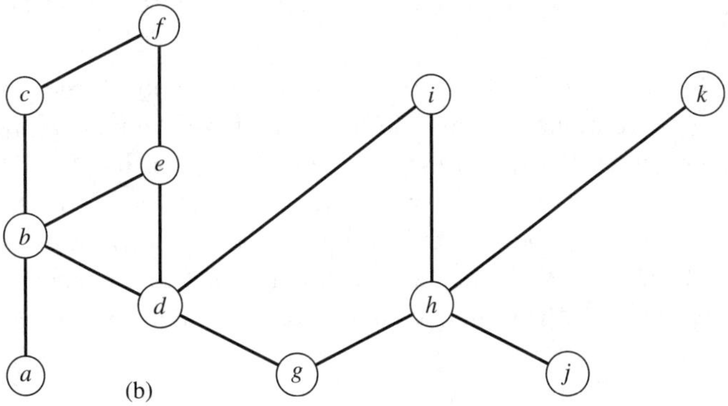

(b)

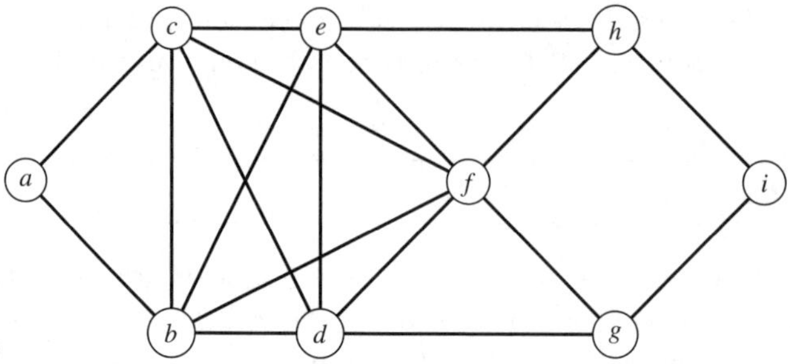

(c)

2. Write a program to find an Eulerian path or cycle in a graph.
3. Write a program to perform a depth-first search through a graph represented by an adjacency matrix. Use the depth-first search to determine a spanning tree for the graph. Use the depth-first search to determine the connected components of the graph.
4. Write a program to perform a depth-first search through a graph represented as a list of nodes adjacent to a given node. Use the depth-first search to determine a spanning tree for the graph. Use the depth-first search to determine the connected components of the graph.
5. Write a naive recursive program to solve the Traveling Salesman Problem. Note that this would be almost identical to a recursive program to enumerate the permutations of the node labels (the difference being that you keep track of a distance function). Run your program on a graph with an increasing number of nodes from 5 to 20, say, and keep track of the running times of your code. To make this a more valid experiment and have the running times comparable from one size to the next, build out your entire graph beforehand and use the first 5, the first 6, the first 7, etc., nodes in your successive executions of the program.

*6. If M is the adjacency matrix for an undirected graph G, representing paths of length one from one node to another node, then the matrix product $M \cdot M$ has nonzero entries that represent the number of paths of length two from one edge to another. The matrix product $M \cdot M \cdot M$ has nonzero entries that represent the number of paths of length three, and so forth. Write a program to compute the matrix products and verify that these are the numbers of paths of the appropriate lengths from one node to another in a graph of your choosing.

A The Author's Idiosyncrasies of Coding Style

Writing in the first person, I freely admit that I write code with a number of idiosyncrasies, and thus my code looks a little different from that written by other people. I have written a lot of code in my life, and I believe that a large part of writing good code that works correctly is simply a matter of forcing oneself to do things to compensate for one's known bad habits. I comment here on some of the peculiarities of the way I write code that have allowed me to write better (in my opinion) and more correct code in less time. Your mileage may vary because you may have different bad habits, so you will probably want to establish your own standards.

A.1 Utilities

To facilitate input, output, and testing, I have a standard `FileUtils` class that has standard `static` methods for opening and closing `Scanners` and `PrintWriters`. These methods take a `String` filename as a parameter and open a file of that name, doing the appropriate error checking. The important thing here is the error checking. By writing and using a utility program, I only have to be that careful that one time, and after having written the program once I can use it over and over again.

Also, to make it easier to test programs in more than one way, I wrote in a hack to deal with I/O to and from the console. If one wants to send output to the console, then by "opening" the `System.out` file as the `outFile`, output goes to the Eclipse console, for example. The code for `FileUtils.java` is shown in Appendix B.

The *prudent programmer*, however, should be aware that odd things can happen when writing to output files under several different names. The order of writing lines to the output files may not be as expected, and it is even possible that output buffers are overwritten so that output lines are lost. Frequent use of the `flush` method may be necessary in order to ensure that the output lines appear in the file in the order in which the user expects them to be written.

A.2 Log Files

I have, in my `FileUtils` code, methods to set up a static log file that can be printed to from anywhere in a program. In some sense, this violates the principle that one should not have global variables because the log file is in fact global to the entire program. I have found writing programs to be a two-step process. First you make it right, and then you make it better, and frequently in making it right it is necessary to trace execution by producing output. In order to avoid the problem of first including an output `PrintWriter` as a method parameter down a food chain of a calling sequence, only to have to remove that parameter after testing is complete, I have found it easier to have a global log file to use during testing. When testing is complete, the global log file should no longer be used, and file output should only be done to `PrintWriter` instances passed in as parameters.

A.3 Labeling Trace Output

I often find it useful to be able to trace the execution of a program through the classes and methods invoked. To facilitate this, I often set up a `TAG` variable that is a string used for labeling the lines of output. This variable is set to

```
FlatFile:
```

(with a colon and a trailing space) in the `FlatFile` class, for example. If nothing else, this can help me follow along through the various method calls to ensure that execution is progressing as I expect it to.

A.4 Naming Conventions

I tend to assign filenames so that they will collate alphabetically. For this reason, I would tend to avoid the Java norm in labeling exception handling classes `BadInputException`, `BadIndexException`, and such, and instead would label these two classes `ExceptionBadInput` and `ExceptionBadIndex`. This way, all the exception-handling classes collate alphabetically together either in the Eclipse IDE or in the normal alphabetic file order in Windows or Unix/Linux. Further, this allows me to see immediately which exception-handling methods are inherent in Java and which I have written myself. For testing purposes, this can simplify things, and Eclipse will be happy to change each such name everywhere in the code if I choose to rename the class.

Similarly, within a Java class, my normal tendency is to sort instance variable declarations first on the complexity of the data type and then alphabetically by variable name. I will sort `boolean`, `int`, `long`, `float`, `double`, and `String` types in that order, for example, followed by the inherent Java types such as `Scanner` or `Iterator`, and then put my own data types like `DLL` or `Record` at the bottom. Again, this is only to make it easier for me to find the variables when I go searching for them during the testing of a program.

A.5 Use of `this` in Java

I try to be especially rigid about the use of `this` in Java as a defensive measure. If I am consistent in using the `this` construct, then anything *not* prefixed with `this` is supposed to be local to the method, and it is easier to distinguish instance variables of the class from temporary variables of the method.

A.6 Labeling Closing Braces

In any situation in which I have a closing brace that is far enough down the page or screen that I will lose track of which open brace is being closed, I will take the leading line of the code block and put that as a comment on the line with the closing brace. Thus, my classes often begin and end like the following.

```
while(notYet != done)
{
   // many lines of code go here
} // while(notYet != done)
```

In some sense, this is overkill because smart editors will highlight the closing brace that the editor thinks matches up with the opening brace. But more information in this context is better, in my opinion. And if what the editor highlights has some other label on it, then I know I am missing a brace in between.

A.7 Keep It Simple

I try to write simple code and not to be overly clever. I don't tend to remember why it is that clever things work, so when I go back to read the code later I have to spend extra effort to understand it. So I normally write code in a style that uses only those things I know I won't forget if I don't use the code for a month or so.

A.8 The Infamous Double Equals

I usually write a test done against a constant with the constant on the left-hand side, as in

```
int thisValue = 0;
if(0 == thisValue)
```

and not as in

```
int thisValue = 0;
if(thisValue == 0)
```

with the constant on the right-hand side. I do this because if I mistype and put only one "equals" sign instead of two, then in the case of the former expression the compiler or the IDE will always tell me that I have done something illegal. The type-checking in the Java compiler is good enough to tell me that the code

```
int thisValue = 0;
if(thisValue = 0)
```

is illegal, but the compiler isn't smart enough to realize that

```
boolean thisValue = true;
if(thisValue = true)
```

is probably a typo. I put all constant expressions on the left-hand side for consistency because it can be all too easy to overlook the typographical error.

(This is also a good habit to get into for anyone who is going to use a language like C++ because those compilers generally *won't* catch the typo done with the `int` variable.)

B File Utilities

It is generally agreed upon that one should not write "utility" code every time one writes a new program. The first time one writes code for some purpose in a given program, it is new code and must be written. The second time one writes much the same code in a different place, the idea of creating a method for that purpose should be considered, and certainly by the third time the same code is written, it's time to write one method with parameters and to get that method right. Obviously it's a method that is common to the computation as a whole, so the code should be standardized.

Almost nowhere is this principle more evident than in the process of opening and closing files. When opening a file, one should always check that the file actually exists and that it can be opened; it should not be the case that this problem is detected when the program crashes on the first read or write.

We have found it to be good practice, then, to build out a standard set of file utilities, mostly for opening and closing files, and we list our code here. This is not to say that students should not write their own code at least once to handle files, but students should not be writing and rewriting that code with each new program.

B.1 Header, Boilerplate, and a Log File

Figure B.1 shows the header and `import` lines of our `FileUtils` class.

Figure B.1 also includes code to set up a static log file. This can be highly useful in testing but also can be a feature that is abused in production code. General practice should be that global variables are to be avoided and that all variables needed in a class or method should be clearly contained in that method or passed in as parameters. Global *constants* are one thing, because they are read-only, but the danger in having global variables is that they can be modified from several places in the code and thus it can be hard to determine, when writing code inside a particular class or method, which value is likely to be held by the variable.

The method to close the file has one line, the `flush`, that deserves attention. The file-handling routines of Java, as with those of many (most?) programming

```
import java.io.File;
import java.io.FileNotFoundException;
import java.io.PrintWriter;
import java.util.Scanner;
/*********************************************************************
 * FileUtils class of static constants and basic file checking routines.
 * This is the header file of constants and methods that might be
 * used in any and all contexts.
 *
 * @author Duncan Buell
 * @version 1.00 Copyright Duncan A. Buell 1 May 2011
**/
public class FileUtils
{
  public static PrintWriter logFile = null;

/*********************************************************************
 * Method to close the PrintWriter class log file.
**/
  public static void CloseLogFile()
  {
    FileUtils.logFile.flush();
    FileUtils.logFile.close();
  }

/*********************************************************************
 * Method to set the logFile given the name of the file.
 *
 * @param logFileName the <code>String</code> name of the log file.
**/
  public static void SetLogFile(String logFileName)
  {
    FileUtils.logFile = FileUtils.PrintWriterOpen(logFileName);
  }
```

FIGURE B.1 ■ The `FileUtils` code, part 1.

languages, do buffered input and output. That is, when a line is written to output, the line is not always written immediately. Since computers are fast and disk operations are slow, it would be inefficient to always write out to disk, perhaps 1 byte at a time. Instead, output streams are buffered in memory before being written. When a new block of output characters overflows the buffer (sized at 1,024 bytes, perhaps), then the buffer in its entirety is written to disk and the characters that would have overflowed the buffer are stored as the first characters of the new buffer to be written in the future.

The **flush** line forces the buffer to be written whether or not it is full. This should be done by the **close**, but it doesn't hurt to ensure that the buffer has been flushed.

In general, when writing data to files, one should issue one's own **flush** commands at strategic points in the program to force output to be written to disk, but one should not always flush the buffer unless performance is not an issue. (If one is writing out log information while testing, for example, then performance is probably not an issue and getting the best information back from the program probably is an issue, so flushing all the time might be appropriate.)

The one instance when writing code in which remembering that output is buffered is required is this: If your program goes into an infinite loop that writes no data, and if finding where the error has occurred requires looking at the absolutely most recent data that you have asked to be written out, then a failure to flush might well mean that the crucial information you need to find your error is in the buffer, not in the file, and thus not available to you. You should be sure, when tracking down infinite loops, that you have not forgotten output data that might not yet have been written to disk.

On the other hand, it can be very useful in testing to have a globally defined log file that is separate and distinct from the "output" file. If one needs to write information to a file in order to show the execution sequence or to document progress of the program through its various classes and methods, then a log file would be an appropriate thing to have. On the other hand, adding a log file parameter when testing and taking it out after finishing can be tedious and unproductive. Used judiciously, a statically defined global log file can be beneficial, and the **SetLogFile** method in Figure B.1 does exactly that. Output to the log file would be done by a program line like

```
FileUtils.logfile.printf(WHATEVER);
```

B.2 Setting Up an Output PrintWriter File

Figure B.2 shows the code for opening and closing a **PrintWriter** output file. We have made these **static** methods, so they would be called by a line like

```
FileUtils.PrintWriterOpen(myFileName);
```

```
/*********************************************************************
 * Method to close a PrintWriter file.
 * @param theFile the <code>PrintWriter</code> file to close.
**/
  public static void CloseFile(PrintWriter theFile)
  {
    theFile.flush();
    theFile.close();
  }

/*********************************************************************
 * PrintWriterOpen method to open a file as a PrintWriter.
 *
 * The main purpose of this method is to do the error checking in
 * a subordinate method so as not to clutter up the code flow
 * in methods that have to open files.
 *
 * @param  outFileName the <code>String</code> name of the file to open
 * @return The opened <code>PrintWriter</code> known to be not null
**/
  public static PrintWriter PrintWriterOpen(String outFileName)
  {
    PrintWriter localPrintWriter = null;

    if(outFileName.equals("System.out"))
    {
      localPrintWriter = new PrintWriter(System.out);
    }
    else
    {
      try
      {
        localPrintWriter = new PrintWriter(new File(outFileName));
      }
      catch (FileNotFoundException ex)
      {
        FileUtils.logFile.println("ERROR opening outFile " +
                                   outFileName);
        FileUtils.logFile.println(ex.getMessage());
        FileUtils.logFile.println("in" +
                                   System.getProperty("user.dir"));
        FileUtils.logFile.flush();
        System.exit(1);
      }
    }
    return localPrintWriter;
  }
```

FIGURE B.2 ■ The `FileUtils` code, part 2.

We have included in our code for opening files a feature that some purists might object to. If the "filename" passed to this method is `System.out`, then the returned `PrintWriter` is not an actual file but instead the console output file built into Java. We have also found this useful in testing. We have often found it to be the case that we have used several different sets of test data, each of which gives us a different output file of results. Sometimes, however, one really just wants to test a particular feature or (what one hopes is) a small change in the code. For this, console input and output might well be more convenient than producing yet another output file. Having the ability to switch between actual files and console input and output without changing the code can make life easier.

We note that in opening an *output* file there should be few occasions on which the open fails. Unlike an attempt to open an input file, an output file need not exist beforehand. If a file does exist beforehand, it is destroyed and the file recreated by the creation of a new `PrintWriter`. The Javadoc from the Web states that the `FileNotFoundException` error is thrown "[i]f the given file object does not denote an existing, writable regular file and a new regular file of that name cannot be created, or if some other error occurs while opening or creating the file," so we will catch that exception, as well as the `SecurityException` that is thrown if a security manager is present and write access is denied to the program for that file.

B.3 Setting Up an Input `Scanner` File

Figure B.3 shows the code for opening and closing a `Scanner` input file. Setting up an input file from which to read is slightly more delicate than setting up an output file but only slightly more so. Here there is only the file exception to be handled, but in this case that exception could easily be triggered for several reasons.

Analogous to what we did with output, we here allow for the special file name `System.in` to refer to the console input rather than a file, thus allowing (among other things) input of specific data from the console for testing without the need to write one or more files.

```
/*********************************************************************
 * Method to close a Scanner file.
 * @param theFile The <code>Scanner</code> file to close.
**/
  public static void CloseFile(Scanner theFile)
  {
    theFile.close();
  }

/*********************************************************************
 * ScannerOpen method to open a file as a Scanner.
 *
 * The main purpose of this method is to do the error checking in
 * a subordinate method so as not to clutter up the code flow
 * in methods that have to open files.
 *
 * @param  inFileName the <code>String</code> name of the file to open
 * @return The opened <code>Scanner</code> known to be not null
**/
  public static Scanner ScannerOpen(String inFileName)
  {
    Scanner localScanner = null;

    if(inFileName.equals("System.in"))
    {
      localScanner = new Scanner(System.in);
    }
    else
    {
      try
      {
        localScanner = new Scanner(new File(inFileName));
      }
      catch (FileNotFoundException ex)
      {
        FileUtils.logFile.println("ERROR opening inFile " +
                                   inFileName);
        FileUtils.logFile.println(ex.getMessage());
        FileUtils.logFile.println("in" +
                                   System.getProperty("user.dir"));
        FileUtils.logFile.flush();
        System.exit(1);
      }
    }
    return localScanner;
  }
```

FIGURE B.3 ■ The `FileUtils` code, part 3.

C Glossary

C.1 The Nature of Jargon

In the next section, the numbers in parentheses indicate the chapter or chapters in which these terms are used and/or defined. In some instances, the reader is also directed to the Jargon File found online (search on the term "jargon file").

The usual notion of a definition is that a definition should read, "An X is a Y that has properties Z," where X is the term to be defined, Y is a larger class to which X belongs, and Z is what distinguishes X from other members in the larger class Y. For example, in the definition "A *tree* is a connected graph with no cycles," we have X = "tree," Y = "connected graph," and Z = "with no cycles."

Unfortunately, there are many important terms in computing that cannot be defined using the classical notion of a definition. In many instances, this is because the term is defined as a phenomenon that has been observed to exist or because the term has come to more or less describe a common feature. Rather than forcing the issue with an artificial definition, we have usually avoided trying to create a true "definition" for such terms.

C.2 Terms Used in This Book

- $3n + 1$ problem (8): The $3n + 1$ problem, also called the *Syracuse problem* or the *Collatz problem*, is this: Begin with any integer n and recursively apply the following transformation. If n is even, then divide n by 2 to produce $n' = n/2$. If n is odd, then multiply n by 3 and add 1 to produce $n' = 3n + 1$. Repeat. The problem is to determine whether repeated applications of this transformation eventually reduce to $n' = 1$. All n ever tested have reduced to 1, and it is conjectured that the repetition of this transformation will reduce any integer n to 1, but this has not yet been proved.
- $f(x) = o(g(x))$(6): See *asymptotic notation*.
- $f(x) = O(g(x))$(6): See *asymptotic notation*.
- $f(x) = \Omega(g(x))$(6): See *asymptotic notation*.

- $f(x) = \Omega_K(g(x))$(6): See *asymptotic notation.*
- $f(x) = \Theta(g(x))$(6): See *asymptotic notation.*
- Ackermann function (8): There are several functions that go by the name of the Ackermann function. The one most commonly used in computer science is the function $A(m, n)$ defined using recursion as follows.

$$
\begin{aligned}
A(m,n) &= n+1 && \text{if } m = 0\\
&= A(m-1, 1) && \text{if } m > 0 \text{ and } n = 0\\
&= A(m-1, A(m, n-1)) && \text{if } m > 0 \text{ and } n > 0
\end{aligned}
$$

- adjacency matrix (13): An *adjacency matrix* for a graph is a matrix of 0 and 1 values. Rows and columns correspond to the nodes in a graph, and 1 in the row-i, column-j position indicates that an edge (a directed edge in the case of a directed graph) exists from the ith node to the jth node. In the case of undirected graphs, this is always a symmetric matrix.
- adjacent node (9): A node v_1 in a (directed) graph is *adjacent* to another node v_2 in the graph if there is an edge (directed in the case of directed graphs) that connects v_1 to v_2.
- analysis of algorithms (6): *Analysis of algorithms* is the subdiscipline of computer science that deals with the determination of the theoretical asymptotic running time of a particular algorithm. For example, it can be shown by analysis that a mergesort on N data items can always be done using at most $O(N \lg N)$ comparisons of different items.
- ancestor of a node (10): An *ancestor* of a given node in a graph is any node that can be reached from the given node by tracing upward through the parent links, just as one's own ancestors can be traced through parents, grandparents, and so forth. See *child node, parent node.*
- arc (7, 9, 13): See *graph.*
- associative search (12): We say that an *associative search* is performed when (at some conceptual level) a sought-for data item is found simply by associating the key to the data item, rather than conducting a search through the data and a comparison of the keys in the data to the key being searched for. If a programmer is using packages like the JCF, then the package may provide the illusion to the programmer of an associative search by a method that returns a data item corresponding to a key, but the underlying code in the package will necessitate a more expensive search operation.
- asymptotic analysis (3): The *asymptotic analysis* of an algorithm or program is done by determining the main growth term, in the expression for the running time cost of the algorithm or program, that dominates the running time cost as the size of the problem being solved goes to infinity.

- asymptotic notation (6): The *asymptotic notation* that is used to express asymptotic running times of algorithms is as follows:
  1. big Oh: We write $f(x) = O(g(x))$ if there exist constants c and C such that $x > c \implies |f(x)| \leq C \cdot g(x)$.
  2. big Omega (traditional): We write $f(x) = \Omega(g(x))$ if $f(x)$ is *not* $o(g(x))$, that is, if there exists a sequence $x_1, x_2, \ldots, x_n, \ldots$, tending to ∞, such that for any fixed constant C, there exists a constant c such that $x_i > c \implies |f(x_i)| \geq C \cdot g(x_i)$.
  3. big Omega (Knuth's version): We write $f(x) = \Omega_K(g(x))$ if for any fixed constant C there exists a constant c such that $x > c \implies |f(x)| \geq C \cdot g(x)$. (The difference between the two versions of Omega is that in Knuth's version the inequality is required to hold for all values of x greater than c, and not just for infinitely many x_i in a sequence going off to infinity.)
  4. big Theta: We write $f(x) = \Theta(g(x))$ if there exist constants c, C_1, and C_2 such that for all $x > c$ we have $C_1 \cdot g(x) \leq |f(x)| \leq C_2 \cdot g(x)$. There is a "little theta" that is used in asymptotic analysis, but it is beyond the scope of this book.
  5. little oh: We write $f(x) = o(g(x))$ if $\lim_{x\to\infty} \frac{|f(x)|}{|g(x)|} = 0$.
- average-case behavior (1, 6, 11): The *average-case behavior* of an algorithm is the behavior that leads to the *average-case running time*. For example, the average-case behavior of insertionsort into increasing order is that an element will have to be pulled halfway through the existing array before its proper location is determined. Average-case behavior usually involves probabilistic analysis. In the insertionsort example, for any new element that should be positioned at location i in an array of length N, there is an equally likely element that should be positioned at location $N - i$, and the average of i comparisons and $N - i$ comparisons is $\frac{1}{2}N$. See *best-case behavior*, *worst-case behavior*.
- average-case running time (1, 6, 11): The *average-case running time* of an algorithm is the running time of the algorithm under the average-case conditions. See *best-case running time*, *worst-case running time*.
- balanced tree (10): A tree is said to be a *balanced tree* if from any node in the tree the split into child subtrees is a split into subtrees of approximately equal size. Since almost no trees will be perfectly balanced, it is rarely the case that this term is used in a precise sense. Rather, a tree will be said to be balanced if the split into subtrees is close enough to subtrees of equal sizes for an algorithm to run with reasonable efficiency.
- best-case behavior (1, 11): The *best-case behavior* of an algorithm is the behavior that leads to the *best-case running time*. For example, the best-case behavior of insertionsort into increasing order is that an element to be inserted belongs exactly at the end of the list, and thus that only one comparison, with the last

element in the current list, is needed. See *average-case behavior*, *worst-case behavior*.

- best-case running time (1, 11): The *best-case running time* of an algorithm is the running time of the algorithm under the best-case conditions. See *average-case running time*, *worst-case running time*.
- big Oh (6): See *asymptotic notation*.
- big Omega (6): See *asymptotic notation*.
- big Theta (6): See *asymptotic notation*.
- binary logarithm (6): The *binary logarithm* of a quantity x is the logarithm base 2 of x: $\log_2 x$. This is usually written $\lg x$ in computer science. Binary logarithms are more often used in computer science than other logarithms due to the ubiquitous presence of divide-and-conquer algorithms and heuristics, which repeatedly split problems in half in order to arrive at a solution. See *common logarithm*, *natural logarithm*.
- binary search (3, 8): *Binary search* is a computational search process in which the size of the space to be searched is cut in half repeatedly, a determination is made as to which half of the search space holds "the answer" to be found, and then the search is made recursively on that half of the space containing the answer.
- binary search tree (12): A *binary search tree* is a binary tree whose nodes hold key values for which the following two properties hold:
  1. For any given node v, the key values for all nodes in the left subtree of v are less than or equal to the value of the key for v.
  2. For any given node v, the key values for all nodes in the right subtree of v are greater than or equal to the value of the key for v.
- binary tree (7, 10): A *binary tree* is a tree in which no node has more than two children, which are referred to as the left child and the right child.
- Boolean satisfiability (13): A *Boolean satisfiability* problem is the problem of determining, for a boolean expression in some number of variables, whether there is some assignment of `true` and `false` to the variables that will result in the boolean expression's evaluating to `true`.
- breadth-first search, breadth-first traversal (10): When a tree is visualized in standard form, with the root node at the top and the tree descending from the root, a *breadth-first traversal* is accomplished by visiting first the root, then all the children of the root, usually in left-to-right order, then all the children of all the children of the root, usually in left-to-right order, and so forth. Equivalently, it is a traversal of the root node at depth 0, then the nodes at depth 1, then the nodes at depth 2, and so forth. See *depth-first traversal*, *depth of a node*, *height of a node*, *inorder traversal*, *postorder traversal*, *preorder traversal*.
- bubblesort (3, 11): A *bubblesort* is an in-place sorting algorithm in which N items are sorted by running N loops, the first of which positions the

largest (or smallest) element in the proper location by comparing it against all elements, the second loop of which positions the second largest by comparing it against the $N-1$ remaining unpositioned elements, and so forth. See *asymptotic notation, heapsort, in-place algorithm, insertionsort, mergesort, out-of-place algorithm, quicksort.*

- bucketsort (11): A *bucketsort* is a sorting algorithm in which N buckets are established for items whose key value is in the range 1 through N, and as elements are examined they are placed in the corresponding bucket.
- bush factor (10): In a tree such as a game or search tree, a node is said to have a *bush factor* of k if there are k possible child paths leading from that node. All nodes in a binary search tree, for example, will have a bush factor of 0, 1, or 2.
- child node (7, 10): When a tree is visualized in standard form, with the root node at the top and the tree descending from the root, a *child* of a given node is a node connected to the given node by a downward arc. See *parent node.*
- class *NP* (13): See *NP-complete problem.*
- class *P* (13): See *NP-complete problem.*
- clique (9, 13): A *clique* C in a graph G is a subgraph of G in which each node in C is connected by an arc to every other node in C. See *maximal clique.*
- Collatz problem (8): See $3n+1$ *problem.*
- collection (5), collection classes (4): In Java, a *collection* is an aggregate of multiple instances of objects. Often these objects are of the same data type, but since all objects are instances of the Java `Object` class, a collection can be formed of instances of `Object` type and thus have no further limitation or specification. See *JCF.*
- combinatorially explosive (1): A computation is said to be *combinatorially explosive* if the asymptotic running time grows as an exponential or factorial of the number of items of data. If a search tree for a game, for example, has a fixed number k of possible subtrees of any given node, then the running time for the search has a combinatorially explosive running time, since there is 1 root node at depth 0, k nodes at depth 1, k^2 nodes at depth 2, k^3 at depth 3, and so forth, and thus k^n nodes at depth n, and the function k^n grows exponentially with the depth n. See *asymptotic analysis.*
- common logarithm (6): The *common logarithm* of a quantity x is the logarithm base 10 of x: $\log_{10} x$. See *binary logarithm, natural logarithm.*
- complete binary tree (7, 10): A *complete binary tree* is a binary tree of k levels and $2^k - 1$ nodes. It is thus a binary tree in which every node in all levels except the level of leaf nodes has exactly two children, and all the leaf nodes are at the same level. See *binary tree, incomplete binary tree.*
- complete ternary tree (10): A *complete ternary tree* is a ternary tree of k levels and $\frac{1}{2}(3^k - 1)$ nodes. It is thus a ternary tree in which every node in all levels except the level of leaf nodes has exactly three children, and all the leaf nodes are at the same level. See *complete binary tree.*

- connected component (9, 13): A *connected component* in a graph is a subgraph of the graph that is a connected graph and to which no further nodes and arcs can be added from the original graph without creating a subgraph that is not connected. See *connected graph.*
- connected graph (9, 13): A graph is said to be *connected* if a path (directed in the case of a directed graph) exists between any two nodes in the graph.
- constant time (6): A computation is said to run in *constant time* if the asymptotic running time is a fixed constant and is independent of the size of the data presented to the algorithm. See *asymptotic analysis, exponential time, linear time, logarithmic time, quadratic time.*
- context (8): The *context* of an executing program includes the memory space allocated to the program, the binary data of the program executable, and the values currently assigned to the variables of the program. The notion of context is that, in theory, the context of the program could be made independent of the rest of the computer in which it is being executed and assigned hardware resources like a CPU, and that all that is necessary for continuing the program execution would be present.
- cycle (9, 13): A *cycle* in a graph consists of a set of nodes $v_1, \ldots, v_{n-1}, v_n$ and a set of arcs $<v_1, v_2>, <v_2, v_3>, \ldots, <v_{n-1}, v_n><v_n, v_0>$ that define a path from v_1 to v_n and then back to v_0.
- data payload (2): The *data payload* of a structure is the actual data carried by that structure, as opposed to other information (often referred to as metadata) used for management of the structure. For example, each Internet packet has metadata fields for source, destination, message ID, and packet ID, in addition to the data payload. The data payload for an Internet packet is the actual portion of the Internet message that is carried by that particular packet.
- decision tree (10): A *decision tree* is a tree representing a nested structure of decisions to be made. For example, any program segment that is a group of nested

```
if()
{
}
else if()
{
}
else
{
}
```

statements represents a decision tree.

- degree of a node (9, 13): See *node degree.*
- deprecated (4): In the world of computing, a feature or practice is considered *deprecated* if it is possible under the rules of a programming language or guidance sheet to use that feature or follow that practice, but it is considered inadvisable to do so. Many methods in Java are deprecated because they have been superseded by other methods. Although the deprecated methods will continue to exist in order to support code already written, the opinion of those responsible for Java is that the newer methods are sufficiently superior that the old methods should simply not be used for new code.
- depth-first search, depth-first traversal (10): When a tree is visualized in standard form, with the root node at the top and the tree descending from the root, a *depth-first traversal* is accomplished by descending from the root all the way to visit some leaf node, then backing up and descending to visit another leaf node, and so forth. See *breadth-first traversal, depth of a node, height of a node, inorder traversal, postorder traversal, preorder traversal.*
- depth of a node (10): The *depth of a node* in a rooted tree is the number of arcs that must be traversed in order to move upward from the node to reach the root. The root has depth 0. The children of the root have depth 1, and so forth. See *height of a node.*
- deque (7): A *deque* is a double-ended queue, a linear list data structure in which data can be added to or removed from the list at either end but only at the two ends. See *queue.*
- directed graph (9, 13): A *directed graph* is a graph in which one or more of the arcs is directed from an originating node to a terminating node and represents a connection only in that direction. See *undirected graph.*
- discipline of programming (3): The term *discipline of programming* usually uses the word "discipline" in the sense of monastic orders to refer to a set of guidelines and practices that curb excessively independent behavior and encourage standards that are felt to be the best practice.
- distributed memory parallel computer (11): In a *distributed memory parallel computer* each of the parallel processors has direct access to read and/or write to or from only a subset of the entire memory in the computer. Read/write access to memory that is directly controlled by another processor must be done by requesting such actions of the processor controlling the other memory. This is the model of computation of a Beowulf cluster, which is essentially a collection of standalone computers with an interconnection network and a software library that facilitates the necessary memory requests. See *shared memory parallel computer.*
- divide and conquer (3, 6): See *recursion, recursive divide and conquer.*
- document authentication (12): *Document authentication* is achieved in a protocol for handling documents when a document that is transmitted can be

verified to be authentic, that is, what it claims to be. See *document integrity, document nonrepudiation.*

- document integrity (12): *Document integrity* is achieved in a protocol for handling documents when a document that is received can be guaranteed to be the document that was transmitted, with no alterations. See *document authentication, document nonrepudiation.*
- document nonrepudiation (12): *Document nonrepudiation* is achieved in a protocol for handling documents when a document received by an individual B and allegedly sent by an individual A cannot be repudiated by A as not having been sent by him or her. See *document authentication, document integrity.*
- doubly-linked list (4): A *doubly-linked list* is a linked list in which links between nodes exist in both directions, forward to the next node and backward to the previous node. See *singly-linked list.*
- dynamic data structure (3, 4): A data structure is *dynamic* when data can be added to or removed from the structure while the structure is being processed. The queue of executable processes in a computer is always dynamic because it is always present and is changing with the user's actions. Payroll data for a company will usually not be dynamic because changes to the payroll data will probably not be permitted during the execution of the payroll check program.
- edge (9, 13): See *graph.*
- edge weight (13): An *edge weight* in a graph is a numerical value associated with an *edge* that usually represents a cost or capacity. A graph that represents cities on a map could have edge weights representing the distance between cities. A graph that represents nodes in the Internet could have edge weights representing bandwidth between the nodes.
- embarrassingly parallel (10): A computation is said to be *embarrassingly parallel* if there is a trivial way in which to break up the computation into a large number of completely independent subcomputations each of which can be executed in parallel with the others.
- encapsulation of data (2): Data in a computer program is said to be *encapsulated* when all privileges for access to that data are tightly controlled, essentially on a need-to-know or need-to-use basis.
- Eulerian cycle (13): An *Eulerian cycle* in a graph is a cycle that visits every edge exactly once. See *Hamiltonian cycle.*
- Eulerian path (13): An *Eulerian path* in a graph is a path that visits every edge exactly once. See *Hamiltonian path.*
- exponential time (6): An algorithm or program runs in *exponential time* if the asymptotic running time is $O(k^N)$ for some $k > 1$ when the algorithm or program is run on data inputs of size N. See *asymptotic analysis, constant time, linear time, logarithmic time, quadratic time.*

- Fibonacci sequence (8): The Fibonacci sequence $0, 1, 1, 2, 3, 5, 8, 13, 21, 34, \ldots$ is the sequence of integers $F(n)$ generated by the formula

$$F(n) = F(n-1) + F(n-2)$$

subject to the initial conditions $F(0) = 0$ and $F(1) = 1$.
- field (1): See *flat file.*
- fixed-format records (1): Records are stored with a *fixed format* if each field within a record is permitted a fixed number of bytes. For example, integer data is almost always stored with 4 bytes for each integer. When a record is stored with a fixed format, the size of each record is fixed as the sum of the number of bytes necessary for each field plus the fixed number of bytes used by the data structure for managing the individual record.
- flat file (1, 3): Data is arranged in a *flat file* if it is arranged in a fashion similar to a spreadsheet, with some variable number of rows, each of which is referred to as a *record*, and some fixed number of columns, each of which is referred to as a *field.*
- forest of trees (9): A graph is a *forest of trees* if as a graph it comprises one or more connected components each of which is a tree.
- free list (4): In many data structures, usually in legacy code, the structure is implemented with memory space preallocated for the structure. In such instances, the *free list* is the memory that has been allocated for the structure but has not been used (yet) for storing data. The need for a free list has been largely obviated by more modern programming languages and environments that do automatic allocation and release of memory from a memory store, which means the programmer does not need to manage memory in such an explicit way.
- generics (1, 3, 5): The use of a Java *generic* permits programs to be written that will operate on instances of any data type whatsoever. A "swap" method, for example, does not need to have any information about the actual data type of the two instances to be swapped; it needs only to be able to create a temporary instance of that data type to be used for storing a value that is overwritten during the swap process.
- graph (9, 13): A *graph* is a mathematical construct $G = \{V, E\}$ comprising a set of vertices V (sometimes called nodes) and a set of edges E (sometimes called arcs), with an edge $e = \{v_1, v_2\}$ between vertex v_1 and vertex v_2 representing a connection.
- greatest common divisor (10): The *greatest common divisor* of two integers m and n is the largest integer g that divides both m and n leaving no remainder.
- greedy algorithm (9): An algorithm is said to be a *greedy algorithm* if, at any stage of the computation, when a choice is to be made, the algorithm takes

the greedy, intuitively obvious, hopeful choice of whatever looks to be best at the time.

- Hamiltonian cycle (13): A *Hamiltonian cycle* in an *undirected graph* is a *cycle* that visits each vertex exactly once, except for the vertex at which the cycle begins and ends and which is thus visited twice. See *Eulerian cycle.*
- Hamiltonian path (13): A *Hamiltonian path* in an *undirected graph* is a *path* that visits each vertex exactly once. See *Eulerian path.*
- hash collision (12): A *hash collision* occurs when two different data sources are mapped by a hash function to the same storage location. See *hash function, hash table.*
- hash function (12): A *hash function* is a function that creates, from some part of the data of a data item, a storage subscript location into which to store the data item. See *hash table.*
- hash table (12): A *hash table* is an array in memory of storage locations into which data is mapped by a *hash function.* See *hash function.*
- hash table load factor (12): The *load factor* for a *hash table* is the fraction of the preallocated storage locations that are expected to be used for actual storage of data. If a hash table is preallocated for 2^{20} entries, and is used for storing 2^{17} data entries, then it has a load factor of $1/2^3 = 1/8$. See *hash function, hash table.*
- heap (7, 10): A *heap* is a data structure that satisfies the *heap property.* See *heap property.*
- heap property (10): An array `A[.]` is said to satisfy the (minimum) *heap property* if for any three locations `A[i]`, `A[2*i]`, `A[2*i+1]` in the array, the key value associated with the data at location `i` is smaller than the key values for the data at locations `2*i` and `2*i+1`. The maximum heap property is defined analogously.
- heapsort (1): *Heapsort* is a sorting algorithm with an $O(N \lg N)$ average-case and $O(N \lg N)$ worst-case running time that can be run as an in-place algorithm and is characterized by recursively creating a heap from the data, removing the smallest element from the top of the heap, and then rebuilding the heap. See *asymptotic notation, bubblesort, in-place algorithm, insertionsort, mergesort, out-of-place algorithm, quicksort.*
- height-balanced (10): A tree is said to be *height-balanced* if no leaf node is "much farther" from the root than is any other leaf node. This is not a precise definition.
- height of a binary tree (10): The *height* of a rooted binary tree is the largest number of arcs that must be traversed in order to move downward from the root node to a leaf node.
- height of a node (10): The *height of a node* in a rooted tree is the largest number of arcs that must be traversed in order to move downward from the node to a leaf node. See *depth of a node.*

- heuristic (1, 8): A *heuristic* is a computational strategy that is not guaranteed to be successful but which, under many circumstances, will work.
- incident, incident node (9, 13): An edge in a graph is *incident* on a node if the node is one of the two nodes that form the edge.
- incomplete binary tree (7): A binary tree is *incomplete* if there are nodes other than leaf nodes at the lowest level that have fewer than two children. See *complete binary tree.*
- incremental update (1): An *incremental update* of a data structure takes place when a small amount of data is added to the existing structure and the organization that characterizes the data structure can be rebuilt without a complete recomputation. Adding one element through insertionsort to a sorted list, for example, is an incremental update.
- indegree of a node (9, 13): See *node indegree.*
- index (3, 12): An *index* is a list of retrieval keys for a data structure, with the list in sorted order, and pointers to where the corresponding data elements are located in the data structure.
- inorder traversal (10): When a binary tree is visualized in standard form, with the root node at the top and the tree descending from the root, an *inorder traversal* is accomplished by recursively visiting first the left child of a node, then the node itself, then the right child. See *breadth-first traversal, depth-first traversal, depth of a node, height of a node, postorder traversal, preorder traversal.*
- in-place algorithm (11): An algorithm is said to execute *in place* if it requires only a fixed amount of storage in addition to the storage necessary to store the actual data on which the algorithm executes. See *out-of-place algorithm.*
- insertionsort (4, 11): An *insertionsort* is an in-place sorting algorithm in which N items are sorted by running N loops; each loop assumes that it is operating on a sorted list of $k < N$ elements and increases the length of the sorted list by 1 by inserting a new element into its proper place in the list. See *asymptotic notation, bubblesort, heapsort, in-place algorithm, mergesort, out-of-place algorithm, quicksort.*
- interior node (10): A node in a tree is an *interior node* if it is not a leaf node. See *leaf node.*
- Internet packets (1): One of the reasons that the Internet works is that an individual message or data file to be sent across the net is broken up into a set of *packets*, each of which contains a great deal of header information regarding source, destination, packet sequence number in the entire message, and a fixed-size block that is a subset of the entire data of the message. In this way packets can be made to have a fixed size and can be sent independently from source to destination, arriving perhaps out of order and perhaps traveling along different paths. It is the job of the router at the destination to put the packets back together so the data is reorganized into the original message or file.

- JCF (5, 12): The *Java Collections Framework* is a set of classes built into the Java package that supports program development by providing routine structures like stacks, queues, priority queues, hash tables, and similar containers for data.
- key (11): The *key* for a data item to be stored, retrieved, or searched for is the information element that is used to identify the data item. Search keys are often names, Social Security numbers, telephone numbers, or driver's license numbers, but can also be other information elements created by the software from the data so as to provide unique identifiers.
- leaf node (10): A *leaf node* in a tree is a node with no children. See *interior node.*
- left child (10): In a binary tree, the *left child* of a given node is the child that descends to the left when the tree is presented in standard form. See *right child.*
- level of a tree (10): The *nodes* at level k of a tree comprise all nodes in the tree whose depth is k.
- level traversal (10): See *breadth-first traversal.*
- linear search (6): A *linear search* is performed on an array of data when the array is processed one item at a time, from beginning to end, comparing the data in the array against the key that is being searched for.
- linear time (6): An algorithm or program runs in *linear time* if the asymptotic running time is $O(N)$ when the algorithm or program is run on data inputs of size N. See *asymptotic analysis*, *constant time*, *exponential time*, *logarithmic time*, *quadratic time.*
- linked list (4): A *linked list* is a data structure characterized by having independent nodes carrying data, a distinguished head node that is the first node in the linked list, and a pointer from any given node (including the head) to the next node in the list.
- little oh (6): See *asymptotic notation.*
- load balancing (10): *Load balancing* refers to the goal of dividing up the work to be done by several processors or processes into roughly equal sizes so that all processors will contribute to the common computation and take about the same length of time to complete their share of the task at hand.
- logarithm, binary (6): See *binary logarithm.*
- logarithm, common (6): See *common logarithm.*
- logarithm, natural (6): See *natural logarithm.*
- logarithmic time (6): An algorithm or program runs in *logarithmic time* if the asymptotic running time is $O(\lg N)$ when the algorithm or program is run on data inputs of size N. See *asymptotic analysis*, *constant time*, *exponential time*, *linear time*, *quadratic time.*
- main term (6): The *main term* in an expression for the asymptotic work required for an algorithm is the function term that determines the big Oh asymptotic

running time of the algorithm. A polynomial $f(x) = a_n x^n + \cdots + a_1 x + a_0$, for example, has x^n as its main term.

- max-heap (7, 10): See *heap property.*
- maximal clique (13): A clique in a graph is a *maximal clique* if no nodes can be added to the subgraph that is the clique without creating a subgraph that is no longer a clique. See *clique.*
- mergesort (1, 11): *Mergesort* is a sorting algorithm with an $O(N \lg N)$ average-case and worst-case running time that must be run as an out-of-place algorithm, and is characterized by a recursive merge of pairs of sorted lists of size k to form single lists of size $2k$. See *asymptotic notation, bubblesort, heapsort, in-place algorithm, insertionsort, out-of-place algorithm, quicksort.*
- min-heap (7, 10): See *heap property.*
- misfeature (4): A computer program is (humorously) said to have a *misfeature* if there is some aspect of the program that decreases its normal ease of use. It is a feature of some email programs that attachments after the first for a given email message have as a default storage location the directory in which the first attachment was stored; it would be something of a misfeature if the mailer reset to a default location because one can imagine most instances of multiple attachments being sufficiently related to one another that saving them in the same directory would happen more often than not.
- multigraph (9, 13): A *multigraph* is a graph in which two nodes are permitted to be connected by more than one edge.
- natural logarithm (6): The *natural logarithm* of a quantity x is the logarithm base e of x: $\log_e x$. This is often written $\ln x$. See *binary logarithm, common logarithm.*
- node (4, 7, 9, 13): See *graph.*
- node degree (9, 13): The *degree* of a node in a graph is the number of edges incident on the node. See *node indegree, node outdegree.*
- node indegree (9, 13): The *indegree* of a node in a graph is the number of edges entering the node. In an undirected graph this is the same as the degree and the outdegree; in a directed graph this is the number of edges directed into the node. See *node degree, node outdegree.*
- node outdegree (9, 13): The *outdegree* of a node in a graph is the number of edges leaving the node. In an undirected graph this is the same as the degree and the indegree; in a directed graph this is the number of edges directed out from the node. See *node degree, node indegree.*
- *NP*-complete problem (13): The class *P* contains all the problems for which we have found polynomial-time algorithms for their solution. The class *NP* contains the problems for which we can check a putative solution in polynomial time. A problem is said to be *NP-complete* if it is in the class *NP* and if any

other problem in the class *NP* can be reduced to it in polynomial time. The Boolean satisfiability and the Hamiltonian cycle problem are both in *NP*. They are also *NP*-complete problems because there is a way to transform, in a polynomial number of operations, an instance of SAT into an instance of the Hamiltonian cycle problem, and conversely.

- objective function (1, 8, 10): An *objective function* is a function to be maximized or minimized during a computation as a measure of success of the computation.
- one-time work (6): Most computer programs are useful because they perform some repetitive computation in a loop. The *one-time work* associated with an algorithm or computation is the work done before the loop begins, perhaps to set up the execution of the loop, or after the loop ends, perhaps to aggregate results from the loop. It is work done once for the entire computation, as opposed to once for every iteration of the loop.
- outdegree of a node (9, 13): See *node outdegree.*
- out-of-place algorithm (11): An algorithm is said to execute *out of place* if it requires, in addition to the storage necessary to store the actual data on which the algorithm executes, additional storage space that is proportional to the storage space for the actual data. See *in-place algorithm.*
- palindrome (4): A *palindrome* is a sequence of characters, such as "radar," that reads the same forward and backward.
- parent node (10): When a tree is visualized in standard form, with the root node at the top and the tree descending from the root, the *parent* of a given node is the node connected to the given node by an upward arc. See *child node.*
- parse (2): To *parse* a sequence of text characters is to break the sequence into syntactic tokens based on separator characters (like blank spaces, tabs, and newline characters) and to obtain a semantic understanding of the text by applying the rules of the underlying language.
- path (9, 13): A *path* in a graph is a sequence of edges that connect tail to head

$$
\begin{aligned}
e_0 &= <v_{i_0}, v_{i_1}>, \\
e_1 &= <v_{i_1}, v_{i_2}>, \\
e_2 &= <v_{i_2}, v_{i_3}>, \\
\ldots, \\
e_{n-1} &= <v_{i_{n-1}}, v_{i_n}>.
\end{aligned}
$$

from an origin vertex v_{i_0} to a destination vertex v_{i_n}.
- pathological cases (1): A *pathological case* of data for an algorithm is an example of data on which the algorithm would perform most poorly. Pathological cases, even if they are highly unusual, must nonetheless be considered as possible when choosing or analyzing an algorithm for a particular computational task.

- portable code (3): Code (programs) are said to be *portable* if they can be moved from one computer to another and still execute correctly. Java, for example, is supposed to be "write once, run everywhere" under the premise that Java is so completely standardized that a correct Java program can run on any machine with a standard Java environment. Realizing that no serious program can really be completely portable, the term is usually qualified to indicate the range of supported machines, operating systems, compilers, and run-time environments.
- postorder traversal (10): When a binary tree is visualized in standard form, with the root node at the top and the tree descending from the root, a *postorder traversal* is accomplished by recursively visiting first the left child of a node, then the right child, and then the node itself. See *breadth-first traversal, depth-first traversal, depth of a node, height of a node, inorder traversal, preorder traversal.*
- preorder traversal (10): When a binary tree is visualized in standard form, with the root node at the top and the tree descending from the root, a *preorder traversal* is accomplished by recursively visiting first the node itself, then the left child of the node, and then the right child. See *breadth-first traversal, depth-first traversal, depth of a node, height of a node, inorder traversal, postorder traversal.*
- primary key (1, 9): The *primary key* used to store data is the key that is assumed to be the key used for the "usual" access to the data. It will usually be the case that the physical storage structure of the data is determined by the structure that would make access by the primary key most efficient because access by the primary key would be assumed to occur more often than access by any other key.
- priority queue (7): A *priority queue* is a data structure in which the "next item to be processed" is at an identifiable "first" location in the structure, and this property is reestablished after the first item is removed for processing, so that the "next" item is present in steady state at the "first" location.
- probe (3, 12): The search through a set of data for an individual item usually requires a process of locating a particular item, comparing that item's key against the sought-for key to determine if they match, and then repeating the location and comparison until the match is found. Each such location and comparison is called a *probe*, and search algorithms are evaluated based on the expected number of probes required before the sought-for item is found.
- prudent programmer (5): The standard navigational charts used in the United States all carry the warning: "The prudent mariner will not rely solely on any single aid to navigation, particularly on floating aids." This carries the force of law, in that a mariner who causes an accident by acting imprudently can be held liable for the accident. By analogy, the prudent programmer will not rely upon best-case conditions to hold true but will instead anticipate possible problems and write code that will be robust under the most hostile of circumstances.

- pseudocode (3): A *pseudocode* description of an algorithm or process is a description that has most of the precision and stepwise sequencing of a computer program, but is written in a form more closely resembling English and without paying attention to the strict syntactic requirements of a programming language.
- pseudorandom number (12): A sequence of numbers is said to be *pseudorandom* if it is produced by a deterministic process but possesses the statistical characteristics that a sequence of truly random numbers would possess.
- push-down stack (7): A *push-down stack*, or more simply just a *stack*, is a list data structure in which all additions to and removals from the structure are made at one end of the list, called the top of the stack.
- quadratic time (6): An algorithm or program runs in *quadratic time* if the asymptotic running time is $O(N^2)$ when the algorithm or program is run on data inputs of size N. See *asymptotic analysis*, *constant time*, *exponential time*, *linear time*, *logarithmic time*.
- queue (7): A *queue* is a list data structure in which all additions to the structure are made at a specific location called the tail and all removals from the structure are made at a specific location called the head. See *deque*.
- quicksort (1, 11): *Quicksort* is a sorting algorithm with an $O(N^2)$ worst-case but $O(N \lg N)$ average-case running time that can be run as an in-place algorithm and is characterized by a recursive splitting of the yet-to-be-sorted data into keys smaller than and keys larger than a chosen pivot element. See *asymptotic notation*, *bubblesort*, *heapsort*, *in-place algorithm*, *insertionsort*, *mergesort*, *out-of-place algorithm*.
- random access (4): A program has *random access* to its data if a particular data item can be retrieved without processing through all the data stored prior to that item. An array or `ArrayList`, for example, permits random access by subscript value; a linked list does not permit random access because a data item can only be reached by traversing the list.
- record (1): See *flat file*.
- recursion (8): A technique for solving a problem uses *recursion* if the problem is solved by using the same technique on successively smaller versions of the same problem.
- recursive divide and conquer (3, 6): A *recursive divide-and-conquer* algorithm is an algorithm that progresses from one stage of the computation to another by cutting the problem into smaller pieces and then calling itself on each of the smaller problem pieces. In many instances, the algorithm tries to cut the problem in half at each stage and call itself on each of the two nearly equal-sized subproblems. See *recursion*.
- recursive program, recursion (8): A *recursive program* is a program that calls itself.

- relation (9): A *relation* R on a set S is a set of ordered pairs $R = \{<s_1, s_2>\}$ in which $s_1, s_2 \in S$. The relation "less than" on the set $S = \{1, 2, 3, 4\}$ is the set of ordered pairs

$$R = \{<1,2>, <1,3>, <1,4>, <2,3>, <2,4>, <3,4>\}.$$

This is the formal statement of what we would normally recognize as

$$\begin{aligned} &1 < 2, \quad 1 < 3, \quad 1 < 4, \\ &2 < 3, \quad 2 < 4, \\ &3 < 4. \end{aligned}$$

- religious issues (2): An issue is considered (humorously) a *religious issue* if there is genuine disagreement as to how that issue ought to be decided or if the issue should properly be viewed as a matter of personal taste. The choice between Emacs and vi as an editor, for example, or the choice between Firefox® and Chrome™ for a browser, is a religious issue. See the Jargon File.
- reverse Polish notation (7): *Reverse Polish notation* (RPN) is the notation for arithmetic expressions that was developed by the Polish mathematician Jan Łukasiewicz. It does not use parentheses or other mechanisms, relying instead on the convention that an operator ($+$, $-$, $*$, or $/$) is to be applied to the two most-recently referenced numerical quantities. RPN was the standard for many years for Hewlett-Packard hand calculators and is a standard example used in discussing stack-based computation.
- right child (10): In a binary tree, the *right child* of a given node is the child that descends to the right when the tree is presented in standard form. See *left child.*
- root of a tree (1, 7, 10): The *root of a tree* is a node in a tree that has been identified as the root. When the tree is presented in standard form, the root is at the top of the display and other nodes descend from the root.
- semantics (3): *Semantics* refers to the meaning of an expression in a language. A program can be syntactically correct, that is, be a legal program in a language, while not being semantically correct, if the effect of the program is to compute something other than what is intended. For example, the program fragment

```
sum = 0;
for(int = 1; i < 10; ++i)
{
  sum += i;
}
```

is syntactically correct as a program fragment in Java. If the semantics of that fragment were to sum the first 10 integers, however, then the program would be semantically incorrect because what it does instead is to compute the sum of the first 9 integers. See *syntax.*

- shared memory parallel computer (11): In a *shared memory parallel computer*, each of the parallel processors has complete access to read and/or write to or from all the memory in the computer. The memory is shared among all processors, and no restrictions are placed on any processor's use of any memory due to the presence of the other processors. See *distributed memory parallel computer.*
- shortest path (13): The *shortest path* between two nodes in a graph is a path with the fewest number of arcs. This may not be unique; there may be different shortest paths of equal length.
- simple path (13): A path in a graph is a *simple path* if each of the nodes in the path is distinct.
- singly-linked list (4): A *singly-linked list* is a linked list in which links between nodes exist only in the forward direction, from the current node forward to the next node. See *doubly-linked list.*
- spaghetti code (2): A program is referred to as *spaghetti code* if the logical flow of control in the program is tangled like spaghetti on a dinner plate. Programs are more likely to be correct from the beginning and maintainable in the future if their flow of control is clean. Programs with a complicated set of controls will be hard to get right and hard for someone new to the program to understand.
- spanning tree (10, 13): A *spanning tree* in a connected graph is a subgraph that is a tree and that contains all the nodes of the graph.
- sparse graph (13): A *sparse graph* is a graph in which there are very few edges compared to the number of nodes. This imprecise term is used very much like the imprecise term *sparse matrix.*
- sparse matrix (13): A matrix of N rows and M columns is a *sparse matrix* if the number of nonzero entries is very small compared to the total number $N \cdot M$ of possible entries. This is not a precise term. Standard matrix algorithms deal with a matrix stored as a two-dimensional array of numbers, processing matrix operations as loops across rows and columns. If the matrix is sparse, it can be more efficient to store only the nonzero entries in something like a linked list and run loops that need only look at the nonzero entries. Because there are separate algorithms and storage structures for dealing with matrices like this, a matrix is usually considered (imprecisely and recursively) to be sparse if the number of nonzeros is small enough that a sparse matrix algorithm is more efficient than a standard matrix algorithm.
- stable sort (11): A sort is considered *stable* if the following property holds. For any pairs A and B in the list to be sorted, if $A = B$ and A appears before B in the original list, then A will continue to appear before B in the newly sorted list. That is, a stable sort does not change the prior ordering of elements with equal keys. Implemented correctly, bubblesort, insertionsort, mergesort,

and quicksort are stable sorts, while heapsort is not. The stability of a sort is relevant to the problem of sorting on multiple keys.

- stack (7): See *push-down stack.*
- state of execution (1): A process is in a *state of execution* if it has begun to execute and has not yet finished executing. A process that has been suspended, either because it needs more of some resource on which to work (such as more data) or because of the usual multiprocessing in any modern operating system, is still in a state of execution, even if it is not actually being executed by the CPU.
- Stirling's formula (6): *Stirling's formula* is one of the standard approximations for the factorial of an integer. Specifically, the approximation is

$$N! = \sqrt{2\pi N}\left(\frac{N}{e}\right)^N e^{\alpha_N},$$

where

$$\frac{1}{12N+1} < \alpha_N < \frac{1}{12N}.$$

- subgraph (9, 10, 13): A *subgraph* of a graph $G = (V, E)$ is another graph $G' = (V', E')$ for which $V' \subset V$ and $E' \subset E$ and the edges in E' only connect nodes in V'. That is, a subgraph is exactly what one would think it is: a subset of the nodes, together with some subset of the edges that join nodes in the subset.
- syntax (3): The *syntax* of a programming language consists of the rules by which one may construct legally correct statements in that programming language. See *semantics.*
- Syracuse problem (8): See $3n + 1$ *problem.*
- token (2): In programming languages and compiling, a *token* is a unit of input consisting of the sequence of input characters in between two instances of white space. To the Java compiler, for example, white space includes blank spaces, tabs, and newline and carriage return characters. Parentheses, open and close brackets and braces, and semicolons would also start or end processing for tokens and would be considered to be separate tokens.
- total order (7): A *total order* on a set of objects is a mathematical relation (which we can refer to as "less than or equal to") such that for any two elements x and y in the set, either "x is less than or equal to y" is true or "y is less than or equal to x" is true.
- transaction processing (1): A computation can be said to be *transaction processing* if the primary computation is the processing of a stream of individual transactions each of which is largely unrelated. The canonical example of transaction processing would be the handling of individual retail

receipts by a large store. Each receipt affects inventory, billing, credit card charges, and so forth but is essentially independent of any other receipt.

- transitive closure (9): The *transitive closure* of a mathematical relation is a subset of the relation such that every element of the transitive closure is related to every other element of the transitive closure, and no element of the set on which the relation is defined can be added to the closure without violating this property of all elements being related. The connected component in a graph is the transitive closure of any node in the component under the relation of "connected by an arc." See *connected component.*
- transitive relation (9): A mathematical relation R on a set S is *transitive* if for any three elements a, b, and c in S, if aRb and bRc are true, then aRc is true. The canonical transitive relations are equality, $<$, $\leq$, $>$, and $\geq$. If, for example, we have $x \leq y$ and $y \leq z$, then we know that $x \leq z$ because the $\leq$ relation is transitive.
- tree (7, 9, 10): The following two definitions can be shown to be equivalent.
  1. A *tree* is a connected graph with n nodes and $n-1$ edges.
  2. A *tree* is a connected graph with no cycles.
- tree search (1): *Searching* through a tree usually refers to a process of traversing a tree whose nodes represent decisions in a process or the status of a game or computation. Chess-playing programs, for example, expand the tree of moves and countermoves from the current position and search among the nodes for the board position most advantageous to the current player. See *tree traversal.*
- tree traversal (10): *Traversing* a tree refers to the following of the paths and the examining of the nodes of the tree in some specified order. See *breadth-first traversal, depth-first traversal, inorder traversal, postorder traversal, preorder traversal.*
- UML diagram (2): Unified Modeling Language (UML) is one of the ways (and becoming the standard way) in which the structure and interactions among various pieces of a software system are described. A *UML diagram* is a graphical display of the variables, methods, parameters, returned values, and public or private accessibility of an object or class in a software package. From the UML diagram one can see among other things which classes are responsible for which parts of the computation and whether the data on which the methods operate is to be passed in as parameters or resides locally within the class.
- undirected graph (9, 13): An *undirected graph* is a graph in which none of the arcs is directed. See *directed graph.*
- unrooted tree (10): An *unrooted tree* is a tree with no node identified as the root of the tree. See *root of a tree.*
- unweighted graph (9): An *unweighted graph* is a graph in which none of the edges has an edge weight associated with it. See *edge weight.*
- vertex (9, 13): See *graph.*

- weighted graph (9): A *weighted graph* is a graph in which one or more of the edges has an edge weight associated with it. See *edge weight.*
- worst-case behavior (1, 6, 11): The *worst-case behavior* of an algorithm is the behavior that leads to the *worst-case running time.* For example, the worst-case behavior of insertionsort into increasing order is exhibited when an item is added to an array of length N and the new item's key is smaller than all other keys for items already in the array. In this case, the new item's key must be compared with all other keys for items in the array and the new item pulled forward to the leading position in the array. This requires N comparisons and is the worst-case situation for insertionsort. See *average-case behavior, best-case behavior.*
- worst-case running time (1, 6, 11): The *worst-case running time* of an algorithm is the running time of the algorithm under the worst-case conditions. See *average-case running time, best-case running time.*

Index

Note: Italicized page locators indicate figures.